Jane Dismore started writing features for well-known women's magazines while she was teaching English Literature to A-level in secondary schools. A complete change of lifestyle saw her running private yachts in the Mediterranean for four years, which led to her writing travel articles – often undertaken between negotiating protection money with local mafia chiefs and trying to avoid floating mines off the coast of Albania. While teaching Spanish students and the British Army in Gibraltar, Jane had a regular radio slot, presenting her features on the British Forces Broadcasting Service.

Inspired by a barrister friend she decided to become a solicitor, and after returning to England, remarrying and wondering if she had gone quite mad, she re-qualified. Jane now practises as an employment law specialist in a Hertfordshire law firm, of which she is a Director, and for three years was the 'legal eagle' on a local radio station. She writes whenever she can and has continued to have articles published, including in *The Times*. Happiest when digging something up, whether from under the ground or from old documents, she is particularly interested in biography. *The Voice from the Garden* is her first book.

The Voice from the Garden

Pamela Hambro and the Tale of Two Families
Before and After the Great War

JANE DISMORE

SilverWood

First published by SilverWood Books 2012
www.silverwoodbooks.co.uk

ISBN 978-1-78132-025-9

British Library Cataloguing in Publication Data
A CIP catalogue record for this book is available from the British Library

Set in Sabon by SilverWood Books
Printed on responsibly sourced paper

In memory of my father

Acknowledgements

I am very grateful to each of the following, who have provided me variously with material, hospitality, time and support in the writing of this book:

Mrs Andrew Gibson-Watt (Pammie), for her lovely, informative letters and photographs, and for her telephone calls; Charlie Hambro, for use of the love letters and much other material; The Lady Hambro; The Lord Cobbold; Anthony Cobbold; Philip Hope-Cobbold, particularly for giving me access to *Baby's Book*; Angus Sladen, for information on his grandmother and others; the late Shirley Somerville of Rannoch Lodge; His Grace the Duke of Devonshire and the Chatsworth House Trust; Her Grace the Dowager Duchess of Devonshire; The Lord Tollemache; Henry Strutt; Gay Strutt; Mrs A M Bonsor; Peter Wallenberg; Peter Hambro; The Foundation for Economic History Research within Banking and Enterprise, Stockholm; Eton College; Natalie Farrar; Charles Morgan; Stuart Whitehead; Adrian Howlett; the Museum of English Rural Life; the Harry Ransom Humanities Research Center; the Buddhist Society; The Royal College of Surgeons of England; Andrew Kidd of Aitken Alexander Associates Ltd; Frances English; Robert Wilson.

I am also grateful to those people working behind the scenes in the grand houses I visited in the course of my research, whose ears they allowed me to bend.

Finally, many thanks to my husband for his constant and uncomplaining support and patience.

Jane Dismore

Contents

Prologue

John was not a religious man. It pained his wife, a regular churchgoer, that he would not go with her and their daughters to the Sunday services at their local church, where her family was buried and the girls had been christened. His mother-in-law, in spite of a strict religious upbringing herself, would berate her daughter for giving him a hard time. John was a good man, she said, and that was all that mattered. That it should be he who had the experience which led to this book, and which was to have such a lasting effect on him, was therefore most unexpected.

The Loch Rannoch region of Perthshire is beautiful, mysterious and remote. On the south side of the Loch lies Tay Forest Park, a surviving remnant of the ancient Caledonian forest. To the west is Rannoch Moor, a melancholy wilderness and the largest uninhabited area in the British Isles, surrounded by distant mountains; and to the south-east the soaring heights of Schiehallion, or The Fairy Hill of the Caledonians. In July 1973 John took his family to stay on a farm on the northern shore, An Slios Min, the Side of Gentle Slopes. They enjoyed walking and holidaying away from the madding crowds, although Rannoch was undoubtedly the most remote place they had yet stayed in. Today its many walking and cycling routes can be considered and assessed in advance via the Internet; in 1973 all that was needed was an Ordnance Survey map and tips from the locals to feel that you were the only person in the world ever to have walked there.

John may not have been religious in any conventional sense but he was very conscious and respectful of nature. He was an avid gardener, loved the countryside and was concerned that man should protect the environment years before anyone talked seriously about saving the planet. On holidays he would usually go for a dawn walk while his family slept, and describe to them over breakfast the creatures he had seen and rare birds he had heard while they slumbered. One day, when it was too wet even for them to soldier through the valleys and up the mountains, they visited the nearby town of Pitlochry, and by the time they returned to the farm the rain had stopped and a warm, clear evening was promised. While the rest of the family loafed around the farm and waited for the evening meal, John, restless at being denied a day's trekking, took the dog and went for a walk.

Nearly two hours later he returned. He was visibly disturbed, pale and shaky. He wouldn't tell the family what the matter was but he said he hadn't had an accident and he wasn't ill. Eventually, after much coaxing, he told them what had happened.

He and the dog, in the stillness of that summer evening, had walked along the quiet road from the farm when he noticed, leading off the road, a rough stony track running alongside a thickly wooded area. They followed the track for a few minutes and then came across a pair of tall, wrought-iron gates, the right-hand one of which was slightly open. Unable to resist exploring John went in, and he and the dog followed a narrow path up a steep wooded hill.

Five minutes later they arrived at a big wooden shed and almost immediately a large creature rushed out from underneath, startling them both. The dog chased on after it and John followed him, along the path up the hill, catching glimpses through the trees of the Loch down below, faintly glistening in the early evening sunlight. As they walked John noticed the dog becoming increasingly agitated for no apparent reason. Suddenly a word flashed into his mind – Pamela. He thought nothing of it and hurried on after the dog. It came again – Pamela. By now the path had become narrower and twisted and turned through the wood, and as it did so the word became more frequent and insistent in his mind – Pamela, Pamela.

And then they were at the top of the hill and in front of them was a large standing stone, facing a wonderful view across a wooded valley surrounding the Loch. As he stood enjoying the scene John realised the stone was the headstone of a grave, and as he peered closely at the front of it and tried to clear the lichen away from the words, he realised he was looking at a name, and that name was Pamela.

At that moment, he said, he was filled with an awful sense of depression despite the beauty of the place, and calling the still-agitated dog to him tried to find the path to return down the hill. Dusk was now falling and the feeling of depression was giving way to panic that he would never find their way out. Eventually he did, and in the fading light as he left the garden – for he realised that, for all its wildness now, a garden was what it had been – he saw that on the iron gates were two sets of letters: at the top OM and at the bottom PH.

John was never a communicative man at the best of times, so the family was surprised but gratified – for they were intrigued by what he had told them – when the next day he asked their host about the grave and who Pamela was. The farmer said she was Pamela Hambro, the PH on the gates, and he gave John and his family the little information he knew about her. He seldom walked near the garden, he told them: if he had his dogs with him, they would never move past the gates.

John refused to speak directly of his experience again, except to allude to it obliquely whenever discussions about life and death arose, his old scepticism less certain, more uncomfortable. He was my father, I was a teenager on that holiday when I saw him troubled in a way that I had never seen before, or since.

The memory of what he told us stayed with me through my various lives until many years later, when on 2 January – on what I thought was a whim but which turned out to be the eve of her birth – I decided to investigate what the farmer had said about Pamela, and to try to find out about this woman who had caused my father to question his whole philosophy. It would lead me through a life that started in the England of 1900 and ended in a different world altogether.

The Hambro Abbreviated Family Tree

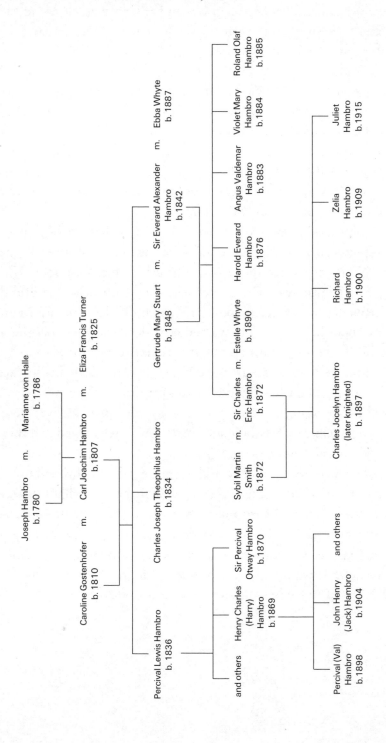

The Cobbold and Murray Abbreviated Family Tree

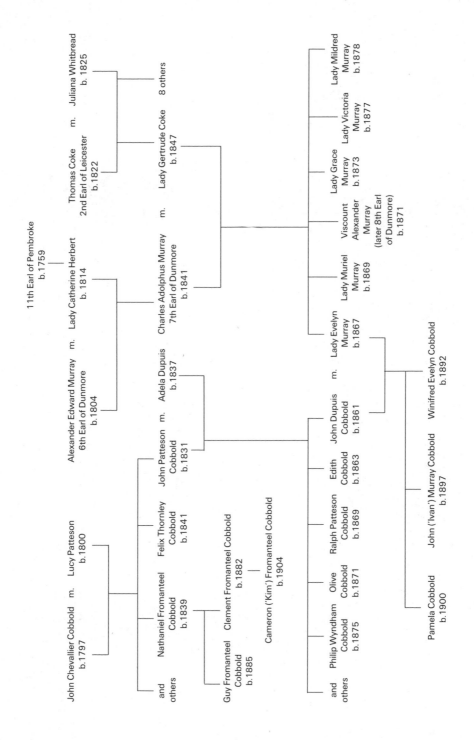

Chapter 1

The Watershed: 1917

In September 1917 on a wet day in the middle of the Third Battle of Ypres, Lt Charles Jocelyn Hambro, nineteen-year-old scion of the merchant banking dynasty, was performing the acts for which he would be awarded the Military Cross. Accompanied by a private, Charles swam to the enemy's side of a canal and rescued two wounded men, one of whom was unable to walk, from close under the enemy's parapet. Later that day he led a patrol in an advance, where he personally accounted for four of the enemy with his revolver and captured several prisoners with his party. On reaching his objective Charles sent back correct and valuable information, at all times, according to *The London Gazette*, displaying 'the utmost coolness and gallantry'.

The battle, which came to be known as 'Passchendaele', had started a few weeks earlier, on 31 July. For Sir Douglas Haig, Commander-in-Chief of the British Expeditionary Force, this major offensive was intended as the Allied Forces' breakthrough in Flanders. The aim was the destruction of German submarine bases on the Belgian coast, and Haig believed, wrongly, that the German army was near to collapse. Encouraged by the capture on 7 June of Messines Ridge, the greatest local success of the war so far, Haig was determined that his tactics for taking Passchendaele Ridge were the right ones.

But abnormal rainfall, the heaviest for thirty years, had turned the fields of Flanders into a quagmire. Ironically the force of the preliminary bombardment had itself destroyed drainage systems, exacerbating the problem. Mud clogged up rifles and immobilised tanks. Men and horses drowned. Then the Germans changed from using chlorine gas as a defence, to mustard gas, causing chemical burns. By the time the village of Passchendaele was captured by British and Canadian forces on 6 November, the battle had proved to be one of the costliest of the Great War in terms of lives.

In a war that measured life on the front line in terms of weeks, Charles Hambro, in the 3rd Battalion Coldstream Guards, was lucky to survive, and relieved still to be part of the regiment with which his family was associated. There had barely been time for him to reflect on the transition from his untroubled life as a schoolboy at Eton, where he was renowned for his cricket skills, to that of an officer at the Front: the moment Charles finished school in 1915 he was packed off to start his army training, foregoing the university education that his father and grandfather had enjoyed, in the pre-war world which now seemed so very long ago.

In Sweden that same year seventeen-year-old Marcus Wallenberg, the youngest son of the Wallenberg family considered to be that country's banking and industrial aristocracy, had just left school and was embarking, with a noted lack of enthusiasm, on his period of military service. Keen to start at the Stockholm School of Economics which was essential for his future career, Marcus was also a talented tennis player; he had won that year's national schools' championship and was determined to become a top international player. He felt that in doing his military service, too much valuable time would be lost: after all, with Sweden's stance in the war being neutral, he was unlikely to become involved in any direct way.

But the reality was that Sweden was not neutral, at least not as far as the Court and the army were concerned. They were very pro-German, and in constant fear of Russia invading the country's eastern borders, to the extent that in 1915 Sweden had imposed licences on British goods bound for Russia, insisting that equal quantities should be allowed to pass to Germany. Britain had been forced to take drastic steps and reduce her trade; the result was that commercial relations between Britain and Russia were in danger of breaking down. The result could have been catastrophic. A four-man delegation was sent to Sweden by the British

Government, with the aim of persuading the Swedish Government to allow the free transit of goods across the country to Russia.

The person to whom the delegation appealed was Marcus' uncle, Knut Wallenberg. Chairman of Sweden's major bank and for the duration of the war Minister of Foreign Affairs, he was considered the most powerful man in the country. The delegate instrumental in helping Britain to achieve its aim was Eric Hambro, father of Charles. Eric used the friendship the Hambro family had enjoyed with the Wallenbergs for nearly forty years to his advantage. The negotiations also cemented the relationship between Eric and Marcus' father, and would soon bring their sons into contact with each other when both families would find themselves in a post-war world economically very different from the old.

In that autumn of 1917, in America, seventeen-year-old Harry Morgan, son of the banker J P 'Jack' Morgan Jnr, must have reflected ruefully on how the term 'the old world' had taken on a new meaning in the last few months since April, when his country had entered the war. The decision to do so, taken by its sorrowful President Woodrow Wilson, represented a dramatic reversal both for the President and for the USA as a whole, which had long obeyed the advice of George Washington to avoid 'entangling alliances'.

In Harry's old world he would by now have joined his childhood friend, Charles Hambro, at Gannochy, the Scottish shooting estate their families had rented together for years since their respective grandfathers, J Pierpont Morgan and Everard Hambro, had become friends in the 1870s. With a large, imposing lodge, excellent salmon fishing and 17,000 acres of upland moors, Gannochy was a paradise of heather, grouse and swiftly-running rivers. There Jack Morgan and Eric Hambro, an excellent shot, both accompanied by that most upper-class English of accessories, a butler to carry their guns, would spend happy days hunting with whomever of their older children, wives and friends wanted to join them. Harry hoped that those times would resume, but for now he contented himself with considering the financial role his father had played so far in the war, which included the raising of a massive loan for the Allied Forces. Having just finished school, Harry turned his thoughts to Harvard and wondered if the war would prevent his going as planned.

In the new post-war world that would greet Charles, Marcus and Harry – three fortunate young men, privileged by birth and by the fact that so many of their generation would not live to see it – were the women they would marry. In 1917 the girls did not yet know this, or each other, and of them only Pamela Cobbold had already met her future husband, the tall, imposing Charles, when her elder brother Ivan had brought him home from Eton in those carefree days before the war. When she learned of her friend's war-time deeds Pamela was not surprised by his courage, for she already knew Charles to be brave and kind, but she did not yet realise that she loved him. Aged seventeen, fair-haired and prettily plump, Pamela was lively, intelligent and sporty with a sharp wit: the perfect foil for Charles' inclination to seriousness.

Pamela was the product of a union between trade and title. Her father was the seventh generation of a respected Suffolk brewing dynasty, her mother an Anglo-Scottish aristocrat. As such, she grew up with a balanced sense of the practical and the privileged; she may have had a good deal of blue blood through both sets of maternal grandparents, but she was also expected to associate with her father's many employees and tenants. Unaffected and popular, she had none of the pretensions of many of her class. Like her best friend Angela Tollemache, always known as 'Angy', from another Suffolk brewing family even older than the Cobbolds, Pamela could talk to anyone, and frequently did.

Although she enjoyed weekends in London and many trips abroad with her wealthy parents, Pamela's home town was Ipswich. Her family's large estate Holy Wells may have been beautiful, but Ipswich – although a significant town, and once home to such luminaries as Cardinal Wolsey and Thomas Gainsborough – was not the most thrilling place for a lively young woman at the best of times, and the war did not enhance its attractions. Even while war raged, nothing very exciting happened in Ipswich: there were two zeppelin raids in 1915 and 1916, but only one death which, although fortunate in being such a small number, did little to render the town more glamorous.

Pamela loved to escape to London but by 1917 it had become risky. In June, German aircraft had carried out the first bombing raid in the capital, marking a sinister development in the use of airplanes in warfare. That same month, King George V finally decided that it may be wise to obscure his German roots, and changed his family's name from Saxe-Coburg-Gotha to Windsor.

To add to her Ipswich-bound woes, Pamela was the last child left at home. Her elder sister, Winifred, had married in 1913 as soon as she reached twenty-one, and was living an odd, itinerant lifestyle with her husband of whom the Cobbolds disapproved; and her beloved brother, Ivan, was away with the Scots Guards in France. Usually Pamela could enjoy herself in Felixstowe, the Suffolk seaside resort with which the Cobbolds had a long association and where she and Angy loved to spend warm summer days. There, Pamela's uncle, Philip Wyndham Cobbold, owned a lovely house overlooking the sea. But since the war had started, the edge had been taken off their pleasure: the town, with all its old fortifications built to defend against a Napoleonic invasion a century earlier which never happened, stood ready to repel another enemy. The girls could no longer even have tea as they used to, in Felixstowe's first hotel, The Bath. Built by Pamela's great-grandfather in 1839, the elegant and famous landmark had been destroyed by fire three years earlier by two aggrieved suffragettes. Pamela found herself looking forward to starting war work, and planned to save any wages she earned to buy a farm in Canada with Angy.

Meanwhile, at least she could still go riding, which was usually guaranteed to cheer her up. As much as Pamela considered herself different from her class and era in many ways, there was one area of her life in which she typified it: her love of hunting. Her parents had taught her to ride and to handle a gun at an early age, so that by the time she was seventeen she was an accomplished horsewoman and a very good shot. If she was not riding side-saddle with effortless ease, she loved walking all day in all weathers, stalking deer, and her favourite place on earth to enjoy this was at Loch Rannoch in Perthshire. It was here that her father owned thousands of acres of prime hunting ground and a magnificent eighteenth-century house, Rannoch Lodge, which stood at the head of the ten-mile long loch. Usually the Cobbolds spent time there every Easter and from August to the end of September, but the war had limited their visits largely due to her father's commitments to the family businesses, affected by so many staff joining up. Rannoch was the one place Pamela really felt alive, truly at one with nature. It seemed to her that since the outbreak of war it was the only part of her life that remained constant, the only link with the untroubled years of her younger life, when all that mattered was playing tennis with Angy and riding her horse.

Pamela and her parents did manage, however, to get to Rannoch briefly in September 1917 and when her friend Charles Hambro was sent home on leave at the end of that month to recuperate from the injuries he had received, she was delighted that he should ask to visit them there. Charles naturally was spending most of his leave with his own family who had also managed a short break at Gannochy, not too far from Rannoch: how envious Harry Morgan would have been.

Pamela wrote to Charles just after he had left to return to France. The earliest known letter between them, it was written on 2 October 1917, the eve of Charles' twentieth birthday:

'My Dear Charles –

Nice – Nice boy! Thank you *so* much for the huge box of chocs I found last night. They *are* good – I'm writing with them at my elbow now & most of the family are out (s)talking so I'm in for a 'good' day – s'pose you are at Gannochy now, slaying poor little partridges by the thousand...'

Pamela was hardly in a position to comment, since she enjoyed her fair share of 'slaying'. Her parents were also accomplished hunters, although Pamela's mischievous sense of humour often suggested otherwise, her mother, Lady Evelyn, a frequent target:

'Let me see, what else has happened since you left Wednesday... Oh yes, the 'wench' pulled out a 25lb salmon from [the] Pool – on a fly, horrible fluke, don't you think? & then proceeded to shoot a stag v. low down near the river with her gun!... Yesterday my 2 Authorities[1] went to stalk T.A.B[2] (Not together!). Dad bagged the low ground! However, they got nothing, Ma indicated clearly that her rifle never left its case!! I went with [Dad] to East Side and got 1 stag about 11.30 at the far end on the flat... Dad says: "Tell Charles that one of his stags was useless, it has so many big bullets in it!!" I think, Charles, that must be an error, it sounds awfully like one of Ma's!'

[1] Pamela's parents.
[2] Talladh-a-Bheithe, a nearby estate, pronounced 'Tel-a-vee'.

Pamela loved the area so much she hated the thought of having to return to Ipswich later that month, lamenting to Charles:

'I s'pose the *awful* day will be about the 16th. 'Tis simply a nightmare to think of dull flat England after being on the top of Corrieich! Think of Loch Ericht & then the typical 'Duck Pond' belonging to every English house! Never mind, these things have to be. How long leave have you got? Heavens! What pages I've written – Goodbye. Thank you understood for chocs.

'Love from Pam.'

Pamela's efforts to keep up his spirits continued when he returned to the Front, entertaining him with more tales of life at home in the jocular, platonic tone of a fond friend who was unaware that Charles would prove to be her soulmate. But her task became more difficult as news of the deaths of relatives and friends reached them; some families had already endured a war, the Second Boer War, in which Britain was engaged a few years earlier when Pamela was born: born into a world which would change faster than anyone could predict.

Chapter 2

New Century, New Life: Pamela

The twentieth century was just three days old when Pamela Cobbold was born at Holy Wells, the estate of her father John Dupuis Cobbold, in Ipswich, Suffolk. There were those who argued, as they would similarly do in 2000, that 1900 was not the start of the new century but the last year of the old one. It was the view expressed in the leader article of *The Times* newspaper on 1 January 1900 and the subject of many letters to the Editor. Not that it was the main subject; Great Britain had far greater concerns at that time. In what was the penultimate year of Queen Victoria's reign, the country was still embroiled in a war in South Africa, the Second Boer War, which had broken out the previous year and which politicians and military leaders had over-confidently predicted would last only until the Christmas of 1899.

'The New Year, the last of the Nineteenth Century, which begins today, is not unlikely to mark a turning point in the history of the British Empire,' the leader article began. 'Two important tasks lie before us, and on the manner in which we fulfil them our future as a ruling people and as a Great Power largely depends.'

These tasks placed an onerous responsibility on the British Tory Government, led by the Cobbolds' acquaintance, Lord Salisbury. The first was to bring the war in South Africa to a speedy and successful end; the second was to review the history of the campaign and learn some lessons from it, for there were serious concerns that the British Army was ill-equipped to deal with the Boers in terms of numbers of troops and equipment.

It was an anxious time too for Pamela's mother, Lady Evelyn Cobbold, as her younger brother Alexander Edward Murray, Viscount Fincastle, was fighting in the war under a government that the Cobbolds had helped maintain in power. But perhaps she need not have been too concerned, for Alexander had already proved himself capable in combat: three years earlier aged twenty-five, he had been awarded the Victoria Cross, the highest gallantry medal, for saving the life of an officer in India.

However, Lady Evelyn's more immediate concern was the health of her new-born daughter, for England was in the grip of a major 'flu epidemic. Killing fifty people a day in London, it had now spread to other towns country-wide. Grave diggers were working night and day and a shortage of nurses, themselves falling prey to infection, meant hospital wards were closing fast. Even without the 'flu, the week before Pamela was born there had been an unusually high number of deaths in Ipswich, higher than elsewhere in Suffolk, largely from bronchial and lung conditions and several babies had died. This was a worrying situation: generally a prosperous town, Ipswich was one of the best in the county for living conditions, in an era when poverty in Britain was still rife. But cocooned in the nursery in Holy Wells well away from the unsanitary dwellings which festered in parts of the town, the baby thrived.

Whether Pamela was born at the end of the nineteenth century or at the beginning of the twentieth, the world that greeted her was still very much a man's world. But times were – slowly – changing. A husband no longer had absolute control over his wife's property, allowing women for the first time to own property and run a company. Women could now aspire to some all-male professions and be admitted into universities previously limited only to men – although not all would award them a degree. The Cobbolds' local newspaper, the widely-circulated *East Anglian Daily Times*, ran a column called 'The World of Women'. A few days after Pamela's birth it reported the appointments of three women lecturers at Royal Holloway College, London, in Modern History, Zoology and Maths.

Recovering after her third child's birth, in her lavish bedroom with its deep Wilton carpet and Hepplewhite chairs, Lady Evelyn may have read the column somewhat ruefully. Had she been born into a middle-class family of bluestockings rather than an aristocratic one, she may have been expected to follow the academic route. She would not have found it difficult; the daughter of a Scottish Earl who was a respected writer and renowned traveller, she was a fluent Arabic speaker, widely read and clever, but higher education for women was just not part of her family's agenda.

Always elegantly dressed, Evelyn probably read with amusement The World of Women's fashion report that day, which discussed, 'Mrs Langtry's khaki dress'. The famous actress until two years previously had been a favourite mistress of Queen Victoria's eldest son, Edward Prince of Wales – a friend of Evelyn's father – when she was superseded in the royal bedchamber by Alice Keppel, great-grandmother of the twenty-first century Duchess of Cornwall. Despite being discarded by Edward whose sexual exploits were legendary, 'the Jersey Lillie', as she was popularly known, still attracted press interest. And khaki, being the colour newly in use by the British Army in South Africa was 'de rigeur' amongst those in the know:

'Mrs Langtry's khaki dress will do much to make that material and colour fashionable when warmer weather comes… It has a high military collar lined with crimson silk and opens in front upon white pleated chiffon with touches of crimson silk.'

To the frustration of Evelyn who with her husband John had always been politically active, the big change that many women had been striving for since at least the 1860s still eluded them: the right to vote. Yet things were looking more hopeful, and by 1900 the National Union of Women's Suffrage had a promising share of supporters including the young Winston Churchill, recently elected to Parliament. But it would take the Great War to persuade the Government that women – and the remainder of adult men – should have the vote.

The idea that all adults, regardless of their wealth and status, should be allowed to elect the country's rulers was not a popular one in Parliament in an age when the poor were deprived of any significant education. When Pamela was born the school leaving age was just ten, and 32% of females over that age were in full-time employment, most of them in domestic service. For the time being at least, there was no shortage of female servants for the fortunate rich.

Pamela's parents had twelve servants at Holy Wells to look after the family, which included her older siblings, Winifred aged eight and three-year-old John, known always as 'Ivan': ten for the mansion house and grounds, and a married couple for their farm. There is little doubt that John Dupuis Cobbold was well-liked and respected by his servants and his other employees. The Cobbolds had been in Ipswich since 1740, and as brewers – John was the seventh generation – they were one of the biggest employers in the town. When Pamela was born, Cobbold & Co owned over two hundred licensed properties across Suffolk and North Essex.

The Cobbolds had fingers in other commercial pies too, and had been hugely involved in all aspects of the town's public life since their arrival. Various Cobbolds over the generations had been MPs for Ipswich, as well as its mayor. A joke published in *Punch* magazine asked, 'Why is Ipswich like an old shoe? Because it is 'Cobbold' all over.' Expectations of the family were such that John could not afford *not* to be a decent master. His wife, coming from ancient Scottish aristocracy on her father's side and English on her mother's – her father was the 7th Earl of Dunmore, her maternal grandfather the 2nd Earl of Leicester – knew of no existence other than that of servanted privilege.

John Dupuis Cobbold and Lady Evelyn Murray had married in Cairo on 23 April 1891, where they had met the previous winter while John was on a world tour. Britain had occupied Egypt since 1882 under the orders of Prime Minister Gladstone, to help put down a mutiny against the Turks. British troops had been sent in to help the Khedive, Tewfik Pasha, who agreed to the reforms insisted upon by Great Britain and assumed the position of a constitutional ruler. Egypt became a popular place for upper-class Britons, with its own social season, and Evelyn's father Charles Murray owned a villa there. John was thirty-one and Evelyn twenty-five. He was not handsome as such but kindly-faced. She was beautiful. What would once have been seen as an unlikely combination – trade, albeit long-established, marrying title – it was perhaps indicative of times just around the corner, when the old aristocracy would be overtaken in the wealth stakes by the new plutocracy.

Charles Murray was relieved at his daughter's choice of husband despite his not being titled, for all the time there was a demand for beer his son-in-law would never be poor. By contrast, Charles had never quite recovered his previous financial position after being bankrupted when Evelyn was a baby. As a result, he and his wife, the Countess Gertrude, had been forced to adopt a more itinerant lifestyle than they may otherwise have chosen, and were conscious of being less wealthy than many of their peers.

Just under nine months after their wedding, on 10 January 1892, John and Evelyn's first child, Winifred Evelyn Cobbold, was born in London and brought home to Holy Wells on 13 February. A few weeks later, on their first wedding anniversary in April, an interview with Evelyn at Holy Wells was published in *The Gentlewoman*, a popular new illustrated periodical. The 'Gentlewoman at Home' section described the surroundings into which Winifred was born and which remained much the same at the time of Pamela's birth eight years later. The unnamed writer described being shown around the house by Evelyn, having been collected in Her Ladyship's pony cart from Ipswich station. Holy Wells was presented as the ideal of late-Victorian upper-class style, an exhibition of John's hunting skills and the individual travels of them both before they married:

'You will not have been five minutes in the house before you will have ample evidence that John Dupuis Cobbold is an ardent sportsman, that is to say, with the gun, for, as Lady Evelyn will presently tell you, the fox is an animal tabooed on the estate, 'the cult of the sacred bird,' the pheasant, being especially revered. Every representative of 'fur and feather,' from home covers and from foreign jungles, seems to have fallen to his unerring aim...'

The luxurious lounge was filled 'with the trophies of the chase, and the spoil of travel from the East and the West. A huge brown bear on his hind legs is so well posed that he seems ready to embrace you, and makes a prominent figure amongst the couches covered with skins innumerable, gaudy Indian sleighs, bright rugs, carved screens and quaint bureaux, whilst the painter's art is represented by many rare works upon the walls.'

The writer, somewhat obsequiously, approved John's choice of wife:

'As you enter the drawing-room and are prettily greeted by Lady Evelyn, you have sufficient proof of Mr Cobbold's good taste and critical judgment in his matrimonial choice. In Lady Evelyn's quiet and gentle manner there is evidently a store of reserved force, and her endeavours to make your visit an agreeable one are tempered with regret that Mr Cobbold's business engagements have that day called him away.'

The drawing room contained such treasures as a mashrabiya screen inlaid with green jade, silver and mother-of-pearl, and another with coloured sketches of Evelyn's favourite views of Egypt. The walls were hung with paintings by Gainsborough, of which John was very proud, for the artist had been a friend of his ancestor Thomas, the first Cobbold brewer. John's private smoking den was panelled with dark oak from the old merchant houses in Ipswich, many of which were bought by the Cobbolds to turn into inns. His library, leading off the drawing room, 'would prove particularly tempting to a studious mind... It is lined with hundreds of volumes, and you may rest assured every work treating of Suffolk may be found there. It is well stored with cabinets filled with rare Delft china, and the quaint wallpaper was sent to Japan to be painted, I am told.'

Portraits of the Cobbolds hung in the dining room, while the billiard room next door boasted a collection of deer heads shot by John. The writer was hoping to meet 'the newly arrived scion of the house, Miss Winifred Evelyn...', but was told that 'excursions from the nursery are chiefly confined to the beautiful grounds, backed by fine woods and watered by a pretty lake, on which black Australian swans disport themselves'.

Evelyn told the writer that she had spent much of her first year of married life away from Ipswich and knew very little of the locality, '... but she feels the strongest interest in Ipswich and its surrounding neighbourhood, and has every wish to improve her knowledge, having the greatest sympathy with her husband's occupation and enterprises...' At the same time, however, Evelyn delighted in talking of agreeable trips in her unmarried days to Albania and Algiers, reminiscing also about her childhood home at Dunmore in Scotland and the romantic scenery of the Isle of Harris which her father's family owned. She spoke almost wistfully of her love of riding and especially of her Arab mare, Sultana.

At the end of the interview Evelyn herself drove the writer to the station 'in her victoria with the high-stepping roans', the writer reflecting, in a manner that was no doubt expected, that 'county society has every reason to congratulate itself on the acquisition of such a charming member'.

The article was illustrated with glamorous photographs of Evelyn and various views of Holy Wells, Winifred being too young to be the focus of an interesting picture herself. However, as with many first-born children, she was the subject of a large photograph album, *Baby's Book*, annotated by Evelyn in the third person, with herself as 'Mamma' and John as 'Dada'. As loving as her notes are, the joy in her first-born undisguised, Evelyn does not appear to have let 'Baby' – as Winifred was known until she was four years old, when it was decided that she was sufficiently grown up to be called by her name – interfere with her social life, in common with other young mothers of her class and era. Although Evelyn's notes mainly concern the early years of Winifred, the Cobbolds' social pattern would remain much the same when they had Ivan and Pamela.

Favourite holiday destinations for John and Evelyn included Monte Carlo for socialising, Egypt for heat and culture, and Scotland and Norway for hunting and fishing. When Winifred was about ten weeks old, her parents left her at home while they went off to Monte Carlo for a month, after which they spent some time in London in May before returning home to Baby. According to *Baby's Book* they were at home with Baby all June, except for a week at Ascot, and spent time 'working hard canvassing as the General Election was taking place' which reaped rewards because, as Evelyn noted, both of Ipswich's Conservative candidates were elected. In October Baby was sent to stay at The Lodge at Felixstowe, the cliff-edge house of her great-uncle Felix Cobbold, with its 'nurseries… which look over the sea' and 'lovely sands'.

Evelyn sometimes took Baby with her on her trips, particularly to visit her friend Muriel Hargreaves at fourteenth-century Leckhampton Court in Gloucestershire, where Muriel lived with her widowed father; her parents' Lancashire forebears had made their fortunes in the cotton industry during the Industrial Revolution. An entry in *Baby's Book* for 1895 reads, 'On the 15th January Father went off to Biskra in Algeria to shoot and Baby and Mamma went to Leckhampton Court for the month of February. We came home again on 5th March and Father came back too.'

Pretty as a child, if serious, Winifred as the first-born was cast early into the spotlight which later she would shun. The 'Court Circular' column of *The Times* recorded her first appearance in public in January 1896, aged four, when she was one of nine bridesmaids at the wedding of Evelyn's younger sister Lady Grace Murray to William James Barry, son of an MP. Evelyn recorded that Winifred, '… was very good but she did not like being bridesmaid & said that "standing so long worried her" – she was given a turquoise & pearl chain & locket.' Whilst she did what she was told on that occasion, her reluctance to do so indicated a rebellious streak that would manifest itself as she grew older.

In apparent contrast, John and Evelyn's son and heir, John Murray Cobbold – Ivan – born five years after Winifred on 28 January 1897, was 'a very happy little boy'. The entries in *Baby's Book*, where it was his turn to be called simply Baby, were not as extensive as Winifred's, although his parents held a big celebration at Holy Wells that August to celebrate his birth which, according to the invitations, included 'free amusements'. John and Evelyn continued their travels but would sometimes arrange for friends' children to stay with Winifred and Ivan to keep them company, such as Sylvia Grenfell, of similar age to Winifred and a niece of society figures Lord and Lady Desborough.

The year Ivan was born was also that of Queen Victoria's Diamond Jubilee. It was celebrated throughout the country, the highlight on 22 June being a six-mile procession to St Paul's Cathedral and back to Buckingham Palace. Undoubtedly the children's maternal grandfather was invited personally to participate in the celebrations. Until 1880 Evelyn's father had been Lord-in-Waiting to Queen Victoria who in turn was godmother to another of Evelyn's sisters, Lady Victoria. As a celebration of the Jubilee and to coincide with the year of his son Ivan's birth, John Dupuis Cobbold gave 11½ acres of his land to the people of Ipswich for use as a recreation ground.

No public celebrations were held or land donated when Pamela, their third January child, was born, although her mother did make some entries in *Baby's Book*, including a photograph of 'Mama's bedroom where Pamela was born January 3rd 1900'. Evelyn wrote that, 'Pamela was born at Holy Wells & weighed 7lbs 5oz. She was very fair, lots of hair & a very pretty baby.' Blonde and blue-eyed, she was of typically

East Anglian colouring and more like her earlier Cobbold ancestors in build too, than her darker and slightly-framed brother and sister. Like them she was christened in the Cobbolds' family church, St Clement in Ipswich, but her godfather the MP William Bromley Davenport – later knighted – was unable to attend because he had just started with the Staffordshire Yeomanry in South Africa, to play his part in the Boer War. Her godmothers were her aunt Lady Grace Barry and, according to Evelyn's notes, a 'Mrs Hay'. She is very likely to have been Lady Hay, wife of Charles Gore Hay, 20th Earl of Erroll; the Hays were friends of Evelyn's, and a photograph of her with the Earl together with Lord Muncaster, appears in *Baby's Book*. The Hays' grandson Josslyn, born the year after Pamela, would later achieve tragic notoriety when, as the 22nd Earl, he became part of the infamous 'Happy Valley' set in Kenya and was murdered in 1941.

In June of Pamela's first year, instead of going to London for 'the Season' as they usually did, John and Evelyn went to Norway; they left all the 'chicks', as Evelyn called them, at Holy Wells with some friends' children. They went to Scotland in August, returning at the end of September for the General Election. But after that the entries trail off: presumably the effort of updating the album for her third child had become too much for Evelyn, for there is very little in *Baby's Book* of Pamela in her childhood. There are, however, some exquisite photographs of Mama on horseback, sitting side-saddle and wearing a beautifully-cut riding outfit which shows off perfectly her wasp-waist and slender figure – perhaps to demonstrate to the children in later years how Mama remained elegant, despite having given birth three times. And given her ancestry, Evelyn had an image to maintain in her wide social circle which included members of some of the oldest families in England and Scotland.

There would have been no need, of course, for Pamela's mother to compromise on style merely because of motherhood. Naturally for a family of their class and era, the childcare was put largely in the hands of a nanny. The three children enjoyed the dedicated care of Jane Cottle, a Hampshire-born woman who was thirty-four when Pamela arrived, assisted by a nineteen-year-old nursemaid, Jane Prime. Nanny Cottle had the honour of being photographed for *Baby's Book*, not just with her first-born charge but with her master and mistress and some of their friends. She served the family loyally, remaining close to Pamela once her nannying duties were discharged and would be rewarded when she eventually retired with her own little terraced house in Ipswich and an annual legacy.

Pamela's first year of life was the last of Queen Victoria's: shortly after her first birthday the Queen died, aged eighty-one, on 22 January 1901, shaking the country and the Empire. The new monarch was her son Edward, short, fat and fifty-nine, of whose sexual philandering as Prince of Wales his parents had despaired. Edward VII nevertheless proved to be a popular king during his unexpectedly short reign. As well as being a friend of the children's grandfather Charles Murray, he was godfather to their uncle Alexander.

That same year Pamela's father was appointed High Sheriff of Suffolk by the King's Privy Council, an important post dating back over a thousand years. In John's time it was the prime office under the Crown, making him the King's personal representative in the county for a year and responsible, amongst other things, for attending royalty when they visited Suffolk. The honour of the appointment demonstrated the esteem in which John was held in the county, making his youngest daughter in particular very proud of him.

In June that year, toddler Pamela and four-year-old Ivan were left at home while Winifred, now aged nine, was allowed to go to Norway, where the family owned a house and fishing rights, with her mother and her friends Lord Aylesford[1] and his soon-to-be-married daughter, Lady Muriel Finch. John could not go with them at first because, as High Sheriff, he was attending a Judge, but he joined the party a week later. They stayed at the family's 'little wooden house', as Evelyn called it: a large, attractive building in the middle of a spectacular gorge, where they fished and Winifred caught her first trout. On returning to England

---

[1] He was Charles Wightwick Finch, prematurely the 8th Earl of Aylesford, whose older brother Heneage, the 7th Earl, a friend of the Prince of Wales, had in the 1870s been unwittingly involved in a scandal. Heneage's wife had an affair with the son and heir of the Duke of Marlborough, uncle of Winston Churchill. The Prince was dragged into it, and it could have threatened his succession to the throne. As a result Heneage agreed to separate from, rather than divorce, his wife, and he died aged only thirty-six, in Texas. Charles had had other tribulations too, as his first wife died aged just twenty-one, after only fourteen months of marriage.

on 20 July, Evelyn 'found the other chicks very well and happy'. It was a trip that Pamela was allowed to take later, and one photograph shows her aged about ten in a rowing boat with her mother, and a man to do the rowing, in the middle of a vast lake, holding a long fishing rod and looking very pleased with herself.

It was usual for children in upper-class families not to see much of their parents on a daily basis, and Pamela was no exception. When he was not away shooting or fishing, her father was busy with his commercial commitments and his public duties, and Evelyn was often an absent mother, but Holy Wells was an enchanting place to spend a childhood with its beautiful grounds and lake for ice skating in the winters and its stable block full of horses. With encouragement from her parents, both keen riders, Pamela was taught to ride at a young age and quickly became very accomplished, as an adult riding side-saddle with ease. As a child she was often photographed with one of her favourite ponies. There were always dogs around to play with too, like Jim the dachshund, and if Pamela's older brother and sister were not interested in playing with their little sister, then she had her best friend Angy Tollemache to keep her company.

The Tollemache family had Suffolk roots even older than the Cobbolds and were the other great brewing family of the county. Since 1490 their family seat had been, and remains, the very grand Helmingham Hall in which Queen Elizabeth I had reputedly stayed twice and left behind her lute. Angy's grandfather, Baron Tollemache, had been close friends with Pamela's great-grandfather, John Chevallier Cobbold, in the mid-nineteenth century when they were both MPs. Angy's father, the Hon Douglas Tollemache, was head of his family's brewing business; he had also joined one of the Cobbold's other commercial enterprises in 1885, the Bacon, Cobbold & Company Bank, so the two families were firmly linked. A few generations later, in 1957, they would go further and amalgamate the two family breweries to form Tolly Cobbold, their beer known as 'Tolly's'.

The girls were the same age as each other, and inseparable. Angy, tall and rangy, was the second youngest of five children; her eldest brother Bevil was eleven years older than her and away at Eton when she was born, and her younger brother Rupert too young to play with, so she spent more time in Pamela's company than that of her siblings. As was usual for upper-class girls of that period, Pamela had a governess, Miss Florence Bartlett, a Kentish woman, and due to the long-standing friendship of the Cobbold and Tollemache families, it was decided that the two girls could share her.

Angy was a lively and outspoken child, and Pamela had a keen and mischievous sense of humour, so their governess had her hands full. The girls were very close and reliant on their friendship. While her parents were pleased that Pamela had someone of her own age as a friend, as the girls got older something made John and Evelyn start to see Angy differently, and they tried to discourage the relationship. Meanwhile the duo had the advantage of almost one-to-one teaching, experiencing freedom from traditional school discipline and being able in their ample spare time to develop, particularly in Pamela's case, considerable skill in several sports, but they were denied the advantages of a more formal education that boys of their class usually enjoyed. Despite wider educational opportunities being available for women and the fact that Pamela's parents were both intellectually bright, there is little evidence that they guided her towards anything other than being of some service to the community – although no bad thing in itself – and hoped she would make a suitable marriage.

That being the way of things, her brother Ivan benefited from a public school education. In 1910 when he was thirteen Ivan started at Eton, following in their father's footsteps. The children's paternal grandmother, Adela, was the daughter of the previous Vice-Provost of Eton, the Reverend J G Dupuis, so naturally there was a certain inclination towards that old and respected establishment. John Dupuis Cobbold had been known at Eton as a brilliant player both of tennis and the separate game of racquets. His son managed to maintain the Cobbold reputation, later becoming Keeper of the Racquets and playing cricket for the Eton XI, a highly regarded team.

Pamela meanwhile had to make do with practising her tennis on the courts of Holy Wells. There she and Angy spent much time playing and getting annoyed with the many visitors the Cobbolds entertained when they were home, who would watch their tennis matches. On one occasion the girls pretended they had lost some balls and looked on amused while the guests, trying to help, searched for a long while in vain amongst the shrubbery. When they told the girls that the balls simply could not be found, they received such black looks that they felt compelled to go back and look again.

Often described retrospectively as a golden time in the light of the horror that was to come, the Edwardian era was characterised at least in part by the ostentation of the upper classes, a period when social standing and hierarchy was paramount. It certainly meant a lot to Evelyn. In July 1910, perhaps as a celebration of the new monarch, Evelyn gave a dance at the Cobbolds' London residence in Berkeley Square. Given the guest list, which comprised many earls and their countesses and hardly an untitled person amongst them, the occasion was reported prominently in the Court Circular of *The Times*, under the heading 'Lady Evelyn Cobbold's Dance'.

Her husband John, however, was missing from the occasion, as he was at Aix-les Bains undergoing 'the cure'. The French spa town had been a favourite of Queen Victoria, and as a result the place had become very fashionable amongst the wealthy and titled; as the American Mark Twain remarked, after a visit nineteen years earlier, the place was always 'a rabble of nobilities, big and little... and often a king or two'.

Why John felt the need to take the reputedly medicinal waters at that particular time is not known, but Evelyn had to rely on her brother, Alexander, to help her receive the guests. Pamela, aged ten, was no doubt required to stay home at Holy Wells with her nanny, so would have missed seeing the guests – including her great-uncle, the 3rd Earl of Leicester and a cousin, Lady Muriel Herbert, daughter of the Earl of Pembroke – arriving in their finery and dancing to Cassano's Orchestra in the elegant drawing rooms, decorated for the occasion with huge displays of crimson ramblers.

The death of Edward VII on 6 May that year marked the start of the second new reign in Pamela's young life, that of King George V and Queen Mary. Edward had outlived Pamela's maternal grandfather, his friend the Earl of Dunmore, who had died suddenly in England in August 1907 and to whose funeral in Stirlingshire he sent his representative. Esteemed for his travels and writing, the Earl's funeral was an impressive

Highlands affair, recorded in *The Times* and described at great length in *The Scotsman* newspaper. Children were not expected to attend funerals in those days, however close the relationship with the deceased, so all his grandchildren were left behind, even Winifred, by then fifteen; a cross of red heather was sent on their behalf.

John accompanied his distraught wife to the service. Evelyn was closer to her father than her sisters had been, sharing his love of travel and of the East and sometimes accompanying him. At the Dunmore family chapel on the Dunmore Estate near Stirling, they joined Evelyn's brother Alexander, by succession now the 8th Earl of Dunmore, and two of her sisters and their husbands. Evelyn's mother, Lady Gertrude Murray, now the Dowager Countess, did not attend, for she was still in a state of shock: her husband had died suddenly on her bedroom sofa.

Alexander was dressed in Highland costume as an officer of the Atholl Highlanders, one of the oldest Scottish regiments, in which his father had served for over forty years. Mourners included Highland chiefs and the Earl's Scottish relations, notably the 7th Duke of Atholl, head of the Murray clan, and his eldest son, the Marquess of Tullibardine. Charles Murray was buried in the family vault in Elphinstone Tower, the Duke of Atholl taking from his cap a sprig of juniper, the emblem of the Murray clan, and laying it on the coffin.

After the funeral, travelling further north with his wife to the hunting estate he rented every year by Loch Rannoch in Perthshire, John Dupuis Cobbold must have reflected on his late father-in-law's life and how, despite several centuries of his wife's aristocratic background and impeccable connections, it was the Cobbolds who had achieved and maintained the greater wealth.

Chapter 3

Water, Water, Everywhere: the Cobbolds

The wealth into which Pamela was born, and the reputation her family enjoyed, were the result of generations of hard work which, fortunately for her father, seldom seemed to have faltered or suffered from family recklessness. John Dupuis Cobbold may have been 'trade' compared with his aristocratic wife, but not only did he have more money, he had the satisfaction of knowing that his family had greatly contributed to the life of Suffolk, something for which they are still remembered in the twenty-first century. John would have been delighted to learn the result of the poll held by BBC Radio Suffolk in January 2004 to find the county's heroes. Two of his ancestors were proposed, one of whom was his grandfather, John Chevallier Cobbold, along with such luminaries as the artists Gainsborough and Constable, Britain's first female doctor, Elizabeth Garrett Anderson, and the cartoonist Giles. The other vote went to John Chevallier's great-great grandfather Thomas, the founder of the family brewing business.

Today, Harwich in Essex is well known as a bustling port, within easy reach of the Hook of Holland for those who want an easy getaway for a weekend break, and like many ports it has plenty of pubs. But in 1723, a decent pint of ale was not easy to find in the town. Thomas Cobbold knew there were plenty of customers for it: not only was it the drink of the working man of the time, but the port of Harwich had been used for passenger and freight sailings to the Continent since the thirteenth century; its shipyard had been building ships for the Royal Navy since 1543; and in 1661 mail packets had started their run to

Holland, so the demand was both local and itinerant. But the essential ingredient of good beer is good water – and Harwich did not have it. Salt water seeped into its wells because the town was almost completely surrounded by the sea. The locals certainly had a problem:

'The sea… maketh the springs so brackish that there is a defect of fresh water, which they fetch some good way off. To eke out the supply, they make conveniences to catch and keep rain water.'[1]

Thomas found the answer that was the start of the family's fortune. Born in 1680 of yeoman ancestry, he was a maltster, 'skilled in turning the barley grown on East Anglian farms into good malt for the brewer's mash tun'.[2] He knew where he could find the perfect water for high quality beer – in the neighbouring county, Suffolk, where the crystal-clear springs of Holy Wells were found. Close to the River Orwell, near Ipswich, the springs had long been known for their purity and their supposedly curative properties used by pilgrims. When Thomas put his plans in place in the early 1740s, he started by renting the estate of Holy Wells, then set in farmland owned by local families.

Thomas had opened the first Cobbold brewery in 1723, in Kings Quay, Harwich. His was not the only brewery in the area, but his idea of bringing the sweet water of Holy Wells to Harwich gave him a distinct advantage. Using a fleet of water schuyts – wooden sailing vessels with tanks for the water and large pumps to empty them – he transported the water from Holy Wells to Harwich. Unsurprisingly this proved hugely successful, and his reputation as a brewer began in earnest.

But the transport costs from Harwich to Ipswich greatly increased Thomas' overheads; the only way forward was to change location. Little is known about Thomas and his family, but in 1746 he moved them and the brewery to Ipswich, a significant town already over a thousand years old, one of whose famous sons was Thomas, Cardinal Wolsey.[3] Erecting the wooden buildings of his new brewery at a spot known to local people as 'The Cliff', beside the River Orwell right below the Holy Wells, he and his family took over Cliff House, an attractive building which, in the

---

[1] F. Walton, *Souvenir of the Bi-Centenary of the Cliff Brewery*, Ipswich, 1923.
[2] R. Malster, *250 Years of Brewing in Ipswich*, Malthouse Press in association with Tollemache & Cobbold Brewery Ltd., 1996.
[3] He had founded a college there in 1528 during Henry VIII's reign, now Ipswich School.

late twentieth century, would become The Brewery Tap public house. Thomas' move to Ipswich heralded the start of over two hundred and fifty years of Cobbold presence and influence in the commercial and public life of the town.

But if Thomas expected to find Ipswich the flourishing, wealthy town it had been between the thirteenth and seventeenth centuries, he would be disappointed, for it was experiencing a downturn in its fortunes. Its wealth had started in medieval times when it was home, as were many other Suffolk towns, to rich merchants in the woollen trade. Many were Protestant refugees from the Continent, who had fled religious persecution with their weaver craftsmen and set up their successful businesses. They contributed not only to Ipswich's wealth but also to its architectural style, building enduringly distinctive houses.

But as religious persecution lessened in Europe, the migrants stopped coming, and gradually the woollen trade moved north. Ipswich became a maritime town and flourished as a port, but little else. However, the Cobbolds took advantage of the merchants' legacy by buying up their beautiful houses, with their rich oak carving and elaborate panelling, and turning them into inns, taking care to preserve their original features. Many survive today.

Ipswich enjoyed a change in its fortunes towards the end of the eighteenth century, but Thomas missed this, as he died in 1752. But during his life he had enjoyed the friendship of the artist Thomas Gainsborough, himself a Suffolk man who later lived in Ipswich. Gainsborough's picture, *Holywells Park, Ipswich,* painted between 1748 and 1750, is the only contemporary record of Thomas Cobbold's enterprise in constructing the reservoirs at Holy Wells, from which the spring water was taken to his Brewery.[4]

The first of the Cobbolds about whom much is known was Thomas' grandson, John Cobbold. After the death of his father in 1767, John found himself head of the business, aged just twenty-two. His older brother should have inherited the Brewery – instead he went into the Church – but at least the young John was in the happy position of taking

[4] Thomas' wife Mary and daughter Anne are thought to be the subjects of another of Gainsborough's works, *Mother and daughter in a landscape with a lamb and ewe* c. 1752. The subjects have never been confirmed but the painting stayed in the Cobbold family until 1995.

over a growing business and also inheriting property in Harwich and Dovercourt.

A well-built man with fair hair and blue eyes, echoed in his great-great-great granddaughter Pamela, he was not only a successful businessman but enjoyed an active procreative role, too. His first wife, Elizabeth Wilkinson, bore him fifteen children in seventeen years before dying, perhaps unsurprisingly, aged thirty-seven in 1790. His second wife, Elizabeth Clarke, widowed after just six months of marriage to the Controller of Customs at Ipswich who was twice her age, was twenty years younger than John and gave him another seven children – six sons and a daughter – in eight years.

When he had time between his lovemaking and his business dealings, John worried about England's involvement in foreign affairs. Due to the Napoleonic and other revolutionary wars, Ipswich had recently become a garrison town, which was good for the brewing trade but had few other advantages. The wars increased taxation, and in 1800 the poor of Ipswich rioted and looted Ipswich market. However, to John's relief they deliberately avoided harming the Cliff Brewery: presumably they looked forward to a good drink after all their thirsty rioting.

To accommodate his vast family, in 1814 John ceased renting and bought the Holy Wells estate, building above the springs the mansion house where Pamela would be born. He also owned the Manor House on St Margaret's Green in Ipswich, as well as Cliff House. It was just as well he and his second wife, Elizabeth Clarke, had a choice of residences, for she did like to entertain; she became a notable society figure in her own right, and her guests are likely to have included Lord and Lady Nelson, either when they bought property in Ipswich in 1797 after his victory at the Battle of Cape St Vincent, or in 1800 when he became High Steward of Ipswich.

Elizabeth was also a significant poet. A contemporary of Jane Austen, her work is still published in anthologies of women poets of the Romantic era. She had published her first work at seventeen and six narrative poems at twenty-one, dedicated to Sir Joshua Reynolds, the Society portrait painter, as well as numerous other works. And although he could not have met her, Charles Dickens, who stayed in Ipswich in 1835 to report on the elections, used Elizabeth in his *Pickwick Papers* as his model for Mrs Leo Hunter who 'dotes on poetry'.

The ample-bosomed Elizabeth was also a benefactor of many local charities and a champion of the arts, making Holy Wells a centre for literature, theatre, music and art. She became renowned for her annual 'Valentine Ball'. For each Ball she made eighty delicate and elaborate valentines which were sent out beforehand to unmarried ladies and gentlemen, who came to the Balls with one aim in mind.

The penniless young Suffolk-born artist John Constable became her protégé and friend, and was tutor to her art students. He frequently stayed with the family, maintaining a friendship with Elizabeth until her death. She was often mentioned in correspondence between Constable and his sisters, Ann and Mary, and his wife Maria, and they were clearly close enough for Ann to feel she should tell her brother about an accident Elizabeth had in 1810. In a letter to John from East Bergholt dated May 8 1810 Ann wrote:

'You have most likely heard of the very lamentable accident of Mrs Cobbold at the Cliff – passing thro' a dark passage at a shop in Ipswich, a cellar door open unknown to her, she fell down without the least warning into the cellar & pitched on her head. I went to the Cliff on Saturday last. She had that morning suffered and endured with her heroic mind, a most severe operation – something similar to scalping, as Harriet [a daughter of Elizabeth and John] told me. The skin had been divided on her head, & compleatly [sic] turned back – to examine what injury the skull had sustained as to a fracture or whether only violent contusion & consequent inflammation on her brain.

It is really dreadful to think on – & really Mr Cobbold looked quite petrified. There were nine of her children with her in the Parlour… William [a son]… was the only one that enquired after you – but this and every other omission was excusable in the present perturbed state of the house and everyone in it.

I shall send tomorrow as while there is life there is hope – besides, the fears & apprehensions that would alone kill many, her heroism is a stranger to. She is surely a wonderful woman, her resolution astonished her surgical attendants. If she can still possess this her strong mind, I hope she will recover, but not to continue an imbecile existence – but what the Almighty ordains, we must submit to...'[5]

Perhaps miraculously Elizabeth survived without becoming an 'imbecile' and continued her contact with Constable, mentioned in letters such as the one he wrote to his wife Maria from Dedham on Easter Sunday 1821, in which he told her, 'I dined with Mrs Cobbold yesterday, very kind of her these enquiries after you...' Elizabeth died suddenly aged sixty in 1824 after she had seemed to be recovering from an illness. Constable's sister Mary, in a letter to him from Flatford in May the following year, gossiped, '*We are told* Mr Cobbold will take a third and *rich* wife, but sure it never can be.'

Indeed it never was, perhaps because John Cobbold was already eighty when Elizabeth died, although arguably he might have managed it in the remaining ten years before his own death in 1835. Why it was thought he might want a rich wife when he had his own wealth is not known, but it may have been related to the banking crisis that occurred in Ipswich that year. The town's bank, the Blue Bank, had severe difficulties, and John, with one of his sons by his first marriage (another John), together with a local solicitor, put money into the business to save it from collapse. Fortunately the scheme worked, even without a new rich wife for him, and the Bank under its new partnership traded for another eighty years: another source of income for the Cobbolds.

If the Bank and the Brewery were not enough to keep John occupied after Elizabeth's death, he had other business interests too. Like his grandfather, Thomas, he was a maltster and had his own maltings in the town; as a sideline he dealt in corn and coal, and with one of his sons he set up a wine merchant's business. Thanks to John the Cobbold name became increasingly prominent in the town, and would shortly become immortalised in literature too.

For John and Elizabeth Cobbold had played a part in saving the life of the family cook, Margaret Catchpole, the story of which was turned into a best-seller of the time, written by Elizabeth's fifth and John's twentieth son, the Reverend Richard Cobbold. Margaret, the illegitimate daughter of a Suffolk woman, worked as the Cobbold's cook in their house at St Margaret's Green. She was treated more as a family member

---

[5] R.B. Beckett, *John Constable's Correspondence*, 1962, Suffolk Records Office.

than a servant, John and Elizabeth teaching her to read and write, and she was responsible for saving the lives of three of their children. After she left their service, she stole John's strawberry roan, a crime for which she was sentenced to death in 1797. Despite the fact that she had stolen from them, the Cobbolds intervened on her behalf and the sentence was commuted to a seven-year sentence in Ipswich Gaol, where Elizabeth and the young Richard visited her.

But in 1800, desperate to go and meet her lover, Margaret escaped from the Gaol dressed as a sailor by scaling the wall with a clothes line. When caught, she again received the death sentence but it was commuted to transportation after Elizabeth pleaded for her life. In 1801 Margaret left Ipswich for Australia, where she became a reformed character, working as a midwife and farmer. She and Elizabeth continued to correspond until Margaret's death in 1819, her letters later becoming historically valuable as some of the only records of the early settlers in Australia, where she became a folk hero. Her story, inextricably linked with John and Elizabeth Cobbold, is still the subject of plays and stories in the twenty-first century.

Of the twenty-two children John had with his two wives, two became particularly significant: the clergyman Richard, novelist and illustrator, and John, the eldest son, who headed the Brewery after their father's death in 1835. John was responsible for increasing the fleet of ships owned by the Cobbolds which traded in India and China, many of them built at the family's own shipbuilding yard, and he added to the wharf they owned next to the Cliff Brewery by buying for £300, 'A strip of land on the Ooze, extending from the Gas Works to the Cliff… with a landing place or right of boatway to be preserved for the burgesses and inhabitants of Ipswich.'[6] Thanks to John, the sources of the Cobbolds' wealth were increased still further.

In 1796 John married Harriet Chevallier from a prestigious Huguenot Jersey family, whose family seat was Aspall Hall in Suffolk. The surname was later given to Chevallier barley discovered on Harriet's family's farmland, which by the turn of the twentieth century was used for three-quarters of the world's barley crops. Harriet was certainly a

[6] F. Walton, op.cit.

suitable wife for John, as her family had brewing connections themselves: Clement Chevallier had started Aspall Cyder in 1728, made from apple trees brought from Jersey. Today it is the oldest cider company in Britain, still run by the same family.

Perhaps wishing to emulate his father's procreative skills, John fathered fourteen children with Harriet. Their eldest, Pamela's great-grandfather, John Chevallier Cobbold, was born in 1797.[7] He played a huge role in the public and commercial life of Suffolk during the Victorian era, being described in the 1861 Census as 'Banker, Brewer, Merchant, MP'; in the latter role for the Conservative Party, the people of Ipswich elected him five consecutive times. He was also a Mayor of Ipswich and a Treasurer of the Ipswich and East Suffolk Hospital. All this while running Cobbold's Brewery and being busy with the family Bank too.

But perhaps John Chevallier's most lasting achievement was the part he played in bringing the railway to Suffolk. A heavily rural county, like much of the East Anglian region it was lagging behind the rest of the country in its rail communications: it had almost none. The railway line went as far as Colchester in Essex and then stopped. John Chevallier decided that the only way of ever getting a train to his home town of Ipswich was to start a company. Contributing his own money and that of some fellow Ipswich businessmen, he saw the start of the Eastern Union Railway. With John leading them they managed to get an Act of Parliament passed in 1844 authorising the Eastern Union Line to continue from Colchester to Ipswich. The line was opened to goods traffic on 1 June 1846, followed by a grand official opening ten days later, with a public holiday being declared in Ipswich.

As the first passenger train left the station at 10.30am on 11 June 1846, according to local press reports six hundred ladies beneath a triumphal arch in a specially erected grandstand waved 'snowy kerchiefs', and a band on the train played 'God Save the Queen'. John joined the train at the first stop and watched the celebratory balloon ascent, while later fireworks by the Wet Dock ended the day's festivities. The effect of the railway's arrival in Ipswich was phenomenal, providing

---

[7] From then on the 'Johns' in the Cobbold family would become distinguished from each other by the use of their first and middle names (which had been their mothers' maiden names).

new opportunities for commerce and industry, and giving everyone the chance for the first time to travel outside the confines of their rural world.

Despite his busy life John Chevallier did find some time to relax with his family – his wife Lucy (née Patteson) and their ten children – and acquired a holiday home for them. Today Felixstowe on the Suffolk coast is the UK's major container port and, with its four-mile long seafront, a popular seaside resort thanks to a visit in 1891 from the Empress of Germany. But in 1839 when John first took a fancy to it, it was a backwater: just a handful of houses and a few Martello towers, built when he was a young boy to repel a feared invasion by Napoleon which never happened.

He liked the place well enough to rent Felixstowe Cottage every summer, much to the delight of his children, who loved the miles of clean, empty beaches. Once a small fisherman's hut, the house had been redesigned by its previous eccentric owner and was perfectly situated on the edge of a cliff at a point later named, and still called Cobbold Point. John was amongst the first Ipswich businessmen to spend the summer months in Felixstowe, and the turreted house with the large garden sloping down to the edge of the cliff became a wonderful legacy for his descendants. The Cobbolds later bought the house, enlarging it and developing it further, and renaming it The Lodge.[8] One of John Chevallier's sons, the MP, banker and philanthropist Felix Thornley Cobbold, lived there until his death in 1909, and being unmarried and without children himself, he welcomed all his great-nephews and great-nieces to stay there with their nannies while their parents were away. As children, Pamela and her brother Ivan loved to stay there.

After Felix died, Pamela's uncle Philip Wyndham Cobbold and her aunt Cicely took over The Lodge. As a teenager, Pamela would spend many happy summer days at Felixstowe with her best friend Angy Tollemache or with Philip and Cicely's daughter, her cousin Joan, spending hours swimming in the sea and drying off in the sun, a pleasure which Pamela revelled in.

Such was John Chevallier's enthusiasm for Felixstowe – as well as his keen commercial eye – that he built its first hotel, The Bath, in 1839

---

[8] The building is still there but is now a residential home.

using bricks from a demolished Martello tower. The elegant building on the seafront was sold after his death in 1882 when it was still doing well, an advert of the time describing it as, '... surrounded by extensive Gardens and Grounds, including Croquet Lawn, Bowling Green, 10 Lawn Tennis Courts...'. The accommodation included, 'Ladies' Drawing Room... Private Sitting Rooms... Smoking Room... Electric Light throughout.'

Closer to home, Holy Wells flourished under John Chevallier's care. In the late 1850s he extended and updated the mansion house, described in newspaper reports as, 'classical Victorian style with colonial style veranda and shutters', and landscaped the park. He and Lucy were keen to put the new-style park, finished in the early 1860s, to good use and make it accessible to the public, and in July 1864 they hosted a couple of events: firstly, the Ipswich Horticultural Show and then a two-day bazaar held in aid of the bluntly-named Essex Hall Asylum for Idiots (Colchester). The idea, according to the *Ipswich Journal* of 23 July 1864, was that 'the highest and most influential ladies in the eastern counties would accord their patronage and assistance'. John Chevallier was praised:

'The hospitable generosity with which Mr Cobbold has so many times, since the improvements at Holy Wells, thrown [the gardens] open to the public, has rendered it a task of mere superficiality and repetition for us to give any description of them.'

The Journal went on regardless to describe the landscape's 'lovely dells, from which may be caught glimpses of the Orwell, wooded glades... a copious spring rising from a cleft in the hill, and running quietly down to the fishpond, on which so many inhabitants of Ipswich have skated'. John also had two lodges built and introduced to the park many exotic plants such as bamboo, rhododendrons, palms and magnolias.

However, there was sadness too in John Chevallier's long life. His eldest son, Pamela's grandfather John Patteson Cobbold with whom he ran the Brewery, died suddenly in December 1875, aged forty-four of, according to a contemporary newspaper report, 'a malignant attack of scarlet fever... in less than a week', leaving his wife Adela (née Dupuis) with eight young children to look after. The eldest of these was Pamela's father, John Dupuis Cobbold, who was fourteen and away at school at Eton; the youngest, Philip, just a baby. In the year before his death,

John Patteson had been elected MP for Ipswich, although a writer in a local newspaper column was dubious about his suitability, declaring that, 'A seat in Parliament is no place for him... Public speaking is not his forte', and suggested that he was a 'different man' from his father, John Chevallier. However, the article spoke highly of John Patteson as a caring employer in Ipswich, saying he was one of the young men who '... saw that... adequate work should be done for money, abuses should be as promptly as possible extinguished, and employment and wages set in healthy relations towards each other'. In 1877 in memory of his son, John Chevallier and other members of the Cobbold family provided all the funds for a children's wing for the East Suffolk and Ipswich Hospital.

John Patteson should have succeeded his father as head of Cobbold and Son on John Chevallier's death in 1882; instead, the role fell to John Dupuis, when he was just twenty-one and still studying for his law degree at Trinity College, Cambridge, where his brilliance in tennis and racquets first seen at Eton had continued. Under his leadership a new Cliff Brewery would be designed and built in 1896, with all the latest equipment and embodying the most modern brewing techniques. Until then, after graduating and familiarising himself with his unexpected responsibility, he indulged in his love of travel and of hunting, and met and wooed his future wife, Lady Evelyn Murray.

Chapter 4

The Murrays

Pamela's roots on her mother's side were thoroughly aristocratic. The Murray clan to which Lady Evelyn's father Charles Adolphus Murray, the 7th Earl of Dunmore, belonged, was one of the most ancient of the Scottish clans. The title of the Earl of Dunmore had been created in 1686 by King James VII of Scotland for Charles' ancestor Charles Murray, younger brother of the first Murray to be created Duke of Atholl. The family seat, where a portrait of the first Earl hangs, remains the fairytale-like Blair Castle in Perthshire. Evelyn's mother was Lady Gertrude Coke,[1] the Norfolk-born daughter of Thomas Coke, the 2nd Earl of Leicester, an even older title.

When Evelyn, first child of Charles and Gertrude, was born in 1867, the construction of his second castle, Amhuinnsuidhe[2] on the Isle of Harris in the Outer Hebrides, was about to finish. There had been no tedious necessity to obtain permission for the castle: Charles' grandfather, the 5th Earl of Dunmore, had bought the island in the early nineteenth century. When Charles' father Alexander, the 6th Earl, died in 1845 at the young age of forty-one, Charles – until then Viscount Fincastle – became 7th Earl at the tender age of four. His widowed mother the Countess Lady Catherine, a daughter of the Earl of Pembroke, continued to run the North Harris estate with her factor until her son came of age.

If that were not enough to keep herself occupied, Catherine set up an embroidery school on Harris in 1849 and did much to encourage the

[1] Pronounced 'Cook'.
[2] Pronounced 'Aven-suey'.

49

fledgling Harris Tweed industry. She commissioned a copy of the Murray tartan from the tweed workers on the island and began to promote and market the fabric amongst her aristocratic friends and London society. Catherine then turned her attention to improving the process of tweed production on Harris. Soon the popularity of the fabric spread and continued, to the extent that modern designers such as Vivienne Westwood and the late Alexander McQueen would use Harris Tweed in their women's wear collections in the twenty-first century.

Charles had built his first castle, Ardvourlie, on Harris in 1863, when he came of age, as a hunting lodge for the North Harris Estate but he never lived there, instead renting it out to his sporting friends. In 1866 he married Gertrude, but if he had hoped to impress her with Amhuinnsuidhe then he was to be disappointed. Rumour has it that she pronounced it not even as big as a hen house or a stable at her father's house. Stung by her barb, Charles built a further wing on to the castle. It is possible that this contributed to his financial problems: in 1868 before the wing was completed, when Evelyn was barely a year old, he was forced to declare himself bankrupt. His bankers in London took over the unfinished castle to repay his debts.

But all was not lost. Charles still had the family estate in Stirlingshire, Dunmore Park; the land had been bought in 1754 from their relations the Elphinstone family by his great-grandfather, John Murray, the 4th Earl. The estate included the nearby village of Dunmore, which Catherine found a miserable and unpleasant place for the local people to live in. Although busy developing the Harris Tweed industry, she found the energy to completely re-model the village, providing it with better housing, a village green and a school. Most of the work was completed by 1879, so Catherine was able to see her plans come to fruition before her death in 1886; the village still stands today, with the status of a protected site.

As the 4th Earl of Dunmore, John Murray had been simultaneously one of the most revered and hated men in the British colonies. Appointed by King George III firstly as Governor of New York and then of Virginia at the start of the American Revolution, he issued a proclamation in November 1775 to any African or Indian slave who would join the British forces and fight for the King. In Virginia and beyond, black mothers named their newborn babies 'Dunmore'. In 1787 he was appointed Governor of the Bahamas and presented himself as the 'Great Liberator'.

After marrying Lady Charlotte Stewart in 1759 he built in the grounds of Dunmore Park, above a garden pavilion, a 23 metre-high stone-carved pineapple, a symbol of welcome in the colonies and of great wealth elsewhere. Still surviving today as a National Trust property 'The Pineapple', as it is known, is considered to be a unique and spectacular architectural folly. It is thought John built it for his new wife, but if he did not then he should have done: it was the least he could do to show his appreciation of her. For after leaving Charlotte and their children at home in 1771 when he became Governor of Virginia, John decided in the winter of 1773 that he wanted them to join him in Williamsburg: he could not have gone home without resigning his post, so he sent for them. With John's personal secretary sent to accompany them, and with ten servants, Charlotte and all but one of their seven children (the youngest of whom she left with her sister) started the forty-four-day crossing to New York. Due to atrocious weather in that city they had to spend a month there, using the time also to recuperate after the nightmarish voyage. Travelling by carriage and the Dunmore yacht, they took another twenty-four days to complete the journey south to Williamsburg.

Not that Charlotte had it all tough. As the highest ranking woman in British North America, the arrival of Lady Dunmore did not go unnoticed. She had been eagerly anticipated: the newspapers which had been keeping the public informed of the family's progress on the journey published three effusive poems in her honour. Williamsburg illuminated its houses with candles in the windows and celebrated her arrival with fireworks, whilst the *Virginia Gazette* wrote of the 'great number of the most respectable citizens, and many from the country' who gathered to see her arrival at the palace in Williamsburg in February 1774.[3] A ball was held in the couple's honour later that year in Norfolk, Virginia, which came to be regarded as the biggest social event in pre-revolutionary Norfolk.

John too was clearly pleased to see his wife again: just over nine months later, in December 1774, Charlotte gave birth to a daughter

[3] Quoted in M.M. Theobold, *The Governor's Lady, Mistress of the Palace*, as published in the Journal of the Colonial Williamsburg Foundation, Spring 2003.

whom they named Virginia, although she would not stay long in that State. In June 1775 the family was forced to flee the colony with John returning to America alone in January 1776, this time to lead the British bombardment of Norfolk, Virginia, as part of the American War of Independence.

Nearly a century later in 1866, when John's great-grandson Charles took Gertrude to Dunmore Park, she found not only the extraordinary Pineapple but a magnificent mansion built by Charles' grandfather, the 5th Earl, in 1822. The oldest part of the estate was the Dunmore Tower built in the sixteenth century, originally called Elphinstone Tower after their kinsmen who had first owned the land. A four-storey turreted building, the ground-floor room was used from the early nineteenth century as the family burial place of the Earls of Dunmore. However, unlike his forebears, and in comparison with his social peers, Charles was a man of limited means, a factor considered by his descendants to have influenced his daughter Evelyn's later choices in life – including her marriage to John Cobbold.

Gertrude, in being dismissive about Charles' castle on Harris, was no doubt comparing it to her father's estate. Since 1609 the seat of her father's family the Cokes and the Earls of Leicester had been, and remains, the Holkham Estate, with its thousands of acres of prime farmland and woodland on the north Norfolk coast in eastern England. With the eighteenth-century jewel of Holkham Hall itself set within 3000 acres of parkland, it is one of England's best-known stately homes. Gertrude's father was Thomas William Coke, the 2nd Earl of Leicester. A cheerful-faced, red-haired man, apparently of great energy and charm, he inherited the estate in 1842 when he was twenty. He was not only an avid agriculturalist, he was also a Member of Parliament for fifty-three years. Thomas' first wife, Gertrude's mother Juliana, bore him nine children, and after she died in 1870 he married his god-daughter, fifty years his junior, who gave him another six. The active life obviously agreed with him: he was eighty-seven when he died in 1908, outliving his son-in-law Charles by more than a year.

The census of 1871 shows Evelyn, aged three, visiting Holkham in the absence of her widowed grandfather, with her mother Gertrude, aged twenty-three, and Evelyn's younger sister, Lady Muriel, then aged one. Apart from their young footman, there were twenty other servants present who formed Holkham's permanent household including a German governess, a male roasting cook and a steward's room boy. Other staff were away accompanying the family in London, for that night the two Earls in the young Evelyn's life, her father and grandfather, were both at the latter's London house, 19 Grosvenor Square. With them were two of Evelyn's aunts, the Ladies Anne and Mary Coke both in their twenties, assisted by a lady's maid and two other servants.

Pamela as a child is likely to have visited her great-grandfather and his second wife at Holkham Hall before he died, not least because her father, John Dupuis Cobbold, sometimes went shooting there. She certainly would have visited her grandparents, Charles and Gertrude, at their London house, 55 Lancaster Gate, where Gertrude continued to live as the Dowager Countess after her husband's death in 1907 until her own in 1943.

Charles Murray's presence in London without his family on that night in 1871 was partly as support for his widowed father-in-law and partly probably for business purposes, to help cultivate his political and royal position. Charles had in 1860 joined the Atholl Highlanders, the only private army in Europe, permitted by Queen Victoria to be retained by the Duke of Atholl, Charles' cousin, at Blair Castle. The Regiment's record book recalls of Charles that, 'During his long service of 40 years his genial kindly presence endeared him to all ranks of the Atholl Highlanders.' Charles retired from the regiment in 1866 but rejoined in 1872 in his former rank as a Major: just in time to help host, with the Duke and Duchess of Atholl, a visit to Blair Castle that September by the Prince and Princess of Wales. The Prince (later King Edward VII) inspected the Highlanders and, to the relief of both the Duke and the Earl, expressed his admiration of them.

Charles' friendship, as it had become, with the Prince of Wales must have helped him in 1876, when Evelyn was nine, to secure the appointment as a Lord-in-Waiting to Queen Victoria in Disraeli's Government, a post he held until 1880; Gertrude, meanwhile, was made a Lady-in-Waiting. The Queen was godmother to one of Evelyn's sisters, Lady Victoria, and the Prince of Wales godfather to her brother, Alexander. The Prince often visited Charles in a private capacity including in 1876 when he spent part of the autumn with the Earl at Dunmore Park; the Prince had just completed a long tour of India with Princess Alexandra and needed time to relax, recuperate, and to indulge in his love of shooting. He may have indulged in his love of loving too, being joined by whichever mistress he had at the time – it was not yet Lillie Langtry, for they would not meet until the following year – but if he did, Charles' discretion would have ensured confidentiality.

Pamela must have regretted being too young to know her grandfather well, for he had many admirable talents. He was also Lord Lieutenant of Stirlingshire and as Colonel-in-Chief of the 4th Battalion of the Queen's Own Cameron Highlanders went on many military campaigns, yet he still found time to do his own travelling. Tall, bearded and handsome, his obituary in *The Times* on 28 August 1907 said that, '… he was a great traveller, and his magnificent physique enabled him to penetrate regions full of hardships'. In fact, the amount of travelling he did by the standards of any period was phenomenal. Amongst the countries he visited were Scandinavia, Syria, Russia, Guinea, Turkey, the United States, Canada, the West Indies and Hong Kong, all the time recording his adventures in beautiful water colours, stunning photographs – sometimes shocking in their honesty – and eloquent words.

Due to the Earl of Dunmore's comparatively limited means the family had an itinerant life generally, and when they were not in Scotland – which Evelyn and her father loved passionately – they stayed variously in North Africa and in Egypt, Charles being a friend of the Viceroy. The British winters were spent at Charles' villa at Bab-el-Look near Cairo, where Evelyn and her siblings were taught by a governess and made many Muslim friends. The Murrays also stayed in Algiers and later, in her book *Pilgrimage to Mecca* first published in 1934, Evelyn wrote:

'As a child I spent the winter months in a Moorish villa on a hill outside Algiers, where my parents went in search of sunshine. There I learnt to speak Arabic and my delight was to escape my governess and visit the Mosques with my Algerian friends, and unconsciously I was a little Muslim at heart.'

In fact, Evelyn later went the whole way and actively converted to Islam, making her pilgrimage to Mecca in 1933 at the age of sixty-six – probably the first British woman to convert to Islam to perform this rite. In her quest for spiritualism she echoed her mother, Gertrude, who herself had experienced many journeys, both spiritual and physical, sometimes travelling without her husband through North Africa. In doing so Gertrude managed, however, to avoid the notoriety of her aunt Jane Digby,[4] also brought up at Holkham, whose name the family would never mention.

Evelyn's chosen religion, apart from being extremely unusual for the age and for her background, was perhaps all the more surprising given that her father was one of the first Christian Scientists. The Church of Christ, Scientist – not to be confused with the Church of Scientology, founded much later – had been started in 1879 in Boston, Massachusetts by the American, Mary Baker Eddy. As a child Mary was regarded by friends and family as having healing abilities, and after a fall in 1866 had left her with a major spinal injury, she turned to the Bible and recovered unexpectedly. She developed an interest in Biblical accounts of early Christian healing, in 1875 writing the tract on which the belief is based: *Science and health with key to the Scriptures*. Eddy's Church Manual states that her Church is designed 'to commemorate the word and works of our Master, which should reinstate primitive Christianity and its lost element of healing'.

Many adherents shun conventional medicine, and it appears that this was the reason Charles Murray was attracted to it, attending the dedication of the Mother Church of the community in Boston. He had apparently suffered for years from a rupture which, according to a testimony he gave to a Christian Science meeting in Aldershot just a few days before his death, could not be cured by even the best surgeons. He had instead, he said, been cured by means of Christian Science by his own daughter. In 1901 Cambridge University Press published Charles' book of poems called *The Revelation of Christianus and other Christian Science Poems*, the same year that the *International Herald Tribune* reported his visit on 25 June, 'with other English visitors and three thousand more Christian Scientists', to Mrs Eddy's residence at Concord, New Hampshire, where they all gathered on her lawn to hear her speak.

[4] Later Lady Ellenborough, who herself had travelled in the East and eventually married a Bedouin sheikh twenty years her junior.

Charles may also have been aware of the unusual health problems that his father's cousin Sir Augustus d'Esté[5] had suffered. Charles' great aunt Lady Augusta Murray had in 1793 married a son of King George III, Prince Augustus Frederick Hanover, the Duke of Sussex. There were complications caused by their marriage, which took place in Rome and was in contravention of the Royal Marriages Act of 1772 and thus invalid. His mother, Augusta, fought to overcome the obstacles created by the marriage to ensure his education and to achieve for him (and his sister) recognition of the prerogatives of the marriage. As a result, Augustus was able to attend military college and enjoy a very successful army career, despite the fact that throughout his life he was the object of much fascinated medical attention: as later discovered from the detailed diary he kept, it is extremely likely that he suffered from what is now recognised as multiple sclerosis. The diary, which he kept until his death in 1848 at the age of fifty-four, is still of great interest to the medical profession, and is thought probably to be the first record of a person having the disease.

If Evelyn's privileged childhood gave her varied travel experience, she had also had in her father an example for travel writing. The 'regions full of hardship' that *The Times* referred to included a nine-month expedition in 1892, with a Major Roche, on horseback and on foot through Kashmir, Western Tibet, Chinese Tartary and Russian Central Asia. Charles wrote of his experiences in diary form which was published in 1893 as *The Pamirs,* still in print in the twenty-first century, and in 1895 he wrote *Ormisdale,* a well-received novel based on people he had met through his travels.

When not travelling abroad with her family, Evelyn had ample opportunity to learn stalking and shooting, which she loved, developing the skills when staying on her father's Isle of Harris. Evelyn became greatly accomplished with a rifle and took her shooting very seriously, a skill that she passed on to Pamela. Her love of hunting and her lust for travel gave Evelyn something in common with her future husband. In an article for the *East Anglian Daily Times* published on 1 January 1890, after a particularly exciting journey, John Dupuis Cobbold wrote:

[5] The surname was an ancient family one: Augustus and his sister Emma could not take the surname of Hanover because of the illegality of their parents' marriage.

'To leave England in the month of May must assuredly denote an insatiable love of travel and sport; that and a chance of visiting regions untrodden by an Englishman's foot was my excuse.'

The article was the first in a series John wrote describing a shooting trip to the Altai Mountains on the borders of Siberia and China which he undertook in May 1889 with a friend and a married couple, two years before his marriage to Evelyn. He also enjoyed shooting in the Rockies and India and, to the satisfaction of Evelyn, rented every summer the magnificent hunting estate at Loch Rannoch.

In 1891 John was a man of significant wealth, heading the family's various commercial interests, including the bank which later became Lloyds, and running the family brewery in partnership with his spirited and handsome younger brother, Philip Wyndham Cobbold: presumably the brothers had an amicable arrangement about whose turn it was to go adventuring and whose to look after the business.

The wedding in Cairo, as reported back home in the loyal *East Anglian Daily Times*, was a sizeable affair despite the restraints and time involved in foreign travel at that time, and the status of the guests gave some indication of the connections of the bride's parents. All Saints' Church, Cairo, was 'beautifully decorated with flowers and palms given by his Highness the Khedive', who gave the bride 'a very handsome and valuable scarabaei necklace'. Guests at the reception held at her father's house included the Khedive's Prime Minister, His Excellency Riaz Pasha; three Consul-Generals – for the King of the Netherlands, for the Czar of all the Russias, and for the German Emperor; and an array of British aristocracy and military, including Colonel Kitchener who was related to the Cobbolds, and Sir Evelyn Baring, Great Britain's Consul-General in Egypt who virtually ruled that country until 1907.

In the centre of a very English scene transported into the middle of the hot Egyptian city was the beautiful Lady Evelyn, in a dress of white satin trimmed with deep Brussels lace, with a veil of Brussels lace and orange blossoms in her hair. Her bridesmaids – her three as yet unmarried sisters, the Ladies Grace, Victoria and Mildred Murray and a cousin, Lady Helena Carnegie – were all dressed in white muslin trimmed with yellow, with yellow sashes, and white hats trimmed with yellow silk and white lilacs. Two of the girls carried with their bouquets white ostrich feather fans, gifts of the bridegroom, while the others had shepherds' crooks and wore turquoise and pearl pins with the bride's initials, also presents from John. Evelyn's mother, Gertrude, the Countess of Dunmore, was dressed in a fawn-coloured gown trimmed with gold. Evelyn's younger brother Alexander, then still Viscount Fincastle, was also there, probably in uniform in keeping with tradition.

After the wedding breakfast John and his new wife, Lady Cobbold – for she would retain a title, whilst John would always be plain 'Mr' – departed under a shower of traditional rice to the railway station near Alexandria, from where they left for their honeymoon in Europe. The newspaper, after reporting the wedding festivities in Cairo, referred to the simultaneous celebration of their marriage in Ipswich, where:

'... the bells of St Clements – a parish church with which the Cobbolds have been identified for more than a century – rang merry peals throughout the day, while flags were also displayed. The healths of the bride and bridegroom were drank most heartily by the numerous employees, and messages of congratulations – necessarily brief – were wired over land and sea by many friends to the happy bridegroom. The general festivities are postponed till the homecoming, a month or so hence.'

On 23 May 1891 the couple returned to the Cobbold family seat at Holy Wells, Ipswich. The *East Anglian Daily Times* again did its duty to the family, describing the homecoming in affectionate terms. At Ipswich station they were greeted by a deputation of the tenants of Messrs Cobbold and Co who had wanted 'to testify their regard and esteem'. A triumphal arch had been erected at the entrance to Holy Wells, which was surmounted by an earl's coronet in honour of the bride's father. On one side were the words 'God bless the union' with the arms of the Dunmore and Cobbold families below, and on the other, 'Long life and happiness to the bride and bridegroom'. The head gardener, Mr Marshall, had picked out the pillars of foliage 'with rhododendrons, lilacs and roses'. They were met at the door by John's mother, Adela, widowed already for nearly ten years and still only fifty-three, 'whose hearty greeting in the presence of the multitude formed a striking example of the unconstrained affection which is the strength of the English home and character'.

If Evelyn hoped that by marrying abroad they could escape involving the people of Ipswich in their celebrations, she would have been disappointed. On the Saturday after their return the newspaper reported:

'Exactly one month after their marriage in the land of the Pharaohs, Mr J.D and Lady Evelyn Cobbold were 'at home' to receive in the picturesque park at Ipswich a notable gathering of the people whose interests are identified with their own. The invitation in the present instance was confined to the employees of Messrs Cobbold and Co and they mustered with their families in force. About 400 of the men and wives sat down to the dinner [in a marquee], some 500 children filed in to the tea, and many personal friends of the bride and bridegroom joining the party, the scene was bright, animated and in several respects unique. Not every owner of such a pretty seat is able to gather around him so numerous a company directly concerned in his prosperity, and not a few employers lack either the opportunity or disposition to do so.'

Unfortunately the weather, in typically British style, was miserable, and Lady Evelyn was 'prevented from leaving the house on account of a cold'. Nevertheless she still managed to welcome the guests, 'and comparatively speaking the day might be described as fine and warm. No rain fell, and the beauty of the country in its rich verdure made up for the lack of sunshine.'

Life seemed to bowl along smoothly for John and Evelyn in their first years of married life. The Cobbold businesses continued to thrive, providing the couple with an enviable lifestyle, enabling them to do as much travelling and hunting as they wished, whilst still being involved, on John's part particularly, in public life. Even Evelyn in the early days embraced local politics, and to cap it all she had three healthy, bright children. But she was a private person and would often be photographed in solitary activities around Holy Wells. And much as she enthused over aspects of the estate, particularly her lovely conservatory with the exotic plants she tended and of which she was very proud, there was no avoiding the fact that she was a social snob. As a young girl, Evelyn had been deeply impressed by her parents' proximity to Queen Victoria and the future King of England, and remained acutely aware all her life of her aristocratic background. In echoes of her mother Gertrude when she snubbed Charles' castle, Evelyn would refer to Holy Wells as her 'little villa'. After all, the Cobbolds, whilst very wealthy, were 'trade': her own family, although not as rich as it had been, came from ancient lineage, with the time-honoured distinction of having inherited estates and of being part of the Royal Household. Her attitude was something that would permeate her relationship with her hard-working husband, and would be a permanent cause of annoyance to her daughter Pamela. The differences between Evelyn and John would later become more marked and Pamela, as the youngest and only child at home, would be there to see it all.

Chapter 5

The Calm Before the Storm

In the frequent absence of her parents, Pamela's childhood at Holy Wells continued with her nurse and governess and best friend Angy, with occasional family forays to Scotland and Norway. In early January 1911 Pamela's mother Evelyn went to Egypt as she often did during the winter, usually with John: not only did they both still love the country, which at that stage continued under British rule, but it was a very fashionable place for the wealthy to holiday and escape the miserable British weather. This time, however, Evelyn left her husband behind with the rest of the family for her plan was to undertake a 'pilgrimage'. In February, with her father's love of travel in her blood, she began a journey with a female companion across what she called the 'Libyan Desert': it was actually Egypt's Western Desert in the vicinity of the Fayyum Oasis. Their adventure lasted just nineteen days but their experiences inspired Evelyn to write her first book, *Wayfarers in the Libyan Desert*, which she published privately in 1912. Amongst lavish photographs, some taken by a professional, and others by Evelyn and her friend, she describes dancing girls, pyramids and Bedouin, taking particular care to relate her retinue's morning prayer as they turned to Mecca. Echoing the narrative skill of her late father, Evelyn conveys poignantly her love of the East and her emotional connection with it, stemming from her childhood days.

Fortunately for John and Evelyn, as had been the case when Winifred and Ivan were young, there was always someone, family or friends, to whom they could send Pamela to stay when one or both of them was away. In January 1911 Winifred had just turned nineteen and Ivan was away at

Eton, so they only had only their youngest child to consider. John's sister Edith was always a reliable option and Pamela liked her aunt. Married since she was nineteen into a wealthy Kentish family, the Monins, who had lived in Dover for centuries, Edith had a son and three daughters. At beautiful Ringwould House near the sea, Pamela enjoyed herself with her cousins – two of the girls were a similar age to her – especially when there was a visit from Guy Cobbold; an unmarried cousin of John and Edith's, he was outlandish and always a lot of fun. On the other hand, both Pamela's governess and her nanny Jane Cottle were sent along too, temporarily swelling the Monins' household staff to eleven and somewhat cramping Pamela's mischievous antics. Still, as she probably shared some of her lessons with her cousins, she no doubt turned the sessions into lively entertainment for the three of them, if not the governess.

Ever conscious of the expectations and conventions of her class, Evelyn is bound to have returned from her travels in time for Winifred to be presented at Court. It was a rite of passage for the daughters of Britain's landed gentry who were starting out in Society, without which an invitation to any social gathering of note was impossible. On 25 May 1911, King George V and Queen Mary held the fourth Court of their reign at Buckingham Palace at which a few dozen presentations were made, amongst them nineteen-year-old Winifred.

A woman wishing to be presented was not allowed to make the application to the Lord Chamberlain herself; it had to be done by the lady who wished to make the presentation, and who in some way was responsible for her protégé. Winifred was presented not by her mother but by Maud Lucia Cazalet, née Heron-Maxwell, a friend of Evelyn's and a relation on the Murray side. A Christian Scientist like Evelyn's father, and an early feminist, Maud was a good role model for the headstrong Winifred. However, in 1911 even she could not advise the young woman to buck the system which provided the only way to get one's existence recognised by that tiny proportion of individuals whose wealth, and therefore influence and power, made up Britain's ruling class.

For Winifred, whose politics were becoming decidedly socialist, the experience, although necessary, must have been uncomfortable. In fact, how she managed to stay sane as part of a wealthy family, where both parents were committed Conservatives and her mother was an aristocrat, can only be imagined. Perhaps she kept quiet to keep the peace, or perhaps part of her enjoyed the privileges she had; after all, life was balanced by her father's businesses which kept her and Pamela in touch with the wider community. But when her mother's family hosted social events they could be very grand and being the eldest daughter and unmarried, Winifred was expected to attend. In June 1912, a year after being presented at Court, Winifred accompanied Evelyn to a dance given by her mother's aunt Alice, the Countess of Leicester, at her London house in Grosvenor Square.

For a budding socialist like Winifred, the desire to sit sulkily in the corner while casting a contemptuous eye over the assembled throng must, on that occasion particularly, have been irresistible for her great-aunt's guests included members of some of the major ruling houses of Europe. At centre stage were Queen Mary's brother Prince Alexander of Teck and his wife Princess Alice; nearby stood Adolphus Frederick, a cousin of Queen Mary and heir to the vast German kingdom of Mecklenburg-Strelitz of which he would become Grand Duke just before war broke out (and to whom Winifred was distantly related, whether she liked it or not). Over there were Prince and Princess Louis of Battenberg who probably chatted to Grand Duke Michael of Russia. The strong connection between Britain and Greece was represented by Prince George and Prince Christopher, two of the sons of King George I of Greece. The Greek King was brother of Britain's widowed Queen Alexandra, so the two princes were her nephews. Their first cousin was Tsar Nicholas II, whose life Prince George had saved when an assassination attempt was made on him in Japan before he became Russia's ruler. Undoubtedly at the party the princes talked to Grand Duke Michael about the Tsar, as he too was related, little dreaming that in six years' time Nicholas and his family would be brutally murdered in Russia's Revolution.

Winifred probably chatted at the dance to the glamorous Countess Zia de Torby, who was the same age as her. She was the daughter of Grand Duke Michael and his wife Sophie. Zia and her family lived in exile in England. This was because her parents' morganatic marriage[1]

---

[1] This was a legally valid marriage between the male member of a sovereign, princely or noble house and a woman of lesser rank, with the provision that she shall not accede to his rank and their children shall not succeed to their father's title, property etc.

was considered illegal in Russia. They enjoyed considerable luxury from her father's Russian wealth; Zia's mother was known for her jewels, as well as her skills as a hostess. But as Michael was related to the Tsar, he would lose all of his wealth after the Russian Revolution. In 1918 after the murder of Nicholas and his family and other relatives, Michael seemed to become unbalanced and, to the concern of Zia and the rest of his family, made life very difficult for those around him. It is thought he had to sub-lease their London home and get a job as a clerk with a Westminster firm on £2,000 a year, forcing him to rely on gifts from friends.

No doubt Winifred behaved with decorum and did not embarrass her family in front of such a gathering with any political posturing. She could not know how the world would change over the next few years and the radical effect it would have on many of the assembled élite. She could not have predicted that just a few months after her great aunt's party, Greece would defeat Turkey in the First Balkan War leading to the assassination of the Princes' father, King George, in March 1913; nor that it would be part of a series of events leading to a war far worse than anyone could imagine. She could not have foreseen that Adolphus Frederick, after becoming Grand Duke, would bring the sovereignty of his kingdom to an end when he committed suicide in February 1918; or that in 1917 events would cause the Prince of Teck to renounce his German titles and honours, taking the surname Cambridge after his grandfather the Duke of Cambridge; while Prince and Princess Louis of Battenberg, who by then were sensitive to perceptions about their German heritage, would follow by relinquishing their titles and changing their name to Mountbatten.

But for now the party was a time to waltz and chat, to talk of European relations and of matters closer to home. Two months earlier, the tragedy of the sinking of the British ship *The Titanic* had shocked the world. No doubt Lady Evelyn told the assembled guests of how she was staying at Claridges Hotel in London as the news broke, the hotel having as usual a good many American guests. Although the majority of those passengers who drowned were British, the total number of deaths was closely followed by that of Americans. There had been some prominent names on board, and Evelyn would have been drawn into the sadness of their countrymen staying at Claridges at the same time. Indeed, the *New York Times* wrote that as so many prominent Americans stayed regularly in London's West End hotels, many hotel staff would be mourning guests whom they had come to know very well.

But on a lighter note, Evelyn would also have shared with the company the reason for her staying at the hotel, which was to meet her travelling companion Mrs William Alexander and embark on a month's trip through Holland – the last chance she would have for a while to travel so freely, although she did not know it. It was also the last chance the guests would ever have to meet all together; her aunt's dance would turn out to be one of the last grand social occasions to be remembered in the difficult years to come.

And as 1913 dawned, who could have dreamed that it would be the last year of normality, the final year of the old world? The upper classes could not know, as they celebrated the New Year on their country estates or in their London houses, that in the swish of a horse's tail they would no longer have the staff to maintain their estates or, in some cases, the estates themselves. Their gardeners and grooms, their gamekeepers and butlers, never imagined that the release of which they had so often dreamed from the jobs that sometimes they enjoyed, and others resented, would come so suddenly and, for many, so finally.

In the spring of 1913 Pamela's great uncle Thomas Coke, the 3rd Earl of Leicester – and since 1910 Aide-de-Camp to King George V and also Lord Lieutenant of Norfolk – entertained a large house party for shooting at his vast Holkham Hall estate in Norfolk. Pamela's father and her brother Ivan, who was encouraged like Pamela to be a good shot from an early age, would have loved to have been there as they sometimes were, for the shooting at Holkham was some of the best in the country.

On this occasion the Earl's guests included the 4th Marquess and Marchioness of Salisbury of that other significant stately home, Hatfield House in Hertfordshire. The Marquess, James Cecil, son of Britain's last Conservative Prime Minister, and his wife Cicely, had been working hard to restore the gardens at Hatfield to their former Victorian glory. They scarcely needed to bother. The following year their grounds would be given up to the testing of the first British tanks, to be dug with trenches and craters and covered with barbed wire to represent no-man's land and the German trench lines of the Western Front. Most of their large and unique deer herd, introduced by the first Lord Cecil in 1610, would out of necessity be culled.

But compared to their host, that was little hardship. Thomas Coke and his wife the Countess Alice did not know, as they entertained their guests in their Palladian mansion, that two years later they would be grieving for their son, killed at Gallipoli, and watching their grandchildren, aged six and eight, come to terms with the loss of their father. And when in March 1913 the 'Cairo Notes' section of *The Times* reported not only the presence there for the Season of Lady Evelyn Cobbold and her aunt and uncle the Earl and Countess of Dartmouth but also that of Mr and Mrs Rudyard Kipling, the writer and his wife could not, in their worst nightmare, have dreamt that it would be the last time they would enjoy themselves so light-heartedly; for the death of their eighteen-year-old son Jack, two years later in the Battle of Loos, would render such frivolity utterly meaningless.

But for now people went about their daily business untroubled by the extremes of fear, guilt and despair that would shortly overshadow their lives. In May that year, 1913, there was a celebration in the Cobbold family when Winifred got married. Although they felt it their duty to make the occasion a lavish and memorable one for their eldest daughter, John and Evelyn were not happy with her choice of spouse despite his background. Algernon Ryder Lambert Sladen had a favourable pedigree, even if not as impressive in the aristocratic stakes as Winifred: his connections were largely military. His father was a Colonel, his mother a Lady, and a cousin was the 10th Earl of Cavan, a significant army figure who in 1913 was enjoying his retirement from army life, unaware that soon he would be asked to come back. One of Algernon's brothers, previously in the Royal Navy, was Chief of the Metropolitan Fire Brigade, while his half-brother was private secretary to the Duke of Connaught in Canada.

To balance the military connections, another cousin, Douglas Sladen, was a noted author, and Algernon's other brother was the vicar of Kidderminster: along with the Sub-Dean of the Chapels Royal, he officiated at the marriage ceremony. Yet John and Evelyn did not trust

Algernon, did not feel he would be reliable. But Winifred had shown herself as she grew up to be an unconventional and headstrong young woman, forever at odds with her mother, and as soon as she reached twenty-one and could marry without her parents' consent she did so, perhaps seeing it as an escape from parental, particularly maternal, rule.

John and Evelyn could not let their misgivings show publicly so, as they felt was expected of them, they made their daughter's wedding a big social occasion. Winifred's socialist tendencies were firstly to the amusement and then consternation of her parents, and she may have preferred to elope rather than putting up with all that fuss. Nevertheless, on 7 May 1913 she bowed to convention and married her handsome, caddish 'Algy' at Christ Church, Lancaster Gate, in London, wearing a wedding dress belonging to her maternal grandmother, the Dowager Countess of Dunmore, of soft white satin, draped with a veil of old Brussels lace. Her bridesmaids were her younger sister Pamela, and Angy Tollemache, both dressed in white silk with blue sashes. The two girls having a mischievous sense of fun, and aged thirteen feeling that they were quite grown up, would have thrown themselves wholeheartedly into the occasion and had a jolly good laugh – except perhaps at the *Daily Mail*'s patronising description of them as 'two little bridesmaids'. The use of the diminutive was also applied to Angy, probably to her disgust, in a photograph of her with one of the pages. These comprised two of Winifred's young cousins, Ralphie Cobbold, son of their racy uncle Ralph Patteson Cobbold, and John Follett, a nephew of Evelyn's. Algy's best man was the Hon Harry Balfour, son of a Liberal peer.

Newspaper reportage of the wedding extended to other publications. The *Manchester Courier* described the occasion as, 'the brilliant Cobbold wedding' and 'a most brilliant ceremony'; the *Daily Express* described approvingly what the titled female guests wore at the 'large reception' at the house of the bride's grandmother, the Dowager Countess, at 55 Lancaster Gate, an elegant house in a grand Victorian development. Winifred and Algy left later in the afternoon for their honeymoon in Italy, a country with which they would become well acquainted.

It was just as well she and Algy did marry that year, for grand weddings were not very much in evidence until after the end of the war. In fact, most of the weddings which took place between 1914 and 1918, from all social spectrums, tended to be low-key affairs with very basic or no celebrations afterwards, time often being snatched while the groom was home on a short spell of leave before returning to his Regiment. When Cynthia Tollemache, Angy's older sister, married Captain Guy Dubs in August 1916 at St Margaret's, Westminster, the advance newspaper announcement said that whilst all friends were welcome to come to the church, there would be no reception. For too many would-be brides, however, the opportunity to have any ceremony at all was denied them, for their men never returned.

After Winifred's wedding – a sparkling occasion despite the undercurrents of parental disapproval – life must have felt a little flat for Pamela and Evelyn. Evelyn, full of misgivings about Winifred's future, wanted something to take her mind off it and took Pamela with her to travel around the country visiting friends and relations, the last time for a few years that it would be quite so easy to do.

They always enjoyed visiting Capesthorne in Cheshire, home of Evelyn's friend William Bromley Davenport, a Deputy Lieutenant of the county and Pamela's godfather. Known affectionately as 'Bromo', he was a man of diverse talents. In the Boer War he had been awarded the DSO and would soon be marked out for significant political roles during the Great War. As a young man he had even played football for England against Scotland and Wales respectively in 1884, scoring two goals in the game against Wales. Bromo was often Evelyn's companion when she went fishing in Norway, where, like the Cobbolds, he owned a house at Romsdalshorn. Capesthorne was a vast Jacobean-style mansion, home to the Bromley Davenports since 1726. As Bromo never married or had children, he must have rattled around in the dozens of very grand rooms and the 100 acres of parkland, but his three nephews, of whom he was very fond, would often stay with him.

Pamela loved her visits to Bromo for there she could pursue hunting, her favourite pastime. She may have been only thirteen but she could also handle a gun very well for she was very much her mother's daughter in that regard, as much as she may have fought against the comparison. In December 1913 *The Sketch* published a photograph of Pamela on a page with other Society folk enjoying the same sport on estates all around the country, entitled, 'Out With the Guns: Society Pheasant-Shooting'.

She is pictured on the edge of woods leaning on her shooting stick next to Bromo and a Miss J Kinlock. Pamela looks pretty, if serious, in a beautifully-cut tweed suit, plus fours and a fetching tweed hat with an upturned brim.

Her mother Evelyn was also a friend of Josslyn Pennington, the 5th Baron Muncaster, whose family had owned Muncaster Castle in Cumbria for several centuries. His wife's sister Mary Caroline was Pamela's godmother, and was married to the 20th Earl of Erroll, Charles Gore Hay. The Earl, too, had the joy and the burden of owning an ancient castle: the imposing and gothic Slains Castle, at Cruden Bay, on the wild Aberdeen coast. And this is where Evelyn and Pamela were heading next. With over 4,000 acres of land, Slains Castle had been owned by the Hay family since 1597. Evelyn's acquaintance with Charles Hay was probably through her late father, the Earl of Dunmore, for both men had been closely connected with King Edward VII, Charles Hay as a Lord-in-Waiting, her father as a friend, and both had served in the Atholl Highlanders. The Hays of Erroll had played a prominent part in Scottish history since the eleventh century, holding important posts and fighting in Scotland's major battles as well as being involved in their fair share of scandals, executions and intrigue.

Slains Castle was described by Dr Johnson and James Boswell when they visited it in 1773 as, 'built on the margin of the sea, so that the walls of one of the towers seem only a continuation of a perpendicular rock... to walk around the house seemed impracticable... the windows look upon the main ocean, and the King of Denmark is Lord Erroll's nearest neighbour on the north-east'.

In the nineteenth century Charles Hay's father, William Harry Hay, the 19th Earl, had spent much of his money on building a new harbour, Port Erroll, to encourage the local fishing trade, and he provided low-rent housing to the locals. He loved to entertain at Slains, where his guests included the author Bram Stoker. After William's death in 1891 when Charles became the 20th Earl and inherited Slains, he spent little time there, living mostly at his estate in Surrey. When he did visit, he liked to take friends with him: in 1895 they included Evelyn and Lord Muncaster. Visitors were more likely to see Charles' eldest son Victor who, as Lord Kilmarnock, stayed at Slains regularly with his family.

Bram Stoker continued to holiday nearby, his novel *Dracula* being inspired by the towering cliffs, jagged sea rocks and wild shores of that part of the coast.

By 1913 the area had become popular with visitors, thanks to the neighbouring Cruden Bay Hotel, built in 1897 by the Great North of Scotland Railway, a spectacular and luxurious place with its own tennis courts, croquet lawns and bowling green and, above all, a championship-standard golf course. With the romantically brooding presence of Slains Castle, the area was flourishing.

Pamela would have loved the wildness and the gothic castle and enjoyed the company of their host Victor – the same generation as her mother – and his three children, of whom the eldest, Josslyn, the future 22nd Earl, was just a year younger than Pamela. It would have deeply grieved Victor if he could have foreseen the disgrace that his eldest son would later bring upon the family.

Meanwhile, Pamela's elder sister and her new brother-in-law returned from their Italian honeymoon and went to the country, probably to Hill House in the historical town of St Osyth in Essex, not far from Ipswich. Then in late October the couple arrived at 262 St James Court, a pied-à-terre in the smart Westminster district of London not far from Buckingham Palace. No doubt Evelyn would have preferred her daughter to live somewhere grander, especially as their arrival was noted in *The Times*, but at least it was a start and in a reasonably fashionable area.

Life for the Cobbolds and the rest of the upper classes in 1913 was, generally speaking, still sweet compared to the vast majority of the population, but for the landowning gentry it was less so than it had been. The Chancellor of the Exchequer, Lloyd George, had already weakened the power of the House of Lords and now he turned to the landlords. All his life he had believed in attacking landlords and in breaking their monopoly of the soil as a necessary prelude to overthrowing their social privileges and political power. He hated the grandees and the gentry and everything they represented; he wanted to break down the remnants of the feudal system.

In 1912 he had set up a Land Inquiry Committee to report on all rural and urban land in England, Scotland and Wales. The first report was published in the autumn of 1913 and formed the basis of the 'Land Campaign', which Lloyd George immediately launched. The programme put the fear of God into the landowning classes – which was exactly what he intended. Its proposals included heavier taxation for landowners; state supervision and adjustment of rentals; greatly improved tenants' rights; much-increased labourers' wages; and increased access to smallholdings. All of this was to be financed by landlords' rents rather than farmers' profits. There were also worrying proposals for urban land.

Although the proposals were not implemented – they were later defeated and the war intervened – the landowning classes were worn down. But it was not only the threats by various Liberal governments that had got to them. From 1880 their land had become an increased burden to them, when cheaper foreign imports had led to a crisis in British agriculture; there was also a new and rival wealthy élite, whose money came from commerce and industry rather than from inheritance; and the political hostility to the land meant it was subject to unprecedented taxation. As a result, by the following year, 1914, many landowners, with a heavy heart, would make the decision that the best thing to do was sell.

Lloyd George had also announced in July 1913 his intention to abolish the House of Lords. This was another attempt to narrow the huge gap between the haves and the have-nots, the main area of inequality still being the lack of the right to vote for all but the privileged few. But another darkness lurked which had the potential to affect everyone, regardless of their class.

In 1908 the eugenics movement had started in Britain, with the founding of the Eugenics Education Society by Sir Francis Galton, a half-cousin of Charles Darwin. He believed that humans could improve their stock by encouraging procreation of the fittest among them and discouraging that of the less fit. There were some surprising advocates of the movement including the Dean of St Paul's Cathedral from 1911-1934, Dr William Inge. One of the most senior members of the Church of England, he was known as the 'Gloomy Dean' for his warnings about overpopulation. In his essay called 'Eugenics' he pointed out that all the males in his family had won scholarships to Eton, Oxford and Cambridge, but that 'Unfortunately the birth-rate of the feeble-minded

71

is quite 50% higher than that of normal persons.' To him the answer was eugenics, starting with 'the compulsory segregation of mental defectives'. In 1912 London hosted the first International Eugenics Conference, addressed by Britain's former Prime Minister, Arthur Balfour, and attended by the Home Secretary, Winston Churchill. Churchill called for sterilisation of the less fit 'so the inferior could be permitted freely in the world without causing much inconvenience to others'.[2] So concerned was Churchill by the 'multiplication of the Feeble-Minded' that the same year the government introduced a Mental Deficiency Bill which proposed compulsory sterilisation.

The result was the Mental Deficiency Act of 1913 in which, thanks to campaigners like G K Chesterton and the MP Josiah Wedgwood, any provision to prevent the pro-creation of the unfit was, in the end, not included. Sterilisation was not mentioned, nor was there compulsory segregation of the mentally deficient. The only real new power was to take the illegitimate children of paupers into care. The Hambro family would be much relieved. In January 1915 Pamela's future mother-in-law, the multi-lingual, exuberant, cigar-smoking Sybil Hambro, thinking her family of two boys and a girl was long completed, would find herself pregnant again at the age of forty-three. It would be clear shortly after Juliet's birth in October 1915 that she was – to use a term coined by the Government – 'feeble-minded'. Given the lack of understanding of mental illness at the time, the situation was worrying enough for the Hambros without the knowledge that some considered Juliet not fit to breed nor even, perhaps, to live.

Britain may have abandoned drastic eugenic measures but other countries made them part of their law, including the Hambros' ancestral home, Denmark, as well as Sweden, Norway and Switzerland, while France practised aspects of the eugenics movement. In America such laws had been in force since 1896 when Connecticut became the first American state to pass explicitly eugenic marriage laws, and by 1917 twenty states had such laws on their statute books. The belief propounded by eugenics, that the human race needed to be protected from 'the unfit' or 'the feeble-minded', would be enthusiastically adopted in Germany

[2] Quoted from Churchill's letters in *Churchill and Eugenics* by Sir M Gilbert CBE, Churchill Centre and Museum, www.winstonchurchill.org.

twenty years later when one of the first acts of the new Reich in 1933 was to pass a sterilisation law, ordering doctors to sterilise anyone suspected of suffering from a hereditary disease.

Fortunately, most Britons were blissfully unaware, and remained so for several decades, of the discussions that had taken place before the final version of the Mental Deficiency Act became law, and of the views of politicians like Churchill; after all, the British Government had recently introduced some very positive measures, like the first sickness and maternity benefits in 1913 under the National Insurance Act. And anyway, there were other issues to be concerned about: rumblings on the Continent and in central Europe indicated that all was not well elsewhere.

The Balkans continued to be a very unstable area, as seen by the assassination of the Greek King. King George had been staying in Salonika since November 1912 when his army captured the town from Turkey, at that time the centre of the problems. On 18 March 1913, aged sixty-eight, he was shot through the heart while taking his usual walk, accompanied only by his aide into whose arms he fell. Despite the Treaty of London, signed in May by Turkey with its erstwhile enemies of the Balkan League, fresh fighting broke out again in July in the Balkans. The allied countries of Serbia and Bulgaria failed to agree on the running of Turkey's previous territory, Macedonia. Bulgaria turned on its allies of the war against Turkey and marched against Serbia; Greece, also attacked by the Bulgarians, allied itself with the Serbs.

While the assassination of King George shocked many people, it was a particular cause of sorrow in the Hambro family for they had enjoyed close professional and personal connections with Greece from the mid nineteenth century. In 1863 Charles' great-grandfather, the Danish-born Carl Joachim Hambro – the first Hambro to set up the family's bank in England – had been instrumental in helping Greece to choose a new King. The Greeks had rebelled against their German-born King Otto whose thirty year reign had been very unpopular. A Greek delegation arrived in London in 1862 in anticipation of Otto's imminent abdication and they wanted Prince Alfred, Queen Victoria's second son, as their ruler. But for many reasons the Queen was not amused at such a suggestion, not least because the Greek throne was very insecure, and in her view it did not offer proper prospects for an English prince. Carl Joachim Hambro's Greek banking colleague expressed his concerns to him one day, saying the Greek delegation did not know where to turn.

Carl, in the process of building the international reputation of his family's bank, had made some extremely important connections in England and Europe generally. He knew of the negotiations in progress aimed at marrying the Danish princess Alexandra, daughter of the heir to the Danish throne, to Prince Edward, Queen Victoria's eldest son and heir to the British throne. He also knew the Danish Navy were due to visit England in July of 1862 while the Greek delegation were there, and that amongst the young naval cadets would be Princess Alexandra's younger brother Prince Vilhelm. Carl considered the young prince would be the ideal choice for the Greek throne, for if the Greeks could not have Prince Alfred, they would surely be pleased instead to have the brother-in-law of Edward, Britain's future King. Carl hatched an elaborate plan which he put into place that year and during 1863 – the year Princess Alexandra and Prince Edward married – to introduce the parties and enable the Greeks to assess the Danes. The result was their choice of Prince Vilhelm as their ruler, for which he was that year elected King George I of the Hellenes.

The result was also very positive for Carl, for he became King George's personal banker and could expect to be invited to float any loans the Greek Government might need: Greece then was a very primitive country, without even a railway. In 1881 Carl's eldest son Everard, Charles' grandfather, negotiated the country's first foreign loan, and the relationship between the Hambros and Greece continued for many years. In 1913 Everard was senior partner of the family's bank so the death of the King, whom he had come to know well, was deeply upsetting and he was pleased when the Hambros' professional relationship with Greece continued with King Constantine, elder brother to Princes George and Christopher.

If only Greece's relationship with its neighbours could have been as felicitous as that with the Hambro family. Following various further disputes between the Balkan countries, in which alliances were made and broken and then re-formed, in July 1913 Greece and Serbia declared war on Bulgaria, which was then invaded by Romania. At least King Constantine would see peace for a short time, for in August 1913 the Second Balkan War was brought to an end by the signing of the Treaty of Bucharest between the King of Bulgaria on the one part, and on the other Constantine and the Kings of Montenegro, Romania and Serbia.

Under the treaty, Bulgaria was made to give up most of the spoils it had gained from Turkey in the previous encounter, and Turkey was permitted to remain in occupation of the strategic town of Adrianople. Nicholas II, the Tsar of Russia, had personally intervened, sending a stern message to the Kings of Bulgaria and Serbia and it looked as though there may be peace in the area, at least for a while.

But in September there were problems in Albania. It had been recognised as a Sovereign State in July that year by the Great Powers[3] but parts of it, including Dibra, remained under Serbian rule. That month three thousand Albanians occupied Dibra causing Serbian troops to retaliate, destroying villages and seizing livestock and carrying out massacres, including of children. At the end of October Serbia withdrew, under pressure from Austria-Hungary.

Elsewhere in the world at the end of 1913 other bizarre, if less threatening, events were happening. In Germany that November the Kaiser issued an order to his army and navy 'requesting' them not to dance the tango, the most popular dance in Berlin, or the two-step, and to avoid families who did so. Failure to comply with this 'request' would result in dismissal. In America, New York's Grand Central Station opened and a couple were arrested on Christmas Day for kissing in the street. In the arts world Paris saw a near riot at the first performance of the ballet *The Rite of Spring*, with its controversial music by the Russian composer Stravinsky, for the audience had never heard anything like its discords and unfamiliar rhythms. At least on New Year's Eve that year Paris was able to welcome back a friend, for the *Mona Lisa*, stolen earlier that year, was returned to the Louvre having been discovered in Florence and an Italian arrested for its theft.

Back in Britain, Emmeline Pankhurst, the Suffragette Leader, was arrested in Plymouth on 4 December on her return from the U S, part

---

[3] Russia, Great Britain, France, Austria-Hungary, Italy, Germany.

of the 'Cat and Mouse' Act passed earlier that year;[4] and Glasgow saw the launch, somewhat prophetically, of *HMS Tiger*, the world's biggest battle cruiser. The Anglo-Turkish treaty gave Britain sole rights to oil exploitation in Arabia, Mesopotamia and Syria, much to the satisfaction of Winston Churchill, by then First Lord of the Admiralty. Less prestigiously a report by Sir George Newman, the Chief Schools' Medical Officer, revealed that one child in twelve in Britain's state elementary schools was suffering from disease or the effects of poor diet, with more than half needing dental treatment and more than a third being unhygienically dirty. And on a lighter side altogether at the end of 1913, while Pamela was shooting on her godfather's estate, her future father-in-law Eric Hambro, an excellent golfer like his own father Everard, was enjoying himself at the Royal Eastbourne Golf Club. There he presented to a lucky winner the Eric Hambro Scratch Challenge Cup, which he had donated to the Club when he was captain in 1902, following the Hambro tradition: Everard had presented the Club with the Hambro Bowl during his own captaincy.[5]

A few months later, days spent so lightly and pleasurably would be, for father and son and so many others, a distant memory.

---

[4] The correct name was 'The Prisoners (Temporary Discharge for Ill Health) Act', under which imprisoned suffragettes who were starving themselves would be released for a set time to get better, and then re-arrested.
[5] Both prizes are still awarded by the Club today.

Chapter 6

The Sterner Conflict: the Hambros and Others Prepare

When Pamela's brother Ivan and his good friend Charles Jocelyn Hambro returned to Eton in January 1914 after their Christmas holidays – Ivan's spent at Holy Wells, Charles' at Milton Abbey, Dorset, the estate of his grandfather Sir Everard Hambro – their school magazine *The Chronicle*, of Thursday 29 January 1914, began on a typically British note with a discussion of the recent weather:

'We live in a day of such short memories that a fortnight's frost suffices to obliterate all recollection of previous fine weather from people's minds; and one hears from all quarters that we are enduring the severest weather for many a year. But those who can make the effort to remember the weather conditions of last Half[1] will recall week after week of irreproachable warmth. In fact, we enjoyed a Christmas Half which it would be difficult to improve on from that point of view.'

How comfortably mundane that subject matter would seem a year later, when *The Chronicle* of Thursday 28th January 1915 began:

'The School reassembled in September [1914] under unprecedented circumstances. Everything had been completely revolutionised by the War: boys and Masters alike were equally affected. On the outbreak of hostilities, M. de Satge, Mr Fletcher, Mr Gladstone and Mr Powell all joined the Forces, to be followed at intervals by Mr Taylor, Mr...'

The year the Great War started had, until August, been like any other at Eton. Ivan and Charles, both seventeen in 1914, were in

---

[1] Eton's name for a term.

the Upper School; other young men in their set B3 VIII included the aristocrats Charles Stewart Vane-Tempest, a relation of the Marquess of Londonderry and a very talented cricketer, and Prince George of Teck, the nephew of Queen Mary. Ivan and Charles were both excelling at sport: Ivan in tennis and racquets as his father had done, Charles as a member of the prestigious Eton XI cricket team, winning matches that year at Lords against the other public schools Winchester and Harrow. As usual in that summer of 1914 Eton celebrated its special day, The Fourth of June, which marks the anniversary of King George III's birthday. The King had been very attached to Eton during his reign, attending many functions and entertaining the boys at nearby Windsor Castle, and the school traditionally celebrated his birthday, as it continues to do, with the Procession of Boats and with games and speeches. Little did the young men and their families know as they celebrated that summer's day, looking forward to the holidays ahead, that the world was just weeks away from war and that many of them would be dead in so short a time. For the Balkans had remained a hotbed of hostility and instability.

In April 1914, while his friend and banker Sir Everard Hambro was enjoying his usual season in Biarritz where he rented a villa every year, the new King Constantine of Greece was faced with the threat of war by Albania. The following month, Serbian troops were reported to be inflicting terrible cruelties on Albanian Muslims. But on 28 June, the event happened which would eclipse everything in the chain of events it would cause. In Sarajevo, the capital of Bosnia, the heir to the mighty Austro-Hungarian throne, the Archduke Franz Ferdinand, nephew of the popular Austrian Emperor Franz Josef, was celebrating his fourteenth wedding anniversary. He and his wife, the Duchess of Hohenburg, were driving in their open-top carriage through the streets of the town where they had earlier been welcomed by the Mayor. They had already had a narrow escape that morning when a bomb was flung at their car. This time there was no escape. A nineteen-year-old student in the crowd fired two shots, the first of which hit the Archduke in the neck, the second striking the Duchess who had thrown herself forward to protect her husband. She was hit in the stomach and died almost immediately, the Archduke about ten minutes later.

The assassin told police that he wanted to take revenge for the oppression of the Serbian people, and was believed to have been assisted with weapons and forged papers by a Serbian secret society of army officers called the Black Hand.

A tidal wave of horror and indignation swept over Europe. In England *The Times* pronounced that the assassination 'shakes the conscience of the world'. In late July Austria issued an ultimatum to Serbia, saying she must allow Austrian officials to conduct an investigation into Serbian complicity in the assassination plot and collaborate with Austrian officials in suppressing subversive movements directed against Austria-Hungary. A reply was demanded within forty-eight hours, by 25 July.

It did not come. Events followed quickly. On 31 July Austria declared war on Serbia. The Tsar of Russia, a first cousin of King George V, ordered mobilisation of his army, followed by Germany and France. On 1 August Kaiser Wilhelm II, another of George V's first cousins, declared war on the Tsar. On 2 August Britain's Royal Navy was mobilised; on 3 August Germany declared war on France. That day, the British Government told Germany that it would stand by the 1839 Treaty of London guaranteeing Belgian neutrality, and would protect the French coast. The Kaiser dismissed the Treaty as a mere 'scrap of paper' according to newspaper reports, and on 4 August Germany invaded Belgium. As a consequence, later that same day Great Britain declared war on Germany. The old world was finished.

Between August and December 1914 one hundred and ten Etonians left school, many sooner than they would otherwise have done, to serve their country. The Masters who remained to teach the rest spent the holidays in training camps preparing those boys, together with some Masters who had joined the Eton College Officers' Training Corps. Meanwhile the school carried on as normally as it could for the sake of everyone who remained. Sport continued to be encouraged, its team-building benefits being particularly important now in the face of combat. In 1915 *The Chronicle* reported, 'At Racquets the School was represented by Cazalet and [Ivan] Cobbold, who beat both Charterhouse and Winchester', while Charles Hambro was made Captain of the Eleven, a significant achievement. *The Chronicle* of 11 March 1915 explained why the boys' sporting training was so important:

'... it is not mere training in the principles of war which makes a really useful officer in the British Army but something else is required which cannot be got from the closest study of military books alone, but which, it is said, is especially inculcated by an ordinary Eton education, so that critics who think that Eton, in these days, gives to athletics greater prominence than they deserve, must remember that the battle of Waterloo was won on the playing fields of Eton, and that while we seem most careless we are most preparing ourselves for the great duty which lies before us as soon as we leave the School... [W]hen we have done with our games and played out our time here, we shall be ready to join the others in the sterner conflict.'

Two months earlier, *The Chronicle* had started to publish a list of old Etonians engaged on active service in France, Belgium, Africa and the Naval Forces. Amongst them were two of Charles Hambro's relatives, Percival Otway Hambro, who had left Eton in 1889, and his younger brother Bertram Emil Hambro, who had left in 1898 and was using his linguistic skills as an interpreter to the Indian Expeditionary Force in France. Bertram survived at the Front until the end of February 1915, but died of trench fever on 25 April leaving a young widow and two small daughters, Diana and Faith.

An anonymous mother, whose son had left Eton in 1914, allowed an extract of her son's letter to her from the trenches in Belgium to be published, a masterpiece of the stiff upper lip:

'Trenches are not exactly comfortable places to live in, even when dry, but on the whole life out here is quite good fun and one has plenty of amusement at the expense of Fritz.'

The Fourth of June celebrations in 1915 were severely curtailed for the second time since the Boer War in 1901. Instead of the usual festivities there were only to be 'speeches in Upper House at noon, which promise, we are told, to be well up to the usual standard in spite of the sad depletion Sixth Form has necessarily suffered'. Also that year a significant amateur sporting event, the Public School's Challenge Cup, was cancelled but other sports fixtures went ahead as planned. A page of photographs in *The Chronicle* entitled, 'Fourth of June 1915' depicted the school's four captains, one of whom was a serious-looking Charles as Captain of the XI. That month he led the school, assisted by Ivan, in defeating two visitors' teams: one led by Charles' father, Eric, and the other by Ivan's uncle Philip Wyndham Cobbold. Ivan meanwhile had the honour of being appointed Keeper of the Racquets, much to the delight of his father.

It was the last sport either boy would play for a while: instead, it was time to put the camaraderie they had learnt into practice. They left Eton at the end of that summer term 1915, Ivan aged eighteen and Charles still seventeen, both going to The Royal Military Academy Sandhurst, and then soon joining the regiments with which their respective families were associated: Ivan the Scots Guards and Charles the Coldstream Guards. Of the thirty-seven boys in their set alone, eight would be killed in action between 1916 and 1918 including Charles' cricket team mate Charles Stewart Vane-Tempest; taken prisoner by the Germans in France, in March 1917 he died of war wounds, aged twenty.

Eric Hambro was in Sweden when he heard the news, just after Charles' eighteenth birthday in October 1915, that his eldest son had been commissioned as an officer. Horrified, he wrote to his wife, Sybil, 'It is wicked to think of sending a boy aged eighteen to lead troops, neither fair to the men or to the boy.'

Eric had been hoping that Charles, as his eldest son, would follow him into the family business, but despite the Hambros' great wealth and the privilege their hard-earned money brought, the fear of losing his son put Eric on the same footing as every other father in the country whose child was going to war. They enjoyed a good relationship and were a striking pair, both tall and handsome. Charles was about 6ft 3ins – short compared with his father, at a towering 6ft 7ins – and well-built, with fair hair, blue eyes and a full, slightly sulky mouth.

Charles and Ivan had met at Eton when they joined in 1910, aged thirteen. They were in different School Houses, so probably forged their friendship through sport. While their families had banking in common, for the Cobbolds it was another string to their bow; by contrast, from the beginning of the nineteenth century until the early twenty-first, the Hambros *were* banking and were amongst only a handful of merchant bankers, including their rivals the Rothschilds, who achieved worldwide renown and respect.

Charles was well aware of the achievements of his ancestors and the expectations placed upon him, should he survive the war. His great-great grandfather Joseph Hambro, a Danish merchant and banker, had been instrumental in starting the family business and bringing it to England. When Joseph was born in Copenhagen in 1780 his parents, Calmer and Thobe Hambro, had only been there for two years. They were orthodox German Jews who had left Hamburg for Copenhagen – then extremely affluent – where Thobe's father had a business, so that Calmer could trade there too. When Calmer was granted his trading licence, he followed the legal requirement for immigrating Jews, abandoning his birth name of Levy and taking as his surname the name of his native town of Hamburg. A clerical error on a legal document misspelt his surname as 'Hambro' and the name stuck. Even his first name, which was actually Calman, somehow became changed to 'Calmer'.

Calmer Hambro became a clothier and started his own business in Copenhagen, sending Joseph back to Hamburg to gain training and experience as a merchant. When he returned home in 1800, Joseph became his father's partner and the firm was renamed C J Hambro & Son. They then experienced probably the worst period in Denmark's history, which in fact paved the way for Joseph to help his country and establish his family's reputation.

For in 1801 Britain was still embroiled in the Napoleonic Wars. Denmark had always been a neutral country, of massive benefit to its international trading relations, and yielded such vast profits to its people that the Government had to issue ordnances to restrict luxury. But Britain could no longer tolerate supplies reaching Napoleon in neutral ships, which were now operating in armed convoys. In April 1801 the British Admirals Nelson and Parker launched an attack on Copenhagen, followed in 1807 by a three-day bombardment of the city in which Britain forced Denmark to hand over the whole of its battle fleet to prevent it falling into Napoleon's hands. The result for Denmark was catastrophic. Neutral shipping traffic was now systematically brought to a halt by Britain; Danish merchants were seized, their cargo confiscated and their crews imprisoned. In essence, Denmark's trading was effectively stopped. With no other way of making any serious money the country's reserves of goods were soon exhausted, its financial situation dangerously precarious.

Calmer did not live to see the bombardment nor the success of Joseph, for he died in 1806. Joseph continued to run the family firm with one of his brothers, Isach, and by 1808 was known as Copenhagen's leading clothier, at the same time building up a trading business. Then in 1813 with the effects of the embargo having taken their toll, Denmark was forced to declare itself bankrupt. Nevertheless, just two years later Joseph was declared one of Copenhagen's wealthiest men, even while other individuals were being bankrupted almost daily. But it was his international role as a Government adviser which would make his reputation.

Joseph went to England for the first time in 1815 to establish business relationships and was soon appointed Danish agent of the insurance company, Lloyds. In 1818 he was asked by Denmark's finance minister to raise a modest but urgent loan to help its troubled agricultural industry. It was not an easy task but Joseph managed to negotiate the loan in England, doing the same again in 1821 when asked to arrange a far bigger loan for his country. The King of Denmark was so impressed by Joseph's efficiency that he made him a Privy Counsellor.

Joseph's success and reputation as a banker and his wealth from interest on the loans he raised grew rapidly. However, his personal life all this time had been less happy. In 1807 he had married Mirjam von Halle, whom he preferred to call 'Marianne'. She was the beautiful daughter of a Hamburg merchant; the fact that there was a history of ill-health in her family did not deter Joseph. But just before Marianne gave birth to their only child, Carl Joachim, later that year, the British bombardment of Copenhagen had taken place and fire bombs had fallen near the centre of the city, setting fire to the church. Joseph realised then the nervous and uncontrollable nature of his wife's temperament.

After seven years Joseph realised he could no longer allow her to look after their young son. He made two very difficult decisions. Firstly he put little Carl Joachim into the hands of foster parents who were Christian, and then a few years later, realising he could no longer look after Marianne at home, gave her into the care of another.

Although Joseph would never have considered formally deserting the faith of his ancestors, he did not want his son to inherit all the problems that Jews faced at that time. Carl Joachim's foster father,

Johannes Reinhardt, was a Norwegian-born zoologist and founder of the Danish zoological museum who, with his wife Nicoline, went on unexpectedly to have four children of their own. Carl Joachim was thus raised as a Christian and as part of a larger family, with his father Joseph still playing his part. After a harrowing series of anti-Semitic riots in Copenhagen, Joseph – following the example of his brother and sister with their respective children – took the major decision in 1822, when Carl Joachim was fifteen, to have him baptised and confirmed. His descendants to the present day would all be Christian.

Although Joseph's removal of their son from Marianne was done for the best possible reasons, it aggravated her mental condition. It was then, with great sadness, but realising there was no alternative, that Joseph found someone to nurse her privately and she spent the rest of her life being cared for by a kind widow, until she died in 1838 aged fifty-two.

Carl Joachim left the care of his foster parents when he was eighteen, being sent to France, Germany and America to learn languages and commerce. Sadly it had become apparent early on that he had inherited his mother's depressive nature. But he was clever, and he knew exactly what he wanted to achieve. After being appointed North American Consul to Denmark at twenty-three, Carl Joachim asked his father if he would let him establish a branch office of the bank in London. Knowing his son's temperament, Joseph had reservations but agreed in order to appease his only child.

So Carl Joachim moved from Copenhagen to London in 1832, the year Victoria became Queen. He loved England and the British mentality and found inspiration in London bankers such as Nathan Rothschild and the Baring Brothers. The London branch of C J Hambro & Son he set up did very well. The following year he married Caroline Gostenhofer, the daughter of a London merchant of German origin, with whom he had four children. Their first two sons and a daughter were born back in Copenhagen, to where they returned in 1834 as Carl Joachim now hoped to become Joseph's partner in the Danish part of the bank. Again, Joseph gave his son what he asked.

Carl Joachim liked success, and next decided he wanted control of the London business too. Moving his family back there in 1839, he persuaded Joseph to lend him £50,000 so that he could prove he could make a success of it. But it was not an easy time because that year a financial crisis hit British and American markets, resulting in the collapse of several banks and bankers. Then in 1840 reports reached Joseph in Denmark of an alleged loss by his son of all the funds Joseph had given him, together with news of his nervous breakdown. Carl Joachim's mental state had become so disturbed that he was admitted to an English clinic where he had to spend a year in complete isolation, much to the dismay of Caroline and the children.

His son's desperate situation saw Joseph leaving Denmark for good that year and taking up permanent residence in England so that he could be near him and run the London business. By 1842 Carl Joachim had recovered his health, although his father took charge of business at C J Hambro & Son's premises in Old Broad Street which, while necessary, caused friction between father and son. That same year, to the great sorrow of Carl Joachim and Caroline, their four-year-old daughter died, but to restore some happiness their last child, Everard, was born. Then in 1843 Carl Joachim was proud to be granted British citizenship.

Father and son became closer before Joseph died, partly due to Joseph's newly-forged friendship with the Danish poet and story-teller Hans Christian Andersen whom Joseph noticed standing in the family bank one day in 1847. Andersen was then forty-three and on his first visit to England to negotiate with his publisher and to be received – he hoped – by Queen Victoria. Joseph became a father-figure to him. Andersen had poor English, so Joseph managed his financial affairs in England and negotiated with his publisher on his behalf.

He invited Andersen for weekends at his country house, Bransbury House at Roehampton, and to Scotland: as an admirer of Sir Walter Scott, Andersen wanted to see the country Scott wrote about, so Joseph took him to stay with Carl Joachim and Caroline who were holidaying there. Andersen made a great fuss of their three boys especially Everard who, at five years old, was already big for his age, calling him 'Goliath': a fitting nickname for a little boy who would not only continue to grow very tall but also become a giant in terms of finance and philanthropy in the Victorian and Edwardian eras.

When Joseph died in October 1848 Carl Joachim, as his only child, was the main beneficiary of his very substantial estate. Joseph's Will took into account his son's mental condition. It included the requirement that he use a specific sum in the purchase of a country house which must remain in the family for perpetuity, never be mortgaged for more than a third of its purchase price, and be inherited by his eldest son. Carl Joachim inherited all of the London bank too, but on the suggestion that he liquidate it if it caused him too much mental anxiety.

He soon found the chance to prove himself worthy of his father's support. In 1850 Joseph's old benefactor Count Moltke, the Danish Minister of State, approached Carl Joachim in London to ask him to raise a massive but vital loan for his home country which was at war following a rebellion in Schleswig and Holstein: Moltke had already been rebuffed by the Rothschilds and the Barings as war loans were no longer favoured in international finance circles, and the view in England, as far as this particular war was concerned, was that Denmark did not deserve to be helped.

Nevertheless Carl Joachim managed it, taking a huge personal risk also in doing so. Anxious not to be accused of profiting from the misfortunes of his birth country, he himself took responsibility for half the loan, risking personal ruin. It paid off, and as an added bonus Denmark won the war. Such was the gratitude of the Danish Government that in 1851 its ambassador in London was instructed to find out what form of appreciation Carl Joachim might prefer. It was not a difficult decision to make. As the Rothschild brothers had already been made Austrian barons and the Barings also ennobled, Carl Joachim wanted a similar social position to that of his closest rivals. He requested the hereditary Danish title of 'Baron'.

Despite a new democratic constitution in Denmark which had abolished future ennoblement from 1849, the King agreed that 'the head of C J Hambro & Son trading house in London, Carl Joachim Hambro, be elevated to the Danish rank of Baron, the title and rank of Baron to be inherited by whoever of his true male issue is considered head of the family and in descending order thereafter'. Contented, Carl Joachim could now turn his attention to the country estate he was required to buy with part of his inheritance and other monies: he had earned a good deal in raising the loan for Denmark and also one for troubled Italy, making him a friend of Italy's statesman, Camillo Cavour. Now he could afford to look at the larger estates in England which would befit both his title of Baron and his position as one of London's most prominent bankers.

Today Milton Abbey in Dorset is a boys' independent boarding school but it is not difficult to imagine what it was like as a country estate when Carl Joachim first saw it in the summer of 1852. He fell in love with the vast hall with its own private Abbey, nestling in the Milborne Valley, as he approached it from the surrounding hills. The estate, which comprised over 8,300 acres, included parkland designed by Capability Brown and four villages including the nearby village of Milton Abbas, which today looks like a film set for a quintessentially English costume drama. But it had a sad history. The estate's past owner Lord Milton was hated by the locals. In 1752 he had dismantled the original village of Milton Abbas, which had been a large settlement for centuries, because it impeded his view from the new hall he was building; in its place he built a new village, the one that stands today, out of sight of his new home. He also destroyed many of the old monastic buildings which had been part of the estate. No wonder the tenants were wary when the new owner, the still heavily-accented foreigner Baron Hambro, arrived.

But within a few years the Baron had rebuilt the Abbey which the previous owner had let fall into disrepair, using one of England's foremost ecclesiastical architects, Gilbert Scott. He opened up the Abbey to all the villagers for their worship, which Lord Milton had never allowed. He also built a new school, repaired the tenants' cottages and carried out other acts of generosity which endeared him and his three sons to the village: tragically, Caroline had died just two months before he bought the estate, aged forty-two.

With his mental history it was not easy for Carl Joachim, with two teenage sons and ten-year-old Everard, to cope with being a widower. Much as he loved the place, he rarely spent much time at Milton Abbey, preferring the smaller house he had also bought, nearer London at Putney Heath. His eldest son, Charles Joseph, moved into Milton Abbey with his wife when he married in 1857. But despite his absence Carl Joachim ensured that Milton Abbey was looked after and that all his family should enjoy it, especially at Christmas and for the hunting season.

Carl Joachim remarried when he was fifty-five, his wife a widow twenty years younger who had nursed him during a spell in hospital.

On his death in 1877 he was buried in the Abbey next to his Hall, his effigy sculpted upon his white marble tomb. In the twenty-first century one of his great-great-great grandsons, while at school at Milton Abbey (appropriately in Hambro House), would walk past his tomb at every assembly.

Unexpectedly, Milton Abbey became ear-marked for Charles Jocelyn Hambro through his much-loved grandfather Everard. At 6ft 5ins tall, Everard Hambro was indeed the giant Hans Christian Andersen had nicknamed him when he was a boy. The only one of Carl Joachim's children to have been born in England, he was generally considered to be more gifted than his older brothers. In the 1860s he went to Trinity College Cambridge, which seems to have been the favoured establishment for other big banking names: his contemporaries included members of the families Lloyd, Barclay and Rothschild. One of his closest friends was Martin Ridley Smith, himself a member of a banking dynasty. The friendship of the two men would be further cemented by marriage on more than one occasion between their families.

Everard entered the family bank C J Hambro & Son in 1864 and was made one of four partners, along with his father, when he was just twenty-seven. When Carl Joachim died, Everard became senior partner at a time which was good for British banks, for London was the centre of the world capital market.

Everard started to finance trade across the Atlantic and, like his father and grandfather, enjoyed arranging the issue of foreign loans, both for private companies and for governments. In the 1880s he was asked to raise a loan for Italy: the Rothschilds had been asked but had hesitated too long. It was a vast and onerous task, and Everard formed a syndicate to do it, which included the bank of Barings Brothers & Co owned by his friend Lord Revelstoke, and a French bank. All was going well until the Paris market collapsed and the burden fell on C J Hambro & Son and Barings. The conclusion of the loan was difficult, and caused immense strain on Everard. Nevertheless Everard managed it, emerging as one of the greatest bankers of his era. A cartoon of 1888 showed the three men considered to be the most important City characters of the day: Lord Rothschild, Lord Revelstoke, and Everard Hambro.

Meanwhile he had the honour of being appointed to the Court of the Bank of England when he was thirty-five, remaining a director until 1924. Everard's wife, Mary, was the younger sister of his friend Martin's wife, Emily. Mary's marriage to Everard in October 1866, when she was eighteen, made the two men brothers-in-law and, later, their children cousins. In London, where they enjoyed a prestigious address in Mayfair, Everard and Mary became friendly with the American banker, J Pierpoint 'J P' Morgan, who had his English country seat nearby. His father, Junius Spencer Morgan, had established his bank just down the road from the Hambros', in Old Broad Street, of which J P became senior partner after his father's death in 1890. The families' friendship would endure for generations.

Sadly for such a family-minded man as Everard, of the five children Mary gave birth to in the 1870s only two survived: Charles Eric, known always as 'Eric', described as 'young Hercules', and his younger brother Harold. In the 1880s, after years of illness, Mary gave birth to three more children in successive years, Angus, Violet and Olaf, who happily survived.

In many ways Everard Hambro typified the philanthropic paternalism of the very wealthy in the late Victorian and Edwardian eras. He considered that his family, and others who enjoyed great wealth, had a moral and social duty to use their wealth for those less privileged – which was the majority of the country. His love of children, for example, saw him buying a house at Roehampton which he turned into an orphanage for girls and paid for himself for years, and he was one of four bankers who donated substantial funds to enable the newly-formed Royal National Pension Fund for nurses to continue.

To balance his pressurised working life, Everard ensured that he and Mary spent what leisure time he had in a varied and enjoyable way. Still keeping their London house, in the 1880s he bought Hayes Place near Bromley, Kent, formerly the home of two Prime Ministers, Pitt the Elder and Pitt the Younger. They also rented a holiday home, Villa Espoir, in the newly-fashionable Biarritz, a place favoured by Everard's friend King Edward VII. Like the Cobbolds, the Hambros loved to spend time in Scotland, and every year Everard rented the Gannochy estate near Edzell in Forfarshire with J P Morgan.

All of the properties Everard enjoyed were happily shared with his family, not least Milton Abbey. He could not acquire it by inheritance, of course: on the death of his father Carl Joachim, it went to Everard's elder brother Charles Percival, and then, on his early death from pneumonia in 1891 without a male heir, to their nephew Harry Hambro.

But Harry was just twenty-two and had no-one to share the burden of responsibility with: both his parents had died prematurely. Due to two unfortunate factors, he found himself unable to maintain the vast estate. The first was a crisis in English agriculture in the 1890s, thanks to cheap American imports of grain, wool and meat, which meant that Harry's tenants on the Milton Abbey estate could not afford to pay him their proper rents; and the second was his being sued in 1895 in the High Court by his step-grandmother Baroness Hambro for a debt he owed her.

He had inherited little money from his father and was not yet earning much at C J Hambro & Son, and without the full rent from his tenants he could not afford the upkeep of the estate which included repair bills for the church and school, the farms and the cottages. Harry's cousin Eric, Everard's eldest son, lent him money to repay the Baroness and more, but by 1899 the debt had become too large for Harry to cope with.

Desperate, he realised he faced financial ruin but in 1900, to his great relief and gratitude, his uncle Everard stepped in and bought the Milton Abbey estate from him. Everard was delighted to return to the place of his childhood and could well afford to restore it to its former glory. With the mansion alone having fifty bedrooms and dressing rooms, eight bathrooms and eleven reception rooms, it was no mean feat. Although his and Mary's main home was Hayes Place, they visited Milton Abbey several times a year including Christmas, when Mary would host lavish parties for family and friends. In rescuing the estate, the line of inheritance shifted; Everard thought he had secured Milton Abbey for his son and for posterity, as Carl Joachim had intended.

Everard's happiness was blighted when Mary died in June 1905, aged fifty-seven, after over forty happy years of marriage. She was buried on a miserably wet summer's day next to the graves of her two little children in Hayes churchyard. Without her, the focus of the Christmas gatherings at Milton changed to hunting, with pheasant, deer and duck all available. *Country Life* magazine described Everard as one of the best shots in the country, although his sons – particularly Eric – were not far behind.

In 1908 Everard was much cheered by the honour of being made a Knight Commander of the British Empire by King Edward VII, and he became an envied part of the 'inner sanctum' of the Royal Family. In June the following year, the King, Queen Alexandra and their daughter Princess Victoria, lunched with him at Milton Abbey, and the King enjoyed it so much he returned in early December to spend several days there on his own, shooting with Everard and other family members. Later that month Everard was delighted to be invited to stay at Sandringham, the Monarch's Norfolk estate, also renowned for its hunting. His last opportunity for socialising with the King came in April 1910, when Edward invited him to his dinner party in Biarritz. The King's death the following month was a great shock, and Everard was honoured to be invited to his funeral.

Everard's eldest son, Eric, had enjoyed a secure and happy childhood. Even taller than Everard, he was dark-haired and charismatic. Like his father he went to Trinity College, Cambridge, where he developed an interest in politics and, already a talented golf player, was immediately selected to play for the University. When back from Eton for the holidays, or down from Cambridge, he spent time with his parents at their various homes, mainly Hayes Place. Hayes was delightful, but the jewel in the Hambros' crown would always be Milton Abbey which Eric now had the satisfaction of knowing he would one day inherit. An outgoing character, he was more extravagant and less cautious than his younger, steadier brother Olaf, who would make the better banker out of the two. Whilst Eric was generous in his extravagance, it would also prove to be a weakness.

Probably engineered by their respective fathers, shortly after leaving Cambridge Eric became engaged to his cousin Sybil, a daughter of Martin Ridley Smith, marrying her in 1894. Petite and vivacious, Sybil was an equally strong character who spoke several languages, was a keen yachtswoman and delighted in smoking cigars in an age when it was not yet acceptable for women to do so.

Their first child, a daughter, died when a baby; their second, Charles Jocelyn Hambro, was born in October 1897, the same year as his friend

Ivan Cobbold, at his paternal grandparents' house in London. Charles spent most of his childhood at Pickhurst Mead, a modern manor house on the Hayes Estate, so he saw much of his grandfather Everard and came to realise that one day Milton Abbey would be his. Meanwhile, as he grew older, it was clear he had inherited much of the humour and easy charm of both his parents, as well as their sporting skills. They had so many hopes and dreams for him. And now in 1915, aged just eighteen, he was going to war.

Chapter 7

Families at War

Pamela was close to her elder brother Ivan and in 1915 when he was preparing to join his Regiment, the thought of his going to war was terrifying. Their uncle Alexander may have won the VC in the Boer War but one hero in the family was quite enough. It was not as though Ivan and Charles were going together and could be of mutual support to each other: Pamela had to face the possibility that the two friends may never meet again and she would lose both a brother and a friend.

And if Eric Hambro was worried by the prospect of his son being sent to war, Charles' mother, Sybil, was already only too aware of what horrors lay ahead. Very soon after war broke out her half-brother, Julian Martin Smith, died in France on 10 September 1914, following an operation for injuries he had received in battle two days earlier. He was twenty-six. A recent Cambridge graduate following in their banker father's footsteps, Julian had left his new career with a city bank to volunteer as an interpreter with the Intelligence Corps. Perhaps Sybil derived some comfort in Charles' absence from the fact that at least her other son, Richard, was too young to go to war – he was thirteen when it broke out and had started at Eton that same year – and she had her baby Juliet, and Zelia, then five, to occupy her thoughts.

Furthermore, she was honoured to be invited to undertake war work of great importance, which drew on her many talents, not least – like her late brother – her linguistic skills, and which kept her fully engaged. She became one of the illustrious members of the forerunner to Bletchley Park: the highly secretive 'Room 40', located in the Admiralty

Building in London, whose task was to serve the Royal Navy by decrypting codes and cyphers intercepted from the enemy. Their skilful decryptions were passed on to a tiny handful of Operations officers within Naval Intelligence, who evaluated the information and decided whether it should be passed on to John Jellicoe, the Admiral of the Fleet.

Under the Director of Naval Intelligence, the much-lauded Admiral Sir Reginald Hall, one of the historically important achievements of Sybil and her co-workers was the breaking of the Zimmermann Telegram in January 1917. This was a telegram sent from Germany's Foreign Minister to the German Ambassador to Mexico, offering territory in the USA – at that time neutral in the war – in return for joining the German cause. It was as a direct result of the deciphering of the telegram that the USA joined the war. Room 40 also decrypted information leading to the interception off the Irish coast in April 1916 of a German vessel disguised as a Norwegian ship, which was carrying munitions for Sinn Fein. Had the weapons reached the Republicans, it is thought the Easter Rising of 1916 would have been much worse.

Sybil was part of a carefully chosen group, an eclectic mix of academics, linguists, musicians and mathematicians, which included individuals as diverse as the composer R Vaughan Williams, Victor Bulwer-Lytton (Earl Lytton of Knebworth), and the actor Gerald Lawrence. Another was one William F Clarke, a young barrister before joining the Royal Navy when war broke out, who was soon recruited into Room 40 as an analyst. In the later days between the two world wars nothing was allowed to be published about the staff of Room 40, and as some of them were re-employed by its successor it was not until the late 1940s that the veil of secrecy was partially lifted.

In 1952 Clarke was asked to write a history of Room 40 which was never actually published, but his notes remain and include a brief description of the staff. His comment about Sybil, who by the time he wrote it had long been titled due to her husband's services to the Realm, was, 'Lady (Sybil) Hambro: Wife of a city magnate. Charming personality. Smoked cigars which startled Captain Hope.' In 1915 smoking by women had not yet become a fashion statement, and when indulged in by a lady as small in stature as Sybil, it must have been quite a surprising sight for her boss, Captain Hope, who later became a respected

Admiral. Of Lord Lytton, Clarke wrote, 'Charming personality. Later became Viceroy of India.'

Clarke's brief comments on the other staff belied their skills and the vital role they played as part of Room 40, perhaps particularly when it came to the women. Of one female member he commented that she was the wife of a city doctor, was known (for reasons he does not explain) as 'the golliwog', and had 'love affairs' with two of the men in Room 40 which 'caused some trouble'. If Mrs M Bayley was indeed having *liaisons amoureux* with her co-workers, it was hardly surprising given the pressures of the job and the close proximity in which they worked with each other. But Clarke's stating whose wives or daughters the women were was not without significance. When Room 40 was set up in 1914, the first permanent British Intelligence agencies were still very much in their infancy having started only in 1909 after lessons learned from the Boer War. A formal process of vetting for recruitment – previously used in the Foreign and Colonial Offices and the Diplomatic Service – was just being introduced into this area. Being from the right sort of family had always been an important factor for hiring men: most of the early secret service officers had élite backgrounds and came from wealthy families with long-standing government, military and commercial connections. In the Foreign and Colonial Offices and Diplomatic Service the importance of wives, too, had never been under-estimated in their role as diplomatic hostesses and for maintaining the familial atmosphere, so important when abroad. But when it came to secret work British officials had concerns as to how patriotic women could be expected to be: after all, they did not have the vote and were not expected to fight for their country. It was instead decided that a woman's true and overriding loyalties were familial ones, and that although a woman might not keep a state secret for reasons of civic or patriotic duty, she would do so for love of husband, parents, children and kin. Intelligence officers also decided to vet women through their male connections; those who were well connected to men of status, integrity or patriotism were deemed acceptable security risks. In short, women were subjected to far more social and political scrutiny than the men.

Sybil's birth into one respected banking family and her marriage into another very prominent one, together with her aristocratic heritage as a descendant of the Marquess of Bute, was therefore most attractive to the recruiters. She also happened to have the sort of skills required for Room 40, as well as a degree of eccentricity which some of her brilliant co-workers of both sexes possessed. Sybil was the supervisor of the women in Room 40 most of whom, by virtue of their privileged upbringing, had had no work experience and no clerical or cryptography skills but were deemed suitable because of their backgrounds.

Among the secretaries, the one appointed to Clarke – himself the son of the Solicitor-General, Sir Edward George Clarke – was a Miss V Hudson, daughter of the soap magnate Robert Hudson whose family had invented Sunlight Soap, the first washing powder. Clarke commented of her, 'Used to arrive at unearthly hour in morning. Very nice child.'

Another of the talents of Pamela's future mother-in-law appears to have been poetry. Amongst the papers of Room 40 is a poem called *The Confidential Waste*, which Clarke attributes to Sybil. Although the references it contains and people it mentions are unique to Room 40 and the Royal Navy of the Great War, it is an amusing piece with a theme still familiar, in these days of security consciousness, to anyone who is obliged to dispose of confidential paperwork and finds that many other odd items end up in the system too. The poem ends:

And when the war is over, I shall contemplate with glee
All enemies of England, whosoever they may be.
Burnt up with all the Confidential Waste.

As it had done for those at Eton, the year the war broke out had started for most of the leisured classes in much the same way as usual. For Pamela's mother, Lady Evelyn Cobbold, this meant socialising and travel. After attending a New Year charity ball in Ipswich with her husband she set off without him on one of her frequent journeys, probably at that stage still with his blessing: his business interests allowed him less time than he would have liked for travel, and he had been well aware from before their marriage of his wife's need to do so. With a small group of friends which included her cousin Lady Joan Legge, the unmarried daughter of her aunt and uncle the Earl and Countess of Dartmouth, and the clever, literary Sir Alfred Cooper, otherwise known as 'Duff Cooper' – then an

John Dupuis Cobbold.

Lady Evelyn Cobbold with Winifred and Pamela, circa 1902.

A Family Groupe with Mummy Amongst.

Family group at Felixstowe with nannies, circa 1906
(Pamela middle row, second from right).

John Murray Cobbold ("Ivan").

Pamela and cousin Ralph Cobbold, circa 1909.

Holy Wells in late 19th century.

The young Charles Hambro.

Wedding group of Lady Blanche Cavendish and Captain Cobbold (Scots Guards) taken at Lansdowne House after the ceremony, April 1919.

Back row, left to right: Miss Pamela Cobbold, the Bridegroom Captain Cobbold, Lady Dorothy Cavendish,
Middle row: Miss Jean Follett, Viscount Calne, the Bride,
the Honourable Elizabeth Elphinstone, the Master of Elphinstone.
Seated on ground: Miss Margaret Mercer Nairne, Miss Felicity Cobbold.
©Devonshire Collection, Chatsworth. Reproduced by permission of Chatsworth Settlement Trustees.

Lot 8. Pickhurst Mead.

Pickhurst Mead.

Winifred
title: Mrs Sladen (née Cobbold) by Bassano, vintage print, 1921
© National Portrait Gallery, London.

eligible young bachelor, soon a notorious womaniser and, in World War II, Secretary of State for War – Evelyn left England in late January on a steamer to the French Riviera. February and March saw her in Egypt, one of her favourite countries thanks to her childhood, doing the Season at Cairo, again with Joan Legge.

While travelling in the Middle East the pair stumbled upon T E Lawrence, later famous as Lawrence of Arabia. He and two others had been sent by the British Government to gather intelligence about Sinai, under the guise of an archaeological expedition. This information would prove to be crucial in the Arab Revolt. As the men were making their return journey north through Petra in February 1914, Lawrence and his companion ran short of money to pay their guides and for the train back to Damascus. He later recounted how he fortunately bumped into 'two English ladies... curious people. At first they were dull, but one of them, Lady Evelyn Cobbold, improved vastly... I borrowed a lot of money from them, since our post arrangements broke down.'[1] The next year he took her out to lunch in London to reciprocate, and they maintained contact for a while despite her privately dismissing him in her usual snobbish way as 'an upstart'.

Back home again by June 1914 she and John, with twelve hundred other guests, including Eric and Sybil Hambro, attended by invitation of Their Majesties the penultimate State Ball at Buckingham Palace to be held before the end of the war. Ten days later Evelyn was off on her own again, this time to Oslo, probably to fish and to stay at the house she and John owned in Norway. Her companions on that occasion included Baron Schröder and his wife, previous neighbours of hers and John at Loch Ericht, near Rannoch, before the Schröders bought another Highlands estate. The Baron, whose title was Prussian, was head of a prominent German banking family – Schröders was by then an established merchant bank in the City – as well as being a leading authority on orchids.

Just the year before, he had been granted a licence by King George V to use his title in Britain, a necessity for those with foreign titles. But the

---

[1] Quoted in *From Mayfair to Mecca*, the introduction by William Facey to *Lady Evelyn Cobbold: Pilgrimage to Mecca*, London, Arabian Publishing Ltd. 2008, as taken from Jeremy Wilson, *Lawrence of Arabia: The Authorised Biography of T.E. Lawrence*, London, Heinemann, 1989.

Baron would not enjoy that privilege for long. When war broke out with the very country whose monarch had bestowed the title on his ancestors, the Baron, like the few others in Britain who bore 'enemy' titles, thought it wise not to use his. After the war the question would arise as to whether the King and Queen should receive at Court those people like the Baron who still formally had the right to use an enemy title in Britain. It was first considered in connection with receiving ladies with German or Austrian titles at Court, including inviting them to Royal garden parties, and the view was expressed that it was undesirable to do so.

Then the wider question arose as to whether royal licences in respect of *all* foreign, or 'alien', titles should be withdrawn. King George was reluctant to make such an order, and suggested instead that the holders apply voluntarily for their licence to be withdrawn. In 1919 the Baron, with five others, formally made such a request of the Lord Chamberlain which also involved the withdrawal of all privileges associated with the licence. The King's consent was granted and the gentlemen, possibly with some relief, were able to disassociate themselves publicly from Britain's enemies.

Pamela, meanwhile, long accustomed to her mother's absences, was good company for her father now that Winifred was married and Ivan away at Eton, and got on with her life at Holy Wells with her governess and Angy for company. As usual she spent her free time riding and playing tennis, and hunting when she could at whoever's estate she and one or other of her parents were invited to. August was always the focus of her year, when they would be back at Rannoch.

It is likely that she met Charles Hambro, through Ivan, before 1914 but the two families knew each other anyway, largely due to their respective banking connections. As well as sharing a love of cricket, the families' sporting enthusiasms included golf, a game which was enjoying its first heyday. In June 1914 Pamela watched with amusement as her father was beaten at a major amateur tournament at Felixstowe by Charles' uncle Captain Harold Hambro, who shared something of the formidable golfing talent of his father, Sir Everard, and his elder brother Angus. Indeed, Everard as usual had already been twice that year to play at Biarritz, the last time in April, enjoying, as *The Times* reported, 'a very good English season'. In fact, Everard was enjoying a very good time altogether, for he was there with his much younger second wife Ebba, née Whyte, whom he had married in 1911 when he was sixty-nine (and, according to one of his contemporaries, still very attractive and charismatic) and she in her early twenties. Unsurprisingly, the family had been very concerned about this union, especially his daughter-in-law Sybil and his only daughter, Violet. However, Ebba quickly endeared herself to all the family, recreating something of the jollity and warmth of the huge Hambro gatherings everyone loved especially at Christmas, which Everard's late wife, Mary, had been so skilled at organising.

Perhaps Ebba enjoyed a round of golf herself. It was a game which Pamela took up with alacrity – she had much natural sporting talent and a competitive nature – and as her father was a member of the Felixstowe Golf Club, she may well have been allowed to play on a casual basis in the ladies' section despite being only fourteen.

It was hardly surprising that Pamela's father found it hard to concentrate on his golf during the tournament, for he had something else on his mind. He was thrilled to have bought at auction just a few days earlier, on 29 May, the Rannoch estates which he had been renting for several seasons and which the whole family loved. The estates comprised over 70,000 acres of prime deer forests and grouse moors and included the magnificent Rannoch Lodge. The previous owner of the Rannoch Estates, Sir Robert Menzies, had died in 1903. Sir Robert's father had left the majority of his land which included Castle Menzies, ancestral home of the Chiefs of the Clan Menzies and Foss, to his widow instead of to their son, who was left a comparatively small acreage. Apparently somewhat litigious in nature, Sir Robert kept lawsuits going against his mother for the next twenty years without avail, and although she left him the Rannoch estates on her death in 1878, by the time Sir Robert died they were heavily burdened with debts. As Clan Menzies had owned Rannoch since the thirteenth century, this would not have endeared Sir Robert to his descendants. On his death his trustees had no trouble renting out the Rannoch estates to keen gentlemen hunters like John Dupuis Cobbold, but eventually a sale was necessary. Originally Castle Menzies and Foss were also put up for sale but later withdrawn: perhaps the trustees were keen to avoid a clan rebellion.

John paid £140,000 for the Rannoch Estates which, despite there being 'a large and fashionable company' at the auction according to a newspaper report, was not much more than the reserve price. The estates were an Edwardian hunting gentleman's dream. Two portions of the estate, Camusericht and Dunan, comprised 25,250 acres, a forty-five stag forest, and an eight hundred to fourteen-hundred-brace grouse moor. Also included were Talladh-a-Bheithe and Craiganour; with them came 21,000 acres, a forty to forty-five stag forest, and a six hundred-brace grouse moor. Then there was Rannoch Lodge itself – big, beautiful and elegant, dating from the eighteenth century and still standing in the twenty-first, following its restoration after a serious fire in the 1980s. At the head of the ten-mile long Loch Rannoch, famous for its trout fishing to which John also gained rights, it was said to command the best views in Perthshire. Before John bought the Lodge its guests had included Andrew Carnegie, the Scotsman who emigrated to America and became one of the world's richest men and, in 1901, Cecil Rhodes, who in turn invited the young Winston Churchill to stay.

What the locals thought about an Englishman buying up the estates is not known, but at least John would stop them becoming neglected after the death of Sir Robert and continue to provide employment to the local people. The fact that John's wife was a Murray, with the ancestral home of their clan, Blair Castle, just a few miles along the road, must have helped. And John was well known for his shooting skills. Nearly a century later he would still be remembered in the marksman's bible, *The Field* magazine, with his wife's cousin Lord Elphinstone, ranked as number 26 in the top 100 shots from Victorian times to 2009; between them they shot 1,292 snipe in eleven days during the winter of 1908 on the Scottish Isle of Tiree.

Pamela was delighted that Rannoch was now theirs, and could not wait until they returned there in August. Meanwhile, at the Felixstowe golf tournament, she and her father reflected on the alternative arrangements that had to be made unexpectedly for the visiting players. Unfortunately the players could not stay as they usually did in their favourite hotel, The Bath, built by Pamela's great-grandfather, for it had been virtually destroyed in the fire two months earlier. First spotted by the coastguard two miles away, the fire had plenty of time to gather momentum by the time the fire brigade arrived, by which time the entire front, with its picturesque verandas, was a blazing mass. Evidence of the suffragette arsonists was found in the garden next to the hotel, where some of their literature was discovered, and on trees on which were tied paper labels bearing suffragette statements. It was the last major militant act of the suffragette movement.

Although the Cobbolds no longer owned The Bath at the time of the fire, they were shocked and saddened by the destruction of the luxury hotel. Since 1839 it had been a well-known landmark on the cliffs, which had long hosted society figures and millionaires. Angy's father, the Hon Douglas Tollemache, was particularly upset, for he had for some time owned the lease on the hotel. However, he also owned the huge, neo-Jacobean Felix Hotel just a little further along the cliff, a much more modern affair which had been designed and built for him in 1903, so the players could stay there instead, recouping for the Tollemaches some of The Bath's lost revenue.

The Bath may have gone by 1914 but the golf course itself, perfectly situated by the sea, was as fine as it always was, lauded that year by the *East Anglian Daily Times* as 'the best nine-hole golf course in the world'. But that soon became a lament, for in August it was turned for the whole of the war into a rifle range on which soldiers practised their essential skills, while the elegant clubhouse became their barracks. And if the loss of the hotel had been a cloud for the Tollemache family, far darker clouds were yet to come.

Douglas Tollemache's eldest son Bevil was also playing in the golf tournament that June. Two months later he was a soldier, having enlisted with the Reserve of the 1st Battalion Coldstream Guards. He was sent to the Front in October and survived for just two months: on 22 December 1914 he was killed at Givenchy, whilst supporting Indian troops in the trenches. He was twenty-five. An old Etonian who had left in 1906, Bevil was mentioned in *The Chronicle* which all too soon was faced with the grim task of listing past pupils killed in action. It wrote of him, 'The loss of this young life, of exceptional vigour and promise, are grievous but the example he set and the noble work he did for his country are imperishable.'

By November that year, the worlds of golf and Rannoch were pushed to the back of John Cobbold's mind, for in those troubled times he became the Mayor of Ipswich. It was in keeping with his family's track record. His grandfather John Chevallier Cobbold had been elected Mayor in 1842; his father in 1867; his uncle Felix in 1896; and, more recently, his brother Philip in 1910. John's election was unusual, however, because he was not a member of the Town Council from which mayors usually came. Following the outbreak of war, many of its members had joined up, and in exceptional circumstances the Corporation could co-opt one of its citizens to the Chair. Coincidentally, the last time that had happened was in 1896 when Felix had been appointed.

Due to the war John had a far more difficult time than his relations had. As his obituary in the *East Anglian Daily Times* would later say, with reference to that time:

'John Dupuis Cobbold and his colleagues in those early days of war were called upon to meet special problems and difficulties; every hand was being turned to the stern purpose of the nation in its struggle to maintain its threatened existence, and having regard to the strategic position of Ipswich in the event of an invasion by the enemy, the situation was one of complexity and no little anxiety. To these varied problems the Mayor of that day directed all his thought and boundless energy.'

The Cobbolds had long been major benefactors of the East Suffolk and Ipswich Hospital, and in his role as Mayor John ensured the provision of two hundred additional beds for the wounded. At the same time he had to manage the effects of the war on the Brewery which saw eighty of his employees joining up, although that represented only about one-seventh of the total. He would have needed all hands to the pumps – literally – for the years 1914-15 saw a significant increase in beer production in England.

Everyone in Pamela's family found themselves well occupied very soon after the war began. Her mother quickly put aside her socialising and helped Stella Cobbold, wife of John's cousin Lt Col Clement Cobbold, to set up a military supply depot in Ipswich, only the second in the country of what would soon be many: the first had been set up very shortly before, in Kensington, London. Stella was an enthusiastic young woman, left at home with a young son while her husband was away fighting. She had already inspired her friend Muriel Bromley-Davenport to suggest to the Mayor of her home town of Hove, in Sussex, a similar venture there. The Cobbolds also knew Muriel, as her brother-in-law was Pamela's godfather William Bromley-Davenport. After Hove had heard the persuasive Stella speak at a meeting, it was agreed that a depot should be set up under Muriel's direction; for that and other war work she would later be awarded a CBE.

Back in Ipswich Evelyn Cobbold worked hard with Stella at the depot in Northgate Street, along with a dedicated group of volunteers almost certainly including Pamela, when she was not having lessons. From there they dispatched medical supplies and items of comfort to various headquarters and naval and military hospitals of the British and Allied Forces, ranging from drugs, bandages and crutches, to socks, mittens and mufflers. At the end of the war, when the depot had served its invaluable purpose, Stella would see her husband return safely to her and their fourteen-year-old son and mentioned in dispatches for his bravery. Tragically, however, she died just a month later aged thirty-six, one of the thousands of victims of the terrible Spanish 'flu epidemic that had started earlier in 1918. Their son Cameron would later become Governor of the Bank of England and the first Cobbold peer.

Pamela may have been a helpful and willing pair of hands at the depot but she found Ipswich boring at the best of times, and now with all the men gone too, and the town turned into almost a fortress due to its position, it was hardly an exciting place for an adolescent girl to be, even a wealthy one. She could only wait to hear from Ivan and Charles, who had not yet been sent to the Western Front, and hope that somehow their going would not be necessary. The death of Angy's brother Bevil brought the reality of the situation closer to home, and she used some of her energies in comforting her friend; in the same way Pamela's parents would have been very supportive of their old friends Douglas and Mary Tollemache in their grief.

For Eric and Sybil Hambro, the death of Bevil and many other young men like him reinforced the danger of Charles' situation. Eric in Sweden felt particularly helpless, although he could not have done anything to change the situation for his eldest son. Eric had been sent to Sweden by the British Government at the end of June 1915, sailing from Edinburgh to Bergen in a Royal Navy cruiser, then on to Stockholm, as part of a four-man British delegation whose aim was to persuade the Swedish Government to allow the free transit of goods across Sweden to Russia.

Eric had been recommended to the British Government by a childhood friend, a member of the Board of Trade and head of the mission, who took into account Eric's personal qualities, such as his irrepressible good humour, and the Hambros' role as bankers to the Swedish government for several generations. The two men, together with a member of the Foreign Office and a noted commercial lawyer with Scandinavian connections, made up the delegation. The four Britons met with a five-man Swedish delegation headed by Knut Wallenberg. That Eric's father Sir Everard had been friends with Knut for many years was naturally an advantage.

But despite such advantages the British delegates did not have an easy task, not least because two of the Swedish delegates were very pro-German, and negotiations lasted for four months. Eric particularly found himself in demand for meetings with influential figures which required all his social skills and tact, and drew heavily on his knowledge and understanding of the Swedes. By the end of October Eric was able to tell the British Government that they had managed to clear all vital materials which had been held up in Swedish ports and free them for use by the Russians, whose situation had thus improved immensely. The delegation had also played a decisive role in combating German influence in Sweden and keeping the Swedes out of the war, and had prevented the breakdown of commercial relations between Britain and Sweden. His Majesty's Government wrote to express its appreciation of 'the ability and zeal with which the delegates coped with the extraordinarily complicated problems encountered during the course of the negotiations'.[2]

As a result of his success in the delegation, Eric was invited to be involved in other aspects of Scandinavian trade during the Great War. He was delighted to do so, not least because it gave him the opportunity to operate away from the shadow of his father Everard, senior partner of C J Hambro & Son, and excel in his own right. In 1916, for example, Eric was co-opted onto a three-man Norwegian committee established by Britain's Board of Trade whose aim was to buy 75% of the Norwegian

[2] Bo Bramsen & Kathleen Wain, *The Hambros 1779-1979*, London, Michael Joseph 1979.

104

fish caught during the main harvest between February and April 1916. The aim was to deprive Germany, normally Norway's biggest fish export market, of a valuable food supply and also of fish oils from which glycerine was obtained to produce high explosives. Britain was sure that Germany would try hard to buy large quantities from Norway. In his role as banker on the committee, Eric had to arrange what was a tricky currency purchase situation in which he successfully involved his family's bank and a recently-established Scandinavian bank, the British Bank of Northern Commerce (BBNC), owned largely by the Wallenbergs, and with which the Hambros would become closely linked after the war. In 1919 Eric would be thrilled to be made a KBE in recognition of his contribution to the war effort.

While Sir Everard was pleased at the successes of his eldest son, he was worried by the effect of the war on business back at home and was anxious for Eric to be able to involve himself directly again in the family bank. Aged seventy-two when war broke out, Everard had for some time been exercising the privilege of attending the office of C J Hambro & Son only on a part-time basis, but he now returned full-time. The glory days of the Bank's Edwardian era had, as a result of the war, given way to the effects of political uncertainty: loss of business. The traditional role of merchant bankers like the Hambros had been to finance the international movement of goods, but in 1914 the old trading network disintegrated because former contacts were suddenly in enemy territory and lines of trust were broken. Merchant bankers were forced to adapt their operations as essential foods and materials for war took precedence over the decrease in trade. Alternative contacts had to be made and new credit facilities arranged. Also, political instability made the Stock Exchange nervous, and many of the existing investments of C J Hambro & Son became heavily depreciated.

In November 1914 the six partners of C J Hambro & Son – Everard and his sons Eric, Harold, Angus and Olaf, and Everard's nephew Harry – had taken the precaution of setting up a guarantee fund of £250,000 in anticipation of future losses they feared may occur. It was a wise move. Although the Hambro partners were able to use their Scandinavian connections during the war to their financial advantage over competitors, finding trading opportunities unavailable to others, their profits were nevertheless severely reduced. Between 1914 and 1917 there was a continual deficit, the worst year being 1915 when the ledger showed an overall loss of £58,000. Whereas the total average withdrawal of their profits in 1912 and 1913 had been £104,000, in 1914-15 this fell to £32,000. The men were therefore forced to exercise severe restraint.

Of the six of them Eric was the worst affected, for although he had been drawing his share of the profits for fifteen years, in December 1914 his capital was only £12. The problem was that despite his significant ability and successes in economic warfare Eric was very extravagant, loving tiger hunts in India, holidays in North America and being very generous to Sybil, which included smothering her in diamonds, despite also having four children to support. Embarrassingly for him he had to seek substantial help from his father, who gave him presents totalling £18,000 from 1915 to 1917. In later years Eric's weakness would have ramifications for his son Charles, although while the young man waited anxiously to be sent to the Western Front family finances were the last thing on his mind.

Chapter 8

From Darkness to Light, 1917–18

Pamela wrote to Charles regularly while he was away at war, fearing constantly for his safety. After his actions in September 1917, which led to his award of the Military Cross – 'For conspicuous gallantry and devotion to duty', as *The London Gazette* later announced – he was sent home that month on leave.

After spending some time with Pamela and her parents, he joined his own family at Gannochy, the Highlands estate which the Hambros had rented every summer since the early 1890s. It was a tradition started by Charles' grandfather Sir Everard Hambro along with his friend, the American banker J Pierpont Morgan; both families would stay at the imposing Gannochy Lodge at Edzell, while enjoying the excellent shooting on the estate. For centuries the owners of the Gannochy estate had been the Earls of Dalhousie, and when in 1913 it became the turn of Charles' father Eric to take over the tradition with Jack Morgan, the owner was the 14th Earl, Arthur George Maule Ramsay. The Hambros had known the Ramsay family for years; Arthur's grandson James, the 17th Earl, would later become a director of Hambros Bank.

Hunting was the main purpose of the Scottish estates for the Hambros at Gannochy and the Cobbolds at Rannoch, about which both families were passionate – and extremely good. Eric Hambro was known as an excellent shot, whilst Pamela's brother Ivan was regarded as one of the best in the country. Her parents, too, were very accomplished, although Pamela seldom showed much respect for her mother's skills.

Both families were lucky they could escape to their Highland retreats during the war years, albeit more briefly than usual. For the Hambros especially it must have been particularly welcome. London, where their business was based, was not the safest of places to be, certainly after June 1917 when the first German bombing raid took place, killing one hundred civilians. While the Hambro men went hunting or fishing, their wives and children occupied themselves by sketching by the North Esk river, reading and walking, joining the men for luncheon and tea. It was a haven of relaxation.

Charles would have been amused to hear in Pamela's letter of 2 October about Ivan's accident the night before when he and a companion, driving in Ivan's car, collided with a cart along the dark narrow lanes around Rannoch, '... but luckily the cart was damaged & not the car!'.

In January 1918 Pamela turned eighteen, and normally she would have been expected to take part in one of Society's rituals: her 'coming out' as a debutante involving her presentation at Court to King George V and Queen Mary, as her sister had done some years earlier. However, there were no presentations during the war and Pamela's loss – although she may not have seen it like that – was noted in *The Sketch* of 16 March 1918. In the social and court column 'Crowns Coronets Courtiers', a none-too-flattering cameo photograph of her appeared as an inset in the column with the caption, NIECE OF A DISTINGUISHED OFFICER: MISS PAMELA COBBOLD. The piece read:

'Miss Pamela Cobbold, who, but for the war, would have been a debutante of the coming Season, is the youngest daughter of Lady Evelyn Cobbold, and niece of the Earl of Dunmore, VC., MVO., DSO. Her only brother, Captain John Murray Cobbold, is in the Scots Guards.'

Also featured in the column were two Society women who were contributing to the war effort, one of them as a nurse in a hospital set up by another Society figure in Grosvenor Square, London, the other 'a keen war-worker'; however, the photographs of them dressed in flowing gowns and draped elegantly over beautiful pieces of furniture do not exactly send out the message of rolling up one's sleeves and mucking in.

The column illustrated the fact that, despite the role that many women were now playing as a result of the war, society was not quite ready to accept them as equal to men. In a piece appearing next to Pamela's with the heading, 'Not yet', a progress report was given on the efforts of a Miss Helena Normanton to become accepted as a barrister at the Law Courts. She had apparently hoped for 'enlightened consideration' but the Masters of the Bench had refused her admission and thus, '… the prospect of a woman barrister at the Law Courts recedes once more into the distance'. While the piece seemed to regret the situation, it ended on a note which would have made her and other feminists furious:

'Whether or not it is true that the public is as ready to employ the female as the male legal luminary, only experience can show, but it is certain that the presence of Eve in the Courts would impart a piquant interest to the dullest of 'Causes.''

Opposition to equal rights for women was not only voiced by men – some of their own sex also disapproved. The column referred to the different views of two women: Evelyn's acquaintance, the brilliant Lady Frances Balfour, and the Duchess of Somerset. Lady Balfour (sister-in-law of Arthur Balfour, the previous Prime Minister, now Foreign Secretary) was the holder of two Doctorates, and was a feminist and active supporter of votes for women. The Duchess of Somerset, on the other hand, had recently confessed publicly that she had been opposed to what she called women's 'interference' in men's affairs. She had, however, now experienced women's 'capacity and resourcefulness', but even so she still thought it best to let men 'imagine' that they did things better.

Happily for Miss Normanton and women after her, the situation would finally be remedied on Christmas Eve 1919 when, within hours of the King assenting to the Sex Disqualification (Removal) Bill, she became, at the age of thirty-seven, the first woman to be admitted to the Bar. Her other 'firsts' included being the first woman to lead a murder trial, the first woman King's Counsel and the first woman to conduct a trial in America. She also campaigned fiercely for the right of married women to keep their maiden name and for women's rights generally, advocating – against much outrage – that they should be free to spend any spare housekeeping money their husbands gave them on cigarettes or anything else they fancied.[1]

---

[1] She is still hailed as a champion of women's rights. In 2002 at an exhibition about Helena's life, Cherie Booth Q.C. highlighted Helena's career when talking about her own fight for greater sex equality and her defence of the right of married women to keep their name.

Meanwhile the war continued to take its toll. Charles would have been very distressed, as would all the Hambro family, to learn of the death of his second cousin, Percival 'Val' Hambro, son of Harry Hambro. A handsome, cheerful extrovert, Val was killed on 22 March 1918 while on active duty in France, aged nineteen.

It was especially important that Pamela keep up Charles' spirits at such a time. If Pamela and Charles wrote to each other between November 1917 and April 1918 – and it is pretty certain they did – the letters have not survived. In April 1918 Pamela wrote to him at his barracks at Windsor. She reminded him of the last time they had met, when they were with two other friends with whom they made up 'the Quartet', as they called themselves. The group consisted of Pamela and Charles, a friend called Pat – the seat of whose car Charles had broken – and Angy Tollemache. Having volunteered for munitions work, on 11 April Pamela started a wartime job as an 'engineering van driver' for Ransomes, a long-established and worldwide Suffolk company which made agricultural equipment and is still trading in the twenty-first century. She was pleased to be paid twenty-five shillings a week.

Just after she started, she wrote to Charles hurriedly during her work break, using a thick pencil – all that was available – rather than her usual elegant dark blue ink, anxious to get a letter to him quickly. Addressing him as 'My dear Charles' she was clearly concerned about his having to go away again:

'Dad tells me that in your letter you may be for France *this* week – But that is *dreadful*. Anyhow, if you *are* in England this week end you *must* come down here, otherwise I shall think nothing of you if you can't work that… I'm writing under difficulties, as I'm seated in my lorry (which carries 2 1/2 ton!!) & they are loading it up with great cases which they let fall every three minutes. So far, so good… Hours are from 8 to 6!

'I'm not feeling very happy about affairs in general, tho' we *ought* to be only too grateful to have Ivan safe in England, *that* is something… London seems a dream of years ago, it wasn't bad fun, though! Don't know when I shall see Ivan, as get the sack from this place if I don't work regularly.'

As always she could never remain gloomy for long, and the letter continued with a cartoon of Charles looking like a garden gnome perched with a fishing rod, depicting:

'Charles fishing at Gannochy. He sees (so he says) a 50lb salmon in the fast-moving water & so he raises his *heavy* rod to cast a *mighty line*. (Let me say that he is about to tumble.)'

But the note of sadness crept back at the end:

'I've just about loaded up, so I'd best end. Anyhow, it's only au revoir, n'est-ce pas? Oh! this war, will it ever cease... Your Pam.'

A few days later, from Victoria Barracks, Windsor, came the first surviving letter from Charles, dated 15 April. He was exuberant after having just seen Ivan on his return from France where he had been wounded, and reported to Pamela that:

'He really is looking awfully well & the swelling has all gone down – I am glad & Harry Forsiter says he will be back for 6 months, thank goodness... But now about my news, I am afraid I shan't be able to come on the 19th because I believe in fact I am almost sure I am going to France next Thursday. I wish I could see you but I am afraid it is almost impossible because I must stay with Ma and Pa & also I must stay at Windsor because I have had quite enough leave. They say!'

His letter regretted the passing of the familiar and the uncertainty of the future:

'What a pity it is the Quartet will be entirely busted & we did have such fun, didn't we, at least I did & hope you did – also good things can't last always & you know what I feel about going out [to France] don't you. Do write to me sometimes won't you, as one does love getting letters out there.

'I shall see Ivan tonight so shall know your movements. Give my best love etc to Ma & Pa and Tollemache & Pat & all the people. How glad I am Ivan is back.

'Yours ever & ever

'One of the Quartet.'

Like Pamela Charles seldom lost his sense of humour, and in a postscript referred to his breaking their friend Pat's car seat and to the size of his bottom, which he always considered too big:

'What about Pat's motor. It is bad luck having such a tiny B.'

As it happened he was not sent into action as quickly as anticipated but had to wait at the base camp at Havre, much to Pamela's relief. Writing from Ransome's Yard on 23 April on a scrappy piece of paper – for which she apologised but said it was preferable to writing on the only other kind available – she implored him not to be in a hurry to move on from there, trying to be optimistic about the situation generally:

'Things look better according to the papers – what do you think of the Budget? 'Tis no use worrying, money must be forthcoming to carry on some'ow!'

The budget of April 1918, under Lloyd George's Chancellor of the Exchequer and future Prime Minister Andrew Bonar Law, was a tricky one to get right because of the cost of the war, not only to Great Britain but also to its dominions, while it was of course not possible to know how long it would last. Bonar Law was a morose and stocky Canadian Scot from Glasgow whose father was a Presbyterian Minister. Recognising the need to raise vast amounts of additional revenue, at the same time he was anxious not make any class feel as though it was being taxed unnecessarily. He made the inevitable increases in income tax on those with incomes of over £500, with an exemption for soldiers and sailors, and raised the duty on tobacco. In addition, he took the unprecedented step of putting up the price of postage on letters to 1½ d and postcards to 1d. Sugar, which was rationed in 1918 to half a pound per person per week, went up too. He massively increased the duty on spirits and doubled it on a barrel of beer, saying that he was aware of the big profits that had been made in this trade during the past year, and that he was confident that those engaged in the trade would still be able to do well. His confidence is unlikely to have been shared by the Cobbolds and the Tollemaches. As the prices of spirits and beer were fixed by a Food Controller, in consultation with the Chancellor, it must have worried those in the trade because it meant that the bulk of the additional duty could not be passed on to their customers.

But the most unpopular part of his budget must surely have been his proposal, following the successful example of the French Government, of a 'Luxury Tax'. The French levied it on items such as jewellery and luxury hotels and establishments but, recognising that people would probably simply avoid such things, Bonar Law decided it was best collected through stamp duty, at a rate of one-sixth of the amount. Stamp duty was payable on a number of fairly ordinary items in 1918, so the effects would be potentially widespread. He at least recognised that the stamp duty would be considered objectionable by those from whom it was collected. The proposal was to be put to the House of Commons, and in the meantime he contented himself with increasing the rate of 'Super Tax' which was payable by those with incomes exceeding £2500.

Thinking about the budget prompted Pamela to tell Charles about her savings. It was clear that she had discussed with him her future plan, in which he was not included, of buying a farm in Canada with her best friend, Angy:

'I earned 31/- last week; I put it all aside for Canada.'

That country, formerly a British colony and still under a British Governor General, was seen as a safe land of great opportunity.

What Charles thought of her plan is not known but he had more immediate matters on his mind. Stationed at base camp for a month, he told her on the 14 May, in a letter stamped in the usual way 'Passed by Censor', that he was at last off and this time it was not a 'false alarm':

'I have been very idle, I know, but I have been very gloomy lately as nearly a month here is enough to make a chap commit suicide. Also all my letters have gone to the Batt. and I was beginning to think everyone had forsaken me. However, I am very bucked with life at present and am in proper Quartet form.

'By Jove, why aren't we all in N.B. [North Berwick] but still if I am careful I may be in time for the grouse shooting yet. You really can write your letters now to the 3rd Batt. Ct. BEF and be good, write nice and often.'

Charles' letter also contained a splendid cartoon, drawn by a fellow officer, of him in uniform, playing cards with a glass of port by his side, and entitled, 'C.J. Hambro M.C.', with the 'M' being formed by two crossed cricket bats and sets of wickets, signifying his love of and skill in the game. The drawing reflected, he said, his life at the base. Charles sent his love to Ivan and to 'East and West', Pamela's nicknames for her parents, and advised:

'...and don't overwork yourself, copy the English working man'.

He sent his love to Jane, being Nanny Cottle who, now that her nannying duties were finished, had become a kind of lady's maid to Pamela. The end of his letter showed their growing familiarity with each other because for the first time, after signing his name, he put in brackets Pamela's nickname for him – Pudge. Pamela loved the cartoon:

'... so *very* like you!! He must have been a clever feller, whoever did it – But I'm sorry, *very sorry* to hear you have gone (you'll be there by now) to the 3rd Batt. Tho' no doubt you are equally glad!'

She did her best to keep him cheerful and in touch with what was happening in her life, however trivial:

'Wonderful hot weather here [Monday, May 20th] & tomorrow I hope to go to Felixstowe & have a dip in the blue, sparkling sea... No work to do till Wednesday. I have great fun driving the lorry, the men told me t'other day that Cobbolds' Beer is only fit to *wash* in!! Nasty one; & I s'pose true... Some boring people are staying here: I spend my time avoiding them! Angy (Tollemache) came over yesterday and we played tennis; of course, I managed to have fun with her; & we kept people looking for 'imaginary' balls which had never gone down, so *we* could continue playing! At last in desperation the unfortunate guests said I don't believe there *is* a ball here!! We looked black so they started to look for it again! This afternoon we are going to some 'sports': how boring.'

What she never found boring, however, was nature:

'I went for a ride at dawn yesterday, to the 'Big Wood' – do you remember you shot it when you were here in the winter? Anyhow, now it's wonderful: a vast carpet of bluebells under wonderful oak trees. Why isn't everything beautiful; I s'pose one would *never* appreciate anything if everything was!

'Loch Rannoch today would look v. blue and not a ripple, so you'd see beautiful shadows of the mountains stretching across. I believe I'd sell my soul to be there; no I wouldn't, on second thoughts.'

But she could not help straying back to her worries:

'Charles, can't you end the war; I don't believe it lies in the power of one individual to do so, not even Lloyd George!! I begin to doubt it lies in *human* power, is everything fate? Well, I haven't given you one sentence of 'news' but there never is any –

'Yours, Pam.'

Perhaps she spoke too soon, for shortly afterwards she had a couple of incidents to report to him. She had heard that he was enjoying life, or at least was pretending to, and she talked about the good news from Italy:

'It is so wonderful to hear of the Italians taking prisoners for a change – you know old Guy Cobbold is out there. Here we've been having rather 'fun' – Ivan has been flying at the aerodrome near here a good deal, & last week Pat came to stay & was taken over there. He went up with somebody in one machine & Ivan in another. They chased each other across the sky but Pat felt frightfully vomitable! & broke the seat of his aeroplane & collapsed on the floor, thereby seeing 0. He can't complain about us breaking seats now! We have wild games of 'fives' on John's [her father's] best billiard table… [he] got furious last night when ball after ball crashed from picture to picture and window to window & refused to play any more!'

That was not the only smashing time she had been having:

'Rather sad things have happened to the lorry. Last week a horrible A.S.C. driver crashed a million miles per hour (slight exaggeration) into my tail end, doing me *no* injury at all but completely smashing himself up – well, then I was summoned to a 'Court of Inquiry' held at Claydon (7 miles from here) by the military – I gave my evidence & I had another female driver as witness, as well as 2 beloved soldiers, so I think it ought to be alright. The whole thing was so 'comic' that I roared with laughter, & luckily the military had a sense of humour & so took it as a joke!! Well, Friday I again had an accident & crashed the front of my car into a cart; (entirely my fault this time!) however, I got some of the most skilled workmen to repair it, & no-one was any the wiser! I flunked reporting 2 accidents in 1 week!!

'Oughtn't you to be getting leave soon? I think you useless unless you arrange to get about 3 months from August till October for Rannoch… Yours Pam.'

As if the poor chap could hope for as much leave as that but he did manage some later in the year, although Pamela was unlikely to see him. In a letter from 'Stagnant Ipswich' dated 17 September 1918, she was pleased to hear of some forthcoming leave and presumed he would go to

Scotland – 'It is the ONLY place to go to' – but she herself was no longer there, unable this year to spend the usual three months at Rannoch, due to work: indeed, she would not have got any time up there at all had it not been for a strike at Ransomes. Neither would Charles have the pleasure of Ivan's company in Scotland this time: Pamela had just seen him in London, back in hospital with a bad leg, and likely to be there for some time, having to give up his good job in France because of it.

Pamela had enjoyed herself in Scotland as always. Angy had been up there for a week and they had spent, 'some glorious days stalking', and the Cobbolds' beloved ghillie, MacNaughton, had 'excelled himself in playing the pipes!' The family had just lost their driver, Mackintosh, to the war – he was 'in France with the Motor Transport' – and Pamela warned Charles that the only person at Rannoch at the moment was her mother:

'Western Front is up there & has all the stalking to herself (Lucky Devil!)'

They seemed fated for a while not to see each other. On 2 October 1918 she told Charles that she was 'v. excited' to get his telegram saying he was coming home on Thursday that week, hoping to stay at Holy Wells for a few days, but said she could not take leave from Ransomes for so long. She was going up to London on the Saturday to visit Ivan but feared Charles may be returning to France that day, so she hatched a plan which was typical of her mischievous nature:

'Big B – I've an idea. You come down to lunch Friday & at 1 o/c I'll say I feel ill and can't work that afternoon & we'll return by an afternoon train to London & if your mother will have me I should simply love to stay Friday night at South Street. On Saturday morning I'll make Jane [Cottle] telephone down I'm worse! Mind you come down here if you can spare the time *Friday.*'

Desperate times, desperate measures. Pamela also wrote:

'The news is very good but ever so many of our friends have been killed, that's the awful part.'

The good news was no doubt the recent weakening of Germany's political and military leadership. In September the Head of the German Army, General Ludendorff, had suffered a breakdown, brought on by the news of the final attack on the German army at Amiens in August.

This he called 'the black day of the German army', with twenty-seven thousand German casualties and twelve thousand surrenders. That was followed by the resignation of Germany's Chancellor, George von Hertling. Germany was at its lowest ebb.

Back on the home front, Pamela and Charles' snatched couple of days were a lot of fun and 'no-one was any the wiser' about her little deception on her return to Ipswich. Plans were made for Pamela to stay with Charles' mother Sybil in London in his absence – a move on his part that perhaps signified the direction in which he wanted their friendship to go – which Pamela said she would 'simply love' to do. Her enthusiasm for staying with Sybil also highlighted her indifference towards her own mother: in the same letter she told Charles of a visit to Holy Wells at the weekend from a friend called Bowker, who she said 'counteracted the misery of Evelyn's return' from Rannoch.

The reason for Pamela's feelings towards Lady Evelyn can only be surmised. There were her absences for travelling, of course, when Pamela was younger, although this was not unusual for her class; and she was considered to be very snobbish, believing that her aristocratic roots put her above the Cobbolds, despite their own long-established wealth. Yet Evelyn was not without humour but compared to her husband, who was easy-going, she could appear very strait-laced. A complex character, she was heavily influenced by her childhood spent amongst the Arabs in Egypt whom she greatly missed, keeping in regular contact with her friends there. Her Muslim faith in itself set her apart from the Cobbolds' conservative and Christian background and values. She loved to garden at Holy Wells, taking great pride in the exotic blooms she grew in their beautiful conservatory, but it seems that she herself wilted when away from her spiritual homeland. Also, it is said that a poem written by her in 1912 shows that even at that stage she seemed to have regarded her marriage as being rather semi-detached; and as Pamela was very fond of her father, anything which might hurt him would no doubt have made her antagonistic towards Evelyn.

Meanwhile the war was having an effect close to home. On 27 September 1918 the husband of Evelyn's youngest sister, Lady Mildred, and thus Pamela's uncle, was killed in action on the Western Front. A military star, Gilbert Burrell Spencer Follett was a Brigadier General, and before he died, aged forty, had already received the MVO (Member, Royal Victorian Order, for personal services to the monarch) and the DSO. He left Mildred with their two children, John, aged twelve, who had been one of the pages at Winifred's wedding, and three-year-old Jean.

Letters from Charles in October and November 1918 were rather thin on the ground, taking a long time to get through, although Sybil tried to make up for it by sending amusing telegrams to Pamela and Ivan. As it turned out, no news was good news, for November 1918 heralded the end of the war. Germany's allies, Austria and Hungary, secured armistices on 3 and 13 November respectively, and Germany itself on 11 November. The country signed the document as a republic, its monarchy in tatters, its leader Kaiser Wilhelm abdicating and fleeing to Holland. On that same day, 11 November 1918, the British Prime Minister, Lloyd George, informed the House of Commons of the conditions of the Armistice and concluded:

'Thus at eleven o'clock this morning came to an end the cruellest and most terrible war that has ever scourged mankind. I hope we may say that thus, this fateful morning, came to an end all wars.'

Chapter 9

Early Days

The war may have ended but unfortunately for Charles, who often told Pamela how much he disliked being in the army, his time in it had not yet come to an end despite the end of the hostilities. He was not sent home on leave but instead to Germany, as part of the British occupation of Cologne under the terms of the Armistice. Answering an earlier letter which took a long time to arrive and which unfortunately has not survived, Pamela wrote to him from Holy Wells on 8 December 1918:

'Yes, it must be wonderful for you that fighting has ceased, it even seems a mighty weight removed to us mere civilians, who've never even heard a gun. The only thing is people who've never been 'in it' can never realise... poor fools!

'Your B. will be v. small by the time you return to England after all this walking – I wonder if you're in Germany now & whereabouts? Ivan is up in Rannoch, lucky devil... Everyone went mad Armistice Day & night & all that week, especially in London. I was down here but of course work ceased, so I got on Picio (the horse) & went for a wild gallop to let off steam & felt calmer afterwards!'

Work at Ransomes had stopped for a few days and Pamela managed to get to London for two nights to see (twice) a revue called *Hullo America*. It had recently opened at the Palace Theatre on 25 September, its star a hugely successful American actress, singer and songwriter called Elsie Janis whose career had started at the age of ten when she was invited to entertain the American President. She had first performed on the London stage in 1914 and became the most popular

American actress in the London theatre, a talented vaudeville performer who combined comedy, dance and impersonations in her act. When the First World War started, despite being at the height of her fame, Elsie left the London stage to travel to the military camps surrounding the city to entertain the British troops who were leaving for France.

Losing her lover, a fellow actor, to the war, Elsie left England in April 1917 when America entered the world stage to go to France to entertain the American and British troops. There she spent six months at the Western Front, often within artillery range of the Germans, being the first female entertainer ever permitted on a military base. Elsie became a fixture at the Front, being allowed to pull the lanyard on one of the big guns which was named 'Elsie' in her honour. She became known as the sweetheart of the American Expeditionary Force. While in France Elsie came across a new form of music played by the black African-American bandsmen whom she met at the Front: jazz. Impressed with the sound, she incorporated it into the revue, taking *Hullo America* to England on her return there in 1918 and later home to America. She may have entertained Charles and his comrades in France – Pamela's letter suggests he knew of the show.[1]

The revue also included a home-grown one-act play, a comedy called *The Boy Comes Home*, about a soldier returning from the war. It was written by A A Milne who, apart from his fame as the creator of Pooh Bear, enjoyed some success as a playwright. He had joined up with the 4th Royal Warwickshire Regiment in 1915, the same year as Charles, and was stationed in France until he contracted a fever and was sent home in 1916, when he started to write plays. The revue was a huge success.

Between her theatre visits Pamela found time to lunch with Charles' mother Sybil but had not managed to get back to London since then, as she was busy back at home: she was still needed at Ransomes and she had become involved in the General Election that December. It was an odd time to have an election as 3.9 million voters were still out of

[1] A friend of Irving Berlin, the composer, and the actress Mary Pickford, Elsie did not achieve the same success in 'the talkies' that she had enjoyed on the stage. She never married, keeping a photograph of her beloved Basil Hallam by her bedside until her death in Hollywood, in February 1956.

the country, but Lloyd George wanted to cash in on his reputation as 'The Man Who Won the War'. Special arrangements were made for the military to vote either by post or by proxy, depending on where they were. Pamela was no stranger to politics with several Cobbold ancestors having been MPs and her parents being involved throughout her life. She seemed to enjoy it, despite a little cynicism:

'At the moment we are frightfully busy with the Election – seems odd even raising a spark of interest in such a fool's game as Politics; but I s'pose it's important to get the right government in *now*. It's going to be a v. hard fight here twixt the Conservative Coalition Candidate & the Labour man, who is a red-hot Socialist. I'm having great fun with the men down at the works & I argue all day, knowing *nothing*, but that's all the better for mere 'talking' – I find they've never asked for so much in their lives before, & it's difficult to refuse them *anything*; shows what bribery does!'

The discontent of Ransomes' workers that Pamela experienced was probably the same as that felt by many civilian workers at the time. Although during the latter stages of the war there had been full employment and rising wages, there was also anger at the increase in food prices during the war and the perception that many businesses had done well out of increased government orders, which was not always reflected in the workers' pay packets. A series of strikes throughout the country had started in 1917 and continued until 1921, much to the concern of the Government.

Pamela's contribution to local politics may not have solved the country's woes but she did make some impact. Ipswich's Conservative candidate Francis Ganzoni, currently in office and hoping for re-election, had asked Pamela to support him at a meeting. Feeling very nervous – 'feeling tiny altogether!' – Pamela 'rose tremblingly' to her feet and '... said about 3 sweet words. There were screams of mirth from the audience!' She did not reveal to Charles what she actually said, but whatever it was cannot have done Ganzoni much harm for he was re-elected when voting took place on 14 December. Other Conservatives elected on that occasion, which resulted in a coalition government which retained Lloyd George as Prime Minister, included the future Prime Minister Neville Chamberlain, and Oswald Mosley, elected for Harrow who, like Charles, had done his time in the trenches, and at just twenty-one was the youngest MP. He would later 'cross the floor' of the House of Commons to join the Labour party, and in 1932 became notorious for founding the British Union of Fascists.

On 7 January 1919 Pamela's job at Ransomes finally ended, freeing her to look ahead to holidays in the more peaceful New Year. The Cobbolds started to make tentative plans although Pamela feared they might not materialise, telling Charles:

''Tween you and me, I live in hope that the Western Front goes abroad!'

The plans were for a holiday in Egypt but, as she had predicted, it did not happen. Pamela told Charles on 19 February 1919, having just recovered from a bout of 'flu, that they had had their cabins booked on a P&O ship and were told only the night before they were due to sail that Egypt refused to let them land. She hid her disappointment by musing on what it would have been like travelling with the 'Western Front':

'Plenty of rows, I s'pect! But of course that would have all added to the excitement. We are now trying (rather feebly) to go to the South of France in March for 3 weeks or so – don't know if we shall have better luck with our passports this time!'

Pamela had also had lunch again with Sybil, who complained that Charles had been back in Cologne for a month but had not written to her, for which Pamela admonished him. Pamela had also just spent a week in London with a friend, Judy Smith, telling Charles:

'… & danced nearly every night; they *are* such a boring lot of fools dancing round London now, that by their conversation you'd say they are quite 'potty'!!'

Pamela was far from a killjoy but knowing of the losses suffered in the war by the extended families and friends of her and Charles, she must have wondered what there was to be dancing about. Not only had Pamela's uncle and Angy's brother Bevil been killed but her parents' friends had lost children, including the Grenfells. Of that family, Lord and Lady Desborough lost two sons: in May 1915 their eldest son, Julian Grenfell, died of wounds in France, and less than two months later their younger son Billy was killed, only one mile from the spot where Julian had been fatally wounded. Lady Evelyn's relation John James Murray, the 7th Duke of Atholl, who a few years earlier as head of the Murray clan had paid his respects at the funeral of Evelyn's father, lost one of his three sons during the first months of the war in September 1914. John and Evelyn's friend the 8th Earl of Aylesford, who had taken some of the photos in her *Baby's Book* and holidayed with them in Norway with his daughter Lady Muriel, lost his eldest son, Captain Heneage Greville Finch. Having survived the Boer War as an eighteen-year-old, he was killed in France, aged thirty-one, in September 1914. Greville left a six-year-old son, Heneage Michael Charles Finch, the 9th Earl, who would himself be killed in action in 1940, at the same age as his father.

The Cobbolds' businesses saw the death of some of their employees but fortunately very few. Approximately eighty of the Brewery staff had joined up, two of whom were taken prisoner and eight killed: a gunner, three lieutenants, and four privates. One of those was Private W A Carter, whose mother wrote to John to notify him of the death of his employee:

'Dear Sir, This is to notify that my son was killed in action on the 20th July, 1917. Thanking you for all your kindness, I am, Sir, his sorrowing mother, Mrs Carter.'

From February 1919 until May no letters survive but Charles finished his time in Germany and was sent home with his Regiment, to be based at Chelsea Barracks. In the meantime some happiness had brightened the gloom, in the form of the marriage of his good friend, Pamela's brother Ivan, to Lady Blanche Cavendish, a daughter of one of the wealthiest men in Britain, from one of its best-known families: Victor Cavendish, the 9th Duke of Devonshire. Precisely how Ivan and Blanche met is uncertain but Ivan must have been unique amongst bridegrooms in not actually meeting his father-in-law until after the wedding. Since 1916 the Duke had been Governor-General of Canada, living in Ottawa, and had not had much opportunity to visit England since then. The reason he did not know about his beloved daughter's marriage plans until March 1919 – only a little over a month before the wedding took place – was because the engagement had only just been announced and as Victor's wife, the Duchess Evelyn (Evie) was due to join him in Canada in May, the wedding had to take place before she left England.

Not renowned for her beauty, Blanche was by all accounts great fun and very popular. She had had a tremendously privileged background.

Since the sixteenth century the Cavendishes had been one of Britain's richest and most influential families, enjoying various political positions and always having the ear of the Monarch. When Blanche was born in 1898 the family still owned considerable estates in England and Ireland, including Chatsworth in Derbyshire into which the family had moved in 1908 when Victor became the 9th Duke. Blanche's mother was a daughter of the Marquess of Lansdowne, the Viceroy of India, and was Mistress of the Robes to Queen Mary. She was also known for being a terrible snob and something of a bully; even Edward, Prince of Wales, thought her 'hopelessly pompous'.

Yet in spite of all this, Blanche's chatty letters written to the Duchess just before and during her marriage to Ivan do not reveal any snobbishness on Blanche's part, certainly not towards the Cobbolds, although there could have been. Despite nearly two hundred years of hard-earned wealth by the Cobbolds and the part they had played in the life of Suffolk during that time, they were not in the same social or financial league as the Cavendishes. But then, few families were. And if they wanted some aristocratic connection for Blanche, then her future mother-in-law Lady Evelyn Cobbold had it in bucket-loads, in background if not in cash. If there had been any snobbery on Blanche's part, her sister-in-law Pamela would never have got on with her, for she had no time for social pretensions. Instead the two young women, only two years apart in age, became very good friends.

The fact that the Duke had not met his future son-in-law did not seem to matter to him, for he had heard very positive things about Ivan. The Duchess Evie had sent him a telegram telling him about the engagement, and he replied in a letter to her from Government House, Ottawa on 17 March 1919:

'It is really splendid about Blanche... I have heard all about [Ivan] and he seems delightful. Henry Cator [one of the Duke's ADC's] is very enthusiastic & says he is a really good sort. I feel no-one can be quite good enough for Blanche and I am sure she will be very happy. You must wire me as soon as arrangements are made for the wedding.'

The Duke also wrote about the news in his diary, saying that his family were delighted by the announcement, and adding that after he got Evie's telegram he 'did not know how to walk off' his feelings: he did not have any members of his family there to share it with, so he:

'... walked up & down the sidewalk which is [the] only place when there is no ice & also telephoned to various people. They were all very nice & I [could tell] that they genuinely liked Blanche.'

The Duke very much wanted to go over for the wedding in April but since the end of the war the political situation in Canada had become very unstable. The rate of unemployment and the increase in the cost of living had led to dissatisfaction among the workforce. Strikes that had started in January that year had become violent, to the extent that on 4 April the government appointed a Royal Commission on Industrial Relations to look at how a permanent improvement could be made to the relations between employers and employees in Canada. But when a general strike broke out in the major city of Winnipeg, which included the police and fire service, and sympathy strikes threatened in other cities across the country, alarm bells rang in Government House. The Duke, fearing this was the beginning of an attempt to overthrow the Constitutional Government, knew it was not the time to leave the country, even for his beloved daughter's wedding.

Blanche was very disappointed that her father would not be at her wedding but she had at least spent time with him in Ottawa in January that year. He had been due to visit Toronto while Blanche was there and no doubt she was hoping to go with him, but, as she told her mother at the time, his trip was cancelled due to the death in England on 18 January of troubled Prince John, the youngest son of King George V and Queen Mary, from an epileptic fit at the age of just thirteen.

As much as he liked the sound of his future son-in-law the Duke however, found a fly in the ointment in the forthcoming union with the Cobbolds, albeit a most unexpected one: Ivan and Pamela's sister, Winifred. Or rather, not so much she as her husband, Algernon Sladen (Algy). In the small world of the upper classes and the military, the Duke's private secretary in Canada happened to be Algy's half-brother who, on the morning the Duke wrote to the Duchess, had warned him that Algy was 'a thoroughly bad lot'. The Duke told his wife that 'Sladen', as he referred to his secretary, was 'very much distressed' about the whole thing, and had told the Duke that his half-brother had 'always been a trouble to his family who have now disowned him'. The Duke said he had learned that Algy had:

'... managed to get a commission in the English army but was tried by Court Martial & cashiered. I gather his offences were connected with accounts. He is now a private in a Canadian unit and Sladen has heard he is coming back to be demobilized... and is bringing his wife back with him. It would never do to have them inside the house here, although one does not want to be hard on the wife.'

Sladen told the Duke about Winifred's parents opposing the marriage but that she was 'very obstinate'. Sladen was now trying to prevent them coming to Ottawa. The Duke told the Duchess that not many people knew about them at the moment, 'and it is most desirable that as little as possible should be said'.

Whether they turned up in Canada after all is not known, but it seems likely Ivan would have been aware of the threat his sister's marriage posed to the harmony of his relations with the Cavendishes, particularly as he was still in the army himself and would have been aware of the seriousness of Algy's court martial.

It seems probable, if harsh, that in the circumstances Winifred was not invited to the wedding. Invitations would have come from the bride's parents, and although the Cavendishes seem to have had a very cordial relationship with John Dupuis and Lady Evelyn Cobbold, such that the Duke and Duchess would no doubt out of courtesy have asked them if they would like Winifred herself to be invited in spite of everything, it seems likely that, given the Cobbolds' now distant relationship with their eldest daughter and their sensitivity of the awkwardness of the situation for the Duke, their answer would have been negative. In newspaper reports of the occasion there is no mention of Winifred having sent a present, let alone being there.

Whilst the relationship between the two sets of parents appeared to be good, there was the delicate matter of a marriage settlement for Blanche to be sorted out before the wedding, which seems to have caused concern on both sides. Although the old law, that a woman's wealth automatically went to her husband, had been changed by the Married Women's Property Act of 1882, amongst upper-class families it was still seen as desirable for the wife to have a settlement in the event that the marriage failed or the husband died and she was left with a much-reduced income: amongst those circles that would have represented a loss of status. Also, the groom needed to know that his bride had some money behind her. Letters from John to the Duchess refer to their having had some ongoing discussion about what the Duke would be settling on Blanche: John seemed to think there was some uncertainty and had been advised by his solicitors to ask certain questions which appear to have worried the Duchess. On 12 April 1919 John wrote to her:

'In deference to your wishes I did not press the point about Blanche's income if she married again but I must confess to being surprised that Mr Macpherson's [the solicitor] original statement that £40,000 would eventually be Blanche's portion should have been discarded and that only ½ would be definitely settled, the other ½ being subject to Devonshire's will – his word is as good as his Bond, and if he would tell me that he intended to make up her portion to £40,000 that is all I want.'

The couple also needed to have somewhere to live in London. John told the Duchess that they had all looked at 12 Hertford Street, actually called Carrington House, a large property in fashionable Mayfair, London, and a stone's throw from Green Park.[2] Ivan and Blanche could rent it until 1 August, with an option to continue until May 1920. John would pay the rent for them because 'it is no use their starting with heavy sums to pay for rent...' In addition to Blanche receiving the settlement money, John would pay Ivan £1000 on the first of May, August, November 1919, and February 1920, '... so they should get along, and I hope... Blanche will be a restraining influence on extravagance – I have been going about in a Taxi with them, it is awful!'

The Duchess must have been concerned by John's points about the settlement, for in his next letter he implores her not to worry about it, because:

'... they are all right and I have written my solicitors that they are to accept everything as you wish – so think no more about the horrid money – the only thing we want is for these 2 to be happy – Devonshire will settle £20,000 now and everything else he chooses eventually to give Blanche is entirely at his discretion. I am so sorry that I worried you but my solicitor

---

[2] It is still there in 2012, turned into luxury flats which sell for up to £2million.

asked me to put the points forward as they appeared to him… Perhaps you would like to cable Devonshire that things are all settled.'

He invited the Duchess to Holy Wells for a long weekend, saying that Evelyn would be so glad if she could come.

In a short timescale that would be unthinkable today, the wedding took place about six weeks after the engagement, on 30 April 1919. An impressive Society affair, taking place at the Guards' Chapel, Wellington Barracks, it occupied many inches in *The Times* newspaper. With the combination of the Cavendishes' and the Cobbolds' connections, the guest list read like a 'Who's Who' of Great Britain, although the Duchess must have reflected sadly upon one missing guest: one of her two younger brothers, Lord Charles Petty-Fitzmaurice, who had been killed at Ypres in 1914.

The day before the wedding *The Times*, under the 'Forthcoming Marriages' section, published a list of wedding presents for the couple, headed by gifts from King George V and Queen Mary. The custom then was for a separate gift for each of the bride and bridegroom, and whether the donor gave a gift to both depended on the relationship to the couple. The King and Queen gave Blanche a diamond and enamel brooch, while their daughter Princess Mary gave her a set of coffee cups, saucers and tray. As the Monarchs' connection was largely with the Cavendishes, it was Blanche rather than Ivan who was the lucky one. From Blanche's parents and parents-in-law came a variety of diamond jewellery, while Pamela – delighted to be one of the bridesmaids– gave her an address book. Ivan did not fare too badly either, although whether he fully appreciated the portrait of his wife from the Duke and the miniature of her from the Duchess, when he had the real thing to look at each day, is not known. Still, the vast amount of silver he received from other guests was no doubt gladly received, even though there was a marked duplication of silver bowls and salvers. Charles, it seems, could not go, Ivan taking as his best man a fellow Scots Guard, although Sybil Hambro was there, which would have pleased Pamela.

In the absence of the Duke, Blanche was given away by her brother Edward, the Marquess of Hartington. She wore a medieval-style cream satin grown finished by a girdle of lace and diamonds, with a satin train embroidered with pearls and diamonds, and carried a prayer book instead of the usual bouquet. The two older bridesmaids, wearing dresses of soft crepe satin and hair ornaments of blue feather and net, were Pamela, and Blanche's younger sister Dorothy, who was pleased to have made it to the wedding, as in late March she had caught German measles, not taken lightly in those days. If Blanche had had a bouquet to throw Dorothy would surely have caught it, for a year later she too would be married: to her father's aide, a brilliant if serious young man named Harold Macmillan.

The reception was held at Lansdowne House in Berkeley Square, London, the eighteenth-century ancestral home of Blanche's mother's family, which included a former Prime Minister. Designed by Robert Adam, it was one of the grandest and best-known private houses in the capital. A formal photograph of the newly-weds with their bridesmaids and pages taken at the House after the ceremony shows the adults looking solemn. Captain Cobbold, with his mother's expression, looks sternly over to one side; next to him his sister-in-law Dorothy looks in the same direction, handsome and regal; Blanche is tight-lipped; only Pamela shows any softness of expression, a hint of a smile around her lips. The six young pages and bridesmaids look warily at the camera, the three titled ones probably feeling the weight of their inheritance already thrust upon them. Little Jean Follett, Ivan and Pamela's cousin, sits holding a bouquet nearly her own size, her small feet in their beautiful buckled shoes barely reaching the floor.

Given Ivan's passion for hunting, the honeymoon was spent in Scotland – naturally at Rannoch. It was the first time Blanche had been to the area and, like the rest of the Cobbolds and particularly her new sister-in-law, she loved it, describing it in a letter to her mother on 2 May as 'the most heavenly place'. No wonder Blanche and Pamela would get on well. The locals were keen to show their support for the son of their landlord:

'All the keepers & people round about turned out to meet us yesterday, they made an arch at the gate.'

Someone made a speech, which Ivan answered, then they all came into tea and danced until two in the morning. The couple motored round the Loch, which Blanche pronounced, 'too lovely', and had 'luncheon' at Blair Castle, the Murrays' ancestral home, presumably with Ivan's relation, the Duke of Atholl, himself. Only two years into the title after his father's death, the 8th Duke and his wife, the beautiful and clever Katharine Stewart-Murray, would have been good company. Already awarded a DBE for public service, she was working towards a political career and would soon be elected as the first Scottish female MP at Westminster.

Writing to her mother from London on 20 May, Blanche said how sorry she was to have left Rannoch when 'everything was looking so delicious'. They were going to join the growing Cobbold contingent up there and buy a lodge at Talladh-a-Bheithe where Ivan's uncle Philip and aunt Cicely owned a property, and had seen one they liked but it needed renovation. Her father-in-law's factor Macdonald, who was an architect, was going to talk to John Cobbold, because he had, 'all sorts of plans, of building on a bit, & putting in another bath which certainly is badly needed & knocking down various walls'.

But John's attention would soon be diverted to other family matters, for the spotlight was about to move away from Ivan and Blanche and fall upon another couple in the family.

Chapter 10

The Young Lovers

After the excitement of Ivan and Blanche's wedding there would be a second celebration that same year, for Charles Hambro had realised Pamela was the woman for him. The precise moment had occurred during one of his periods of leave when she had given him a two shilling piece for a taxi, and as he told her later in a letter, 'It was the night that I really knew!' Their absences from each other and their relief and gratitude that the war was over, and that Charles had survived, must have made them realise that time was too precious to waste. On the night of 23 May 1919, both of them sitting on 'terribly hard chairs & frightfully conspicuous covers', he proposed and she accepted. Pamela was nineteen and Charles twenty-one.

An ecstatic Charles wrote to her from his barracks at 3am the next day:

'Am I in a wonderful dream & shall I wake up in the Trenches or worse still in the ball-room of a typical London House. I am writing on purpose with the dear pencil. How I have treasured it. Do you remember what we said when we bought it...'

He was going to return the two shilling piece to her:

'I have kept it ever since & now I am returning it to its owner, the most wonderfull[1], beautifull girl in the world. It is only a 2/- piece but it is the greatest treasure I possess even before the pencil. Oh my darling how I love you. How happy I am going to make you... I have built such

---

[1] Spelling was not Charles' strong point and he consistently spelled such words with a double 'l'.

131

wonderfull castles for you and I to live in, never daring to dream that it could ever come true.'

If he had been able to do things his way, it seems he would have told her of his feelings before then:

'How hard it was for me when I could not tell you how I felt. But I had to keep my promise. But the weight is off now and I feel happy, blissfull, in fact I know that at this present moment no-one is happier on earth...'

If the 'promise' was not to tell Pamela he loved her until after the war was over, the person to whom Charles had made such a promise can only be guessed at. It could have been John Cobbold. His protective instincts as a father, once he realised what Charles felt, may have caused him to extract the promise because he thought it would worsen his daughter's loss if Charles was killed: Charles would no doubt have deferred to John's wish in the interests of future harmony as his son-in-law. Or perhaps it was made to her brother, his friend Ivan, for the same reason: as a fellow soldier, Ivan would have been acutely aware of the risk that Charles may not have returned. It is hard to imagine that it would have been Charles' parents, for they would have had their son's happiness at stake, and if that had meant securing the love of this woman, giving him hope for life after the trenches, then that is surely what they would have wanted for him.

Although Pamela had accepted his proposal, Charles wanted her to be absolutely sure:

'But my darling, if you are not sure, wait a bit. I shall wait 20 years if necessary. But lately I have known you were sure. Else I would not have said anything... Oh my darling, how I love you... Can anything be as perfect as our love. God is very, very kind.'

Pamela's reply written later the same day, from Claridges Hotel in London, must have removed any doubt in Charles' mind of her certainty:

'Now I KNOW I love you. Of course, there was never really any doubt, there never could have been anyone but you, but till you put it into words last night I hadn't realised – thank God for giving us this.'

Pamela was going to tell her father that evening. Charles responded in his second letter of 24 May from the midst of what he called a 'duty party' at Wakehurst Place in Sussex, a beautiful Elizabethan manor house owned by a friend, Gerald Loder.[2] Despite being a sociable person like Pamela, Charles often found parties boring, and this one was particularly so because she was not there. Still in his ecstatic state, Charles wanted her with him in the lovely garden so that they 'could walk about and be in Paradise', instead of which he had to make 'stupid conversation'. He told her:

'I am so happy with everything that I want to shout out and tell all & everyone that I have got the only girl in the world and am in heaven... When am I going to see you? Just think what an awful long time it is until June 2nd.'

Charles thought it wonderful that she was going to tell her father all by herself and said he would be writing to him the next day; he would also be telling his parents that day when he dined with them, and anticipated that they would say he was, 'the luckiest man on earth'.

Naturally Pamela could not wait to see him either, but in her letter to him of 27 May, addressing him by his nickname, Pudge, she realised he would not be able to get away properly until after Trooping the Colour, which was to take place on 3 June in Hyde Park. That year it was the turn of Charles' Regiment, the 3rd Battalion Coldstream Guards, to troop their colour before King George V. The last time the Regiment had done so was in 1904 and so this would be the first time Charles had taken part. In 1919 the event was particularly significant because it was the first one to take place since the war had started. Normally an annual event to mark the official birthday of the Sovereign, the ceremony had been suspended during hostilities and had not taken place since June 1914. At that time the King had still enjoyed his family's German surname, untroubled by the fact that Kaiser Wilhelm II was his first cousin. How so much had changed in such a short time.

Pamela ended her letter, 'Goodbye most wonderful of human beings – For eternity', and went on to muse in her next one about the 'wonderful things just Love makes one do':

'I have chucked over Canada & thrown over my best friend all

[2] Later created Lord Wakehurst, he was a passionate gardener and conservationist, and later a President of the Royal Horticultural Society. Lord Wakehurst is credited with creating the garden, which is today managed by the Royal Botanical Society and is the 'country garden' of Kew.

because I love you so, & now nothing else counts… But it won't make any difference to my friendship with Angy; you see, till you came she was the biggest and greatest thing in my life!'

As Charles had predicted his 'Ma and Pa… were awfully pleased', and his mother 'wept for joy'. But he was nervous about Lady Evelyn's reaction:

'I wonder if she will be pleased, I think she likes me, don't you.'

Charles was longing to see Pamela and could not wait for another six days until 2 June, wondering if her parents had room for him at Holy Wells during the coming weekend if they were not full up. He was also desperate to get out of his 'beastly' London office. Like many soldiers who had seen action, he hated desk jobs. But later that day, 27 May, he received the very welcome news that he was going to be relieved of his job on 10 June. After that he reckoned he could be 'practically always on leave'. By the time he wrote to Pamela later to tell her this, he had already sorted out their immediate plans. He had written to her mother to tell her of their engagement and asked if he could go down to Holy Wells the next weekend, 31 May; from 3 June Pamela would stay with his mother for a few days at his parents' Mayfair house in South Street; then she would go with Charles to his parents' country house, Pickhurst Mead in Kent, and after that, they and both sets of parents would visit his grandfather at his estate at Milton Abbey, where Pamela would be introduced to the great Sir Everard and the engagement would formally be announced. It was important that she go to Milton, not only to meet his grandfather but:

'Because one day you will have to boss Milton. Oh how happy you will make all the poor people there. You Darling, how they will all love you!'

The prospect of being mistress of a vast estate like Milton, where the house itself dwarfed even the ample proportions of Holy Wells, must have been daunting to a young woman unused to such responsibility, but perhaps she consoled herself with the thought that the task would not fall upon her yet: even after Everard died it would be expected to pass to Charles' father, Sir Eric Hambro, first, and so by the time Charles inherited it, Pamela should be ready for the challenge.

As delighted as Charles' parents were about their son's engagement, Sir Eric did not think they should rush into it. Charles told Pamela:

'My Pa says he thinks we ought to wait 6 months before getting married. It is an awfull long time. But what is time when we love each other. It won't make any difference. How I love you, my wonderfull girl.'

Excited about seeing each other again on 31 May, for the first time since the proposal, they wrote four letters between them over the next three days, Pamela doing a sort of count-down:

'My darling Pudge. There exist 72 hours before I can possibly see you (12 seconds gone!)...'

She was thrilled to have received a 'perfectly wonderful' letter from Sybil, and even her own mother had taken it very well and seemed 'delighted'. Pamela commented, however, on how typical of Evelyn it was that her letter to Charles had been 'curious'. She was not at all perturbed by Eric's suggestion that they wait six months and suspected he was quite right, saying, '... 'cos it's not as if we were not going to see each other for the next 6 months'. Even visiting Milton sounded 'too heavenly', although she was anxious about meeting his grandfather:

'Is he alarming?! Will he hate me? & be furious with you for even *thinking* of getting married!'

There were clearly things they still had to discover about each other that had not been possible in the short time during his periods on leave. She told him about having a 'ripping time' at Felixstowe with Angy, bathing in the sea, and asked him if he liked the sea. Writing from his barracks on 28 May he told her he had been to see *La Bohème* at Covent Garden during that week, and wondered if she liked opera.

Ivan was delighted that his little sister was marrying his good friend, and wrote to his mother-in-law the Duchess on 3 June:

'Pam and Charles Hambro are engaged. They are competing to be as happy as we are. We hope it will be a drawn match. You know Charles, don't you? he is such a good fellow and of course he has been a friend of the family for years.'

Pamela's first visit to Milton in early June 1919 must have been inspiring, for while she was there she wrote a poem:

There is no joy in life but Love
Travel the Earth where e'er you may;
Heaven itself descends in love
Tho' this is not what the public say.

Pay no heed to the rushing crowd
That is yet unsatisfied still
For amusements you hear them cry aloud
As they climb the scale, the social hill.

My God, my God, this wondrous world
Surely was made for something fine
Now Charles & I indeed have learned
That I am his, and he is mine.
We've found the Truth that here in
Life itself is a paradise.

Great literature it may not have been but it was heartfelt. Charles and Pamela spent the following weekend with her family at Holy Wells, and on 9 June from South Street Charles wrote to her at The Lodge, Felixstowe, saying that it was 'a wonderful weekend, I didn't think it possible to be so happy. I think I shall remember it until our dying day.' He was also pretty cheerful because he was just off to Chelsea Barracks, where he was going to write his application to resign from the army, telling Pamela, 'I don't think I can bear it much longer.' He had also 'bagged' her photograph from the drawing room at Holy Wells as he did not have one, and could not wait until he saw her again, four days later:

'But still, what does space matter. I can imagine you playing fives now and wondering if I am at home or still trying to mend a puncture. Thousands & thousands of people and motors on the road but of course we hardly noticed them as usual… If only I could put into words what I want to say to you my darling, the English language is so bad & inadequate…'

Writing to her again the next day from the Guards Club, his impatience with his current situation continued:

'My Darling

'Such a day! Cricket, soldiering, another Court Martial etc.

'How I hate London, more every day & soldiering in particular. Have just been made very angry by a fellow I like very much but he was not minding his own business. I hate people prying into other people's affairs, don't you?

'It was Eric Mackenzie, I really didn't think he was such an ass. He is so nice!

'Told me I was not wearing proper clothes and ought to be ashamed of myself...'

The normally mild-mannered Charles gave him a piece of his mind. Whether the two ever spoke again is not recorded, but Pamela was very pleased Charles told Mackenzie what he thought, as she considered it 'ridiculous' that he should make such a fuss over such a trivial matter. She, meanwhile, waiting for their next weekend together, was love-struck by the sea:

'To think there is nothing that can cure 'Love'; when it comes it is overwhelming, & now we can never be again as we were because we have it with us for ever. There go two swallows, sapphire against a turquoise sea. Let's ask 'It' (if we dare ask ever anything more) if we may be swallows if we *have* to be re-incarnated again. Would my Pudge care to be a swallow?'

But she too had cause to be ill-tempered, although for quite a different reason from Charles:

'For the first time since we were engaged I feel cross! You see, I want you so terribly badly & everyone else (bar Angy of course!) at the moment seem to get on my nerves; I am so stupid I can't talk to them. I'm thinking about you. There were a whole heap of people at Holy W. at lunch & they were all hateful. Must go down to the sea & talk to it about you. It will understand perfectly, it *never* interrupts one's train of thoughts or asks futile questions, it merely murmurs, how wonderful you are.'

The energy that seemed to connect them revealed itself increasingly over the next few months, caused by their continuing absence from each other. Charles wrote on 26 June from South Street:

'How black everything seems here tonight. I just feel so lonely. At least only materially because I can feel you all the time. I wonder if you are thinking of me at this moment, I kind of feel that you are just off to bed and you are thinking of me a little bit before going to sleep. I wonder if you miss our good night, I hope you do!... I am going to sleep loving you more and more...'

Pamela, also bound to carry on with some degree of normality and always having shared with her father a sense of duty, visited with him the troubled Pond Hall Farm, a farm since medieval times on the outskirts of Ipswich, then owned by the Cobbolds, where they were shown calves with ringworm and pigs with their stomachs on the ground. But even such ghastliness and the fact that they walked all the way there – no small distance from Holy Wells – failed to make much impression on Pamela. While John talked concernedly with the farmer, she was thinking of Charles so hard, she told him later, that she was convinced he must have felt it.

In mid June Pamela went to London to stay with her sister-in-law Blanche at the couple's London home in Hertford Street, for the week. Blanche told her mother in a letter on 16 June that it was 'such fun' having Pamela there, and how she and Charles were planning to be married in about October. She said Charles had 'sent in his papers' to leave the army, and that Ivan had just done the same thing but that it could take months for their demobilisations to be processed. After leaving the army, both young men would quickly have to establish themselves in careers to support their wives in the style expected of their class and their respective families. Fortunately for both of them, their fathers had businesses into which they were happy to follow – and indeed, being the eldest sons, it was expected of them. As Blanche said of Ivan:

'As he has got to get out sometime and go into the Brewery, it seems better to get out at once.'

On the evening of 16 June, Charles joined Pamela and her father in playing tennis at another house belonging to Blanche's family, Devonshire House in Piccadilly, London seat of the Dukes of Devonshire since the eighteenth century: not a bad place for a bit of indoor sport. It was probably, like Lansdowne House, one of the biggest and best-known private houses in London. In 1897, the year Ivan and Charles were born, it was the venue for the huge Queen Victoria's Diamond Jubilee Ball, attended by the Prince and Princess of Wales in fancy dress. To her regret, Blanche could not play tennis with them that evening because she did not have the right shoes which, naturally, were to be hand-made. She told her mother plaintively:

'I am still waiting for my shoes, they do take such a long time to make them but it is no good trying to play in ordinary ones.'

With Charles and Pamela's passion also came the practicalities. In a letter dated 1 July 1919, written from his barracks, Charles told her of his father's financial intentions for them:

'Had a long chat to Dad last night. We are lucky people. Heard all about our future income etc. They are kind people our parents. Also learned such a lot about running things. Very difficult my 'poppit'. In fact, you have most of the difficulties. It will cost roughly 1200 a year to run Pickhurst Mead counting the house books. That means we shall have 2800 and 1000 to find other things with. No fearfull riches but it will augment every year as I earn 1000 the first year at the office & then anything up to 10 or 20 thousand if I am a clever boy! But my darling all this will bore you fearfully so less of it. But one must think a little of these things. I am now going to sit on a court martial, so goodbye. Keep your darling self well. What rot I have written! However, there always was madness in my family, I will try to do better in future.'

Apparently not having received Charles' letter despite the post usually being delivered on the same day, Pamela wrote to him blithely about the enjoyable day she had just had. The morning was spent 'whacking the golf ball' about until she got so tired walking after it that she was very thankful when it got lost; then she got on her motor bike to deliver pieces of wedding cake around the Holy Wells estate, 'rushing from cottage to cottage, depositing 1 piece at each'. Finally in the evening she went for a horse ride, taking one of Ivan's hats with her 'which unfortunately blew off, & it was too much trouble to stop', so she carried on riding until she came across one of their estate workers, Searlie, feeding some young pheasants. She told him about Ivan's hat:

'Searlie's legs didn't want to walk so he made me practice picking up *his* cap with riding whip till I was well skilled, then he told me to go & pick up Ivan's! When I got to place, hat had gone!'

Pamela loved her motorbike almost as much as her horses. Motor cycling had become very popular and was a cheaper option to cars, which very few people owned at the time. Describing to Charles her sadness after he had left after a weekend visit, she said she; '...went on a long ride on motor bicycle; & spirits rose: *wonderful* effect it has!'

Meanwhile Charles had had a 'horrible day' due to the Court

Martial which went on for four hours. He had found it hard to concentrate, writing in his notes 'Pam darling' instead of 'Guardsman Jones.' He admitted to her:

'I'm afraid I was very lenient, as I could not possibly have been hard on anyone, when I really was about 80 miles away quite near Ipswich.'

As their wedding was to take place in Ipswich the arrangements were to be left to her father, so there was not too much for the couple to do except think about pages, bridesmaids and presents. She wanted to have Angy, her cousin Joan, and Charles' younger sister, Zelia, with a page to match her, probably Toby, '...unless we have taught him too much!' She also suggested Charles' four-year-old cousin, Nigel Hambro. Charles did not mind how many they had, even if it was 'dozens': he wanted whatever made her happy.

Time passed slowly for Pamela between the weekends when she saw Charles. Although she had plenty to do on the social front, it was a rare occasion that elicited her enjoyment or approval, and she seemed to prefer being on her own, free from the annoyance of other people when the only person she really wanted to be with was not there. In early July she had a 'wonderful day' at the Newmarket races with lots of Charles' relatives, even though she 'didn't make a lot of money', and although she enjoyed being with his family, it seemed to emphasise the fact that Charles himself was not there. She always enjoyed herself at Felixstowe, and described to him a particularly wonderful day she had just spent there because she was *absolutely* alone', at least until that evening when her father, her Uncle Ralph and their cousin Guy Cobbold, would be arriving.

Pamela always enjoyed their company, especially Ralph's. A younger brother of her father, aged fifty, he was racy and exciting. Ralph had enjoyed a brilliant military career, had been imprisoned by the Cossacks and become known for his explorations of Asia, writing a book about the Pamirs which remains a classic in the twenty-first century. He was now a Colonel, had recently fought in the war and had received a DSO. His love life was quite varied too: he had had two wives so far and would later take a third. Ralph's only child, also Ralph, aged thirteen, was a favourite cousin of Pamela's. Yet despite enjoying her uncle's company, she told Charles, 'How I wish it was my Pudge coming!' Small things irritated her:

'Oh! that clock! It keeps ticking, I feel it ticking our lives away. Of course that's silly, as they are only just beginning, but every moment that goes is a moment gone… *for ever* & anything irretrievable always annoys me.'

Her restlessness made her almost feverish:

'Ah, there is a lovely bird, I must ask it where it has come from. The little bird tells me it has come from a far, far country, by name Afrique; it also tells me this country is devoid of colour & seems v. dark, in fact it thought we had perpetual night, but I told the bird this is not so, night is many degrees darker.'

As always, though, her sense of fun and the absurd was never far away. She wrote to Charles from Holy Wells on 6 July to tell him about Uncle Ralph:

'Ralph is nagging me to write to you. He *is* funny! I can't stop laughing, he has just given a graphic description of you & I in the heart of Africa, clad in a string of beads; the beads being his wedding gift to us. The only really useful present that we shall have! You can't make a remark but Ralph turns it into an 'arriere pensee'; is that the expression; no I don't believe it is. Guy has just offered to give us a Hammock (7/6) as a present; only we want it at once! Funny idea giving people gifts when they get married; I used to think it so very foolish, but I now see a vast amount of sense in it. If people get married two or three times, do they go on getting presents?!! You can't imagine how hideous they all look snoring loudly on the Tudor room sofa, Ralph, Guy & Audrey. *Ve* look much more attractive.'

A few days later, while Charles was at Pickhurst Mead and she was at the dentist's in Ipswich waiting for the car to collect her, she regaled him with the ordeal she had just been through:

'*What* a man. The pukka dentist is away, this one is here v. temporarily, he hails from Yorkshire; I shd think he's spent most of his time extracting miners' teeth. His strength & velocity were terrible. Having spied a minute hole in my wisdom tooth he proceeded to hack away with an axe-like instrument & use my tooth as if it were a flint. In despair when I saw him coming at it again with *renewed* energy I bethought myself of the bowl of running water my left hand could *just* reach. This I dipped in & put 4 or 5 great drops on & under my eyes.

141

The effect absolutely miraculous! The man *has* a heart after all, 'cos in 2 seconds the instrument of torture was *flung* away & he gently but firmly filled the tooth with cotton wool!'

Her fellow victims in the waiting room did not escape her observations while she impatiently waited for the car: the nervous-looking woman who resembled an Angora rabbit, whom she wanted to startle by dropping something heavy, and the 'pretty boy who is breathing so heavily'.

They may have missed each other but neither Charles nor Pamela were ones to sit around moping. They kept themselves very fit, not for modern reasons of 'body image' but because they both enjoyed physical activity. Charles still spent much of his spare time when he was not seeing her playing cricket, at which he continued to excel as he had at Eton, his name appearing every now and then in the sports pages of the national press. She thought nothing of walking many miles in a day, especially when at Rannoch, and she loved her golf and tennis. Visiting some friends for lunch with her father, she said they played 'about 12 sets of tennis, thundering good tennis too!'

Lady Evelyn meanwhile had been in Norway fishing since early June, and Pamela and Blanche were concerned because she had said that one day she would take them to a garden party at Buckingham Palace. In her absence an invitation had arrived for Evelyn for 11 July but the girls were not sure if she would be back by then. Assuming they would not be able to go without her – both girls were under twenty-one – and anxious that his daughter and daughter-in-law should not be disappointed, John Cobbold wrote to Lord Sandhurst, the Lord Chamberlain, asking if the date of the invitation could be changed. Happily for them, and presumably in an acknowledgment of both Blanche's and Evelyn's family's connections with the Royal Family, Lord Sandhurst said the girls could go without Lady Evelyn. She eventually returned in late July and joined the girls in London for a few days. Blanche had just had it confirmed by her doctor that she was pregnant, and in the absence of Ivan at his barracks with the Scots Guards – like Charles, awaiting his demob papers – she was at least able to share her news with Pamela and Evelyn, together with her doctor's recommendation that she carry smelling salts and eat acid drops!

It is hoped Blanche felt well enough on 26th July that year to enjoy the fête her parents-in-law held in the grounds of Holy Wells to celebrate hers and Ivan's marriage. On a fine Saturday, John Dupuis Cobbold hosted a luncheon for many of the Cobbolds' tenants and other guests, mainly to share with everyone his joy in his son's marriage but for other purposes too. As the *Evening Star & Daily Herald* of Ipswich reported:

'[John] complimented the wives of the licensed tenants who had been temporarily absent during the war. He thanked the employees who had stayed at home for the devotedness with which they had carried on and remarked how pleased he was to see them and those who had returned from service around him on that day. That day, he pointed out, was an exceptional one in many respects, and not least because his only son had come of age and returned alive from the war, and had 'captured a very charming young woman.''

John also used his speech to make 'his introduction of the name of Captain Hambro as the fiancé of Miss Pamela Cobbold', which resulted in much applause and probably blushes, too, on the part of the engaged couple. Toasts followed, and then sports for everyone, Pamela coming third in the two laps women's walking race. Blanche presented the prizes to all the winners.

Music and dancing carried on into the evening, when a nine-gallon cask of Murray ale was opened which had been brewed when Ivan was born, and was eagerly drunk while the partygoers watched a splendid firework display. There was even the opportunity to buy a momento: a photo postcard of the bride and groom, as well as one of Pamela, with all proceeds going to the Ipswich and East Suffolk War Memorial Fund for an extension to the East Suffolk and Ipswich Hospital .

A few days later, on his own again, Charles had to fulfil a family duty in London and chaperone his cousin, Gracy McRae, at a dance. Most of the time he was bored, grumbling that he had to spend his time 'dancing with females who cannot dance or talk', until he found someone who knew Pamela and they spent the rest of the evening talking about her. The thought that next year they would be going to dances together cheered him, as long as it was, '... just a few select ones', and he mused on how they would laugh at 'all the unfortunate people still on the waiting list'. But then he worried that Pamela would be claimed for a dance by all her old friends, and he would have to sit in the smoking room waiting patiently for her to come and dance with him.

When he had the chance Charles would motor down to Pickhurst Mead to continue making arrangements for the preparation of their rooms. He imagined himself with Pamela at Holy Wells:

'I am at present sitting in Jane's room, in other words the nursery. Can't you feel me, I know you can. Here, you have just put your arm round my neck as I write & are saying 'Poor old man'. There, I've taken your hand, in fact I can smell your dress & hear it rustling. Darling, you've been here for the last ½ hour, the house simply breathes of you… There you go again, my beloved, you now made some priceless remark, pulling my leg: now you've thought better of it & have given me a kiss like only you can give! I've just buried my head on your chest. My darling!… This is just as I feel you here now, exactly as if you were here… What do distances matter!'

As her youngest child was marrying, Evelyn thought it a good idea to take her on a pre-wedding visit to friends and relatives around the country on their way up to Rannoch: once Pamela was married the opportunity to do so would be limited for she would have responsibilities to the Hambros too, and perhaps children. Perhaps also the increasing threats to the landed gentry made such a visit feel more urgent than before. During the Great War a Super Tax had been introduced for the first time on incomes in excess of £10,000. Now, in 1919, death duties were increased from 15% to 40%. The future for the wealthy did not look hopeful.

Having decided before the war to sell up, many landowners in England had found it hard to do so during it as the market had slowed down, so sales were postponed. However, in Scotland, although many estates were vast, they seemed to sell quite easily. Between 1912 and 1920 the land agents, Knight, Frank and Rutley, alone claimed to have sold 1.6 million Scottish acres, equivalent to more than one-twelfth of the land area of the country. Amongst those families who sold, there were a few whose estates were so large that, even after selling several hundred thousand acres, they remained substantial magnates. These included Evelyn's cousin, the Duke of Atholl at Blair Castle; he also took advantage of the option of making over his estates to his successor in good time to avoid death duties, giving half his remaining estates to his son. Amongst the smaller estates, Slains Castle had been sold in 1916 which Evelyn and Pamela were no doubt sad about, as they would not be able to stay with their friends, the Hays.

Evelyn also intended to take her grandson with them on their journey. Born on 17 May 1916, he was the only child of Winifred and Algy. His full name was Algernon Ivan Sladen but he would be known always as 'Toby'. Evelyn seems to have despaired of Winifred and what she considered to be her rootless, often impecunious, lifestyle with her husband which resulted in John Dupuis Cobbold often sending their eldest daughter financial handouts. Concerned for Toby's future, Evelyn effectively adopted him. He would become her favourite grandchild and benefit substantially from her generosity all his life.

On 5 August, as Pamela was preparing to leave with her mother and little nephew of whom she was very fond, Charles wrote to her with a progress report on Pickhurst Mead. Giving rein rather endearingly to his creative streak, which must have been a welcome respite from his 'bloody soldiering' as he called it, he told her he had chosen 'a whole lot of paints and papers' which would be ready for her approval in October. For her bedroom – indicating their intention to follow the upper-class tradition of having separate bedrooms – he had found 'a really beautiful light blue paper. I think light blue walls and pink fittings are prettier than vice versa.' He also referred to a 'lovely grey' he had chosen for her boudoir, with a dark blue for his room. The other rooms he did not anticipate would be a problem, as there were twenty colours and patterns he had picked out as the best. The garden too had had the benefit of some changes, although he was keeping 'the big idea' until she had made her suggestions. She would not have minded what colour schemes they had. Although she thought his suggestion of blue and pink sounded lovely, and that the beauty of one's surroundings made for happiness, she replied:

'… when you are with me I never notice anything; the walls might be magenta, & the carpet orange, & the doors apricot & I'd never notice anything the *least* ugly about them!'

Charles ended his letter:

'God bless you, my lady of the mist. Thou shortener of distances.'

The notion that their physical separateness was irrelevant, and that each could transport themselves to where the other was, regardless of time and distance, became stronger over the next two months before their wedding day. Writing to Pamela the next evening from Pickhurst, at the end of a hot and boring day fulfilling one of his amateur league cricket obligations at Lords, Charles told her that that she was 'there' with him at Pickhurst and they had just been for a walk in the garden. Replying on 8 August from Patshull House in Wolverhampton, where she, Evelyn and Toby were now staying, she apologised for not being able to 'get to' Pickhurst until very late on the night he was thinking of her. She wanted him with her at Patshull:

'Thine own, I *must* call your spirit *here* this evening, I know it won't refuse to come.'

As she looked at the moon from her bedroom window, she silently willed him to her.

Chapter 11

Travels by Road and Space

The wedding arrangements are not mentioned much in the couple's correspondence. In the absence of both the bride-to-be and her mother who were on their way to Rannoch, it seems that Pamela's father was left to get on with it all, as Pamela said he would.

The honeymoon, however, was too special for anyone else to sort out and Charles was doing his best on that front. Both of them were very keen to go to Egypt, Pamela's enthusiasm probably stemming from her mother's love of the country. However, it was not the best holiday destination that year. As the Great War ended, Egyptian nationalists had resumed their fight for independence from Britain, and in September 1918 made the first moves towards the formation of a *wafd*, or delegation, to voice its demands for independence at the Paris Peace Conference. Then in November a group of prominent members of Egypt's Umma party had met with the British High Commissioner, Sir Reginald Wingate. They demanded complete independence, with the proviso that Britain be allowed to supervise the Suez Canal and the public debt. They also asked permission to go to London to put their case before the British Government and formed a *wafd* for that purpose.

Despite Wingate's efforts to persuade the British Government to give permission, it was refused. On March 8 1919 members of the *wafd* were arrested, thrown into prison and the next day deported to Malta. It led to a major uprising in Egypt in which Egyptians of all social classes participated. Within a week the whole of Egypt was paralysed by general strikes and rioting, with Egyptians and Europeans being killed or injured when the British attempted to crush the violence. On 16 March a demonstration by upper-class Egyptian women in veils took place against the British occupation, marking the entrance of Egyptian women into public life. Women of the lower classes demonstrated in the streets with the men, while those in the countryside engaged in activities like cutting rail lines.

Wingate meanwhile was replaced as High Commissioner by General Edmund Allenby, the Great War hero known for his liberation of Jerusalem, who had led the Egyptian Expeditionary Force. Through him a deal was struck with the nationalists in April, under which they would urge the demonstrations to stop and the *wafd* leaders released and allowed to proceed to Paris.

The protests became fewer and less violent as the year went on, as proper negotiations about independence took place between Britain and Egypt. However, the situation there remained delicate. Charles told Pamela she would have to get a certificate from her doctor saying she was suffering from something chronic, and that the only thing to save her would be a trip to Egypt. Charles also said he was sending her a form to sign, which was probably for a passport, as it was only recently, in 1915, that the modern British passport came into being for foreign travel, under the British Nationality and Status Aliens Act 1914. As a result of the Great War, countries around the world started issuing passports as a way of distinguishing their citizens from others they thought of as 'foreign nationals'.

Nearer to home, driving back to Pickhurst Mead, Charles had just been the victim of a speed trap, doing 23 ½ mph, against a speed limit – since 1903 – of 20 mph. Speed traps often took the form of policemen sitting in trees and bushes armed with stop watches, trying to catch the unwary. Apart from campaigning for better roads, the Automobile Association (AA) since it began in 1905 had also organised patrols to warn motorists of what they saw as over-zealous police. In a somewhat subversive role, it published maps showing the favourite places for police ambushes and if an AA member drove past an AA patrol man near a trap, the patrol man would warn the member by not giving the usual salute. No doubt the police justified their traps by saying they were concerned about the number of often fatal accidents. Indeed, the Prince of Wales, after taking his first flight in 1918, wrote to his mother, Queen Mary, that flying was far safer than motoring! Accidents were hardly surprising given the lack of motoring laws at that time; and the situation was not helped by the casual, even light-hearted approach of the Government and drivers generally towards what was, until the Great War, still regarded as a sport, afforded only by the very wealthy.

Perhaps Charles had not yet joined the AA. In an uncharacteristic display of what seemed like boasting – and behaving exactly like the sort of motorist Kenneth Grahame had satirised a few years earlier in Toad from his book *Wind in the Willows* – Charles told Pamela:

'Such a nice policeman. He told me that I was unlucky. I told him I passed every day & that next time should be going 55 mph. not 25. He laughed & said it would cost me a sovereign this time. I told him I had no intention of attending the Court & he said a military certificate was all I required.'

Charles was not the only imperfect driver. Lady Evelyn had caused her fellow passengers on their journey to Scotland much consternation when she insisted on taking over from the chauffeur. Pamela complained:

'... about 100 miles on our way, Evelyn displayed [a] wish to drive; chauffeur & I, Nannie & Toby in vain used persuasions to prevent this at all costs! Every hill we descended the 2 brakes were rammed heavily downwards & the car crawled down at 6 miles per hour. Then my darling would you believe it, every town we came to we rushed through at 25 miles per hour!'

Still, they managed to arrive safely on 6 August at Patshull House, which Pamela pronounced:

'... a wonderful place; big hills & you can see miles across Staffordshire, till the little hills fade into blue so pale that you can see them no more. House is nice 'cos it smells good wherever you go, & the garden, 2 comfy chairs under some cool yew trees, which throw their reflection, nay shadow, onto a red path glaring in the hot sunshine.'

Today Grade 1 listed and used as a wedding and conference centre, the eighteenth-century mansion, with sixty rooms and fifty acres of gardens designed by Capability Brown, is regarded as one of the most important Georgian mansions in England. For over a hundred years it belonged to the Earls of Dartmouth. The incumbent in 1919,

Sir William Heneage Legge – the 6th Earl of Dartmouth, previously Viscount Lewisham – was Evelyn's uncle by marriage; his wife was Evelyn's aunt, born Lady Mary Coke, one of the Earl of Leicester's daughters. The Cobbolds' stay would only be two days at Patshull so they would have missed the fourth anniversary, on 9 August, of the death of the Dartmouths' second son Gerald, Evelyn's cousin, killed in action aged thirty-three.

No idle aristocrat, Sir William was a graduate of Christ Church College, Oxford; he had held the political post of Vice-Chamberlain to Queen Victoria's Household; he had been MP for West Kent and later Lewisham; his current positions included being a Justice of the Peace for Shropshire and for Staffordshire, as well its County Alderman; and he was the recipient, amongst other honours, of the KCB and an Honorary Law Degree from Dartmouth College in New Hampshire, USA.

An article published in October 1904 in the *New York Times*, following the visit of the Earl and Lady Dartmouth to the College, said he was not even typically English because '… unlike the average Englishman he has no fondness for fishing or shooting'. The article attributed this to his Italian background, from the Legge side of his family. (No doubt Evelyn was a little disappointed by her uncle, for she tended to rate people by their willingness, and particularly their ability, to hunt.) Sir William's connection with the USA was that one of his ancestors had married a descendant of George Washington, as the article was pleased to point out, giving him the right to fly the American flag which had appeared on Washington's coat of arms.

Evelyn's Aunt Mary was not ignored in the feature:

'The Dartmouths' country residence is at Patshull, near Wolverhampton, and as Lady Dartmouth is fond of horticulture, she has done much to improve the grounds. One of the attractions of the place is a beautiful rock garden.'

Lord Dartmouth preferred golf to gardening and he and his son would play on the nine-hole course in their grounds which no doubt Pamela, being fond of the game, would have liked to have played if they had been staying longer.

At the time the article was published the Dartmouths also owned, like many of the wealthy aristocracy, a London residence: the article said that their '... large house on Charles Street, London, formerly the property of the late Lord Revelstoke, is the scene of balls and dinners'. In fact, the 'large house' was Dartmouth House in Berkley Square, one of the city's most significant properties, which survives in the twenty-first century as a Grade II listed building. It had famously been remodelled and refurbished by Lord Revelstoke, head of Barings Bank, in the 1890s. But by the time of Pamela and Evelyn's visit, the Dartmouths no longer owned it, having felt compelled to sell it earlier that year.[1]

For it was not just the country estates that were being sold. The land agents' bible, *The Estates Gazette*, said, 'The tendency of the great territorial families to sell a considerable proportion of their land is now extending to their expensive town houses.' Ivan Cobbold's father-in-law the Duke of Devonshire had agreed in September 1919 to sell Devonshire House for £750,000; and the ex-Prime Minister Lord Salisbury, whose country seat was Hatfield House, sold his house in Arlington Street which had been the London seat of his family for generations, for £120,000. Many other London properties were sold and some demolished, including Lansdowne House in Berkeley Square, built by Robert Adam and home of the Duchess of Devonshire's family for many years.

The Dartmouths were able to hold on to Patshull for a little while longer, and Sir William was spared the disappointment of learning that on the death of his son and heir William, in 1958, the house would be given to the Crown to pay death duties. The Duke of Devonshire, as well as selling his London house, also sold some of his land in Ireland and, as an alternative to decreasing further his land ownership, did what others were doing as an alternative, and sold part of his art collection at Chatsworth.

The Cobbolds' visit to Patshull was a fleeting one: they had to move on to Capesthorne in Cheshire, home of Pamela's godfather Bromo, William Bromley Davenport, a Deputy Lieutenant of the county. Arriving there on 8 August, Pamela wrote to Charles that he would love Bromo and he would love the place. As usual, Bromo had his three nephews staying. Pamela told Charles about the boys fishing all day at the great lake, where they caught pike, roach, perch and bream, together

---

[1] In 1926 it was sold again to the English Speaking Union, which still owns it in the twenty-first century.

with Toby, who was thrilled to be allowed to join them. She was feeling particularly fond of her godfather at the time, as he had just given her a wedding present: '… a wondrous Lynx fur'. Clearly Charles was thinking along similar lines for his present to his future bride because Pamela gave him a pointer in the right direction:

'Darling, if you *want* to give me silver fox Evelyn says she knows an American lady, by name McCreery, who gets the most beautiful skins from America for 70 pds. (Whether the story is true we shall have to find out.)'

Pamela wondered about the future of houses like Capesthorne:

'I wonder if we, you and I, will come here in the future? I think Bromo wld. ask us, but will big places cease to exist in the near future? *We* would not mind, 'cos, lump, we could find happiness with a large H. anywhere but it must be awfully sad for people who've lived in their places for years, & then have to give them up.'

In fact, Capesthorne was one of the survivors. Although it would be used during the Second World War as a Red Cross Hospital, it never passed out of the Bromley Davenport family and in the early twenty-first century it is lived in by Bromo's namesake, William Bromley Davenport, the Lord Lieutenant of Cheshire, and his family.

The Cobbold family is certain that Evelyn and Bromo at some stage became lovers. By 1919 she and John were spending more and more time apart, although it is not known when exactly her relationship with Bromo began. His attractiveness lay at least partly in the diversity of his talents. Not only had Bromo been a sportsman, he had also been a Conservative MP and Financial Secretary to the War Office under Arthur Balfour. In the Boer War he was awarded the DSO, and in the Great War he had commanded part of the Egyptian Expeditionary Force as Brigadier General. He had been Assistant Director of Labour from 1917-1918, and very recently had been made a CBE.

Whether Evelyn would have slept with Bromo at Capesthorne while her daughter and grandson were there can only be guessed at, but the house was big enough for lovers' trysts to take place without anyone knowing. Evelyn would very likely have risked the wrath of Pamela if she found out about any affair, for Pamela would have hated the thought of her father being duped; however, it is believed that at some stage John also took lovers, but again it is not known when. If Evelyn and John conducted any extramarital relationships in the dignified way they ran their everyday lives, no-one would have been any the wiser. Whether Evelyn was ever aware of the French lady who was the other 'interest' in Bromo's life, according to one of his nephews' children, may never be known.

Meanwhile, Charles at Pickhurst Mead was missing Pamela badly, imagining he had 'arrived' at Bromo's while she was there, and was looking forward to her reaching Rannoch so that he could join her later. He wanted them to row on the loch together, to go stalking with their ghillie Mackintosh, and to sit looking down on Loch Ericht 'and across to Ben Alder with the sun setting behind'. Pamela had also received a letter from Angy who had just arrived in Perthshire and was staying, as she always did, at nearby Talladh-a-Bheithe. Part of the Rannoch Estate John Dupuis Cobbold had bought at auction back in 1914, Talladh-a-Bheithe was itself a stunning estate. It comprised at that time approximately 13,500 acres of forest, including a forty to forty-five stag forest, a four to five hundred-brace grouse moor, and an imposing stone hunting lodge built in 1840, on the edge of Loch Rannoch, with seventeen bedrooms and several cottages. Angy too was missing her friend, writing in her melodramatic manner:

'O! my Pam. *All* time not spent here must be wasted! The loch is so wild and cruel tonight, great black waves with creamy crests. A wonderful glowing light all around Rannoch Lodge, O! why aren't *you* there. No *here* I want you. Darling I almost burst with wild joy akin to sorrow when we sped past Rannoch Lodge this morning, then every stone of the Kinloch Road recalled to me our bycyle [sic] ride.'

Angy had arranged for hers and Pamela's motorbikes to be sent up from Ipswich a week earlier so they could ride them while they were in Scotland, but she was furious to find they had not yet arrived. However, on a lighter note, she regaled Pamela with an amusing incident on the train travelling up involving her dog Mac, a fellow passenger and a bottle of lemonade. But for Angy the journey was still dull:

'O! *how* boring the journey was last night, compared to our journey together last year. I *had* to have a fit in the carriage & make a woman hysterical to make up a bit!'

Angy was anticipating her best friend's forthcoming marriage with some gloom:

'Pam darling. Life is real & Life is ernest [sic]. Inshallah, the next 6 weeks will be some of life's best and sparingly given moments. Then the autumn, then what for me? Write O! Write.

'God bless thee, Your Angela.'

Charles, on hearing about Angy's letter, asked Pamela to give her friend his love and to tell Angy she was a wonderful person, with an imagination surpassed only by him and a love for beauty which came halfway to Pamela's. He thought it lovely that his fiancée should have a friend like her.

Still fretting about what to buy Pamela as a wedding present, and in a manner typical of men across the centuries, Charles put the ball back in her court:

'About the furs. What would you like, my little one? Furs or a gold purse or what. I want you to have something you will want to carry about. Just think of something you really want!'

One item he had confidently bought for them both was the complete set of books by Stephen Leacock, the English-born Canadian writer, who at that time was the most popular humorist in the English-speaking world: he thought they would be a good start to their library.

In that second week of August 1919, Charles Hambro was a happy man. His letter of 10 August from Pickhurst Mead captured the contentment of a young man in love, with everything to look forward to:

'A perfect Sunday as far as weather was concerned. A round of golf in the morning. A real good wallow in the lake after lunch and tennis in the evening. Then the most lovely of all sitting in the moonlight listening to a gramaphone [sic] playing all our old tunes. You were as near to me tonight, my own lady, as if you were two feet away. I was putting on the tunes for you!'

At last Charles could look ahead to shortly leaving the army. His resignation had been confirmed, and he was about to start on the last job, at Pirbright, with his leaving date of 6 September: he would have preferred to leave before then but he realised he would be letting people down if he did. And he was looking forward to all the travelling they would do together:

'Tell Ma [Evelyn] I am examining a lot of aeroplane photo's of Egypt, Mesopotamia & North India. Such lovely views. But very desolate, just what we want to see. Darling, we must travel a lot!!! Just you and me. Can anything be more wonderfull than our prospects for the next fifty years. Darling mine, if only I can make you perfectly happy I shall have done my job on earth...'

As Charles sat writing to her in the moonlight, she was doing the same. Having left Capesthorne the day before, she now wrote from Crathorne Hall in Yorkshire but her thoughts of travel were of a different dimension:

'It is such a wonderful night that I must put my thoughts on paper to you. 'twould be a waste to go to sleep. Unless you come to me soon my spirit will get angry, it is simply aching to be away, away stealing over the dew-bespattered grass, all cool and fresh, down the steep hillside to the river, all shimmering blue and silver in the moonlight – Darling, my darling, are you looking at that moon?... (She is so beautiful.) I can't write sense to you tonight. We can't talk about the things that have been happening, we can't even speak of the future, it must just be one of the strange letters that everyone else would think entirely senseless, but We, Us, with our great understanding UNDERSTAND. Our spirits are travelling at a great pace, each moment the wonders of this hot August night are being revealed to them, but they are ever trying, trying to find something that they know exists but they cannot name, it is the ESSENCE of something they seek, their faith tells them they will find it one day, but as they are together they do not hurry so much!... where are we?'

The notion of journeying without each other, however they travelled, was, on that hot summer night of 1919, inconceivable. Just two months before their wedding, it seemed they had the whole of their lives ahead.

Chapter 12

Nearly There

Pamela was very impressed by Crathorne Hall – hardly surprising, since it was the largest country house in England to be built during the reign of Edward VII and probably the last of its kind to be built. Completed only thirteen years previously, after three years of building, it had one hundred and fifteen rooms, requiring twenty-six live-in servants.

It was built by the Cobbolds' friend Captain James Lionel Dugdale, whose great-uncle had bought the Crathorne estate in 1845. 'Lionel', as he was known, used only local building materials and staff, and paid London-rate wages to his workmen. He was not only concerned with his house but totally dedicated to the village, being responsible for much of its re-building from 1887 onwards. Crathorne Hall was the centre of an agricultural estate and so was the focus of many village activities, such as children's Christmas parties, sports days and charity events. The Dugdale family's events which the village attended were the coming-of-age parties. The first was for Tom, the son of Lionel and his wife Violet, who was twenty-one in July 1918, but his party had to be delayed for a year because he was still fighting at the Front at that time. Despite being in the thick it for eighteen months, when life expectancy was a matter of weeks, Tom had survived. His family and the village celebrated his coming-of age – and presumably his return, too – in July 1919 instead. Tom went on to have a significant political career, becoming the first Baron Crathorne, and the Hall would stay in the Dugdale family until they sold it in 1977, the year of Tom's death.

Pamela enthused to Charles:

'This is a *heavenly* place, the air feels like Scotland, it is literally the *most* comfortable house I've ever been in. They built it about 15 years ago & the comfort: sandal wood soap! Bath salts! Douche in your own bathroom! Latrine that you press a pedal with your right foot, like driving a motor (only no change of gear!)... Another attraction here is a Pianola, worked by electricity, so you don't *even* have to pump away with your feet.'

Her enthusiasm for the bathroom turned Pamela's thoughts to the decoration at Pickhurst Mead that Charles had been talking about:

'Let's make the bathroom, at least our bathroom, at Pickhurst a *dream*. White paint for walls; p'raps it would be better if the douche is left out, 'cos though I had great fun with the douche here, I left the bathroom here a swimming, floating mess!'

The Hall was only just getting back to normal after the war; in November 1914 Lionel and Violet had opened it as a Voluntary Aid Detachment (VAD) hospital for Belgian and British troops. The VAD organisation had started in 1909, the result of the British Red Cross joining up with the Order of St John of Jerusalem, to provide help in hospitals where there was a shortage of nurses. Some VAD nurses had completed short courses before war broke out, but often there had been conflict between fully qualified nurses, who had undergone three years' training, and the amateur volunteers. With the outbreak of war the Joint War Committee strived to overcome these differences, so that both groups could work together. Violet herself, in charge of the Crathorne Hall VAD, was said to have considerable skills as a nurse.

The Dugdales were not the only friends of the Cobbolds to put their home to good use during the war. Evelyn's friend Muriel Hargreaves, now Mrs Elwes, of Leckhampton Court, had put her house at the disposal of the British Red Cross, and from 1915 to 1919 it was used as a hospital for sick and wounded soldiers. Over one thousand seven hundred British, Commonwealth and Belgian soldiers were treated there, and after the Somme offensive the number of beds reached one hundred.

Pamela may have enjoyed herself at Crathorne but she had not had the happiest time getting there after leaving Capesthorne the day before, telling Charles:

'We seem to hit all the big towns of England yesterday, Manchester, Halifax, Bradford, Harrogate. Ma's temper was *awful* yesterday, she has a habit of *screaming* at the chauffeur; he *can't* get accustomed to it & almost leaps out of his seat!'

Pamela was also worried about something that Charles had asked her to do as part of the process for getting permission to travel to Egypt for their honeymoon; he had asked her to sign a form in her not-yet-married name. She started her letter of 10 August most concerned:

'Charles darling – I think I shall be locked up, 'cos I've forged a signature! However, we must hope for the best. Of course, I could have written my name as P Cobbold; & so the authorities should not think it fearfully improper, you could have sent an explanatory note!'

As for the need to say she would benefit health-wise from going to Egypt, she would write to Dr Brown:

'... who is a bosom friend & I think he will perjure his soul, he also must fill in my name as Hambro I s'pose – I think it sounds awfully nice, in a way it's a pity it's H. because the 'set' I live in cannot possibly pronounce their H's – !'

The last stop on their journey to Rannoch was North Berwick, which Pamela adored. It must have been a relief to get there, for there had been more 'excitement', as she gamefully referred to it, en route. They were going down a hill:

'Ma driving, & she would keep both the brakes on hard down all the time till smoke emerged from various parts of the car & we pulled up & the chauffeur shouted "Fire!!" We leapt out & dragged Toby onto a heap of stones, then found a bottle of lemonade in the back, threw it over the gear box where there was a flame, turned off petrol, needless to say the chauffeur did all this! & raced up & down to a stream... throwing water over everybody but the car! It was funny! We then waited ½ hour for the brakes to cool down!'

It was worth the delay. On the east coast of Scotland, twenty-five miles from Edinburgh, North Berwick's beautiful, long sandy beaches, accessible islands full of birdlife, and gentle green verges, had made it popular as a resort in Victorian times, followed by fame in the early twentieth century for its golf courses. In the 1890s golf had become a popular game for the middle and upper classes, the latter congregating in North Berwick in the summers, creating a mini Season there before the shooting season began. In fact, Pamela and Evelyn arrived on the Glorious Twelfth when 'a good many people will be walking the moors today to find a grouse', yet it was still busy. Jane Cottle and her young charge Toby were spending the day with the Elphinstones, Evelyn's relations – presumably so they could catch up with young Toby's development now that he had been unofficially adopted by his grandmother – while Pamela and Evelyn were joined by the sister of a friend from the Hay Drummond family, whom Pamela pronounced 'quite good fun'.

Pamela enthusiastically described the scene to Charles:

'This is the most fascinating place... I'm looking... at stretches of golden sand, & the bluest of blue seas, with great purple, crimson & violet rocks spread about... literally boiling hot sands, stretching away for miles, all ribbed & delicious.'

Charles may not have been there but she still managed to have a whale of a time:

'Have been hunting for winkles; there are millions & we're going to have a huge tea of them: so good! We did some *absolutely* mad things in the town & altogether had a v. good morning!'

She had also bought:

'... a bathing dress: I got a BEAUTY for 5/6, then plunged into the foaming brine, never cold... This afternoon we are going to try & get a boat to fish; all he [Charles] says is don't sink the boat with your sickness!'

They were to continue travelling the next morning by putting the car on the ferry at nearby Granton and crossing the Firth of Forth to Burntisland – there was no Forth Road Bridge then, only the Forth Bridge for the railway – and driving from there to Loch Rannoch, hoping they would arrive the same day. In the absence of motorways, or indeed many decent roads at all, driving to Scotland in 1919 was not for the faint-hearted, even with a chauffeur. Had it not been for wishing to visit friends and relations on the way, their journey would have been much easier by train, to Rannoch Station itself. The section of the West Highland Railway Line that passed through Rannoch had been completed by five thousand Irish labourers in August 1894, making travel far easier to the otherwise near-inaccessible Loch Rannoch. Rannoch Station is one of only a handful of stations along the line which also passes Fort William and ends at Mallaig, after a stunning journey across a beautiful plateau dotted with lochs and then across the desolate wilderness of Rannoch Moor. Still a lonely outpost today, the railway must have been a godsend to the local people. Today the journey is to Glasgow, picking up the West Highland Line to Rannoch Station, but Pamela told Charles that he could get the train from King's Cross, London at about 7pm and arrive at Rannoch at 8.40am, with no change. Perhaps it should not be surprising to find that the journey in 1919 was easier than in the twenty-first century.

Charles, meanwhile, was not having the best of times. Writing on 12 August from Pirbright Camp, he told Pamela:

'I had a slight mishap today which has put me hors de combat for a few days. My horse fell down and rolled on my right foot. Consequence crushed foot, only slightly hurt but rather painfull, nothing broken. I am not sorry because it prevents me from taking an active part in the musketry... I am walking about on two sticks, & limping just like John with gout.'

As it would turn out, he had underestimated his injury but at least for now he had two things to keep him cheerful: the fact that on the 13 August he was 'gazetted' out of the army – the announcement in *The London Gazette* being the final formality to leaving, although he was still staying to finish his last job – and the thought that he was soon to join Pamela at Rannoch. Meanwhile she had 'come' to him the night before and eased his pain, and he would 'travel' to Rannoch that evening, to row with her on the loch.

It had taken them rather longer than expected to get to Rannoch. As planned, Pamela and Evelyn had arrived early on the morning of the 13 August at Granton to take the 9.30am ferry to Burntisland, only to be told by the captain that he could not take them because the tide was too low. They could either wait for the next ferry at 1.30pm or drive the 100 miles to Rannoch via Stirling. Unsurprisingly they chose to wait, killing time by visiting Edinburgh where Pamela persuaded her mother to have her hair washed, and mused about the way in which she had been so 'odd' on the journey up there. Eventually they arrived at Rannoch at 9.30 that night, weary but happy.

Pamela, as always, was in her element. The next day she sent Charles a sketch she had made of the view from Rannoch Lodge looking down along the Loch with the little rocky island in the middle, Eilean nam Faoileag or Gull Island, with its strange old tower once used by the

Robertson clan as a prison; and across to the heights of Schiehallion. She could see the purple of Talladh-a Bheithe and the blueness of Craiganour, and marvelled at how it all looked even more wonderful than she remembered it from the summer before. She looked forward to seeing her father and Guy Cobbold, who were out walking Cruach, and the friends who were staying with them who had gone shooting. But meanwhile Pamela was enjoying the peace of solitude while she renewed her acquaintance with her favourite place on earth.

The Victorian and Edwardian eras saw the heyday of hunting and shooting, and between 1883 and 1908 the acreage of deer forests in Scotland increased by nearly 50%. Sheep farming was dominant here in Perthshire and other counties, but farms were often cleared of stock to give the deer free range, and small tenant farmers were disappearing. As a result, the number of farm servants had decreased but at least the number of gamekeepers had increased, and John employed several. There was, however, concern (and in some quarters, criticism) that deer hunting did not bring in sufficient money to justify itself. The local people in the area may have tolerated John Cobbold because not only would he have been a reasonable employer, he would undoubtedly have been a decent landlord too, with his experience of his many tenants in Suffolk, and possibly a better one than his predecessor, Sir Robert. The Parish historian had summed up Sir Robert:

'He was a strict game-preserver and strongly asserted his rights as a landlord. Nevertheless in his own way he could be kind to his tenants and dependants and to such others as knew how to flatter him.'

John may also have earned extra kudos because of his wife's connection with the area; after all, just down the road was the Murrays' seat, Blair Castle, long owned by Evelyn's relations, the Dukes of Atholl. According to the Scottish Landownership Return of 1879 the 7th Duke, who had died in 1917, was recorded as being the second-biggest landowner in Perthshire.[1] With an estimated 201,640 acres, size-wise

---

[1] The first was the Earl of Breadalbane, owner of Taymouth Castle, with 234,166 acres. However, his family was off the list by 1970, their lands allegedly lost through gambling; by then the Duke of Atholl was in first place although, as with most private owners, he had fewer acres than a century before, largely due to the public ownership of forests and water boards.

this put him just above the Duke of Devonshire at around the same time, although the annual rental which Atholl received for his acres was less than a quarter of Devonshire's gross income. The fact that John was a brewer rather than an aristocrat may have endeared him to many too, in a county where almost two-thirds of the land was owned by two dukes, four earls, a baroness and half-a-dozen lesser nobles. Some were criticised for furthering their own interests rather than considering the long-term future of the land and its people, such as the 6th Duke of Atholl. He had made himself deeply unpopular in the mid-nineteenth century by trying to keep pedestrians out of Glen Tilt, his land in the north of Perthshire, in an attempt to protect his game: a case was brought against him by the Scottish Rights of Way Society, which succeeded. The Duke's actions were seen as typifying the arrogant attitude of landowners of the time.

At least the start of the Forestry Commission in 1919, and the thousands of acres it planted, was seen by many to be putting Perthshire's uplands to better use, and it provided more work per acre than other rural work. What John thought about the planting is not known but if he could see the Rannoch area today, especially along the road from the Lodge going back towards Kinloch Rannoch, he would hardly recognise it, for it is more forest than open land.

That year John's ownership of the Perthshire estates was proudly marked by his introduction of the 'Cobbold Tartan', a hunting tartan in colours of light brown, beige and black, in which Pamela thought their stalker MacNaughton and the others looked very smart. They would wear it for the local Highland Games, which were to take place on 16 August, and for which preparations took several days. Pamela was worried that Charles, with his injured foot, would not be able to make it up to Scotland at all:

'Darling, I *know* your foot hurts like blazes, promise you won't walk or do anything to make it worse, 'cos you *must* be right for Scotland – I writhe with agony when the *little* pony at H.Wells just steps on my toe; so what it would be like a great horse rolling all over your foot!'

People had been asking about Charles, hoping to see him there; he was missing out on the fun. Ivan and Blanche, nicknamed variously 'Blinks' or 'Blinky', had arrived in their car the night before, their friends the Colquhouns had turned up, and they had all gone rowing on the Loch under a 'lovely, great big moon'. Pamela was looking forward to having a 'proper walk', where she would go out 'alone with a beloved stalker, from 7 am till 11 pm!' and boasted to Charles of her further fishing feat; she and Ivan had caught thirty-six trout in Loch Rannoch, compared with the mere two which Guy Cobbold and their friend Dickie had managed in another loch. However, as Guy had been insisting that everyone ought to bathe in a loch every day before breakfast and, according to Dickie, had flung himself naked into the one they then went fishing in, Pamela thought he had probably frightened the fish away. Meanwhile her father was not enjoying himself very much. The stags were late that summer and John was miserable about the lack of grouse, especially when Ivan told him that at Wellwood, just a few miles away at Pitlochry, they had been getting over a hundred brace each day.

Although she was enjoying herself, Pamela was still worried about sorting out the formalities for their Egypt trip. She told Charles that Dr Brown, whom she had confidently thought would 'perjure his soul' for her, had decided he would not: he refused to provide any certificate for her without examining her first, but he did give her a piece of advice:

'… he says I must take up a disease, such as consumption or Brights' disease![2] 'Cos Egypt is always prescribed for these & also continue to "look the part." I feel the latter would be the most easy to feign as I think it has something to do with swelling! & as you say I can look big in pants I might put it down to Brights' disease!'

How Charles wished he could be there at 'the place eternal' with her: '… the air is full of you tonight… ', he wrote miserably from Pirbright Camp, where he was having to put up with having his foot massaged three times a day by a man who seemed to him 'like the devil incarnate'. To make matters worse his men were all smelly after getting hot playing football, and all that was going on was firing practice, 'Nothing but firing, firing at inanimate objects', when he wanted to be at Rannoch shooting at real targets.

The next day, 17 August, he was a bit happier, his friends having

[2] A now obsolete classification for what is now known to be different types of kidney disease.

163

done their best to cheer him up:

'My friends have been amusing me in bed tonight, consequence several broken things in my room & everything upside down. Not to mention the fact that I am minus about 50 cigarettes. They found a box & I think have all filled their ones. Still, it was very good of them to come and amuse me! Hurrah! a man has just brought me my evening drink. Your health darling! How good it tastes.'

He imagined he was at Rannoch:

'I am sleeping in a hut just like the Bothy with trees rustling outside & I sit and pretend I can hear Ericht & the stags roaring on Ben Alder. There goes one. How lovely it is. Darling, we have just had such a good supper & you have bagged all the blankets & the room with a fire as you say that being the thinnest you feel the cold worse.'

He teased her that she had just wounded two stags – the mark of a poor hunter and much frowned upon – which she had never done, and boasted of having himself '... killed two beauties 14 points at 300 yds'.

Charles would have enjoyed the local Highland Games, which Pamela said were great fun and involved 'hundreds'; she had not realised so many people lived around Rannoch. MacNaughton had done them proud, winning the tug-of-war for their side of the Loch, pulling 'till he nearly burst'. Their party had grown in the last couple of days. Angy and her younger brother, sixteen-year-old Rupert, had arrived by motorbike, her uncle and aunt Philip and Cicely Cobbold, their son Robert and 'dozens of boys' had settled in their lodge up the road and, much to Pamela's delight, their old stalker and friend 'beloved McPhee' had turned up after being away in the war. Pamela had not seen him since 1916, when she and he had been thrilled to get four stags and a grouse at Corriech. He teased Pamela about having been a 'fat little girl' then, and said how he remembered Charles in 1915 – probably at Rannoch at Ivan's invitation – as a 'fat little boy'. Since arriving the day before, their friend Ruby had managed to shoot a stag at Craiganour, and their acquaintance Macintosh, who lived on the Loch, had paid a visit. Evelyn had not yet shot anything but had had a near miss; Pamela always played down her mother's skills as a hunter, but the formidable reputation that she would acquire in the 1920s would be evidence of her daughter's unfairness on that point.

At Pirbright Charles was cheering himself with the thought that time would pass very quickly until he joined her but in any case:

'Thank God that with us time and space do not matter. I really am at Rannoch all the time.'

There was a potential obstacle to his actually getting there; his father, Sir Eric, wanted him at Gannochy, the estate where the Hambros shot every summer and to where Pamela had been invited in September, but Charles thought he could manage to get to Rannoch first. Not wanting to lessen his time with Pamela, he suggested asking his father if she could go Gannochy earlier than planned. Pamela, anxious not to upset her imminent father-in-law, insisted Charles should not mention it, and anyway, due to their various guests, she could not leave Rannoch before 8 September.

Pamela had a very active time over the next couple of August weeks, neither she nor her doughty friends being deterred by the elements. One windy day she, Lady Colquhoun and Blanche – despite being pregnant – took out a boat on another loch:

'When we got there the gale was so terrific we could hardly launch our boat! However, we did eventually & floated at high speed to t'other end, catching 4 wee fish en route, lunched in a hailstorm, until all our lunch was washed away; then we struggled to row back, which took *ages* – we walked back, as we hadn't ordered motor 'til 5.30. Luckily we found the shooters & their motor so we seized it & they walked! Unfortunate men!'

She and Angy were amused one afternoon to visit an old lady living at Rannoch who spoke only Gaelic. Pamela proudly reeled off the only Gaelic sentence she knew, whereupon the lady stared at her incomprehensibly, and the three of them sat and laughed. She and various friends played noisy games in their boats on Loch Rannoch; she tried unsuccessfully to catch salmon but more successfully, one early evening out on her own, shot four rabbits in the birch woods behind the Lodge whilst marvelling at 'a great rainbow, thick and clear, from one side of the Loch to the other'. Going out shooting with Blanche one day, she was pleased when her sister-in-law managed to shoot a buck 'beautifully' near Dunan. With her thirteen-year-old cousin Ralphie Cobbold they shot a roe, and the two of them triumphantly carried it home with the blood pouring down their backs. Evenings were spent enjoying long dinners at the Lodge with their various guests, who seemed to increase every few days, and either going out on the Loch in the moonlight or playing games like bridge, which Pamela refused to take seriously.

The only irritant was her mother. It seemed sometimes that everything Evelyn did got on Pamela's nerves. She complained to Charles:

'Shells, railway men, more wages, curse! Ma insists on reading out to poor Blinky boring bits out of a week-old paper... Oh God, from bad to worse, the paper is no longer being read but words of wisdom are flowing forth from Evelyn's mouth; such as "those damned Americans", "Trade of the world". Oh! darling lump, I *wish* you were here so terribly much; *how* we would laugh at all the rot!'

Pamela was pleased to receive from the doctor the certificate to help get their passports for Egypt – he had relented after all – but she fretted that he had put her name as 'Cobbold' when Charles had thought everything should be in her married name and she thought it might complicate things. But at that moment it must have seemed to Charles that they would never get to Egypt for he had discovered that he had, after all, broken a bone in his ankle. Pamela begged him to rest it, even if it meant he may be delayed in getting up to Rannoch, and not to get too downhearted. It was not easy. He had been admitted to the army hospital, the Cambridge, at Aldershot in Surrey, his window had a depressing view of a yellow stone wall, two drainpipes and a slate roof and, not being allowed to walk until the bone had set, he had to urinate in a bottle. Two of his fellow patients were low-rank soldiers who would sit on his bed and use 'the most awful language between each sentence', and he suggested she get Ivan to tell her what he meant by 'simple private soldiers' language'. The only bit of brightness was in the entertainment provided, unwittingly, by some of the nurses. Violet Dugdale doing her bit at Crathorne would have been disappointed, for the nurses of whom Charles was most critical were the VADs:

'I don't think much of the nurses here. The older ones are good but the VAD's seem more for other things & flirt with two officers at the other end of the room most of the time. I asked one today what bone I had broken, it is called the Astapolous or something like that, she said she did not know what bone that was. However, the trained nurses seem to be quite sensible.'

He also had his first experience of the 'Wrens', the popular name for the Women's Royal Naval Service (WRNS). The WRNS was still a very new organisation, founded in 1916 as part of the Royal Navy – the first armed service to recruit women – and the women were used in all parts of the war effort, from cooks to nurses to engineers:

'The officer in the bed next but 4 has the most lovely visitors, WRENS or something like it, with starched caps & assisted complexions. I don't know when they do any work as they seem to be continuously up here. However, they interest me as they do such funny things. They don't care how they behave. I know one of them wears pink knickers, the other has white ones, I think. I'm not sure, however!'

Charles forwarded to Pamela a letter he had recently received from Angy, written since she had arrived at Talladh-a-Bheithe, which showed her fears:

'Pam has given me your messages. *How* happy I was to get them, it's somehow made such a great big difference. Pam is *everything* to me, she is my 'life' – Always her sorrows have been my sorrows, her happiness my happiness, except when I thought you were taking her away from me. Ever since I can remember *anything* our lives have always been bound up together, and there had never been anyone else, only just 'Pam and me' with the glorious future of we two together on a farm in Canada. Impossible I love Pam too much; then it becomes a 'selfish love' and I wasn't prepared, couldn't imagine this great parting of the ways; it was as if the whole object of my life had been swept away... Pam has given me your messages, and explained to me that it is *not* a parting of the ways; instead in the future we are to see more of each other and with no difficulties, as then her parents will no longer be able to use their influence to keep us apart. How happy this has made me. Thank God that fate brought you and Pam together, who else in the world is worthy of her?

'Goodbye Charles and do not take my Pam too far from me.'

Exactly what the Cobbolds had been concerned about in the relationship between the two young women, given that the families had known each other for generations, is not known. Certainly Angy was a gregarious character, in her adult life quite outspoken: they may simply have considered her a bad influence on Pamela, or they might have suspected the nature of her feelings went beyond friendship. Perhaps a clue can be found in Charles's letter to Pamela in which he enclosed Angy's:

'Tell her from me that the sooner she follows your good example and finds out that the *stronger* !? sex are not all pretty boys, the better. I know she will soon, she can't fight against it. Specially when she sees how happy we are!'

If it was a dislike of men that she had, she would certainly overcome it in later life.

From his sick bed, Charles was making plans to take the sleeper train up to Rannoch; his parents had agreed he could postpone Gannochy until his foot was better and Pamela's father, keen to keep his daughter happy, said they would find room for Charles at Rannoch. Charles was thoroughly fed up with being in bed:

'First you feel hot, then you take a blanket off & the sister says you are untidy, then you turn over and get wound up with the sheet & get more sweaty than ever. Then you kick off the clothes, come out at the end & you get a draft up your legs. Horrible!'

Charles had his foot in plaster and was getting thinner, too – 'mad and very thin!!' – which he put down to all the water he was drinking, but as he always considered himself on the heavy side, it was no bad thing. Pamela's desire for him was strong in her letters and he entreated her to '… hold on a little longer, I'm coming as fast as I can… [I]f you feel hot like I do when you want me you must be boiling a bright red when I think of the amount I want you.'

Not to be deterred by his bad foot and thrilled he would be up at Rannoch on the 30 August, Pamela arranged fishing trips for them so he would not have to walk too much, and cheered him with news of what she and their guests were getting up to. Apart from the usual grouse and stag shooting, they played 'Navies' on the Loch, crashing into each other at twenty miles an hour, and cricket with her father's walking stick, and in the evenings were entertained by her Uncle Ralph's 'thundering good' tales of his explorations, especially the one about his hunting a lion at night in Africa and hiding in a thorn bush with a goat as bait. It fired Pamela's lust for travel more than ever, and she was excited that he knew the director of the Ellerman shipping line, who might be able to help them in their passage to Egypt. Apparently passports were becoming less of a problem; it was which route they took which was more likely to be the issue. The quickest route was from the south of France:

'… but getting our luggage across to Marseilles is apparently the v. Dickens, & everyone advises starting from England & *enduring* the Bay of Biscay! I *will* hold your head & no doubt be sick on it!!'

Pamela was kept well entertained by Ralph and Bouker whose humour, when they got together, could be rather bawdy, but as she confessed, 'I must admit I enjoy it awfully!' One afternoon Ralph amused them by calling in at all the 'huts' around Loch Rannoch and asking for a glass of beer, and was intrigued by a woman in a purple petticoat whom he just had to investigate but, fortunately for her, aged about thirty she turned out to be too old for him.

Pamela was pleased that Charles was going to get his chauffeur Curly to drive him to Scotland after all, instead of getting the train – not easy on crutches. Charles' car was a Sunbeam, a stylish make of car first produced in 1905 and available in 1919 in either 16hp or 24hp; most useful for getting to Gannochy and around the place generally.

Pamela warned him that her mother was writing to the newspapers with an announcement of their marriage on 22 October – she did not want him to get a shock when he saw it, and reminded him that it ought to bring them lots of presents. It seems that etiquette demanded that once a wedding announcement was made, then all those who knew the couple were expected to send something, even if they were not invited to attend.

Charles was relieved to be discharged at last from hospital on 27 August and suggested Ralph book their passage for them and two servants; he said he knew the Governor of Khartoum, so thought they would be all right once they got to Egypt. Even better, the next day would be his very last in the army:

'It is rather a wonderfull feeling that one is one's own master. That is, that one is regulated by one person & that person is the most wonderfull person in the world.'

But Charles could not give up his allegiance to his Regiment that easily. His leaving for Rannoch was delayed for two days because Curly, on whom he had become totally reliant because of his foot, had to stay to finish his musketry course, and while he waited for him he watched the 3rd Battalion Coldstream Guards become champions in the Army Tug-of-War competition. Charles had started the team the previous April and since then they had won three events:

'I am proud of them & so I had to stay to watch them. It was really most exciting & they only won after a hard tussle.'

When Charles finally got to Rannoch their reunion must have lasted at least three weeks, for there are no letters between them until 26 September; instead, Blanche takes over, keeping her mother the Duchess up-to-date with goings-on in Rannoch, as she and Ivan were visiting again. Writing from Craiganour Lodge on 2 September Blanche told her that young Toby, whom they thought had bronchitis, in fact had whooping cough. She and Pamela had been near him when he whooped, and as it was highly contagious she hoped Pamela would not catch it for her wedding.

The Duchess was now in Canada with the Duke, and they were intending to come over to England the following spring for the wedding of Blanche's sister Dorothy to Harold Macmillan. Blanche was keen to see her sister with her beau, writing from Rannoch Lodge on 22 September:

'I should like to see Dorothy & Captain Macmillan, it must be rather funny. I am sure Dorothy would never really care for him, would she? but I suppose he is interesting & has got a good deal to talk about, which I should not think the others have… I don't know if he is like that when you get to know him but Dorothy never really cares about people like that, does she? & as you say, I should not think Macmillan could ever feel very strongly, he doesn't look that sort. After all, Dorothy likes to have someone she can talk to & flirt with wildly!'

Pamela and Charles had returned to Rannoch that day from Gannochy after spending time there with his parents and friends, including Jack Morgan and family. John had also joined them at Gannochy but, stricken with gout, had to stay longer.

He was not the only one stricken. While Pamela remained in Scotland,

170

popping back and forth between Rannoch Lodge and Craiganour Lodge to see Ivan and Blanche, and making the most of the late summer before she would have to return home to finalise the wedding arrangements, Charles was admitted to a nursing home in Wimpole Street, London. Dreaming of looking across to Craiganour instead of at the sooty brick outside his window, he lamented on 26 September, less than a month before their wedding:

'The verdict on my leg to be frank is not fearfully good! I shall not be operated on but am to be managed. [The doctor] says that the bones have all been frightfully squashed & I shall never have a perfect foot again! However, it won't affect my walking, except that my right foot will pain me at times & will get tired quicker than my left. Darling, it is really very lucky it was not worse.'

He cheered himself up by 'accompanying' her on a stag hunt, imagining her standing with her hat off on Corriech with 'a N.W. wind & sunny weather & a few clouds', and gave her a running commentary on her performance as though he were her stalker.

If he was depressed by his foot, he would feel worse later when, at midnight that day, 26 September, a nationwide railway strike started, crippling the whole country. It was in fact just one of a series of strikes that had taken place across the country since the end of the war, the result of changing conditions and reduced wages and benefits suffered by various groups of workers. The Government was prepared to fight it and took immediate steps to reduce the size of rations of various foodstuffs. It remained concerned about the supply of milk and mail but made it clear that, if necessary, the military would be called in. Charles was worried that Pamela would not receive his letters, writing to her on the 27, still from Wimpole Street:

'Darling, whether you will get this or not I don't know… All the same, I hope the government hold out. By Wednesday next the men's wives will be grumbling, then I think they will start considering. I have not been outside but I believe the gov. have taken over Hyde Park as a huge motor depot for food distribution. Everyone very excited! I wish I was fit then I could go & drive a motor lorry. What fun that would be.'

The British spirit that would be epitomised in the Second World

War was seen, with the crisis bringing out the best in people:

'Everyone is lending motors, so I suppose I shall have to lend mine.'

Like many, Charles was not particularly sympathetic to the workers' cause:

'I wish to God they would shoot a few people pour encourager les autres. Don't come back to England yet, you are far better off where you are!... I hope to God this blasted thing does not go on long because we shall have to fly for our honeymoon if it does.'

The country for which he had so recently fought suddenly did not seem the place to be:

'How I hate my country at the moment. I really think England is no place to live in. Let's go to the South Sea Islands. There you do have complete autocracy & rest & quiet. I hate being disturbed and just after 2 ½ years of war, too. We used to sing Keep the home fires burning in France. By jove a lot of coal the blasted people at home have put on them.'

But the next day he had calmed down a little and turned his mind onto a more important matter: their wedding. At just over three weeks until the event it is surprising, especially by modern standards, how relaxed the couple seemed to be about the arrangements. Charles had ordered the bridesmaids' presents but wondered whether the wedding cake and bouquets were his province or not, and urged Pamela to 'wake Ma up about the invitations!' Meanwhile he was keeping his mind on Scotland by making a plasticine map of Gannochy from memory, a rather tame way to pass his time but he was very proud of it, and there was not much else to do whilst confined to bed in his pyjamas, with a jumper that Pamela had knitted him over the top.

The strike continued. For John Cobbold it added insult to injury. He was still fed up with the lack of grouse at Rannoch and the strike made everything worse. Writing to the Duchess he was uncharacteristically depressed:

'My Dear Duchess

'It is ages since I heard directly from you and I expect you are horribly busy travelling & touring with the P of W gone before – We are all here and the best place too, because things look bad in the south and anything might happen – but news is hard to get, we may get letters

3 times a week, anyhow there is enough to eat & no fear of rioting. Blanche is I think well considering everything and walks about & has shot a roebuck… but they are fixed here & couldn't go south to Cadogans & Northbrooks… Pamela is to be married to Chas Hambro on the 22nd October – if there are trains running and they want to come here for their honeymoon & then go to Egypt for the winter… We are killing stags, wretched herds and I can get up no enthusiasm but want a big cariboo [sic] in Newfoundland & a big moose in Alaska – in fact, after Pam goes shall want to take to a roving life again – so don't be surprised if I turn up in Canada next summer – The Edmonton people want me to build shops & offices on a corner lot there but I funk it and at any rate must go there before deciding. Everything seems so risky & the future so doubtful that I feel inclined to dig a hole & put one's savings into it… I am rather sick of the place, there can't be any quantity of grouse for 3 years, the stags don't amuse me and there are no roads to get about on & it is impossible to make them now… I am seriously thinking of letting or selling this portion & going into one of the other places or perhaps back to Duke of Richmond's place, Glenfiddich, if he will let it to me again… but when will trains begin to run again, I fear three weeks at least.'

John could not have realised that the Duke of Richmond had other things on his mind, for his grandson had just died, aged twenty, from war wounds sustained in Russia. Neither could he know that when the Duke himself died, he would leave his son and heir, the 8th Duke, with financial difficulties that resulted in having to sell off part of the land that John was thinking of, to cope with death duties.

John's desire to start 'roving' again was a clear indication of how separate his and Evelyn's lives now were, and for him to even think about selling the Rannoch estate would have been unheard of just a few months earlier. John also commented to the Duke on the sale of his family's London house:

'Various rumours about Devonshire House but I suppose it is sold and I hope for a good price.'

Victor Cavendish had the misfortune of being the victim of several events which badly affected him financially. He was the first Duke of Devonshire to be hit in 1908 by the new death duties upon the death of his uncle, the 8th Duke, leader of the Liberal Government; there were the ongoing debts built up by the failed business ventures of the 7th Duke; and like many landowners, Victor was affected by the political and social changes caused by the war. From Chatsworth he was forced to sell some rare and priceless collections of books, he had to put Devonshire House on the market after one hundred and eighty years of family ownership, and also had to sell another of his houses, Chiswick House.

The Duke was not the only one of the Cobbolds' friends and relations to be affected. Slains Castle had been sold by their friend Charles Gore Hay in 1916. He had discovered that the generosity of his father William, the 19th Earl of Erroll, coupled with the effects of the agricultural depression of the late nineteenth century – the one which had seen Harry Hambro selling Milton Abbey to his uncle Everard – had reduced the family fortune considerably, and there was insufficient to pay the crippling death duties. Charles Hay's income as an army officer – he was head of the Household Cavalry and served as a Major General during the Great War – was simply not enough to pay the death duties. The castle and estate were sold to Sir John Ellerman, the shipping magnate, and then sold on again to an absentee landlord in 1922 who let the castle fall into disrepair. It was de-roofed in 1925 so that rates did not have to be paid, and although a decision was made to demolish it in 1927, the year Charles Hay died, this never happened, probably because of the huge cost involved. Instead, it fell into a ruin, albeit a spectacular one. Charles Hay's death at least spared him from sadness other than the ruin of the castle. His son Victor, succeeding him as 21st Earl of Erroll, held the title for less than a year, dying in 1928. Local legend, enduring into the twenty-first century, says that Victor haunts the ruins of his family's castle.

Charles updated Pamela on the strike in his letter of 30 September:

'... I believe the arrangements in London as far as food is concerned are wonderfull. Hyde Park is a huge 'dump', thousands of lorries, milk cans... everything. Everyone is doing something & it really makes me very wild to think I can't go and flag a train. Humphrey Tollemache [Angy's older brother] is driving an engine with Jack Head [her uncle] as stoker, not bad. Also anyone who was in any motor thing before is now back. The strikers are getting a bit frightened & I see in tonight's paper that they are starting to hedge... The miners were going to have a large meeting in London, now they can't because of the railway strike. What fools, how ignorant people do cut each other's throats when they try to run things. I believe the miners are dead fed up with the railway men! I am sorry to say the devils are starting to try to wreck trains, that is the last straw! Personally I'm never going to tip a porter more than 2d any more if I give him that!'

All bedridden Charles could do was to carry on with his plasticine map of Gannochy, and had got as far as modelling the moor and had even added grouse drives, looking forward to showing it to Ivan when he was next down that way. With few trains, and private cars being put to community use, Pamela was stuck in Scotland. Even the local timber lorries had left the area to carry supplies between Perth and Inverness. Despite the inconvenience, she hoped the Government would not give in to the strikers. Normally she would have been thrilled to be at Rannoch still, but she was dying to see Charles, to comfort her war hero whom she was dismayed to hear may never walk properly again. The post was somehow still being delivered, although later in the day than usual. She wrote on 1 October:

'Tis awfully funny being stuck up here, feels as if we were in the ark; I think it's time we sent a dove out & see how far it could get; but I want to be the dove! I bet I could get to London & find my way to 29 Wimpole Street.'

She wondered how arrangements were going for the second part of their honeymoon in Egypt – they would be at Rannoch to start with – and was delighted to hear back that the passports were in hand, although he needed six photographs of her; he had written to people in Alexandria and Cairo to arrange 'the best duck shooting in the world bar Mesopotamia' for them, and was arranging to borrow some rifles, although he pointed out that Pamela could take her own with her. He was also pleased to report that his foot was 'passing all expectations', and transport was now running more smoothly in London, with a regular tube service manned by volunteer drivers. Things were looking up at last, and he could turn his mind to the practicalities of the wedding, which was now less than three weeks away and for which he had already received many wedding presents. Their friend Thelma Cazalet, who would become a feminist and well-known Conservative MP, had sent them a present, the merits of which Charles was uncertain:

'[It] is an objet d'art of some kind. What it is for I don't know, but I suppose it is awfully nice. I'm sure you will be able to put it on your table or something.'

Charles was arranging to have his banns published in the second week of October and wondered if she had arranged hers yet: there was no requirement that they should be read together but it was a legal requirement that he live in Ipswich for fourteen days before the wedding in order to be married there. He asked if she knew of a pub in Ipswich where he could take a room for that period. Meanwhile a friend was going to book their passage to Egypt at Thomas Cook's, and he was grateful to his imminent father-in-law for making the rest of the arrangements for their 'approaching torture'. They were young to be marrying by today's standards – on 3 October he turned twenty-two while Pamela would still be nineteen – but the effects of the war had turned people's minds to marriage earlier than before, although Charles expressed the view they both held, that really they would rather be together without any of this fuss.

Still stuck in hospital on 4 October, looking at the passport photos she had sent him and feeling lonelier than ever, he drew an 'insane' comfort from his now-completed relief map of Gannochy, with its 'little hills all covered with heather & grass', and dreamed they were living on Ben Alder, in Cluny's Cave, with Pamela wearing kilts and he a red beard. He told her a cartoon joke from Punch:

'Man & pretty girl walking past shop with wedding cakes for sale. Man says, "Well, old scream. What about it?" Darling, did I do it like that!'

The whole wedding process was exhausting him, despite having done little so far:

'Talking of cakes, has John ordered ours from Ipswich or shall I order one from London. Also bouquets, that's my job isn't it?

'What a life, I never knew it was so difficult to get married. How much more sensible to go to a Registry office. S. Leacock is wonderful, he really does cheer me up. Also Zane Grey makes me want to go away with you where no-one else lives, where there is no money, no strikes, no trains, nothing, no great Aunts. (Two arrived today.) Oh gawd!!

'Darling, let's lose ourselves in the great unknown, just you and I and nature.'

He was fed up with long-distance connection with Pamela through their spirits: now he wanted material connection:

'I'm a man. I really do prefer you in reality, really I do.'

Fortunately the next day, 5 October, the rail strike was settled, following intervention from Downing Street. The country could get back to normal, although Sir Eric Hambro had started for London from Gannochy a few days earlier and had not been heard of since. And still the wedding invitations had not been sent out! People were asking Charles when he was getting married, although they should have seen the announcement in the newspapers.

On 6 October, in the last letter Pamela would write from Rannoch as a single woman, she was overcome with happiness knowing that the next time she was there would be with Charles:

'The Hills have told me to give you their messages. Ben Alder standing huge & stern says, what matter the boring fortnight that lies before you two when after that you can come & gaze at me! T.A. Bheithe cries, "Think of the days you'll have roaming over my rocks when I shall show you some wonderful things." Corriech – ah! Corriech says nothing; it only speaks by changing from deepest violet to golden pink, by letting you stand on its precious heights & gaze & gaze till you feel you must burst with joy, at peak after peak of such changing colouring & then tells you the most marvellous secret of Life, in fact the whole motive of life, that we have a soul.'

Thoughts of their future together overwhelmed her:

'It seems hard to realise what a wonderful future lies before us & that it's coming *true*: Rannoch, Egypt & God knows what; I suppose there will be a million troubles, a thousand disappointments; what matter though if the big thing, ie. whether we understand each other... Charles, it's 12 o/c. This time tomorrow (all being well of course!) I shall be with you, materially as well as spiritually.

'My lump, God bless you.

'Bogie'.

Chapter 13

Religions

Pamela's letters to Charles were full of references to time and distance being irrelevant, and to the idea of a kind of psychic ability to 'travel' to each other. These notions, along with her passion for nature, were either inspired by, or were the reason for, her interest in Buddhism – still an unusual religion for the time, because in the early twentieth century, little was known in Britain about it. The British had first encountered Buddhism in the late eighteenth and early nineteenth centuries when the Empire expanded to Buddhist countries like Ceylon and Burma, and contacts made with places like Nepal. Some of the first people to study Buddhism seriously were British civil servants stationed in those places, and in the late nineteenth century translations of Buddhist texts were made available for academic study in Britain.

The introduction of Buddhism to a wider public had started in the United States in 1875 with the birth of the Theosophical Society, which still exists today. The period from the 1850s onwards was a period of intense intellectual ferment and uncertainty, with natural sciences making great strides in explaining the world in terms which challenged the traditional, religious views. The Theosophical Society was one of various bodies which attempted to deal with this. Pamela's sister Winifred was an enthusiastic member of the Theosophical Society, probably from about 1915.

Essentially, Theosophy means 'knowledge of the divine'. It restores the ancient belief that humans are divine beings whose true home is the universe, not only the physical planet on which they live. The universe is a 'boundless plane' allowing infinite growth of consciousness; every being, including mankind, alternates between a physical life and a spiritual one, in a continual sequence of action and rest.

As a member of the Society Winifred was in good company, for it attracted a wide range of intellectuals. Some of the literary giants of the late nineteenth/early twentieth century were either members or had an interest in Theosophy. Among them were Oscar Wilde, George Bernard Shaw and W B Yeats, the latter a friend of Pamela's acquaintance Wilfrid Meynell. The founders of the Theosophical Society were a strange couple: a Russian occultist, Helena Petrovna Blavatsky, and an American spiritualist, Henry Steel Olcott. Their initial objective was to investigate, study and explain mediumistic phenomena but after a few years the pair moved to India and became interested in Eastern religions. They are thought to have been the first Westerners formally to become Buddhists, which they became in Ceylon in 1880. Olcott designed the Buddhist flag used universally today.

The aims of the Theosophical Society were: 'To form a nucleus of the universal brotherhood of humanity without distinction of race, creed, sex, caste or colour; to encourage the study of comparative religion, philosophy and science; to investigate the unexplained laws of nature and the powers latent in man.' Although the Society would also come to be linked to various secret societies and sects, it did much in the late nineteenth century to promote the understanding and tolerance of Buddhism, for which Olcott became regarded as a hero, especially in Ceylon.

Its promotion in Britain came a little later, when in the 1890s a restless, clever young Londoner called Allan Bennett, an asthmatic scientist and devout Catholic, started to question and then abandon his faith. He experimented with various drugs and became interested in Eastern religious and Western mystic and occult systems, which led him to join the Theosophical Society. In 1900 Bennett left Britain for the East to study Buddhism and in 1902 was ordained in Burma as a Buddhist monk, taking a Buddhist name. He wanted to start a Buddhist community in England, saying he thought the West needed a religion of truth based on a belief compatible with science, asserting that Buddhism was that truth.

Bennett established the International Buddhist Society and started a journal on Buddhism which was sent to organisations sympathetic to the Buddhist message, including the Theosophical Society. Then in November 1907, in a private house in London, twenty-five people interested in Buddhism formed themselves into the Buddhist Society of Great Britain and Ireland, and were amongst the first Westerners to practise Buddhism as a living religion. An educated group of people with an eminent scholar as their first president, they were supported by the Theosophical Society. The following year they welcomed Bennett to Britain, where he gave lectures and helped to increase the understanding of Buddhism, which he continued to do from Burma and later back in England, where he died in 1923: despite the Burmese climate helping his asthma, other aspects of his harsh life as a Buddhist monk were detrimental to his health. After his death a separate 'lodge' of Buddhist Theosophists was formed in Britain, which eventually became the Buddhist Society. Similar groups were growing in Europe, and in 1930 the Buddhist Society of America would be formed.

One could be a Theosophist without being a Buddhist, and vice versa; there is no evidence that Winifred was anything other than a Theosophist, or that Pamela's interest in Buddhism included a wider involvement in the Theosophical Society. Winifred's interest in the Society may have been encouraged by her husband's cousin, Douglas Brooke Wheelton Sladen. A traveller, historian and writer, he went to live in Australia for a while in the late nineteenth century, and became a major authority on Australian literature. Douglas also had an interest in the occult, publishing poems and essays and contributing to the long-running *Occult Review* in Britain, to which the famous author and keen spiritualist, Arthur Conan Doyle, was a contributor. Douglas and Winifred also corresponded separately with a major publisher of the day, John Lane, whose company – John Lane the Bodley Head – was well-known for publishing esoteric and controversial works by unconventional authors like Oscar Wilde. Some of Douglas' letters to John Lane concern his proposed travel books, including one called *Queer Things About Japan*: he became known as an expert on that country and so was familiar with Buddhism. Winifred's letter to Lane reminded the publisher of a recent meeting she had had with him and invited him to tea, perhaps to discuss the latest ideas expressed by the authors on his list.

Such ideas included those of the Theosophists, for John Lane also published books about the movement's supporters including Annie Besant, its international president after Olcott's death in 1907, and its co-founder Helena Blavatsky. Blavatsky was a woman of mysterious origins. The core of her ideas is thought to have stemmed from Edward Bulwer Lytton,[1] whose family seat was Knebworth House in Hertfordshire. An acclaimed Victorian writer, politician and close friend of Charles Dickens, he was also an occultist into whose family, by coincidence, one of the Cobbolds would later marry. His interest in the occult started when he was a Cambridge undergraduate, where he became known for his passion for predictions, using a crystal ball, and for the casting of horoscopes. Edward was visited in 1854 by Eliphas Levi,[2] a French occult author and magician, who considered him to be one of the principal exponents of occult studies in Britain.

It was one of Edward's novels which impressed Blavatsky: written in 1871 it was called *The Coming Race*, later reprinted as *Vril: The Power of the Coming Race*. One of the early science fiction books, its subject was a subterranean species, rather like angels, called 'Vril-ya' who have access to an extraordinary force that can be controlled by will: they can heal and also destroy. Their source of energy comes from 'an all-permeating fluid' called 'Vril'. Blavatsky seemed to take the view that Vril[3] was based on a real magical source, which she endorsed in her book called *Isis Unveiled* in 1877, in which the Vril power and its attainment by a superhuman elite are worked into a mystical doctrine of race. The existence of a secret Vril Society was later alleged, perhaps unsurprisingly suggesting links to Nazi organisations.

The Cobbolds' connection with Edward Bulwer Lytton was through Pamela's second cousin Cameron Fromanteel Cobbold; four years younger than Pamela, Cameron shared with her and her siblings the

---

[1] 1803-1873. Famous as the creator of the saying 'The pen is mightier than the sword'. Today the book for which he is best known is *The Last days of Pompeii*. In 1866 he was created the first Lord Lytton of Knebworth.

[2] Pseudonym of Alphonse Louis Constant.

[3] More prosaically, it gave rise to the name 'Bovril': the beef tea product was developed in the same decade.

same great-grandfather, John Chevallier Cobbold. In 1930, continuing the Cobbold trend of marrying title, Cameron – known as 'Kim' – would marry Edward's great-granddaughter Lady Hermione Bulwer Lytton. The marriage secured for that branch of the Cobbolds one of Britain's best-known stately homes.[4] Kim Cobbold shared the house with abundant evidence of Edward's interest in the occult, still seen in his study, where magic markings adorn the ceiling above his crystal ball, and cabinets display some of the tracts he read, such as *An Essay upon Reason and the Nature of Spirits* and *Full and Plain Evidence Concerning Witches and Apparitions*.

Britain had also seen the rise of spiritualism. Interest had started to increase and spread widely during Edward Bulwer Lytton's lifetime. In 1882 the Society for Psychical Research began in Britain. Its purpose was to investigate mesmeric, psychical and 'spiritualistic' phenomena in a strictly scientific manner. The Society was started by Henry Sidgwick, Professor of Moral Philosophy at Cambridge University, who had enormous standing and authority in the intellectual circles of the day. The leaders of the Society turned psychical research into a science, with disciplined experimental methods, and founded a scholarly journal for reporting and discussing psychical research worldwide. Prominent early members included two eminent physicists and two philosophers: Arthur Balfour, Britain's Prime Minister from 1902-5, and his younger brother Gerald Balfour, a classical scholar, MP and President of the Board of Trade. Their sister, Eleanor, was also a member: a mathematician, she married Henry Sidgwick and later became Principal of Newnham College, Cambridge. Each of them was at some time President of the Society: Arthur in 1893, Gerald from 1906-7, and Eleanor from 1908-9 and again later.

Coincidentally, the Balfours were twice connected by marriage to the Cobbolds. Firstly, Evelyn Georgiana Mary Balfour, another sister of

---

[4] Kim later became Governor of the Bank of England and Lord Chamberlain, and managed to acquire a title at last for the Cobbolds, being created the first Lord Cobbold in 1960. Knebworth was a mixed blessing: when Lady Hermione inherited it from her father Victor in 1947 it was in need of much attention and therefore money. The couple opened the main rooms to the public on summer weekends from 1950. In 1974 their son David (the second Lord Cobbold from 1987) and his wife Chryssie raised its profile and fortunes further by starting the rock concerts in the park for which Knebworth became famous.

the brilliant trio above, after founding the Soil Association and marrying an eminent physicist John William Strutt, 3rd Baron Rayleigh, had a son called Robert. He married Lady Evelyn Cobbold's cousin Lady Mary Hilda Clements. Then, like the Cobbolds, the Balfours married into the Lytton family: Gerald Balfour's wife, Lady Elizabeth Edith, or 'Betty', was a granddaughter of Edward Bulwer Lytton, and aunt to Hermione. It is tempting to imagine that Betty inherited her grandfather's interest in the occult and initiated her husband Gerald; more likely, however, it was because Gerald, Arthur and Eleanor had developed their interest in the study of psychic phenomena when all were students at Cambridge University, which is where they met Sidgwick.

The interest in spiritualism was revived at all levels of society after the Great War, when people who had been bereaved turned away from the more orthodox forms of Christian religion to seek comfort elsewhere, trying to establish contact with their dead relatives. The war played a part in establishing the credibility of supernatural intervention in human affairs, and stories abounded of strange experiences on the battlefield. Séances became popular again, and spiritualism generally was endorsed by the involvement of famous names. The Duchess of York, the future Queen Mother, had lost her older brother, Fergus, in 1915 in the Battle of Loos, and as a result was said to have shown an interest in spiritualism; Rudyard Kipling's son, Jack, was killed in the same battle – the writer's second experience of a child's death – and subsequently wrote stories about sympathetic visions and ghostly healings; Arthur Conan Doyle, who had always been interested in spiritualism, became more involved after some of his relatives were killed, claiming to speak to 'the other side'. It was he who travelled to Yorkshire in 1920 to interview the two girls who famously – and, as it turned out, untruthfully – claimed they had seen fairies at the bottom of their garden, resulting in his book *The Coming of the Fairies*.

The Great War also played a part in raising an interest in Buddhism in Britain: the history of Buddhism contains stories of people whose lives were greatly changed by the death of someone close to them. With its emphasis on rebirth, it provided a spiritual answer for some. One such person was the future eminent criminal Judge Christmas Humphreys, or 'Toby' as he was known to his family and friends. Born the year after

Pamela, he was a Christian until he lost his beloved elder brother in Belgium during the war which led him to question the existence of a benevolent deity. He tried other faiths and then, whilst a law student at Cambridge, came to fully embrace Buddhism. Early on he was also a Theosophist and a strong supporter of the aims of the Society and of Blatvasky. It was Humphreys who in 1924, the year he was called to the Bar, started the Lodge of Buddhist Theosophists after the death of Allan Bennett. However, he came to see a divergence between the principles of Theosophy and Buddhism, and in 1926 steered the Lodge away from the support of the Theosophical Society. His group came to be called the Buddhist Society, the biggest of its kind outside Asia, and Humphreys would be its President for forty years, writing many books on the subject.

It is unlikely that Pamela's interest in Buddhism resulted from the losses her family and friends experienced as a result of the war: the ideas she expressed to Charles in her letters are not obviously linked to loss. Instead, she probably gleaned something of Buddhism from her sister via Theosophy, and also from their uncle Ralph Patteson Cobbold who had travelled in and written about Asia. Above all, she would have read the now classic book by her maternal grandfather, Charles Adolphus Murray, about his travels on horseback through the Pamirs, which included his experiences of Buddhism in Western Tibet. In fact, of the several variants of Buddhism that exist, it seems likely that Pamela's interest indeed lay in Tibetan Buddhism: for one of its central practices is chanting mantras (prayers), and the initials 'OM' on the top of the gate to the garden where she is buried are the beginning of the well-known mantra, 'Om mani padme hum'. The prayer cannot be translated into a simple phrase or sentence, but saying it either out loud or silently is thought by Tibetan Buddhists to invoke the powerful benevolent attention and blessings of 'Chenrezig', the embodiment of compassion. Viewing the written form of the words is said to have the same effect.

Most Tibetan Buddhists, as well as those from China and several other countries, refer to themselves as 'Mahayana' Buddhists, as opposed to certain other types, such as 'Theravada' Buddhists. Mahayana is characterised by its diversity. It is not a single school of Buddhism in the way that Theravada is, but a convenient label for a whole variety of teachings and practices, suitable for different sorts of people in different cultures at varying levels of spiritual development. That would make it more attractive to a lay person in the Western world, such as Pamela. The goal of Mahayana is to become a *bodhisattva*– a person who dedicates herself to obtaining enlightenment, not for herself but in order to help others – and eventually a Buddha.

Pamela would have known that all Buddhists believe in the Four Noble Truths; the three marks of life; *karma*, rebirth, enlightenment, and compassion. Features that distinguish Tibetan Buddhism include the vast variety of supernatural beings; a belief in the *Bardo*, an intermediate state of forty-nine days between one life and the next; an elaborate variety of rituals; and a belief in *tulkus*, which are *bodhisattvas* in human form, taking several rebirths. After death there are several stages to go through during the *Bardo* either before one is reborn or achieves *nirvana*, the perfect state.

Exactly how far Pamela embraced Buddhism in practice is not known. Oddly, in some of her letters to Charles she used an Islamic expression, 'Inshallah,' meaning 'If Allah wills', referring to something she hoped would happen: she probably heard her mother, a Muslim, using this term at home, but it is clearly nothing to do with Buddhism. If Pamela became an actual lay Buddhist, rather than just having a sympathy with its general philosophies, then she would have had to undertake to keep its five precepts of morality: to abstain from killing, from taking what is not given, from misusing sensual pleasures (mainly meaning sexual misconduct), from false speech and from drugs and alcohol. Even if she kept to most of these, the one she would have had a problem with is the first – killing – because this refers not only to humans but to any 'sentient being', including animals. Although some Buddhists eat meat they will not kill the food themselves, using a butcher of another faith to do it. And Pamela did love her hunting, delighting in the conquest of a stag or a rabbit; however, it was not the fact of death itself that she enjoyed but rather the process of stalking and then accurately shooting the creature, a testimony to her judgment and skill. Nevertheless, it was not compatible with the teachings of Buddha.

However far her leanings went, what were Charles' views of his wife's interest? He would have indulged her but not in any patronising way: she was too bright to deserve condescension, and the study of Buddhism, like Theosophy, was not for the intellectually feeble. Charles is unlikely to have shared her enthusiasm, however, for the Hambros had given up Judaism three generations previously, and since then had fully embraced the Church of England. They had become mainstream establishment and saw no reason to change that; an interest in Buddhism would have been tolerated as the eccentric inclination of a family member. After all, Pamela's religious background was not exactly consistent or orthodox, with her maternal grandfather a Christian Scientist and her mother a Muslim. With John Dupuis Cobbold and his side of the family being long-standing Church of England followers, it was time for another religion to be thrown into the melting pot, and Pamela did just that.

Chapter 14

The Newly Weds

Pamela left Rannoch for Holy Wells on 8 October to finalise the wedding arrangements. Her parents were staying on longer, cutting it rather fine for the 22nd. According to Blanche, writing to her mother from Rannoch Lodge, John would be leaving Scotland on the 16th and Evelyn on the 18th or 19th. Blanche herself anticipated leaving in a few days' time and joining Pamela at Holy Wells to give her a hand. Writing from Holy Wells on 19 October, she told the Duchess:

'Lady Evelyn got back from Scotland yesterday. Pam has been awfully busy, she was in London a few days this week finishing off clothes & things. Her wedding frock is lovely. Marte made it. We got her writing table things from you & father, they were a little over the £20 but we thought you would not mind, it is [sic] so nice. They said they wanted that sort of thing. I think she is very pleased with it.'

Meanwhile Winifred and Algy, just back from America, had visited Holy Wells the day before, and would soon be going off to Budapest where, according to a rather disapproving Blanche:

'... he has got some job of some sort, I don't quite know what it is. She is staying for the wedding but he is not. He doesn't look up to much.'

What young Toby thought about seeing his parents again, and knowing they would be going off once more without him, can only be guessed at: as an adult he would rarely talk about them. Blanche was concerned for him, as well as how he might perform as a pageboy at his Aunt Pam's wedding, as he had recently been ill:

'Toby I suppose will stay here. He is very well again now, I don't think the whooping cough was bad, but having bronchitis at the same time made him rather ill for a few days, he still coughs a bit from time to time, I hope he won't get a violent choke at Pam's wedding. I expect he will, he generally does when he gets excited, as long as he is not sick when he is carrying her train, it will be all right.'

Blanche's thoughts were also on another couple: her sister Dorothy and Harold Macmillan who were to be married the following year. She was still doubtful about her sister's choice, writing to her mother:

'I should have loved to have heard your interview with Captain Macmillan, it must have been rather funny but I should think very awkward! I am sure he is awfully nice but he doesn't look Dorothy's sort a bit really.'

Delighted on the other hand at her sister-in-law's choice, Blanche helped Pamela in a flurry of last minute preparations, supervising the arrangements at Holy Wells and sorting out her clothes for the first part of the honeymoon at Rannoch. No doubt Pamela had a few rows with her mother before the day itself, with Evelyn anxious that everything should be done in accordance with the social etiquette of the day, and Pamela disdainful of anything that smacked of pointless convention.

At last, Wednesday 22 October 1919 arrived. St Clement's Church in Ipswich, as the *East Anglian Daily Times* reported, had not been such a centre of interest for a very long time, but as the Cobbolds had been associated with the church and the town itself for the best part of two centuries, 'a widespread desire on the part of the public to see something of the proceedings' was not surprising. The head gardener at Holy Wells, Mr Davis, was responsible for the beautiful floral arrangements for which he was widely complimented; this was well-deserved, for he would have been under the unerring eye of Lady Evelyn, an avid gardener, to get everything just right. Flowers of 'various hues' adorned the font just inside the church door, while the chancel displayed large clusters of white flowers amongst 'handsome foliage plants and waving plumes of pampas grass'.

The service began at 2.30pm and was conducted by the Bishop of Edmundsbury and Ipswich, who commented on what a beautiful day it was, with 'the mellow light of an October sun streaming through the windows of the ancient church'. As Blanche had said, Marte, the Italian designer of Grosvenor Square, London, had done a lovely job with Pamela's dress, which was of white and silver brocade. It had:

'... a diamond girdle passing loosely round the waist, one end being caught up on one shoulder at the back. The train was of the same brocade lined with net, and over all the gown was a long tulle veil, held by a wreath of orange blossom.'

Pamela's jewellery was simple, just a pearl necklace and the Coldstream Star of Charles' Regiment, and she carried a bouquet of lilies and white heather.

Fortunately the procession was not marred by Toby being sick over his aunt's train, as Blanche had feared. Pamela was attended by seven bridesmaids and two pages. The bridesmaids were Angy Tollemache; Joan Cobbold, Pamela's young cousin; Charles' younger sister Zelia, and cousin Mary Martin Smith; and the daughters of family friends, the Hon Judith Gurdon, daughter of Lord Cranworth, and Pamela Schreiber, whose father was the Chief Constable of Ipswich. The elder bridesmaids wore apricot satin veiled in chiffon, with tulle veils and wreaths, and the two little girls wore mob caps. Carrying striking bouquets of copper-beech leaves and yellow roses, they also wore gifts from the bridegroom which Charles had managed to organise after all: diamond brooches for the older girls, diamond and pearl for the little ones. The two pages were Toby and Charles' four-year-old cousin, Nigel Hambro, who were dressed, no doubt self-consciously, '... en suite with the dresses of the bridesmaids'.

John Cobbold proudly gave away his youngest daughter, probably relieved that Pamela's choice of husband was someone reliable and solid, with a certain future and an unblemished army record: quite different from his other son-in-law. Charles' best man was one of his fellow officers from the Coldstream Guards, Captain Acland-Hood.

The service sheet, like the invitations, was simple and elegant. Helped by the 'hearty singing' of the choir, the congregation sang 'Oh God our help in ages past', 'Fight the Good Fight' and 'Now thank we all our God'. The couple made their vows standing on a white rug at the front of the altar, and listened to the Bishop's address on 'the happiness to be gained by married people who sought it in self-surrender to each

189

other, and not in gratifying their own inclinations'. Charles and Pamela signed the register to the accompaniment of Miss Ivy Lush from the Royal Opera, Covent Garden, singing 'O perfect love', and left the church to Mendelssohn's 'Wedding March'. Outside they passed underneath the crossed swords of the guard of honour of the Coldstream Guards.

As Ivan reported a few days later to his parents-in-law, both in Canada, the couple got through the wedding without any mishaps. The Duke and Duchess' gift to Pamela – a writing case and blotter made of crocodile skin, which Blanche had bought on their behalf – joined a present which by modern standards would be deemed unacceptable: a seal and musquash long fur coat with skunk collar and cuffs from Pamela's uncle and aunt, Philip and Cicely Cobbold. Her present from her brother-in-law Algy was typically obscure, described by the newspaper as a 'freak ornament'. Winifred's gift, however – a silver biscuit box – was more conventional and more in the style of the others Pamela received. Ivan and Blanche gave a silver kettle and stand; her grandmother, the Dowager Duchess of Dunmore, a large single pearl ring; her great-aunt and uncle, the Earl and Countess of Dartmouth, a gold bracelet with star sapphire; from family friends and other relations, trade and title alike, came silver sugar tongs, china ornaments, books, goblets, various types of boxes and scent bottles, ashtrays, a blue leather bridge box, telephone books, mirrors, silver trays and lamps.

The couple's desire to travel was reflected in their gifts. Pamela's explorer uncle, Ralph Cobbold, gave her a Kodak camera and Charles a travelling watch, perhaps showing the time in various zones, while a Cobbold cousin gave Pamela a grey suede travelling cushion. Charles' presents reflected the outdoor life of the upper class gentleman, with silver flasks, shooting sticks, walking sticks, silver cigarette boxes and cartridge cases, and on the more domestic front his younger siblings, Richard, Zelia and Judith, gave him a breakfast set. He was clearly expected to do his bit of correspondence too, receiving several writing aids and two writing tables. The couple also each received gifts from their parents' respective employees and tenants – Pamela from the Cliff Brewery staff and offices, and from the tenants of the Rannoch estate, and Charles from his father's bank staff in London and parishioners of Milton Abbey. The amount of duplication of presents suggests – somewhat refreshingly by twenty-first century standards – that there was no presumptuous wedding list sent out beforehand.

Holy Wells, where the reception was held, looked stunning on beautiful autumn days like this. The two families, with their outgoing and often eccentric characters, threw themselves into the celebrations, although never before had a toast for absent friends been so poignant. It may not have been a favourite topic for discussion that day, but the war was a common theme amongst the guests. Those who had recently fought included Lord Cranworth, father of Pamela's bridesmaid, Judith Gurdon, winning both the Military Cross and the Croix de Guerre. One of the early British settlers in East Africa, he had been living in Kenya with his wife and family when war broke out, and returned to England to play his part.

Guests were from a diverse mix of business, aristocracy and the arts. Combining title with artistic talent was the Hon Marion Saumarez, a daughter of the 4th Lord de Saumarez, of a prominent Guernsey family who, for at least a century, had lived at Shrublands Park in Suffolk, an eighteenth-century mansion known for its 1000 acres of gardens. Marion was a very successful painter of character portraits, whose work is still in evidence today in Suffolk and Guernsey. There was Lady Kathleen Pilkington, a champion of and expert on French toy bulldogs, whose book written in 1905 is still referred to by enthusiasts. There were budding politicians and war heroes and their families, including Mr and Mrs Chevallier, close relations of Lord Kitchener and the Cobbolds. The Cobbolds' good friends and fellow brewers, the Tollemaches, were there in force, Angy's father, the Hon Douglas Tollemache, probably making mental notes for when it was his daughter's turn. Pamela's co-workers from Ransomes were guests too, and they would enjoy a good laugh with her, reminiscing about their still-recent war efforts.

After the reception, the newlyweds travelled up to Rannoch by train with a car to collect them at Rannoch station. Like Ivan, when he had married Blanche, Pamela, the youngest child of John Dupuis Cobbold, would have received a warm welcome from her father's tenants when she returned there with her new husband. They had a wonderful time there. Pamela knew her soul would never really leave Rannoch, wherever else they may travel, and it must have been while they were on honeymoon that she expressed the wish to be buried there with Charles, in a spot which would give a perfect view of the Loch. Not that they were alone the whole time: Ivan popped up to see them, and whilst there he managed to secure his reputation as one of the greatest shots in Britain when, as *The Times* noted, he killed two woodcock with one shot, an extremely rare feat.

After a couple of blissful weeks Pamela and Charles left Rannoch at the beginning of November to prepare to travel to Egypt, but it was not to be. Updating her mother on November 5 from Sutton Hoo, where she and Ivan were temporarily renting a country house, Blanche told the Duchess that her sister-in-law and Charles were coming down to Holy Wells on the Friday, then going to Milton Abbey for a few days. They were supposed to be leaving for Egypt on 8 November but the ship had been delayed until the 15th. On the 11th, as they waited patiently, they experienced the introduction of the two minutes' silence, commemorating the first anniversary of the Armistice. Unfortunately, they then received a telegram from Charles' parents to say that Egypt was now impossible. There had been another uprising and all foreign entry was banned. All their hard work and preparation had been in vain. They were hugely disappointed. Nevertheless, they were still determined to get away and travel abroad for the rest of their honeymoon.

They did get away, even if not to the destination of their choice. Ivan told the Duke on 11 December:

'Pamela and Charles have got to Gibraltar. They had a wretched time in the Bay [of Biscay] where both very sick. They are now sitting on the Rock wondering where to go next. They wanted to go to Egypt but cannot, owing to the war. Then they thought of Morocco but discovered there is a war going on there. I think they will probably end up in Monte Carlo or one of those places.'

Although the term 'jetsetter' was not yet invented, Monte Carlo, with its international social scene, was not so very different in 1919 to today: not Charles and Pamela's idea of fun. Neither was Gibraltar a place to stay for very long in 1919, despite its being the gateway to the Mediterranean and the stepping stone to North Africa. Today it is multi-cultural with native-born Gibraltarians and British expatriates living

Drawing Room at Holy Wells, 1890s.

Bedroom at Holy Wells where Pamela was born, 1900.

Charles and Pamela engagement photo
1919.

Charles and Pamela's wedding,
taken at Holy Wells.

Marcus Wallenburg and Dorothy ("Doie") Mackay – engagement photographs.

Diana & Cynthia Hambro with Peter and Desmond Strutt, circa 1929.

Delcombe Manor.

Pamela and Charlie 1931.

side by side, a popular place for a holiday in itself, and even more so with the attractions of Spain and Morocco nearby. But in 1919 it was not renowned as a tourist haven. Although it had become a British Crown Colony in 1830 – much to the fury of Spain – in 1889 the Governor of Gibraltar decreed that only native-born inhabitants had a right of residence there. Pamela and Charles were therefore visiting 'aliens', despite having British passports. Yet those same residents did not have the right to vote, and it was not until 1921 that the first elections were held; even then, only male ratepayers could vote, making the colony backwards compared to Britain where the vote had been available to almost everyone since 1918.

Gibraltar's position at the entrance to the Mediterranean had always made it a place of immense strategic importance, and the opening of the Suez Canal in 1869 increased its value to the Royal Navy. In 1905 the building of the vast Admiralty dockyard was completed, which proved to be of vital importance during the Great War when Gibraltar was in control of the Straits as an assembly point for convoys. When Charles and Pamela arrived, there would still have been much naval activity, but they could escape from the remnants of the war and the greyness of the dockyard by enjoying one of the secluded bays on the east side of the Rock; or they could take the steep path to the top and savour the breathtaking views: down and along to Spain in the west, and south across the Straits to Morocco, easily visible on a clear day. That is, as long as they did not experience the Levante, an easterly wind for which Gibraltar is notorious that can blow for weeks, bringing with it a depressing cloud which clothes everything in a grim dampness.

Where Charles and Pamela stayed is something of a mystery, for the first hotel in Gibraltar, the Rock Hotel, was not built until 1932. Perhaps they found a boarding house, for the locals would have been used to offering accommodation to wealthy travellers from northern Europe who were waiting for the next ship to carry them on the rest of their journey. However, the war had meant a distinct lack of travellers for pleasure in Gibraltar for the last four years, so the couple's custom, along with that of Pamela's maid whom she insisted on taking with her, would have been welcome. (The idea of her taking a servant with her even on her honeymoon became a source of hilarity in the family in later years.)

193

Their daughter Pammie believes that Pamela and Charles eventually went to Morocco. There were two ports easily accessible from Gibraltar where travellers to Morocco in 1919 could disembark, as now: Ceuta, which belonged to Spain, or Tangiers. But it would have been risky; Ivan was right when he wrote to the Duke. In July 1919 Moroccan nationalists had begun an insurrection against Spanish possessions in Morocco, which would have included Ceuta, and was the start of the Arab resistance movement. Then later that year there were rumblings in the area of Mellila, east of Ceuta, also Spanish, which erupted into the Rif War in 1920, lasting until 1926. As romantic and exotic as it was, Morocco was not, therefore, the ideal place for a honeymoon. And apart from the fighting, no guidebook existed for the country in 1919; although that may have added to the adventure, the roads – if they could be called that – were precarious.

Perhaps in the end they went to Algiers: Blanche had mentioned that as a possibility when she wrote to her sister, Dorothy, in November. After all, Pamela had a family connection with Algiers, as Lady Evelyn as a child had spent winters with her parents there: no doubt family friends still lived there, who would have welcomed Evelyn's daughter and son-in-law. But wherever it was they went, Pamela and Charles would have made the most of it.

While his youngest daughter was enjoying her honeymoon, John Cobbold was helping his daughter-in-law, Blanche, to find a suitable doctor to look after her when she gave birth to her and Ivan's first child, which was to be in May 1920. The Cobbolds' long-standing association with the East Suffolk and Ipswich Hospital gave John many useful contacts, and the family were particularly popular at that time because of their recent donations for the building of a new war memorial wing: John had donated £5000, his brother Philip £1000, and Evelyn and Ivan £500 each. Blanche was pleased to report to her mother that John had been able to recommend a particular doctor to help her, while Philip's wife Cicely had been 'awfully nice' and had also done some research.

Meanwhile the union of the Cavendishes with the Macmillans was getting nearer, and Blanche was still worried about her future brother-in-law, Harold. Writing to the Duchess on 15 December 1919, Blanche

194

recounted the visit of Harold's mother to 'Granny Evans'. Apparently Mrs Macmillan had read out to Granny Evans pages of letters from Harold and kept talking about him and their family. Granny complained that she was 'so boring & tiresome' that she did not bother to listen. It convinced Blanche even further that Harold, who was about to return from Canada and go into his family's publishing business, was unsuitable for Dorothy:

'I don't think he would suit Dorothy at all, I should like to see her with Mrs Macmillan. She sounds such a bore I'm sure Dorothy would fight with her at once.'

Pamela and Charles' honeymoon lasted until about March 1920, and when they returned they moved into Pickhurst Mead, where Charles had lovingly overseen the redecoration of their part of the house. Although Eric and Sybil lived in the lion's share of the mansion, they were usually in London during the week and so joined the young couple only at the weekend.

Pickhurst Mead was part of the Hayes Place Estate in the village of Hayes, near Bromley in north-west Kent. The area was beautiful with the benefit of two commons, Hayes and Keston, and open countryside all around. Charles' grandfather, Sir Everard Hambro, still owned the estate, which he had bought in 1880 when his sons Eric and Harold were eight and four respectively; his other three children, Angus, Violet and Olaf, were born there within the next five years. Everard himself lived in Hayes Place Hall, famous for having been, in the eighteenth century, the home of the statesman William Pitt the Elder, before he passed it to his son William Pitt the Younger; the latter became Chancellor of the Exchequer at the age of twenty-three and then Prime Minister. The imposing house even came with its own ghost, that of poor Miss Dehany, its owner after the Pitts from the mid-eighteenth to the early nineteenth century. She was engaged to be married to the 11th Earl of Caithness, Lt Col John Sinclair, but on the morning of their wedding, 8 April 1789, he was found dead from a gunshot wound in London, apparently having killed himself. When Miss Dehany died in 1832, still unmarried, she left the house to her dead fiancé's niece, a Miss Traill, from whose nephew Everard bought the house. Miss Dehany's portrait continued to hang above the staircase throughout the Hambros' occupation of the estate, and her presence continued to linger.

In 1882, two years after Everard moved in, the Mid Kent Railway line in Hayes was opened, providing a direct link with London. Not only did this make access to the Bank much easier for Everard, but overnight Hayes became 'the country', opening to Londoners an opportunity of spending their leisure time in the heart of the English countryside. The railway's advertising sold the attractions of Hayes, particularly the Commons and Keston Ponds, which it painted as being a passable substitute for the seaside. On a particular day in the early 1900s the number of passengers was said to exceed eleven thousand. However, when Pamela and Charles moved to Hayes in 1920, it was still a peaceful, if slightly busier, village, and had not yet become part of the conglomeration of Bromley just down the road.

Everard must have sold the attractions of Hayes to his brother-in-law, Martin Ridley Smith, also a banker, for in 1882 Martin bought a newly-built mansion in the village called The Warren, which sat in 6 acres of land, with landscaped gardens, lodge and stables. It may have been to make a new start after the death of his wife, Emily, in May that year, when his daughter, Sybil, was just eight. As relaxation from the pressures of high finance, Martin became well-known in horticultural circles around the world for his cultivation of a new species of carnation which he raised at The Warren; Sybil's brother, Nigel, followed suit, raising a yellow one which he named 'Cecilia' after their stepmother, whom Martin married in 1884. Spending much of her childhood at The Warren with her father, stepmother and siblings, Sybil knew the village of Hayes well, and became close to her first cousin Eric Hambro – a union almost certainly engineered by their fathers, who believed that family ties could only strengthen the bonds of business. Besides, there was much affection between Everard and Martin: they had been friends even before Everard married the sister of Martin's first wife, and they must have hoped that their children would further the family link. The mental impairment suffered by Eric and Sybil's youngest daughter, Juliet, has been suggested to have been caused by the close blood tie between the couple, but fortunately Charles, Richard and Zelia were apparently unaffected.

When Charles and Pamela moved into Pickhurst Mead, Everard

still treated Hayes as his main home, even though he had by then also owned Milton Abbey for some years. Pickhurst Mead itself was a much younger house than Hayes Place Hall, and replaced an older property that had once stood on the site which had been occupied in 1830 by Lady Clementina Hawarden, later one of the first women pioneers of photography.

After passing a Lodge at the entrance, a wide double-carriage drive wound through shrubbery which shielded Pickhurst Mead from the road, and led to the ivy-clad brick house with its mellow tiled roof. With three gables and tall chimneys reminiscent of Tudor times, Pickhurst Mead was dignified and attractive. Its size meant that having to share with her in-laws would not have been too burdensome for Pamela. There were six to seven 'entertaining rooms', including a drawing room measuring 31ft 6ins by 15ft 3ins and a dining room of 25ft 6ins by 19ft, with a large bay window. Also on the ground floor were a telephone room, library and study. Central heating – a very modern convenience – had been installed in several rooms. The electric generator, situated outside, apart from providing electric lighting enabled the Hambros to summon the servants by electric bells in each of the rooms.

On the first floor, reached by the principal staircase with its carved oak balusters and newels, was the Principal Suite. The main bedroom – probably for the use of Eric and Sybil – was an apartment stretching across the entire width of the house, measuring just over 32ft by 16ft, with wide bays at each end. This had a tiled fireplace and an ensuite bath-cum-dressing room and WC. A further seven bedrooms were on this floor, all good sizes. As Charles had talked in one of his letters about their having a bedroom each, he and Pamela probably had the two inter-connecting rooms, one 21ft 3ins by 19ft 6ins, and the other 17ft 9ins by 16ft 6ins, each with a fireplace and bookshelves. They would have had the use of the other bathroom on the floor, which had a radiator and a heated towel airer: another very mod con. A housemaid's closet with a 'wash-down' (a form of sink) and a WC was along the corridor, and above them the servants' accommodation, comprising another seven bedrooms, bathroom and WC.

A separate wing of the house contained such necessities as the kitchen, servants' hall and butler's pantry, along with dairy and wine cellars. Outside, the 13 acres which Pickhurst Mead occupied included a beautiful walled garden, with a lily pond and the rose beds whose glory Charles had described to Pamela in his letters; and there were terraced gardens and a wild garden, reached by a series of lawns and walks. Four heated glass houses stood in an acre of well-stocked kitchen garden; a gardener's cottage and other useful outbuildings were dotted around the yard and, to Pamela's satisfaction, a hard tennis court stood at the lower end of the garden. It was a glorious spot to begin their married life.

Fortunately, being on honeymoon the couple missed the outbreak in Hayes of diphtheria in January 1920, the respiratory disease which, according to the local *Bromley & District Times*, necessitated the postponement of concerts and various social functions. Although children up to their mid-teens were the main victims, it was highly contagious generally, and a vaccine would not be available until 1926.

There was much to get involved with in the village, and Everard, who had taken an active part in village life ever since he arrived, would have expected his grandson and new wife to keep the side up. Since 1895 Everard had been the first chairman of Hayes Parish Council; he was a Justice of the Peace, and he was very supportive of the local church, St Mary's, donating three bells in 1886.

When Pamela was introduced to the village, she would have been moved by the Hambro family memorial, which still stands in its churchyard, the elaborately carved wall erected by Everard in 1905 when his beloved wife, Gertrude Mary, died. Her tomb reads, *'Absent from the body to be present with the Lord'*. Near her lie the graves of the two children whom she and Everard lost before Eric was born: eight-year-old Hermione Cecilia in 1878, and six-month-old Maurice Christian in 1875. At the foot of the wall lie other Hambro graves. Charles' older sister, Hermione Sybil, his parents' first-born child, is there, just seven months old when she died in March 1897, with the simple inscription *'Thy Will be done'*; his youngest sister, Juliet Carin Hambro, would be buried in the Hambro plot in 1992. Some of Sybil's mother's family, the Stuarts – descendants of the first Marquess of Bute – are buried there too, including her aunt, Octavia Henrietta Mary Stuart, who died unmarried in 1940.

Pamela may have been shocked too by the brevity of the lives of so many Hambro wives compared with their men, which bizarrely seems to have been a recurring feature throughout the generations. None of the women's deaths was apparently associated with childbirth – throughout history a common cause of death – yet in almost every case the wife died first, despite the family having access to all the medical expertise money could buy. Amongst the graves, Pamela would have seen that of Charles' aunt, Rosamund Maud Hambro, wife of his uncle Angus, Everard's youngest son and one of Britain's leading amateur golfers of the day. Rosamund died in January 1914 aged twenty-nine, of tuberculosis. She left three young children, the youngest of whom, Michael, was just three months old. Michael is buried with her, having died the month before his third birthday in September 1916.

The Hambro men, all being sporty, helped to maintain the tradition of many English villages which helped to bind communities together. Everard was a keen member of the local Bromley and Bickley Golf Club, and its President for many years. Pamela may have joined, as she enjoyed the game, although Charles hated her playing it: he thought it ruined her hands, and would rather she used them for playing the piano. But the game with which the family was most associated in Hayes was that quintessentially English of all sports, cricket. With his own background in it, Charles could not resist getting involved with the Hayes Cricket Club, one of the oldest in Kent, thus also following in the footsteps of his father and uncles.

The history of the Club, written in 1978 to commemorate its 150th anniversary, names all four of Everard's sons as having played cricket for the Club when Charles was still a baby, although it is the skills of his uncles, Angus – not just an accomplished golfer – and Harold, which are mentioned most often. The twenty-one-year-old Harold, for instance, had a 'great season' in 1897, when 'he returned some sensational figures', and managed to top even that when the next year he 'produced the finest bowling performance by a Hayes bowler'. Both brothers were described as 'fine all rounders who returned many fine performances, although not playing regularly'. Every now and then they would be graced with the presence of really major players like local boy Maurice Bonham Carter, later a leading Liberal peer under Asquith, who gained his Oxford Blue in cricket in 1902 and played for Kent.

The Hambro brothers were often joined in the team by their friends, two of the sons of Martin Ridley Smith who, like the Hambros, were keen and talented players and strong supporters of the Club. One of the sons, confusingly also called Everard, fell in love with the rather plain Violet Hambro, much to their fathers' delight, and their marriage in July 1906 was a major event in the village, as it saw the uniting of its best-known families from two of the 'big houses'. It was, incredibly, yet another familial bond between the Hambros and the Smiths. Led by Angus, Violet's proud big brother, a team of forty volunteers spent several days beforehand decorating the whole village with poles and arches adorned with flags, bunting and flowers. For her lavish church wedding, Violet had nine bridesmaids, and then walked along a lane strewn with flowers to an open carriage. The reception was held at Hayes Place, where in the evening the grounds, illuminated by fairy lights, were open to the public, and the day ended with a magnificent firework display for all to enjoy.

But life in an English village at the turn of the twentieth century was not always the golden idyll that is often portrayed, certainly not for the ordinary person. The popular picture of Edwardian life before the Great War, of a countryside of milk, honey and sweeping lawns, was very much for the likes of the Hambros and the Smiths and the landed gentry of the time. However, nationally wages were poor and poverty rife, especially in the countryside. The shadow of the workhouse still cast its gloom over the average family, who were afraid that the ill health or death of its breadwinner may see them ending their days there. The pre-war class system was still rigid, although since the 1890s there had been more opportunities for the emerging middle classes to start businesses, so that social movement was becoming easier. Of course the Hambros and the Smiths were themselves trade, albeit long-established, and perhaps it was this that distinguished the families from the aristocrats of the time. Nothing had 'landed' on their laps: they had worked for it, and therefore they had no problem in sharing with others less fortunate, whether by financial benevolence or by contributing their time to village activities. Contemporary accounts demonstrated the popularity of the two families in the village.

Although many games of cricket were played on Hayes Club cricket ground, and were the ideal opportunity to bring together all the villagers, the Edwardian era was also the period of country house cricket, where the wealthy often had their own pitches in their grounds and invited friends to spend the weekends, the men playing and the ladies sometimes watching but otherwise finding other ways to amuse themselves. Everard Hambro had his own cricket pitch at Hayes Place, and the Smiths may have had their own at The Warren. Another wealthy house owner at Hayes let the village team host a match every August Bank Holiday on his estate, Ballards. Although there is no record that Everard opened his gates for community cricket, he made up for it by providing employment on his estate, often from one generation to the next. Frank Keech, a stalwart of the Hayes Cricket Club, for example, worked on the Hayes Estate for many years, as had his father. There were also many farms in and around the village providing employment, so Hayes was actually better off than many other villages of the time.

During the Great War, families in Hayes, as in other Kent villages, had contributed in their own ways to the war effort. Martin and Cecilia Ridley Smith opened up The Warren as a VAD hospital from October 1914 to May 1916. When Charles and Pamela moved to Hayes in 1920, like so many villages it was still recovering from the war. It had lost some of its men, while those who returned found there was little work. Owners of some of the other large houses, whose fortunes had been affected by the war, had sold up. Even the Cricket Club needed a rebirth: the pavilion had been dismantled during the war and the ground used for farming, and in 1919 it was still being grazed by the farmer's cows. But the villagers rallied round, and with help from some of the local wealthy families, the Club was resurrected.

On 21 April 1920, not long after Pamela and Charles had moved into Pickhurst Mead, Dorothy's marriage to Harold Macmillan took place, despite Blanche's misgivings. As fond as Blanche was of her sister, she must have been jealous of the fact that, not only did their father come back from Canada to give Dorothy away when he had not been there for her, but this time royalty was attending the wedding in person, rather than just sending a present. Queen Alexandra, widow of King Edward VII, attended the service at St Margaret's, Westminster, with her children,

Princess Victoria and Prince Albert, and the siblings of her late husband: Princess Christian, the Duke of Connaught and the Duchess of Albany.

Ivan, as Dorothy's brother-in-law, was an usher, and Pamela sent a porcelain bowl as a present. She is not mentioned as a guest in *The Times* report, although it seems to list mostly the titled guests, of which there were many; however, considering the Cobbolds' relationship with the Cavendishes and the occasions Pamela had met Dorothy, it is very likely the Duke and Duchess would have invited her and Charles. The reception was held in Lansdowne House, at that stage still the London home of the Duchess' family, as Blanche and Ivan's had been.

Blanche's view that Harold was an odd choice for Dorothy would sadly prove right. Bookish, still affected by his war wounds and lacking in self-confidence, Harold would later find he was the opposite to the outgoing Dorothy. His lack of experience with women made him frightened of them. But in 1920 the Macmillans started married life as a happy young couple, as the Hambros had done a few months earlier. Both husbands naturally were expected to support their wives, regardless of the means of their respective fathers-in-law. That year, having finished in his post as the Duke of Devonshire's ADC, and well before his career in politics started, Harold joined his family's eponymous publishing firm as junior partner. When he had asked the Duke for Dorothy's hand in marriage, the Duke – with Blanche's husband in mind – had apparently replied, 'God, trade again – but I suppose books are better than beer!'

As for Charles, now that his honeymoon was over, he too was starting with his family's firm, C J Hambro & Son. However, it came as rather a shock to him and Pamela, just as they were settling in to their first home together, to find that their financial situation was not quite as secure as they had thought.

Chapter 15

Bright New World

In May 1920, seven months after her wedding, Pamela fell pregnant. She was twenty, Charles twenty-two. They had only just settled into Pickhurst Mead but, unusually for her, she was doing what was expected for those times: if you were young and healthy you got on with having children as soon as the ink was dry on the marriage certificate. If you did not, people wondered what was wrong. Her mother had done it, producing Winifred in slightly less time than necessary; her sister-in-law Blanche had done it in under a year, giving birth to Pamela Maud Cobbold on 1 March 1920; generations of Hambro wives had got on with it impressively quickly. Only Winifred managed to avoid childbirth for three years before having Toby.

On the other hand, it was difficult *not* to get pregnant at that time. The British Medical Association opposed the provision of information on childbirth even to married women, and would continue to do so until 1930; and old-fashioned GPs were still known to lecture young wives on their duty to populate the Empire, refusing to advise them on contraception. Couples did practise birth control but it was largely of the unreliable kind: mostly withdrawal and the 'safe period'. Rubber sheaths, known as 'male appliances', had been available since the late nineteenth century but were largely used in the context of extramarital sex, particularly where prostitutes were involved.

There was, however, a glimmer of hope in the form of Marie Stopes, the birth control pioneer. Her book *Married Love* had been published in 1918 and was a sell-out, followed the same year by her guide to contraception, *Wise Parenthood*, in which she explained the application of rubber caps and soluble quinine pessaries by women. The Establishment had responded predictably: the Catholic Church was outraged, *The Times* and *The Morning Post* refused to accept advertisements for a meeting she had organised in London in 1921 to promote birth control, and two of her supporters would be prosecuted for obscenity in 1923 for giving out pamphlets on the subject. Nevertheless, she managed to open her first voluntary birth control clinic in 1921, with twenty operating by the end of the decade, although the subject would remain a very volatile one to Church and State for years to come.

The last baby at Pickhurst Mead had been Charles' sister, Juliet, born in 1915. Whilst the Hambro's nursery equipment would still have been in the house, it was expected that, like most young mothers-to-be, Pamela would want to start afresh – and anyway, Sir Eric did not want to be seen stinting on the needs of his daughter-in-law and first grandchild. He promised to buy the couple everything new and to have the nursery re-furbished. But he had overestimated his financial position. Things were not looking good.

For the war years had not been kind to the merchant banks, and C J Hambro & Son was no exception in still feeling the pinch in the aftermath. A world war lasting four years could not have happened without leaving its mark, not just on the domestic front in terms of jobs and people's expectations, but further afield. The traditional role of the merchant banks was to finance the international movement of goods, but suddenly in 1914 the old trading network had disintegrated because former contacts were found to be in enemy territory and lines of trust were broken. The main requirements during 1914-1918 were essential food and materials for the war, and these came to dominate the dwindling volume of trade, so merchant bankers had to adapt their operations. Alternative contacts had to be made and new credit facilities arranged. The political instability of the war had made the Stock Exchange nervous, and C J Hambro & Son's existing investments became heavily depreciated: the total value of the Bank's portfolio dropped by 33%.

A major headache was the number of loans the merchant banks had made to countries that had become enemies: nearly £600,000 was owed to C J Hambro & Son by Germany and Austria. Fortunately, just after the beginning of the war, the Bank's partners – Everard and three of his sons, Eric, Olaf and Harold – had wisely established a guarantee fund of £250,000 in anticipation of losses they feared may occur. That – and their long-established relationship with Scandinavia, largely through Eric – gave C J Hambro & Son another advantage over some other family-run banks and helped to minimise losses. Eric's negotiations with Sweden in 1915 as part of the Swedish delegation, which had earned him his knighthood in 1919, had led to C J Hambro & Son being instructed in January 1916 to act as agent for the British Government in the purchase of a serious amount of Norwegian Krone. The amounts involved meant the operation was tricky and had to be done secretively over a period of time to avoid alerting the Germans. In June 1916 C J Hambro & Son was authorised, along with the British Bank of Northern Commerce Ltd (BBNC), to negotiate the loan with various Scandinavian banks, giving the British Government the option to repay the money in either gold or currency.

The BBNC was already known to the Hambros, owning shares in C J Hambro & Son. A recently-established Scandinavian-orientated bank based in London, one of its founders was Knut Wallenberg. One of the most powerful men in Sweden and its minister for foreign affairs during the war, Knut was also a friend of Sir Everard Hambro, which undoubtedly helped Eric's dealings with the BBNC. Eric Hambro described Knut as 'a very splendid type of man with a head very like a mixture of father's and Natty Rothschild's'. The two Banks worked successfully together, which would lead to a significant event in the Hambros' history. But they were still very lean years as far as the Bank's profits were concerned, despite the success of C J Hambro & Son in acting as agent for the British Government during those difficult war years, which had kept the wolf from the door.

Although all the partners had to adjust their lifestyles radically, Eric was the worst hit. Despite having received a share of the profits since becoming a partner fifteen years earlier, his capital on New Year's Eve 1914 was just £12. But then, Eric did like to spend. Apart from being generous to his wife, and spending money on tiger hunting, he liked to spend money on his favourite sport, golf. An excellent player, he had represented Cambridge University and been lauded in the USA as a strong player, and he enjoyed control of the Royal Ashdown Forest golf course. And, crucially, he liked to gamble, particularly enjoying roulette. Unfortunately he was not very good. Mindful of having four children to support, he had found himself in the embarrassing situation of having to ask his father for money. In 1920 Eric realised he should warn his lately-married son not to be too profligate about his own finances because he would be unable to help him out. In a letter sent some time after May that year, from his London residence, Norwich House off Park Lane, he said:

'My dear Charles

'Things are going to be very difficult this year & you will have to be most economical, house books will have to be kept as low as possible i.e. entertaining people to stay etc. kept as little as possible. After I have paid for your nursery equipment I really can't do anything more, and if you require more you must take it out of your spare rooms.

'Times may not be as bad as they look but we must all be prepared: I must remind you that your income is bigger than Uncle Angus's & he manages to keep Hill House, a house in London & a boy at school plus a nursery & governess.

'I have to cut down here: Dick [Charles' brother] at Cambridge is but an economy: and I have to keep this house up, as an advertisement for the Bank, as a place to entertain important clients. Excuse this letter: I hate to write it: you know if I could I would do all I possibly could for you.

'Your loving

'Pa.'

Norwich House from where he wrote was in the prestigious area of Mayfair, in what is now called Dunraven Street. Certainly a London address would have been a necessity for a partner of C J Hambro & Son; he must not appear the poor relation when compared with the likes of the Rothschilds or any other of their rivals. The Georgian-style house was built between 1913 and 1916 and was large even for that area, with several storeys and six bay windows. The owners chose not to live in it, allowing it to be used as a military hospital in 1917. Eric had moved there in 1920 just before he wrote to Charles, and would occupy it – probably renting rather than buying – until 1926. Charles' uncle Angus, while not busy playing golf at home and abroad for the British amateur team, was at that time pursuing a parliamentary career, so his income, although respectable, would have been less than Charles' at C J Hambro & Son. Eric was clearly at pains to try to justify what he feared may otherwise have seemed to his son a sign of meanness on his part, and he would have hated that.

His father's situation must have greatly concerned Charles. It was not that he had been expecting too much from his father, but he must have been worried that it would adversely affect them, particularly as he and Pamela were expecting their first child. So when the BBNC approached C J Hambro & Son in the summer of 1920 to see if it would be interested in merging, it was seen as a golden opportunity to get the finances of the long-running and previously independent Hambro family bank back on track. The Hambros knew from the accounts of the BBNC that it was a very efficient organisation, with a modern accounting system, good management and an excellent growth record: by 1920, just eight years after it had started, its balance sheet had reached nearly the same figure as C J Hambro & Son. Also should the Banks merge, the Hambros would have the security of being part of a limited liability company, rather than a partnership where each partner was liable for any losses; in the war years it was Everard who paternalistically shouldered most of the financial burden himself but losses were there to be borne by all of them. The merger was also advantageous to the Wallenbergs, because they wanted the BBNC to be seen as a British bank: its capital was mainly foreign, with only 13% from England, and only by enlarging its British interest could it achieve this. And there was the big advantage that the main players in both families already knew and respected each other.

It was this proposed merger about which Eric wrote to Charles one Tuesday in that summer of 1920, from Gannochy:

'My dear Charles

'I told Dick to write to you about the grouse in order to give him something to do. I thought Grampy was going to Rannoch and would give you all the news about the merging. I think it is a good thing for many reasons. We live in difficult times. Competition is so great and while we undoubtedly had a big business in order to maintain it we were taking accounts which others were refusing and in many cases cutting corners. Now we have joined up with a good money making concern which made larger profits than we did and which managed by Hambros ought to make big money. As regards yourself, your present position will remain, that is to say you will receive the £500 a year plus the extra £1000 you get from me. As you get on you will be made say in over the year a Managing Director the same as Olaf & H.C.H [Harold], so much a year and a share of profits but definitely arranged. If we had remained as we are, you would in a year have been made a partner, 1% as we all started = about £1000 a year. When Grampy goes I shall step into his shoes and you into mine. I am going home next week and shall I but find that the accountants have brought the accounts up to date, HCH is then looking after it: I refused to let my holiday be tampered with.

'Glad to hear Pam is keeping well, give her my best. I shall attend to your grouse.

'Your loving Pa.'

Clearly, as a result of the change to a company, Charles could no longer be a partner, but greater things were on the horizon for him as a result: ultimately more money, less personal risk and the chance of becoming a director of Hambros Bank. The merger would also bring him and Pamela into close contact with the man who would later have an unforeseen effect on their story: Knut Wallenberg's nephew, Marcus, the scion of that Swedish dynasty.

Meanwhile Pamela coped, probably not always graciously, with the physical confines of pregnancy, reluctantly curbing her desire to play tennis and golf and putting on hold her hunting pursuits. She read widely and acquired interesting friends and acquaintances, which would not have been difficult for she was very good fun. Amongst her acquaintances were Wilfrid Meynell and his literary family. A Roman Catholic convert despite being born into a well-known Quaker family, Meynell was a publisher, writer and literary agent who discovered, amongst others, the poet Francis Thompson. His wife, Alice, was a significant writer, critic and suffragist, now remembered largely as a poet. The Meynells had a wide circle of famous literary friends, including W B Yeats and G K Chesterton, and of their nine children two of them – Viola and Francis – respectively became a writer and a publisher. Although they lived mostly in London, the Meynells also had a house in Greatham, near Pulborough in Sussex, where an artists' colony had been founded. There they met D H Lawrence who rented a room in their house for a while during the war with his German wife, Frieda; Viola was an early supporter of Lawrence.

Pamela clearly made an impression on Wilfrid. In March 1925, three years after Alice's death from depression and migraine, he wrote to her at Pickhurst Mead from Greatham, after she had been to see him:

'My dear Mrs Hambro

'I really must send you a line of thanks for the pleasure your visit gave us – & especially gave me. At my age I *must* be a better judge than the best of these young 'uns; & when I see the exact right thing, great indeed is my delight.

'As you live in Pitts house, I am sending to you, for your idlest moment, some doggerel I have just soothed my toothache by setting down – as a sort of skit...

'Again blessing you for the picture you have left in the gallery of my mind.

'I am your faithful

'Wilfrid Meynell.'

The poem he had written was based on clever puns about Lord Chatham – one of William Pitt's titles – and was amongst the few personal letters she kept.

Amongst the other friends she and Charles had in Kent were the Cazalets, whom the Hambros had known for a couple of generations. Naturally they were another wealthy family, whose fortune had been made in Russia. Their home was Fairlawne, a 3,000-acre estate standing partly in the village of Shipbourne, partly in Plaxtol, near Tonbridge and not far from Hayes. There were four children of Pamela and Charles' generation: Edward, who had been killed in action in France in 1916, aged twenty-two; Victor, who had been at Eton with Charles and Ivan; Thelma, the feminist and Conservative MP; and Peter, the youngest. They were related to the Murrays: their mother, Maud Lucia Cazalet, was the lady chosen by Evelyn to present Winifred to Court.

Thelma and Victor had both attended Pamela and Charles' wedding. Victor was an army captain, then aged twenty-three, and like Charles had been awarded the Military Cross. In 1924 he became

Conservative MP for Chippenham, which he remained for twenty years, and during the Second World War would be appointed as the British Military Liaison Officer to the Polish wartime leader, General Sikorski. Nobody could foresee, in those peaceful interwar years, that in 1943 he would be killed with his Polish boss when their converted RAF Liberator bomber crashed into the sea seconds after taking off from Gibraltar. It would be the subject of conspiracy theories for many years to come.

Their youngest sibling Peter, aged twelve at the time of the wedding, was not invited but was a likeable lad of whom Pamela was very fond. Fairlawne was already known throughout the racing world for its stables, and Peter had a natural affinity with horses. Neither he nor Pamela would have dreamt when she visited Fairlawne in 1920, longing for the day when she could take up riding again after her pregnancy, that thirteen-year-old Peter would later achieve worldwide fame as the Queen Mother's horse trainer, securing around two hundred and fifty winners for her from 1949 until his death in 1973. His brother Victor moved to nearby Cranborne, buying an estate called Great Swifts, easily accessible for a visit by Pamela and Charles, on the infrequent occasions when Victor was at home.[1]

Pamela and Charles' other friends in the locality included the Astors of Hever Castle at Edenbridge. The owner, since 1919, was the public-spirited John Jacob Astor, then MP for Dover, the youngest son of the American millionaire William Waldorf Astor and his wife, Mary. John had been brought up at his father's other English estate, Clivedon, and when William died in 1919 John inherited at the age of thirty-three the magnificent castle, former home to Anne Boleyn. William's death was the second time that decade that the Astor family had been touched by sadness. In April 1912 William's cousin, his son's namesake, Colonel John Jacob Astor, had died on the *Titanic*, although miraculously his pregnant wife survived. John moved into Hever with his wife, previously Violet Petty-Fitzmaurice, whose first husband had been Blanche's uncle, a brother of the Duchess Evie, killed in action in the Great War.

Angy of course was still on the scene. Pamela had the chance to see her properly for the first time since returning from honeymoon in

[1] A willing visitor to a cottage on Victor's estate was the film star Elizabeth Taylor to whom Victor was made a godfather on her birth in 1932.

May 1920, when she was invited to a Tollemache family christening in Knightsbridge, that of Angy's nephew, son of her sister, Cynthia. Angy would probably have stayed with Pamela and Charles in Kent, and she and Pamela would have enjoyed time out in London too. Charles' work meant he was in London during the week at the Bank's headquarters in Old Broad Street in the City, and so he would usually stay in Norwich House, where Pamela would sometimes join him.

London was an interesting place in the 1920s. By then, the old social system that had given precedence to landed wealth and ancient alliances was breaking down. After the restrictions of the war the decade also saw the increased freedom of women, both politically and in terms of employment, the introduction of the exciting sounds of jazz recently imported from America, cocktails, smoking, short dresses and daring dances like the Charleston. During the 1920s there emerged a group of mostly, but by no means exclusively, aristocratic, confident, often university-educated young men and women, who delighted in decadence, throwing wild parties at the new London nightclubs, and flaunting their sexuality, particularly the men: it has been said that no other English youth movement has ever contained such a high proportion of homosexuals, or – in an age when homosexuality was still illegal – been so indulgent of their behaviour. Cosmopolitan and sophisticated, they initiated styles and fads, and provided rich pickings for the social magazines and increasing newspaper gossip columnists. They became known as the 'Bright Young People' (BYP).

Shocked by losing many of their generation to the war, some of the aristocratic BYP also found their family's money had been diminished by taxation and other political changes, so their inheritance was threatened. Those who had relied on anticipated inheritance found they would have to earn some sort of a living after all. As a result, the BYP reacted against the pre-war expectations and behaviour of their class, developing their own code of social conduct. A kind of 'smart bohemia' formed, which was open to both the avant-garde artist and the peer's son or daughter.

Some of these BYP, shortly to be immortalised in novels like Evelyn Waugh's *Vile Bodies*, were complete wastrels, drinking or drugging away what was left of their inheritances; others were writers and artists underneath whose flamboyance or eccentricity lay real talent. This latter group included Cecil Beaton, who became a noted photographer; the homosexual writer Beverley Nichols, a former high-profile President of the Oxford Union and author of *Cry Havoc*, a much-read indictment of war which called for world-wide disarmament; the Honourable Nancy Mitford, eldest of the Mitford clan, writer and coiner of the term 'U' and 'Non-U' to describe language which was acceptable and what was, in modern terms, 'naff'; and Evelyn Waugh himself. By the end of the decade the two leading lights of the BYP were considered to be Nancy Mitford's sister, the noted beauty Diana, and her first husband, Bryan Guinness, heir to the brewing dynasty – before she divorced him for Oswald Mosley. Bryan, however, was appalled to be linked with such a juvenile group whom he considered to be sensation-mongers. As the decade went on, Pamela was often seen at the same social functions as Nancy and Diana who, with two of their sisters, Jessica and Unity, were often in the newspapers for one reason or another, much to the concern of their parents, Lord and Lady Redesdale.

As bizarre and attention-seeking as the behaviour of some of the BYP often was, the changes in society that they epitomised provided a golden opportunity for talent from non-aristocratic circles to mix with those who still were part of that gilded group, and to become trend-setters of the post-war era. Evelyn Waugh, for example, was middle class, being the son of a publisher, and Cecil Beaton's father worked in the timber business. Beaton made no bones about wanting to be accepted by 'smart' society and worked very hard to get invited to all the right parties.

Charles and Pamela, apart from being a fraction too old to be part of the BYP – Charles by about five or six years, Pamela by about three – also lacked other attributes to be part of the group, although they would not have sought to be part of it. Whilst not absolutely necessary, neither Pamela nor Charles had a title, nor an expectation of one, even though Pamela had aristocratic blood through her mother; and as far as inherited wealth was concerned, although Charles would inherit from Eric, he was still expected to earn his living, while Pamela knew she would lose out to Ivan on their father's death. This lack of expectation gave Charles and Pamela a certain protection that many of the BYP did not have, as did the sense of purpose that Charles possessed, knowing where he was going career-wise. The only characteristic they probably regretted not sharing with the BYP was a university education, which a significant number of BYP, particularly the men, enjoyed: thanks to the outbreak of war at just the wrong time for Charles, he had lost that opportunity from which his father and grandfather had benefited, whilst for Pamela it had never been part of her parents' plans. Also, although they liked to have fun, and Pamela particularly enjoyed high jinxes, they did not possess the wild party animal instinct that characterised so many of the BYP, even though they undoubtedly enjoyed some of the new nightclubs that had opened in the Capital, and may have been invited to some of the headline-grabbing parties. For despite not being part of the BYP themselves, Pamela and Charles did have connections with them. Victor Cazalet was a good friend of Beverley Nichols, sharing his political persuasion, and when Victor became a Conservative MP in 1924, they shared the same social stomping ground in Mayfair. One particularly prominent BYP with whom Charles and Pamela were acquainted was the Hon Patrick Balfour, later Lord Kinross, whose uncle, Harry Balfour, had been best man at Winifred and Algernon's wedding. An Oxford-educated historian, Patrick was a significant social commentator of the time. He was 'Mr Gossip' for the *Daily Sketch* in whose columns Pamela or someone in her family often appeared, he wrote many books about Islam and was known to be homosexual: he did try marriage once, but it ended in divorce without children.

One of the best known of the BYP was the Hon Stephen Tennant, of whose family Pamela and Charles knew at least one member. Stephen's older brother, Christopher Grey Tennant, had attended Charles and Pamela's wedding. Sadly, their elder brother, Edward, had been killed in France in 1916, aged nineteen. The Tennants were descendants of an eminent nineteenth-century Scots chemist and industrialist. In November 1920, on the death of their father who had been made a Baron and was the first Lord Glenconner, Christopher inherited the title. The two brothers could not have been more different. Stephen, born in 1906, was so precious and highly-strung that he sometimes went to bed for months at a time. His eccentric lifestyle and extreme show of his homosexuality, with his golden finger curls, extravagant makeup and jewellery, was said to have made him the model for Sebastian Flyte in Evelyn Waugh's

Brideshead Revisited and for other fictional characters.

Apparently achieving little of note other than having a well-documented affair with the war poet Siegfried Sassoon, Stephen turned doing nothing into an art form, with wit and elegance. Christopher, however, took his responsibilities as Lord Glenconner seriously, to the extent that Charles considered him sufficiently suitable to propose him as a director of Hambros Bank, which he became in 1931. Christopher's son the Hon Colin Tennant, born in 1926, would, like his uncle Stephen, also embrace flamboyance, later buying Mustique; there, as the 3rd Lord Glenconner, he would throw wild parties and famously entertained Princess Margaret. Colin later married a cousin of Pamela's, one of the Coke family. In the 1990s his granddaughter Stella Tennant would continue the aesthetic bent of Stephen, albeit much less eccentrically, by becoming one of the 'super-models' of the decade.

There would also be a connection between the Hambros and Cecil Beaton himself. In 1934 his favourite of his two sisters, Barbara, known as 'Baba' – photographs of whom had helped launch Beaton's career – married Charles' cousin Alec Hambro, son of his uncle Angus. Ever the social climber, Beaton had always dreamed of Baba and their other sister, Nancy, marrying title. In Baba's case, Beaton had to be content with the fact that she married into a well-known, wealthy family, albeit for too short a time: in 1943 Alec would die of war wounds at Tripoli, leaving Baba with two young children.

Pamela's view of some of the BYP, with their posturing and antics, would have been that of contempt, although she shared with some of their most brilliant a lively mind and a sharp wit. As long as she could escape from the metropolis back to the country before her dread of closed doors and windows engulfed her, she may even have enjoyed herself in London in the 1920s. Wealthy young people like she and Charles could be entertained at clubs like The Gargoyle, The Bat or The Night Light, or at out-of-the-way places that opened almost all night, like The Windmill in Great Windmill Street, where it was possible to eat bacon and eggs until dawn, provided by a butler-like person in a tailcoat. And there was always the elegant Café Royal in Regent Street or the Restaurant de la Tour Eiffel in Percy Street.

Meanwhile, during the summer of 1920 Charles and the Hambros were busy with preparations for the merger with the BBNC, which took place officially on 31 October, when the new bank, Hambros Bank of Northern Commerce Ltd was born. To the Hambros the opening meant a complete break with the past, turning one of the great merchant banking houses into limited liability form. The event was a huge and, for the Hambros, emotional event, at which King Christian X of Denmark, monarch of their ancestral homeland, was the guest of honour, and after which parties were held to celebrate the union, not only of the Banks but also of the two families and their new roles. Psychologically the Hambros dominated: Sir Everard was Chairman, his eldest son, Sir Eric, a Vice-Chairman jointly with the former Chairman of the BBNC. Eric's brothers Harry and Olaf were managing directors, along with the former general manager of the BBNC, Gerard d'Abo. Ten months later the Bank's name was shortened to Hambros Bank Ltd, and although it continued for a while to operate from the separate premises of the two previous banks, in 1926 it opened new and elegant premises at 41 Bishopsgate, where it remained until 1988.

While Pamela and Charles' financial future now seemed more secure, and they could look forward to his burgeoning career and their first child, life was not so good in the Cobbold camp. Pamela's parents had grown further apart, her father was depressed and her uncle Ralph seemed to have bothered their friend and Ivan's father-in-law, the Duke of Devonshire. Adding to that the rumblings of post-war discontent that sounded in the country generally, the skies looked grey.

Chapter 16

Discontent at Home and Away

In August 1920 a friend of the Cavendishes wrote to the Duchess of Devonshire saying he had been to stay with Blanche and Ivan at their house in Milden, Suffolk. He praised Blanche for being 'splendid' with the Cobbold family, and for keeping 'old Mr Cobbold' amused. John certainly needed a bit of cheering up. With Pamela, his favourite daughter who had played that role, now married, and with no more children at home he was left to contemplate the rest of his life with Lady Evelyn. It was no longer an edifying prospect. Much to their regret, even if their family was not surprised, they had drifted apart over the years. They are both thought to have had lovers – on Evelyn's part, Pamela's godfather, Bromo – but although the acquisition of a lover may have been common amongst the upper classes, the union of Evelyn and John had been a love match, even if John's money had been part of the initial attraction.

Adultery was more likely a symptom rather than the cause of their estrangement. As happy as Evelyn and John had seemed to be in the early years, there had always been signs that she could never have been entirely content with life in England. Significantly, in 1889, two years before they married, Evelyn had written a poem in Cairo anticipating her leaving Egypt. Although she was a young woman who should have been looking forward to life with her husband-to-be, it demonstrates a love of Islam and a longing for the world she was leaving behind. In her poem she stands on the roof of her home at night and surveys the city sleeping beneath her, saying a prayer:

To Him, the One, the Essence of all

And I felt His Presence within and around.
Divine, soul-enhancing His Love I Found.

She writes of the 'vague longings that filled my soul' and recalls 'the weird cadence of the Mueddin's cry' which calls the faithful to prayer. It is a haunting piece.

When Evelyn came to England to live in Ipswich with John after their marriage, her family had returned to the Dunmore estate in Scotland, which she also loved and missed. It was not as though she was not made to feel welcome by the people of Ipswich. As the Cobbolds had played a prominent part in the life of Ipswich, and Suffolk generally, for a good hundred and fifty years by the time the couple married, due respect was paid to John's wife, and at least one road, Murray Road, was named after her, still there today in a residential area. But their regard was never quite reciprocated: Evelyn's snobbery always got in the way. Perhaps she chose to overlook the fact that, despite her aristocratic ancestry, her father had been bankrupted, his wealth much diminished. Evelyn's husband was richer than her father had been when he died, although if a comparison were made between the Cobbolds and her mother's family, the Cokes of Holkham, the result would have been less favourable.

As John had told the Duchess of Devonshire at the time of Pamela's marriage, he intended to return to the roving life after Pamela married; after all, his wife had done her fair share in the last few years, including more travelling in the Near East. Evelyn went to Egypt every winter and in February 1915 met T E Lawrence again, by then an Intelligence officer in Cairo, when he wrote to his mother that he was having dinner with her.

While his wife was away adventuring, John had been left at home at the outbreak of the war to cope as Mayor of Ipswich at one of the town's most difficult times, as well as overseeing the running of the brewery and the family's other business concerns with the problems of reduced staff. Of course Evelyn had played her part in the war effort, but by 1920 there was not much to keep her at home. Whilst she enjoyed the company of intelligent children, the prospect of two new babies – Pamela Maud, Ivan and Blanche's child, and Pamela's, due in February 1921 – was not enough to quell her wanderlust. She spent as much time as possible either in Scotland or in London, taking her grandson, Toby, with her wherever she went. Later, when he reached thirteen in 1929, he would be sent to the recently-opened public boarding school, Stowe in Buckinghamshire: a departure from Eton, the Cobbolds' traditional choice, because Eton was situated on the River Thames which Evelyn thought would aggravate Toby's asthma.

Certainly by 1920 Evelyn's husband was not a sufficiently exciting prospect, a fact of which he was all too aware. To add to John's marital woes, he was rather embarrassed by his brother, Ralph, who had tried to buy Devonshire House from Victor Cavendish, apparently on behalf of a third party, and was now attempting to buy one of the Duke's other family properties in Eastbourne, Sussex. Eastbourne's development as a seaside resort in the nineteenth century had been largely due to the 7th Duke, and the Cavendishes still owned part of the town. On 3 December 1920 one C G Hamilton, a private secretary to Victor Cavendish, wrote to him in Canada from 30 Lower Sloane Street, London, saying:

'I am sorry you have been troubled by Ralph Cobbold. I know him well – he is quite impecunious & unreliable & always on the prowl for a commission. I don't believe for a moment that his principals who were G Clare & Co even had £800,000 at their bank & were prepared to buy DH [Devonshire House] out & out – what they wanted was an option so they would have time to hawk DH about in the market... R.C. now wants an option on Eastbourne.'

It seems that prior to the sale of Devonshire House, Ralph – clearly taking a break from his travels, and having the Cobbolds' banking credentials to his credit – had been tasked by his employer, the bank G Clare and Co, to enquire about its purchase. Now here he was again, seeking an option from the Duke on his property in Eastbourne – probably relying on the Cobbold/Cavendish family connection. Ralph may have been acting on behalf of a third party rather than himself, but one thing John would not want to do would be to antagonise his son's father-in-law; and he himself enjoyed an amicable relationship with the Duke and Duchess, which he did not want to spoil. Mr Hamilton also presented a gloomy picture to the Duke of the economic situation in Britain generally:

'Things in the City are bad. Trade is very bad & there are bound to be big failures. Manufacturers can't sell at a profit & most are afraid to realise their losses. I don't see how any landowner can live on his income from land.'

Having already sold some of his assets, Victor Cavendish was already all too aware of the poor time Britain and Ireland – where he also owned property – were having in 1920, with the effects of the war really taking hold: a million unemployed, a decline in foreign markets and therefore in exports, and wage cuts and discontent generally.

But amidst the gloom, John could at least look forward to his next grandchild. In December 1920 Pamela, heavily pregnant, was making preparations for the birth. She had no problems in finding a suitable nanny, for she would be using the Cobbolds' trusted old nurse, Jane Cottle. Her sister-in-law, Blanche, on the other hand, was at the same time fretting to her mother because her nurse had been in hospital for an operation and was still recovering and Ivan was away for three days at Holkham – since 1909 owned by his great-uncle, the 3rd Earl of Leicester. Not only that, but soon to arrive for the weekend were Harold and Dorothy, she being heavily pregnant with their first child, as well as Blanche and Dorothy's older sister, Lady Maud. Maud was a worry to the sisters. Like Dorothy she had married an aide-de-camp of their father's in Canada, Angus Alexander Mackintosh, but he had died in October 1918, when Maud was twenty-two. Married for just eleven months, Angus had just managed to see their daughter, Anne Peace Arabella, born the month before he died. Maud was mentioned in many concerned letters from Blanche to their mother, her bereavement having apparently affected her health, but fortunately she eventually re-married.

Ivan, Blanche and the Macmillans, along with Maud and Arabella, met up that Christmas of 1920 but it was unlikely to have been at Chatsworth, as the Duke and Duchess were still in Canada. They had not yet seen their granddaughter Pamela Maud, now twenty-one months old; writing to his mother-in-law on 23 December, Ivan said how much he and Blanche wanted to go to Canada and he wished she and the Duke could see the child, who was already past babyhood. Charles and Pamela that Christmas probably divided themselves between Milton Abbey and Holy Wells, to keep both their families happy.

Charles and Pamela's first child, Cynthia, was born on 21 February

219

1921, and was very much the image of Charles – much to the delight of Eric and Sybil, for whom she was their first grandchild. Pamela was glad she was born early in the year, for 1921 turned out to be a year of intense heat and prolonged drought. It was also another year of strikes. Pamela took Cynthia to visit Blanche at Sutton Hoo in the March but their next visit in April was doubtful, Blanche writing to her mother on April 8, 'Pam & the baby were coming today but they thought they had better not because of the strike. I wonder if the railwaymen will come out, it looks very bad.'

The strike to which Blanche was referring was the miners' strike. It had begun a week earlier when, on 31 March, the mines were handed back to private ownership after their state control during the war. While they were Government run, Lloyd George – who declared that 'In peace and war King Coal is the paramount lord of industry' – had been unwilling to impose wage reductions, as this would provoke strike action against the Government, with political implications. But once the mines were returned to their previous owners, things were different.

The strike resulted from the standoff between the miners' union, the Miners' Federation of Great Britain, and the mine owners' organisation, the Mining Association of Great Britain. In 1920 the Government had announced its plans to return to privatisation in 1921, and as a result the miners demanded a wage increase and prepared to strike if it was not granted. But the demand for coal was slowing down, as was its production, and the mine owners, never generous at the best of times, rejected the miners' demand out of hand. The miners looked to the Triple Alliance for support, an organisation formed in 1914 between the three unions for transport workers, railwaymen and miners, as a vehicle for united action. However, although this was now revived, the dockers and railwaymen refused to rally to the miners' cause. The threat of strike action faded and the mine owners exploited the weakness of their workers' union. The mine owners wanted a new wage agreement: the basic wage was to be cut and the 'national pool', which guaranteed a decent wage to miners in less profitable pits, was to be abandoned. It meant that some miners would be paid less than the reduced national rate. The miners refused even to negotiate. In retaliation the mine owners declared a lock-out. Miners who did not accept the terms would be refused employment.

The strike began at midnight on 31 March 1921, when one million miners chose unemployment in preference to wage reductions. As an indication of how serious it expected things to be, the Government invoked the recent Emergency Powers Act, and declared a state of emergency in Britain. This could only be done 'if any action has been taken or is immediately threatened by any persons or body of persons of such nature and on so extensive a scale as to be calculated by interference with the supply and distribution of food, water, fuel, light or with the means of locomotion, to deprive the community or any substantial part of the community of the essentials of life'. In such a situation the Government could make whatever regulations it deemed necessary to preserve peace and to secure the necessities of life.

The Government this time looked to the mine owners to try to settle the dispute, but made it clear that if necessary it would put into action the schemes it had prepared previously for maintaining the essentials: Britain's food supply, the lighting of London and the keeping open of the country's ports. What Lloyd George feared most looked likely to happen. Anxious that their own members may face a wage cut, especially as the state control of the railways was due to end in August, the National Union of Railwaymen, together with the Transport and General Workers Union, agreed in principle to strike in the miners' support and to call their members out on 15 April.

The first step the Government took when the miners' strike began was to ration coal. A week later, as a precaution against the threatened general strike, it recalled all three military services and appealed for 'all loyal citizens capable of bearing arms', aged between eighteen and forty, to volunteer for ninety days' service in new units of the regular army, which would be called 'Defence Units'.

The response was overwhelming, particularly from reservists and others keen to rejoin their wartime regiments. The Royal Family returned to Buckingham Palace from their stay at Windsor Castle much earlier than intended, and King George V held an urgent interview with his Prime Minister. By 9 April mines in some areas, particularly Wales, were already in danger, because the miners refused to let volunteers man the pumps to keep out the water, and they were flooding and becoming ruined. Fires and looting were also breaking out, and in some places the

Salvation Army had taken to distributing food.

However, on the eve of the expected general strike the General Secretary of the miners' union, Frank Hodges, announced he was prepared after all to negotiate new wage rates, area by area, and in the early hours of 15 April he met with Lloyd George and the other two union executives to formalise the terms of a settlement. But the miners insisted that the decision on how to proceed was theirs alone and refused to let the other unions participate in the negotiations. Hodge's proposal was rejected, although by a majority of only one, and he resigned. Denied the right to comment on the strategy or the tactics, neither the dockers nor the railwaymen felt obliged to support the miners in their dispute, and they were left to fight on alone.

The abandonment by the two unions was disastrous for the miners and led to them afterwards referring to 15 April 1921 as 'Black Friday'. They went for ten weeks without wages, at which stage they were still two-to-one in favour of continuing the strike. After three months, starvation saw them returning to work. The miners then agreed that wages could be negotiated area by area and that some pits could pay wages which were below subsistence level. The debacle convinced the whole trade union movement that, for future reference, it was mass action that was needed, rather than action by individual unions. However, how this should be done and financed became itself the cause of much argument. As for the coal industry itself, things would go from bad to worse.

The deal which was reached in July 1921 saw the miners about 20% worse off than they had been in 1914. During those three months much hardship had been suffered by the miners' families and great inconvenience by the British people generally, with those in many areas fearful of the sporadic outbreaks of violence and looting.

Not that the strike deterred Lady Evelyn who, as it began, was looking for someone to go to Scotland with her. Blanche complained to her mother on 8 April that her mother-in-law had 'tried hard' to persuade her to go to Edinburgh, but she did not want to. Blanche said that, 'She is under the impression that no-one can survive without Scotland.' Unless Evelyn was planning to stay with relatives en route, given the amount of time it took to drive there in 1921 she was presumably intending to go by train: a ridiculous idea, given that the number of passenger services was greatly reduced because of the coal rationing. And like Wales, Scotland was a particular place of unrest, with naval ratings being dispatched there to pump out the mines where the volunteers were prevented from doing so. Much to her chagrin, Evelyn ended up having to stay put at Holy Wells until it was over.

The miners returned to work in early July and the country resumed normality. With transport running freely again and no more worries about petrol supplies, travel between country and town became feasible again. Charles could get home to Pickhurst Mead at the weekend rather than having to stay up in London all the time, and occasionally at the weekends he followed his uncles' example and played cricket at Hayes. Not that he was always supporting the home team: in July that year, 1921, he raised a team and on the 16th, a baking hot day, Hambros Bank took on Hayes. The local team was slaughtered. Charles made the Bank's top score of 32 runs out of a total of 98, supported by Simon Keech, the son of one of the Hambros' long-serving estate workers; his older brother, Frank, played on the opposite side, achieving the top score for Hayes of 39 out of 66. The number of runs may not have been very many by today's standards, but the method of cutting the grass in 1921 was not conducive to short turf and fast games.

It was a gloriously festive occasion, with the village band playing on the cricket ground throughout the day. Refreshments, consisting of the Club's customary sandwiches, cakes and scones, and plentiful tea from the huge urn, were laid out in the interval under the mulberry tree near the entrance. As a relatively new Hambro incumbent at Pickhurst Mead, Pamela would have been expected to watch the match in support, along with baby Cynthia and, of course, Nanny Cottle, anxious to keep the child well protected against the heat. Pamela may even have provided the refreshments, for since the revival of the Club in 1896 it had become the custom for the ladies from the 'big houses' to take it in turns to provide the teas on match days. Since it was her husband's team which was playing, it would have been the hospitable thing for her to do – even though, of course, she was unlikely to have cooked anything herself, but rather given orders to her cook. By that time Pamela should have got over any morning sickness she may have been experiencing – for she was already pregnant again by three months, with their second child, due in January 1922.

While Charles was playing cricket at Hayes that July, Ivan was playing at Winchester. In his absence Blanche stayed with her in-laws at Holy Wells, and wrote to her mother on the 24th saying how glad she was that Ivan was back, for '... Lady Evelyn is spending most of the time in bed, or resting, she has got neuritis or something in the leg, but I am pretty sure it is not really bad, & I have been left with four people I practically did not know...'

Whatever her problem was, Evelyn's leg clearly improved in time for her to enjoy her usual summer season at Rannoch. After the cricket, and with the railway strike finished, Pamela too probably went up there for part of that summer of 1921, although it seems she was not there at the end: no mention of her is made in a report in a Scottish newspaper of the end-of-season dance given by her mother at Rannoch Lodge. About one hundred guests accepted Lady Evelyn's invitation to 'an evening's amusement and enjoyment prior to her departure for the South'. Amongst many of the Cobbolds' Scottish tenants and their servants, there mingled a few guests from neighbouring estates. The dancing – the main entertainment for these gatherings – took place in the dining room and the front hall, which was decorated inevitably with 'various trophies of flood and field'. These included many stags' heads shot by Evelyn and a preserved salmon weighing a massive 44lbs, which she had caught the previous year in Norway. Music for the dancing, which started at 7.30pm and was 'fast and furious', was provided by three local pipers and three violinists, with Messrs M'Naughton and MacIntosh acting as Masters of Ceremony.

The only ladies who merited specific mention in the article were Evelyn herself, recently recovered from what was described as a severe illness – probably the problem with her leg – who was dressed in champagne-coloured crepe-de-chine, with a blue shawl and blue suede slippers; her friends Lady Tweedmouth and Countess O'Brien; and the sister of the Cobbolds' estate factor Macdonald. Most of the men were dressed in traditional Gallic costume, while 'the ancient language was much in evidence during conversation'. Fiercely adhering to the fact that she was 'Highland by birth and [belonging] to one of the ancient families of the North', Evelyn announced that only Scottish dances should be indulged in. Risking the wrath of her Ladyship, one of her young English guests, described by the paper as 'a little Sassenach maid', later asked one of the MCs in a whisper to announce a particular English dance. Her hostess overheard and 'curtly rejoined, "M'Naughton! No English dances"', apparently to everyone's amusement except, it is presumed, that of the rebellious young lady.

Evelyn provided an 'ample and satisfying' supper to keep her guests going, which was eaten very quickly, and at the end of the evening Mr Duncan Robertson, from a very old local family, gave a vote of thanks, to which Evelyn 'briefly replied'. Naturally the newspaper said that everyone proclaimed it 'the best night ever experienced in Rannoch Lodge'.

With her husband busy familiarising himself with his new job, Pamela learnt to deal with motherhood with the help of Nanny Cottle, and, being forbidden to ride in her pregnant state, occupied herself instead with one of her other interests: dog breeding. It was likely to have been cocker spaniels that she favoured, as her family had always owned them and her father-in-law was never without one. On 22 November 1921 she won a prize at a show of the Ladies' Kennel Association, although the report in the social column of *The Times* the next day does not make it clear which breed it was for. Dog-breeding had always been a traditional male domain, but the Ladies' Kennel Association, founded in 1895, made it acceptable for the first time for women to take part, and it introduced breeds that were popular as pets for women. According to the report, in 1921 these were Alsatian wolf dogs, Pekinese, Sealyham Terriers and Cairn Terriers. Pamela did well to win: the number of entries for the show 'came up to the pre-war standard', and there were many new exhibitors. The President of the Association, Princess Helena Victoria, a granddaughter of Queen Victoria, visited the show and presented the prize for the best bitch '... to Mrs Charles Hambro's C. Rufflyn Veda'.

Although it was not the intention of the Ladies' Kennel Association to limit membership, in practice in those early days it was only a few privileged women with the time and money to spare who could take part in dog breeding. One of these was Lady Evelyn's friend Lady Kathleen Pilkington, a guest at Pamela's wedding. She was from a very old Anglo-Irish family, the daughter of the 4th Earl of Desart of

County Kilkenny. A leading light in the Ladies' Kennel Association, Kathleen had been responsible a few years earlier for introducing the French Toy Bulldog to Britain. But her attention would soon be focused on weightier matters. On 6 December 1921, two weeks after she supported Pamela at the show, Lloyd George signed the historical Anglo-Irish Treaty. This established, after much fighting and negotiation, the Irish Free State, which gave Ireland the right to self-govern as a Dominion within the British Empire. But within a few months a bitter civil war broke out between the Provisional Government of the Irish Free State and those who felt the Treaty fell far short of Republican ambitions.

Just two months later, in February 1922, while Kathleen's uncle, the 5th Earl, was in London, a small group of Republicans with fire torches marched one night up to Desart Court, the family's home in Co Kilkenny for countless generations, and burnt it down. The whole family was devastated; they did not know why they were targeted, as the Earl had obeyed the Irish Land Act of 1903 and sold much of the family's estate to his tenants. The family had not realised there was so much antagonism towards them. The Earl was inconsolable. With neither the money nor the inclination to rebuild the house, he and his wife moved to Sussex and he gave the title of the house to Kathleen. With the help of an architect she restored Desart Court and reopened it in 1926. But in the 1930s a rise in anti-English sentiment in Ireland would compel her to abandon it. During World War II it was used to billet soldiers and was eventually demolished in 1957; no sign of it now stands, although local legend plays its part in resurrecting the old house on certain moonlit nights.

Meanwhile, on safer and more domestic matters, Pamela's second niece was born. Having endured her pregnancy during that cripplingly hot summer of 1921, Blanche gave birth to Jean Cobbold on 7 October. Blanche and Ivan chose Pamela to be one of Jean's two godmothers, her christening taking place that Christmas at Chatsworth, in its beautiful chapel with the seventeenth-century painted ceiling depicting the resurrected Christ. Just a month away from giving birth herself, Pamela must have hoped she would not go into premature labour in the middle of the service. Jean's second godmother was her aunt, Lady Mary Cavendish, wife of Blanche's eldest brother Edward, the Marquess of Hartington. Five years older than Pamela, Mary was a rather grander godmother than she. Apart from being a Marchioness through her marriage, her father was the 4th Marquess of Salisbury, and her grandfather Robert Cecil, the 3rd Marquess, had twice been Prime Minister, in whose second government Blanche's father had served. It is tempting to imagine Blanche and Mary comparing notes about their lives, as they had both enjoyed hugely privileged upbringings in two of Britain's most historic houses: Blanche largely at Chatsworth, and Mary at Hatfield House, Hertfordshire, home to her father's family since about 1607. However, it is more likely that they simply accepted their respective backgrounds as a given. The fact that their fathers bore two of England's oldest hereditary titles and still enjoyed, like their ancestors, much wealth and power (albeit these were now less than they had been), made the two young women a breed apart from the rest of womankind in 1921.

Keeping pretty much apace with her sister-in-law, Pamela gave birth to her second child, Diana, on 27 January 1922. If Charles was disappointed that he still did not have an heir, it is unlikely he would have expressed this to Pamela. Having done what was generally expected of her by producing two children in just over two years, Pamela – still aged only twenty-two – could now turn her attention once more to her sporting interests, like golf. Despite Charles not being keen on her playing the game, she had the support of various others in the Hambro family, particularly Sir Everard and his son Angus, the brilliant amateur. Pamela had a keen fellow player in her friend Angy, and a full-page article about golf in *The Sketch* on 20 September 1922, by an eminent golf writer, was illustrated by a photograph of the pair ready for action. Captioned 'Golfing at North Berwick: Miss Tollemache and Mrs Charles Hambro', the photograph makes the two young women look a good ten years older than they are, for the golf wear of the period does not flatter them. Whilst neither of them was conventionally beautiful, they both had striking features but unfortunately the cloche hats they wear seem to cover half their faces, especially Angy's. The heavy, shapeless golfing skirts, with their indeterminate pleats, hang mid-calf, while their legs are encased in thick woollen stockings, ending in masculine-looking brogue-type shoes. Yet their outfits were of the style worn by every self-respecting woman golfer of the time, and would have been of the best quality; and Pamela was clearly quite happy, for she smiles at the camera, poised with one hand on hip, the other holding her golf club. Angy, on the other hand, unusually looks rather reserved.

While *The Sketch* was primarily a Society magazine, priding itself on its standard of photography, it also contained features and short stories by eminent writers such as Walter de la Mare and Algernon Blackwood. Under the editorship of Bruce Ingram, it would be the first to publish short stories by Agatha Christie, starting in March 1923. Ingram, who had won the Military Cross in the war, was one of the bright young men of journalism of the time, and was also the editor of *The Illustrated London News*.

However, undoubtedly journalism's most talented and influential figure of the time, until his death on 14 August 1922, was Alfred Harmsworth, Lord Northcliffe, who owned *The Times* and the *Daily Mail*, and is generally credited with being the father of modern journalism. Tragically, following a mental breakdown he contracted streptococcus, and was found dead, aged fifty-seven, inexplicably in a wooden hut on the roof of the Duke of Devonshire's rented house at 2 Carlton Terrace, London. His estate was inherited by his brother Harold, 1st Viscount Rothermere, who found himself having to sell *The Times* to pay the death duties on Alfred's estate. Harold did in fact make a bid from his own private fortune but was beaten by Pamela and Charles' friend, John Jacob Astor: for £1,580,000 Astor became the new owner of the world-famous and already long-established broadsheet. In 1934 the Hambros would make him a director of their bank: not a bad relationship for either party to have.

Meanwhile, Pamela would not have been surprised to learn that her parents had decided to formally separate. She was probably upset, although if she knew her father was unhappy, she would have considered it the best thing for him. Divorce was not an option for John and Evelyn, for in 1922 the only ground was adultery: if the husband was the petitioner, he had to prove his wife had committed adultery, while a wife had to prove not only adultery but another offence too. It was a messy and inevitably public business and, despite the acceptance by the upper classes that extramarital dalliances went on in their circles, such conduct was supposed to be discreet, and divorce was still frowned upon. A formal separation, until either of them wanted to remarry, was by far the better option. Pamela of course would no longer be able to take the children to visit her parents conveniently together, although the settlement that John and Evelyn agreed upon meant their grandchildren would have even more beautiful houses to visit when they went to see either of them.

If John felt the need to commiserate with anyone over the end of his marriage, he could do so with his brother, the raffish Ralph. Coincidentally, that same year Ralph was divorced by his wife, Minnie. Apparently not deterred by the stigma that attached to divorce, it was Ralph's second; his first wife Millicent, mother of Ralphie, Pamela's younger cousin, had divorced him in 1903. However, demonstrating the maxim that marriage is the triumph of hope over experience, Ralph would marry for a third time in 1929.

Charles was saddened by the separation of his parents-in-law, for he got on well with them both, although he was well aware of their shortcomings. In John he sometimes saw a pompous streak, which he recognised in Ivan, and Evelyn's lack of humour and snobbishness he found tiresome, the more so because he knew how it made Pamela react. But he would not have taken sides, and he ensured that the children would not see any less of either of their grandparents.

Charles was an unusually involved father for the times, and was delighted with his new daughter, even though he was unlikely to have been able to spend much time with his growing family during the week. Learning the ropes at the Bank in the footsteps of his father and his esteemed grandfather – Sir Everard was the first Chairman of the newly-formed Hambros Bank Ltd – was not easy, and expectations of him were high. Like his wife, Charles had a great sense of humour, but he sometimes let his sense of responsibility weigh heavily upon him, and Pamela would soothe him as she had done when they were courting. But Charles was not the only son with the spotlight on him. His counterpart in the Wallenberg family, Marcus, was also coming to terms with his new position in his family's growing empire, and although the two young men had already met, soon their paths would cross more permanently.

Chapter 17

Three Young Lions

In August 1996 in an interview with *TIME* magazine, Dr Peter Wallenberg, second son of Marcus and Dorothy Wallenberg, said his father told everyone, including the newspapers, that he was not competent and capable, that he never did anything good. Marcus did not consider his son would ever be able to head the family empire, which had been Sweden's leading industrial dynasty since the mid-nineteenth century, when they founded Stockholm's Enskilda Bank (SEB). His father's lack of faith in him led Dr Wallenberg to recall, 'He gave me calluses on my soul.' But his father's scorn made him more determined, and not only did he continue the family's success, he had awards and honours heaped upon him from all over the world. Sadly his older brother Marc was less able to bear their father's approbation and the pressures he felt were upon him, and took his own life in November 1971, aged forty-seven.

The harsher side of Marcus Wallenberg was probably disguised as youthful determination and ambition when he met Charles Hambro in around 1920. Born within a couple of years of each other – Charles in 1897, Marcus in 1899 – they could not have been more different in character, yet they managed to remain friends for some years. This may have been partly out of necessity, given their families' long-standing association and the uniting of the two family banks in 1920. But they did have in common the expectations put upon them by their respective families, both having to learn quickly the complex and competitive world of merchant banking. In Charles' case it helped that his family had achieved success and had learned to live with pressure in the world-wide market, as well as in Britain, acquiring worldliness and tolerance on the way, never being afraid to embrace eccentricity; the Wallenbergs, on the other hand, were top-dogs in the comparatively small country of Sweden, where pressure to conform to the social expectations of one's class was far greater than in Britain. Those factors, and Marcus' position in his family as the youngest of six children, spoiled by his domineering mother, saw him grow up with confidence bordering on arrogance, and a defiant streak.

Although Sweden had pro-German tendencies it had been neutral in the Great War, so apart from doing his military service in 1919 and qualifying as a Reserve officer, Marcus had not faced the challenges that young men like Charles had encountered elsewhere in Europe. In March 1920 when Charles, already honoured for his bravery and recently married, began his training for entry into what was still C J Hambro & Son, Marcus had just graduated from the Stockholm School of Economics; like Charles, he was starting his training for his family's bank. He seemed to have accepted his destiny from early on, writing aged eight to his father, one of SEB's Board members, on notepaper from one of SEB's branches, 'How do you do. Here I am sitting doing business.'

Both men were well-built, good-looking and sporty; while Charles' skills lay mainly in cricket, Marcus' game was tennis. In 1920, aged twenty-one, he became the Swedish Men's Singles Champion. In Sweden the game was the preserve of the upper classes, and the Wallenberg family was one of that exclusive circle of people who, along with the Swedish Royal Family, introduced the sport to the country. Marcus' aunt Elsa had also been a national tennis player, and had represented Sweden in the Olympic Games in London in 1908.

Intellectually Marcus' forebears were impressive: apart from their banking and industrial expertise, one uncle, Knut, was the Swedish Minister for Foreign Affairs (with whom Charles' father had dealt during the war), and his great-grandfather had been a Bishop. Yet in spite of this, Marcus did not show any particular religious or cultural interests: the family as a whole occasionally went to the opera and to divine service on special festival days but did not go any further than the expectations of their class. That Marcus managed to woo and win the love of his wife, the cultured Dorothy Mackay, known always as 'Doie',[1]

[1] Pronounced 'Doy'.

who was not even Swedish and, unlike most women of the time, had a university degree, was perhaps surprising.

But in the spring of 1920, as newly-weds Charles and Pamela were considering their financial situation, and Marcus was sent off to Geneva to start his training in foreign banks – in between the diversions of tennis competitions in Switzerland, Germany and France – Doie was not yet on the horizon. Marcus' girlfriend at that time was one Alice Hay, whose family moved in the same circles as the Wallenbergs. Her father was Lord Chamberlain-in-Waiting to the King of Sweden and the Managing Director of one of Sweden's largest companies. They became secretly engaged, much to the concern of Marcus' mother Amalia, who somehow found out, the way mothers do. Neither she nor Marcus Senior wanted their son to commit himself until his training was finished. It was a long-distance relationship due to his training and, after getting a didactic letter from his father on the subject, telling him that marriage 'is not only based upon a fancy', and not having seen Alice for two years anyway, Marcus jilted her in a letter that was partially guilty and largely matter-of-fact.

Meanwhile, Marcus' future wife was having quite a different upbringing in Britain. Although university education had been accessible for women since the late nineteenth century in Britain, it was not an opportunity that many women could take advantage of. A scholarship was vital in the days before any kind of financial assistance was available, and although money was not normally a problem for the upper classes and aristocracy, they tended to regard university education as a waste of time: after marriage women would be supported by their husbands and not need to earn a living, considered anyway to be incompatible with having children and managing the family estates. There was little notion of higher education for its own sake. And regrettably some women themselves still thought intellectual ability was not to be encouraged in the female sex lest it make men feel inferior. Doie's family was different: her parents were 'mad on education', as hers and Marcus' daughter Ann-Marie later said; perhaps it was because, although wealthy, the Mackays were more middle than upper class.

The family was Scottish and owned a large estate called Glencruitten in Oban, a small coastal town northwest of Glasgow. Doie was born in

232

1900, the same year as Pamela. Her father, Alexander Mackay, was a partner in a firm of chartered accountants in London and New York, and was described by Marcus' father in a letter to his eldest son, Jacob, as 'an old fashioned Scottish businessman with a wide education'. Alexander was also a very successful entrepreneur. He cleared swamps in Florida and encouraged people to grow oranges, making the place desirable enough for him to buy a bungalow there, on Lake Alfred. In Texas he became involved in cattle ranching and was one of the first people to find oil there, becoming a founder of Shell, and he was variously chairman or director of many substantial companies. Doie's mother, Edith Helen, was the daughter of a Scottish clergyman and very musically inclined.

Doie won a place at Newnham College, Cambridge, to read English and German Literature and Language. Ironically, although her future father-in-law would write to his son in the language of whatever country Marcus was doing his training in, and expect him to answer in that language, German had been Marcus' weakest subject at school. Like the very few other female students of the time, Doie was not allowed to attend lectures in the University, which was male-dominated, but had separate lectures in her all-women's college. Fortunately she passed her final exams in 1921; had it been earlier, as a woman she would not have been allowed a degree, only a University Certificate.

Doie and Marcus met in November 1922 when they were both travelling on the SS *Mauritania* to New York. She was going to visit her father; Marcus had just finished part of his traineeship with various banks in London, where he cemented his relationship with the Hambro family, and was about to start his next training stage in New York, with First National City Bank. The pair continued to see each other over the next few weeks while they were in New York, and quickly decided their future lay together. Writing in January 1923 to tell his father about the future 'Mrs Marc Wallenberg Jr', Marcus described Doie as being 'of medium height, slender but at the same time strong and shapely with a nice, perhaps even pretty, face framed by blonde hair, from the centre of which peeks a pair of blue eyes'. He referred to her many good qualities, including her sense of humour, good judgment and 'versatile intellect', in a letter which also lapsed into bank-speak when he talked about their relationship being a 'long-term investment'. No doubt hoping it would please his father, as well as his exacting and bossy older brother Jacob, he said that Doie 'has the ambition and interest to take part in her husband's work with pleasure'.

If Doie ever read that letter, that sentence would have rung warning bells, for she had heard worrying stories about Swedish women being confined to their homes. During their engagement, which was announced in June 1923 – after their fathers had met in Paris and approved each other, and after Marcus had satisfied his father that his marriage plans would not interfere with his training schedule – Doie wrote to Marcus:

'You *won't* expect *me* to be a sort of *Hausfrau*!! will you. You know how that would *kill* me – I hate & loathe those sort of girls & women.'

If Marcus Wallenberg Senior had read that, it would probably have confirmed his opinion of Doie, whom he described rather disapprovingly in his letter to Jacob as '… a modern type of girl'. He also remarked that she had 'little screwed-up eyes… She was mostly on the defensive.' Despite his acknowledging that his future daughter-in-law was a Cambridge graduate, it was clear Marcus Senior thought his son could have done better, writing;

'… with his excellent prospects [he] should have managed a more advantageous match, although he could probably also have got himself into something far worse. After all, everything depends on the real temperament of his wife to be.'

Doie had some idea of what the family thought of themselves and what she was marrying into. Marcus Senior had written to her, referring to the public-spiritedness of his family, saying that the 'envy created by their success' had been 'modified by the undeniable fact that several of the members of the family have substantially contributed to the progress and prosperity of Sweden. It is my desire that my sons will follow in the same track…'

At least the apparent arrogance of Marcus Senior had foundation: the family is credited with being predominantly responsible for the industrial development of Sweden from the late nineteenth century. But his attitude also reflected one of the criticisms of the Swedes by those of his many countrymen who emigrated to the USA in the late nineteenth century: the innate feeling of superiority of many upper-class Swedes towards the rest of the world. This and other reasons, not least the religious repression practised by the Swedish Lutheran State Church, saw Sweden from the 1840s until the Great War have the third highest rate of emigration in the world after Ireland and Norway. By the early twentieth century one fifth of all Swedes had made the USA their home, and such was the concern of the Swedish Government that in 1907 it formed a Parliamentary Emigration Commission to study the problem, which it continued to do until 1913.

Urgent social and economic reforms were recommended as a result, particularly universal male suffrage, better housing and economic development, as well as broadening popular education to counteract what were considered to be class and caste differences. This was because class inequality in Swedish society had been a strong and recurring theme in the Commission's findings, perpetuated by the Swedish monarchy. Ignorance and hatred towards America by the aristocracy had also been observed. And Doie was not wrong in thinking that women were not treated well. There was a history of this, for Swedish emigrants, on visiting their home country in the 1880s and comparing attitudes with those of their adopted one, had commented on the disrespect shown in Sweden towards its women.

Apart from her concerns about Swedish women, Doie had a few criticisms of Marcus himself. Letters were written between the couple while they were apart for six months before their engagement, during which Doie and some of her family went on a cruise from Britain through the Mediterranean. Perhaps tellingly, their correspondence hardly compared to the passion and humour of the letters between Charles and Pamela. Doie complained, for instance, that Marcus seldom wrote and that when he did, his letters were pedantic, trivial and written in poor English. She discovered that he did not like criticism, for he responded angrily that she was very rude to say such things, stressing the weaknesses of her arguments and the character they mirrored, and said he only wrote in English because she was too lazy to learn Swedish.

Nevertheless, they survived their time apart and were married in Oban on 22 August 1923, the reception being held at Glencruitten. Charles and Pamela were probably unable to attend, for that summer they spent a few weeks in Iceland. Although they indulged in one of their favourite pastimes, fishing, in which Pamela had excelled since a child,

Charles was there on business. In 1920 Iceland had been recognised by Denmark as an independent sovereign state and its development was beginning to accelerate. Hambros Bank Ltd was keen to offer its services, and Charles helped to build up a relationship which would last for many years. But other Hambros were likely to have attended the wedding, for given the professional relationship of the two families, Marcus' parents are bound to have invited Eric and Sybil, and possibly Sir Everard too. They would have joined some notable guests. Marcus and Doie's witnesses were the Swedish Prime Minister Ernst Trygger and his wife, and others included Lord and Lady Salisbury and Viscount and Viscountess Astor – that is, Waldorf, the elder brother of John Jacob Astor, Charles and Pamela's friend and Kentish neighbour, and Waldorf's wife, Nancy Astor MP.

The Wallenbergs may have been revered in Sweden as its industrial aristocrats but at the time of the wedding the country was virtually unknown in Britain, except perhaps for its neutrality during the Great War. The war had seen Sweden continuing to trade with Germany in violation of the Allied blockade, which led to hunger and political instability in the country. It was the situation which Marcus' uncle Knut had tried to resolve as Foreign Minister, and which was achieved by Sir Eric Hambro. And while Marcus' father may have been somewhat diffident towards Doie, according to Marcus and Doie's daughter Ann-Marie, known always as 'Anis', the Mackays were 'rather appalled' by the marriage, because they considered Sweden to be backwards compared with Britain.

Since the 1920s Sweden has come a long way – in the twenty-first century seeming to represent everything that is liberated and laid-back, with a modern, relaxed monarchy. But in the early 1920s even the average Swedish household was some way behind Britain. Despite marrying into a family of great wealth, the new Mrs Wallenberg discovered, for example, that her dressing table stool doubled as a bidet: her maid would open it and fill it with hot water when she had finished using it as a stool. The Wallenbergs' domestic staff would have had to work harder too, compared with the Hambros'. Electrical washing machines were still unknown in Sweden, only entering Swedish homes after World War II – and then slowly, and were still absent in the majority of households in the 1970s. By contrast Hotpoint had begun in Britain in the early 1900s, and the year Doie and Marcus married, Hotpoint in Britain started to produce washing machines under its own name; while many households still had to do without, the British housewife could at least aspire to owning one, unlike her Swedish sister. Britain also saw the refrigerator first, in the 1890s, and it managed to beat Sweden in the vacuum cleaner stakes, for the machine was invented by a Briton, Hubert Cecil Booth, in 1901. But Sweden could claim superiority over Britain for introducing the mobile version, thanks to the giant Swedish company Electrolux, which started in 1910 and of which Marcus and Doie's grandson would become Chairman in 2007.

As the 1920s progressed, there was a sense of increased freedom in Sweden: the changes in outlook, fads and fashion promulgated by other European countries in the post-war period had reached it at last. Women shortened their skirts and those in the upper echelons of society, like Doie and Marcus, enjoyed 'the most amazing parties' during that decade; according to Anis, everyone went 'completely mad'.

Doie and Pamela, introduced through their husbands, got on very well, sharing a similar outlook on life. They were both outgoing, and Doie thought Pamela was tremendous fun. Charles and Marcus' work permitting, they saw each other as often as they could, although at the beginning this was less than they would have liked. However, in October 1923, while Marcus and Doie were enjoying the first flush of married life, the two men coincidentally were each sent by their father to the USA, their wives accompanying them, for the next stage of their on-the-job training. Both couples travelled to New York from Southampton. The Wallenbergs sailed on 13 October on board *RMS Aquitania*, a very luxurious ship owned by the Cunard line, who advertised it as 'the Ladies' Ship' in the hope of attracting the growing number of post-war bachelor girls who were seeking freedom and adventure. *Aquitania*'s reproduction period décor and elaborate furnishings were designed to make passengers think they were in a stately home, rather than on a ship.

Charles and Pamela left Southampton on 26 October on *RMS Majestic*, which at that time was the biggest ship in the world. Previously named *SS Bismarck*, and launched in 1914 by the granddaughter of the nineteenth-century German Chancellor, she never sailed under the German flag except for her sea trials in 1922 because the war intervened: the Treaty of Versailles demanded that German ships be turned over to the Allies as reparation for those destroyed in the war, so she was ceded to Britain and became the flagship of the White Star Line.

That crossing on 26 October broke a record in carrying 2,622 passengers, the White Star Line's greatest number. With about a thousand crew to look after them, the experience was a very comfortable one, especially for those travelling first class as the Hambros would have done. The facilities included a luxurious marble swimming pool holding 120 tons of sea water, which offered either gentlemen-only bathing or mixed – although curiously not ladies only – surrounded by electric baths, thirty dressing rooms and a spectators' gallery. Pamela and Charles would have enjoyed use of the library, holding about one thousand books, and the tennis court. There was also a gymnasium, a nursery and playroom, a smoking room and many restaurants, bars and decks at various levels, the best being the sundeck for the first-class passengers.

The purpose of Charles' journey was to gain experience at J P Morgan and Company, the bank of the Hambros' old friends. In New York he and Pamela spent much time with Charles' friend since childhood, Harry Morgan, who, the same age as Pamela, had just celebrated his twenty-third birthday. Harry was fourth generation of that famous American banking family. His great-grandfather Junius Spencer Morgan had founded the bank, J S Morgan and Company, in London in 1864, which was when the two families' friendship began. Harry's grandfather, John Pierpoint Morgan (known as 'JP'), met Charles' grandfather, Everard Hambro; they were near neighbours in London and JP was also a frequent attendant at the Court of King Edward Vll.

In 1898 JP brought his son J P Morgan Junior ('Jack') over to London – where Harry was born – for his bank training, and he became close friends of Charles' father, Eric. Ever the ardent anglophile, Jack loved London, for so long the world's leading financial centre. He played a major part in the financial aspects of the Great War, including raising a massive Anglo-French loan in 1915, which helped the Allied victory, and established his name as one of the world's leading financiers. When his father, JP, died in April 1913, Jack took over renting Gannochy with Eric and their respective families.

There was, however, a significant difference between the Hambros and the Morgans: money. Despite the great wealth of the Hambros, it was less than that of their American friends, who in 1937 would be listed the second-richest family in the USA, thanks to the success of J P Morgan & Co. The various luxurious properties Jack owned in America and England, the priceless art collection of Rembrandts, Turners and other great artists lavished on him by his father, and his yacht *Corsair IV*, which needed a fifty-man crew and had accommodation for eighty-five passengers, made the Hambros' wealth look almost modest. It made no difference to the families' friendship, however, which continues in the twenty-first century.

Harry Morgan also knew Marcus. Although the Wallenbergs at that time did not have such a long-standing relationship with the Morgans as the Hambros, the professional positions of Marcus and Harry's respective fathers meant their paths had crossed. In the next ten years the young men would become more closely connected, as Harry would become a founder of the investment bank Morgan Stanley, in which successions of Wallenbergs would gain training. He and Marcus also discovered a shared passion for sailing, and Marcus let him moor *Kong Bele,* his 12.7m oak-timbered yacht, in Sweden under his supervision. For the moment, however, Marcus was focused on his training in New York, which was with Brown Brothers, the oldest private bank in the USA.

Harry had something else in common with Marcus: he too was newly married, having also tied the knot that year, 1923. Like Marcus and Charles, Harry was another young bridegroom. His engagement had been announced in June the previous year when he was still a twenty-one–year–old student at Harvard, and he married a year later, one week after graduating. When Pamela and Charles arrived in New York on 2 November, it was the first time they had met Harry's wife, the formidable Catherine Adams. From an eminent old Boston family, Catherine was a direct descendant of no less than two American presidents: the sixth president, her great-great-grandfather, John Quincy Adams, and the second president, his father John Adams. The successor to George Washington, John Adam's life and achievement in persuading Congress to sign the Declaration of Independence would be revived in the twenty-first century following a television series, inspiring celebrity-style interest in this father of modern America.

Charles, Harry and Marcus: three young men who were good-looking, clever, from successful, rich families, and with glittering fortunes and futures ahead of them. Leaving aside the ever-enduring allure for an unmarried girl of a blue-blooded aristocrat with his family estates still more-or-less intact, these young lions were, nevertheless, surely amongst the most eligible bachelors of their time. Except they had married – and so early too. Why had they not gallivanted like archetypal playboys, spending their handsome incomes and allowances on boys' toys and beautiful women, spreading their bonhomie while they could? Because they knew, from their fathers and their grandfathers, that the continued success of each of their family's businesses depended exactly on that: family. In banking, personal connections count: it has always been a question of who you know, who you trust and who trusts you. Personal connections handed down from one generation to another are vital in engendering trust, and the best way of doing this is by the continuity of family via good marriages and dynastic succession. Walter Bagehot, the famous nineteenth-century economist, noted this, saying that, 'The banker's calling is hereditary; the credit of the bank descends from father to son; this inherited wealth brings inherited refinement.' As one of Hambro Bank's chairmen said, 'Our job is to breed wisely,' whilst with the Morgans, the Protestant-driven convictions of Harry's father Jack, concerning family, were so great that even the employees at his bank were not allowed to divorce.

Hardly surprising then, that Charles, Harry and Marcus should tow the family line and find themselves suitable wives as soon as possible with whom to continue the dynasties. Having achieved that, they could concentrate on their careers. Not that any of their wives was the quiet, acquiescent type, for they would not have been able to cope either with the social expectations demanded in their positions as the wives of eminent bankers-to-be, or with the personalities of the men they had married. And although for the Morgans their uniting with the family of American presidents might have been another useful connection, for the Wallenberg family there was no obvious benefit in the marriage of Marcus to Doie, as made clear by his parents, although Marcus himself had clearly considered the sort of wife Doie might make. As for Charles and Pamela, for them it was certainly a love match, happily blessed by both families. While the banking interests and other associations of the Cobbolds linked them with the Hambros and gave the two families a mutual understanding, it was an advantage rather than a necessity.

There were several factors that the three women had in common: the friendship between their husbands; their marriages to well-connected, wealthy men who had the capacity to become even richer; and the expectation upon them to have children. But their backgrounds were quite different.

It is perhaps ironical that while the Morgans were treated in America like the aristocracy their country had overthrown, and the Wallenbergs in Sweden enjoyed close contact with their Royal Family, it was Pamela and Charles, behaving with typical British sangfroid, who possessed true aristocratic heritage. Charles, through Sybil, was a direct descendant of the 1st Marquess of Bute and of his father, the 3rd Earl of Bute, who had been a Prime Minister under King George III. And of course, Pamela's aristocratic lineage, through two sets of grandparents, was something she took for granted and certainly never used to her advantage, for she was acutely conscious of her mother's snobbery in that respect; however, she may have experienced a new awareness of her background when meeting Catherine.

Dark-haired, handsome rather than pretty, and impeccably dressed – which would have pleased the Morgans, who set great store by looks and 'elegance of conduct'[2] – Catherine had the cool self-assurance that came with belonging to one of America's oldest families, secure in the knowledge of its role in the country's history and in the wealth and prestige of her recent marriage. But while Catherine's ancestor may have been largely responsible for America's independence from Britain, Charles' ancestor, as Prime Minister, had served a British King who had enjoyed sovereignty over America; while Pamela's ancestor John Murray, as the 4th Earl of Dunmore, had held a position of great

---

[2] As quoted by David Landes in *Dynasties: Fortune and Misfortune in the World's Great Family Businesses*, United States, Viking Adult (Penguin Group), 2006.

power in America as the last British Governor of New York and then of Virginia. And going back along the Coke side of Pamela's family, recognition by England's Monarch of that family's service to the Crown went back to the sixteenth century, before America was even settled.

Thus Pamela, if she had felt the need to do so, could have drawn favourable comparisons with Catherine and derived quiet satisfaction from her background. She may have smiled to herself when thinking that, while Catherine may have been proud of America's ousting the British monarchy for being contrary to the principles of true freedom and democracy, Catherine's father-in law, Jack Morgan, revelled in his connections with it, as his father had done, and was immensely proud of the personal cable he had received from King George V after the war thanking him for his help.

Like the good hostess she was expected to be, Catherine had recently started a guest book to record the visitors she and Harry would receive, and the Hambros were among the first. Pamela and Charles visited them again on the 17 December and once more in the New Year on 29 January 1924. Harry and Catherine's home in the early days of married life may have been JP's previous house, famous in the 1890s for being the first in New York to be entirely powered by electricity, thanks to Thomas Edison, whom JP had supported financially; or it could have been the thirty-roomed house just outside Oyster Bay on the island which Jack Morgan had bought in 1908, called East Island. Although the couple entertained the Hambros at home on the days they visited, at some point over those few months, while Charles was doing his bank training, Harry is bound to have taken him, and probably Marcus too, to the place which has officially become an historic landmark in New York City: the Metropolitan Club.

The Metropolitan was, and remains, the most exclusive private social club in New York, and it was started by Harry's grandfather JP in 1891. Angry when a friend of his was refused membership at another club because the 'new money' of bankers was considered unfit for New York society, JP commissioned the building of his own club. He was determined that it would upstage everything else in the city, by its position – in Fifth Avenue, then a street of huge private mansions owned by other rich, like the Vanderbilts – and by the sheer opulence of its interior, masked by a deceptively modest exterior. With JP as its first President, it was completed in 1894 at a cost, even then, of $2 million, and boasted a foyer made entirely of marble, two ballrooms, a Great Hall with a triple-height ceiling, a reading room, dining rooms and bedrooms.

When Harry took Charles there in the early 1920s the private mansions along Fifth Avenue had been replaced by skyscrapers, but the Club itself was unchanged. Membership in those days was exclusively male, so Catherine and Pamela would have had to find alternative entertainment. Its membership then, as now, included world leaders and the super rich, but also a wide range of professions, for JP was determined that it should not be stuffy or elitist, like the club which had excluded his friend.

While Harry and Charles draped themselves over the leather and silk of the Metropolitan, quaffing the finest wines and discussing the latest on Wall Street, Catherine would have shown Pamela the club of which *she* was a member: the Vincent Club. If the name does not have quite the same cachet as the Metropolitan, it is because it was not the same beast at all. Rather, it was a very worthy charitable institution. Founded in 1892 in Catherine's home town of Boston, its sole purpose was to raise money for the fledgling Memorial Hospital, newly established to treat the diseases of women, ranging from gynaecological problems to cancer. As a young woman in such an elevated position in American society, through her ancestry and marriage, it was important that Catherine be seen to serve her community and set an example by doing good works. Pamela would have done her best to show interest. And although neither woman could have foreseen it, Catherine's sense of charity would, much later, be of great help to the Hambros.

Chapter 18

The Adulterers

While 1923 ended for Pamela and Charles in the USA, the year had started on a very British note, with the announcement in January of the engagement of the Duke of York, second son of King George V and Queen Mary, to Lady Elizabeth Bowes-Lyon. They would later become – unexpectedly and reluctantly, following the abdication of the Duke's brother as King Edward VIII – the King and Queen of Great Britain. The union of Elizabeth and Albert, or 'Bertie' as she called him, was considered very romantic, because for the first time in history a British monarch was marrying a non-royal, instead of it being the usual alliance between the royal families of Europe.

Their wedding took place on 26 April at Westminster Abbey, the first royal wedding to be held there since 1382, rather than in the private chapel of a royal residence, and was a very public occasion. King George granted all schoolchildren the day off and provided a special feast for eight thousand London children, as well as money for children's parties all over the country. The wedding gave the British people the first opportunity for public celebration since the end of the Great War, which was still very fresh in their minds. Conscious of that, and no doubt thinking of her own dead brother, the last act Lady Elizabeth did before her marriage was to place her bouquet on the Tomb of the Unknown Warrior, which had been installed in the Abbey in November 1920 to honour all the unknown dead. The groom was the first royal to be married in military uniform, that of the newest service, the Royal Air Force.

Although there was no television coverage, parts of the occasion were filmed by Pathe News including the royal couple standing on the balcony at Buckingham Palace. It could be seen impressively quickly, being screened that same night in all the major towns in England. Scotland, however, where the Queen Mother's ancestral home of Glamis Castle stood, had to wait until the following afternoon, because distribution of the film was made by rail and road, rather than by aeroplane. Of the many hundreds who attended the service, only one hundred and twenty-three guests were invited to the wedding breakfast, where the centre-piece was a spectacular ten-foot high wedding cake. The public had the chance to see it later on display in Reading, before it was cut up and distributed.

Pamela and Charles were not among the guests in the Abbey, headed of course by the King and Queen, as well as by the elderly Queen Mother, Alexandra, but they could hear all about the occasion later from the various friends and relatives of both their families who had been in attendance. One of these was Pamela's second cousin, the Hon Elizabeth Elphinstone: her mother, Lady Mary Bowes-Lyon, was a sister of the bride, and her father, the 16th Lord Elphinstone, was a cousin of Pamela's mother. Aged twelve, Elizabeth had the honour of being one of the eight bridesmaids.

Charles would also come to have a connection with the newly-weds. His widowed uncle Angus Hambro had remarried in 1916, and just two months before the royal wedding his wife, Vanda, gave birth to a daughter, Jean, a new cousin for Charles. Jean's first husband would be killed in World War II, and in 1946 she remarried. Her second husband was the Reverend and Hon Andrew Elphinstone, brother of the bridesmaid Elizabeth, and thus a nephew of (as she would be by then) Queen Elizabeth, consort of King George VI.

The Times naturally gave a long and detailed account of the wedding, devoting four columns alone to the gowns that some of the most important female guests wore. Pamela's relation the Duchess of Atholl, elected as an MP that same year, would have looked as beautiful as usual in 'a grey georgette dress with green and gold ribbon trimming and a gold lace toque with ostrich feather'. In her official capacity as an attendant upon the King and Queen was Ivan's mother-in-law Evie, the Duchess of Devonshire, who wore a complicated-sounding draped gown in taupe, its long sleeves merging into a cape slung from its shoulders, with a lace overdress. The Duke of Devonshire was there too, of course, as well as the Cobbolds' friends Lord and Lady Desborough, the Earl and Countess of Erroll, the Astors and the Balfours. Pamela's mother may have been put out by the lack of an invitation – after all, the Murrays had enjoyed close connections with the monarchy since the reign of George III. Not even her brother Alexander, the 8th Earl of Dunmore, was listed as a guest. However, in 1930 he would be appointed as a Lord-in-Waiting to the King, so clearly he had done nothing to blemish the family's royal record.

There was, however, one guest in attendance who was a blot on the royal landscape: Freda Dudley Ward. Invited with her husband, a Liberal MP, by the time of the wedding her adulterous affair with the bridegroom's older brother and best man David, the Prince of Wales, had been going on for over five years, and would continue until she was replaced by Mrs Wallis Simpson. Ivan Cobbold had met Mrs Dudley Ward at an early stage in the affair, mentioning her in a letter he wrote to his mother-in-law in October 1919. Ivan mused as to whether Evie and the Duke, through their close connection with the Royal Family, had been 'blessed with the company of Mrs Dudley Ward'. Ivan said that he disliked her very much, and thought her an 'influence for bad'.

Meanwhile, Evelyn Cobbold need not have been too concerned that her family's links with the Royal Family were weakening. One of her relatives, Lady Coke, was sharing with Mrs Dudley Ward a favoured position as another of the Prince of Wales' close women friends, although she would be dropped in favour of Freda. Another familiar name on the guest list was Keppel: one of the royal attendants was the Hon Sir Derek Keppel, whose brother had the dubious honour of being married to Alice Keppel, the longest-standing mistress of the late King Edward VII. Perhaps unsurprisingly, she does not appear on the guest list.

While the royal union was a love match, the Duke and Duchess of York becoming an example to the public of stable family life, it made little difference to the rest of the upper classes. There, bed-hopping continued to be acceptable, provided it was done discreetly. Divorce continued to be difficult for women, due to the requirement to prove both adultery and a further offence. The Cobbolds' acquaintance Nancy Astor, by then four years into her position as the first female MP to take up her seat in Parliament, initially refused to support any changes in legislation, even though, being American-born, she had taken advantage of American law to divorce her first husband. But her postbag was full of correspondence from ordinary women trapped in unhappy marriages, who had assumed she would help them. She reluctantly bowed to pressure and voted for reforms which led to a bill being passed that year, 1923, by which women could also obtain a divorce solely for adultery.

However, she prevaricated over any further reforms. Until 1937 the position for both sexes would remain that the only ground for divorce was sexual misconduct. As divorce for either sex still carried a stigma, affairs were often seen as the better alternative amongst the upper classes who knew, in those days before the paparazzi, how to keep such matters within their own circle, whether they were extramarital affairs or homosexual ones. Given that homosexuality was still a crime, discretion was particularly important where that was concerned.

Amongst some of their Majesties' wedding guests were some serial male adulterers, like Oswald Mosley, then an MP and still married to his first wife, Cynthia; Duff Cooper, an intellectual aristocrat and later politician, who was a known philanderer despite his wife Diana being considered the most beautiful woman in England; and Lord Londonderry, who had a well-known actress as a mistress, with whom he fathered a child. His wife Edith would come to have a close, although not necessarily sexual, relationship with the first Labour Prime Minister, Ramsay MacDonald.

Pamela may not have gone to the royal wedding, but her opportunity to put on a lovely gown and have a party did in fact happen that same year: she was to be presented at Court, having missed out the first time because of the war. It was, however, more likely to have been at the instigation of her mother than of her own choosing. Given her background and the ongoing connection of her brother with the Royal Family, Evelyn probably thought it politic for her daughter to be presented to their Majesties in order to formalise her acceptance into Society. Charles is unlikely to have been unhappy about the idea: he probably accepted the inevitability of the process, and would only have objected if Pamela had been against it.

So in June 1923 Mrs Charles Hambro was presented to their Majesties, along with a few dozen other well-connected married women and a few unmarried. As many ladies had missed the opportunity to be presented because of the war and had since married, the old rules were relaxed. This time they could either be nominated by their mothers, provided they themselves had been presented, or by another acceptable lady.

Traditionally the debutante's dress was virginal white, although a few colours were tolerated and anyway, given that so many debutantes at that presentation were married, white would not have been appropriate. *The Times*, in its account of the occasion, reported that Pamela wore a dress of silver broche, with a chain girdle of diamante and a train of old Brussels lace. Once she had been presented, curtseying deeply to their Majesties without getting her foot caught in her train, she would have walked backwards for several paces without turning her back on them, in time-honoured fashion. While Pamela would have treated the ceremony itself seriously, she would have found something funny to recount later at the party that would have been held.

The occasion would have given John Dupuis Cobbold something to smile about too, in a year which was the first complete one on his own following his formal separation from Evelyn. It was certainly an expensive one for him. He was in the process of buying a magnificent Tudor mansion, Glemham Hall in Suffolk, for Ivan and Blanche, which remains in the Cobbold family today. Conscious of the fact that Blanche had been brought up in the spectacular, if chilly, surroundings of Chatsworth, John's pride meant he wanted his son to be able to show that he could provide for his wife if not as grand an estate as Chatsworth, then at least one that could hold its own in terms of beauty and history. Also, Ivan's reputation as one of the country's finest shots had increased; and thanks to that and his marriage to Blanche, his social circle now included the Prince of Wales and a number of top Conservative ministers. The Prince was a very keen shot, and Ivan was expected to provide suitable field sport for him and anyone else he needed to impress. It must have helped that Ivan's close friend and shooting companion was Tom Purdey, whose family in 1814 had founded, and in 1923 still owned, what was considered the world's most prestigious firm of makers of firearms, James Purdey & Sons Ltd, having held the royal warrant since 1868.

Since leaving the army Ivan had joined his father and uncle Philip in the family businesses, and although John was buying Glemham for him, Ivan would have been expected to use the handsome salary he earned for its upkeep. Negotiations for the purchase lasted for months. With 3,000 acres and all its history, Glemham was an expensive property. Blanche told her father in October 1922 that the asking price at that stage was £74,700, although no doubt John eventually managed to knock that down. Fortunately for everyone, Blanche's mother approved of the property. Evie wrote to the Duke in February 1923 from Sutton Hoo, where Ivan and Blanche were still renting a house, that Glemham was 'nicer' than she remembered. She was going to luncheon at Holy Wells the next day, where presumably she expressed her approval to John about the house in which her daughter would be living and raising her family.

It says a lot about the success of the Cobbolds' businesses in 1923 that John could afford to buy Glemham even after the settlement with Evelyn. As John had anticipated, one of Ipswich's other two breweries, Catchpole's Unicorn, closed that year, leaving just the Cobbolds' and the Tollemaches' breweries. Between them, the two families bought up all Catchpole's public houses. As a result, the number of Cobbold public houses rose to two hundred and seventy, bringing with it a very healthy increase in revenue. This helped John in his payments to Evelyn of £10,000 a year tax-free, a huge amount in those days, as well as the purchase of a Scottish estate for her at Glencarron, in Wester Ross.

Glencarron comprised 15,000 acres of prime deer stalking estate, an eleven-bedroom Victorian shooting lodge, excellent fishing rights, a second lodge, a keeper's cottage and a staff cottage. To keep her happy in London John also bought her a smart mews house in Mayfair, at the bottom of whose garden the fashionable French couturier Molineux had his studio. A keen fan of fashion, Evelyn befriended him, and always travelled in the latest chic even when visiting Arab countries, rather than adopting the local dress.

The estate was bought for Evelyn on the understanding that she would no longer stay at Rannoch, such was the apparent state of relations between her and some of John's immediate family. Perhaps surprisingly, one of the first people to visit her at Glencarron was Pamela, but then she never could resist the opportunity for a good deer stalk. Evelyn recorded all successes in the Glencarron game book, and wrote that on 22 August 1923 Mrs C Hambro killed a stag weighing 15 stone.

Living in Hambro property in Kent, Pamela was on neutral territory as far as her parents were concerned, but whatever her feelings were about who was to blame, she wanted to appear even-handed. In the absence of her mother, she was pleased to support her father on 30 July that year, in what was a very important occasion for the family: the bi-centenary celebration of the Cobbold Brewery. John and his brother and business partner Philip, helped by Ivan, provided entertainment and games at Holy Wells for everyone in Ipswich, including barrel-rolling competitions and pillow fights, and grand feasts were provided for all the many Cobbold tenants and staff.

A special commemorative book was produced by Felix Walton, a writer for the *East Anglian Daily Times*, containing a history of the Brewery since 1723 and of its oldest public houses in Suffolk. Some of these were historically significant and had been restored by the Cobbolds between 1914 and 1922. There were tributes to loyal members of staff, and details of the Cobbold family past and present, listing their achievements and – as the writer would have felt was expected of him – acknowledging their benevolence. The book was well illustrated with photographs, including one taken in 1918 of a plumper Pamela with her motorbike, when she was working at Ransomes, with a narrative attesting to her popularity. Quite why Felix Walton could not have found a more recent photograph, or even mentioned the fact that she was now Mrs Charles Hambro, particularly as his paper had carried an extensive account of her wedding, is not known.

The Tollemaches were at the celebrations too, of course, except for Angy: she had had celebrations of her own recently, for on 12 July, much to Pamela's delight, she had married, and was now on her honeymoon. The lucky man was Algernon Henry Strutt, 3rd Baron Belper, aged forty and so seventeen years older than Angy. They had been introduced by Charles. Algernon's first wife, formerly Eva Bruce, had divorced him the previous year after eleven years of marriage on the grounds of his desertion and adultery, when women were still required to cite a ground for divorce in addition to adultery. According to Eva, they had spent a good deal of time apart when he was in the army, and their relationship had deteriorated since 1916.

Algernon was descended from a Derbyshire family of MPs, architects and textile manufacturers who had been a major force in the county's cotton industry since the Industrial Revolution. He also happened to be Evelyn Cobbold's first cousin: his mother, born Lady Margaret Coke, and Evelyn's mother, Gertrude, were sisters. The fact that he was related to Pamela meant that his marriage to Angy further cemented the link between the two young women.

As a boy, Algernon had not expected a title. His elder brother, William, should have become 3rd Baron Belper on their father's death but tragically, in October 1898 at the age of twenty-three, he was found drowned in the bath in his hotel room in St Louis, Missouri, when on a trip with members of his family. Amongst them was his Aunt Gertrude, the Countess of Dunmore, who told the coroner quite definitely that it could not have been suicide because he was subject to fainting spells and must have suffered one while in the water. After the coroner reached the same verdict, the grieving family took William's body back to England. When their father died in 1914, Algernon took the title.

Angy and Algernon were married at the Queen's Chapel of the Savoy in London, after a civil ceremony. She wore a soft white French silk dress draped with a long tulle veil and carried a sheaf of lilies. Her tiny attendants were a page and her god-daughter, Pamela's daughter Cynthia, aged just two-and-a-half. Taking the title of Baroness Belper, she also acquired three step-children, aged eleven, nine and seven, the youngest of whom, Lavinia, would one day marry a title herself and become the Duchess of Norfolk.

Angy's home became the imposing Kingston Hall in Nottinghamshire, built in the 1840s for Algernon's grandfather, the 1st Baron Belper. It was not as grand, nor anywhere near as old, as the Tollemache family seat, Helmingham Hall, but with 3,000 acres and pretty gardens, it was not a bad substitute. Given the part her husband's family had played in the life of the village for nearly a century, Angy involved herself in the local community in her outgoing and inimitable style. She seems to have been an affectionate and committed stepmother to Algernon's children, who visited often, as of course did Pamela, marital commitments permitting. These were about to become greater. Charles' training, which ended in New York with the Morgans in early 1924, had paid off. His father and grandfather were obviously pleased with his progress, for in 1924, aged just twenty-seven, he was made a director of Hambros Bank. Life was looking good for Charles and Pamela.

Chapter 19

A Prince Made of Butter

Having had two children in just under a year during 1921 and 1922, Pamela was more than happy to leave that activity to others for the next couple of years, watching delightedly as her friends Angy and Doie both produced their first-born during 1924. Like Pamela, they shared the fecundity of falling pregnant soon after their wedding, fulfilling expectations of them. Unlike Pamela, however, they both dutifully had boys, heirs to their respective families' businesses and fortunes. Coincidentally the two women gave birth within days of each other that June, the Hon Peter Strutt arriving on the 18th and Marcus Wallenberg Junior, known as 'Marc', on the 28th.

Pamela's sister-in-law Blanche was also having a childbirth break in 1924. She was too busy organising Glemham Hall so that it was a suitable house in which to live and entertain their circle, and she was becoming involved in local life, which included persuading her father to open charitable events, for a Duke was bound to be a crowd-puller. Blanche was also providing support for Ivan in the changes taking place within the Cobbold empire. In April that year the two main Cobbold businesses were brought together: the Brewery, Cobbold & Co was merged with the wine and spirit business of Cobbold & Sons, to form a limited company, Cobbold & Co Ltd. John Dupuis Cobbold was the first Chairman and Ivan was appointed to the Board of Directors, with his uncle Philip still playing a prominent role.

In the national arena, 1924 was a significant year for Britain in several ways. Firstly, much to the concern of the largely Tory-supporting

Cobbolds and Hambros – indeed, to the concern of many Conservative supporters – the first Labour Government, formed by Ramsay MacDonald, took power. The illegitimate son of a Scottish farm worker and a ploughman, he had been the Labour Party Leader but resigned in 1914 because of his opposition to Britain entering the war, and did not become leader again until 1922. By then, Labour had replaced the Liberal Party as the main anti-Conservative party, and became the governing party – by a minority – on 22 January 1924.

It was largely the recently-enfranchised working classes who had voted for the new party: they made up approximately 78% of the British population, and since 1918, when women over thirty had been given the vote (provided they met a minimum property requirement) along with the remainder of adult men, they had made their voices heard.[1] A great intellectual talent, Ramsay MacDonald nevertheless caused much national anxiety, including on the part of King George V, who was dismayed by his new Prime Minister's determination to repair Britain's damaged relations with the Soviet Union. The assassination by the Bolsheviks in 1918 of the King's first cousin, Tsar Nicholas II, and his family, was still fresh in the King's mind, not least because the murdered Tsarina, whose body had been thrown down a mineshaft, was one of Queen Victoria's grandchildren. Hardly surprising, then, that when Ramsay MacDonald invited a Russian trade delegation to London, he provoked an outburst from his Monarch, who said he hoped that MacDonald would do nothing that would compel him to shake hands with the murderers of his relations.

The two treaties that MacDonald wanted to be drawn up, one for the settlement of diplomatic differences between Britain and the Soviet Union, the other for loans, excited much opposition generally. Lloyd George, the Conservatives and the Press united to attack the Labour administration with the slogan, 'No money for murderers'. MacDonald would not be in power for very long. The Foreign Office got hold of a letter purporting to be sent by the head of the Communist International

---

[1] The age of thirty requirement was to ensure women did not become the majority of the electorate. If they had been enfranchised based upon the same requirements as men, they would have been in the majority due to the loss of men in the Great War. They would eventually attain equal voting rights in 1928.

Party in Moscow to the British Communist Party, urging British communists to do all they could to ratify the treaties. The letter arrived at the British Conservative Party and at the *Daily Mail*, which published it. Although the Prime Minister did not see it until later, the damage was done. The British public saw the Labour Party as the benign face of communism. The result was another General Election, in which Labour was defeated, to be replaced by the Conservatives under Stanley Baldwin in a second term. The anti-Labourites could breathe again – at least until 1929, when Ramsay MacDonald would be elected once more.

On a brighter note, everything that was good and creative about post-war Britain and its Empire was celebrated that year in the vast British Empire Exhibition at Wembley. This was a huge propaganda exercise designed to remind the rest of the world that Britain was more than ever a force to be reckoned with. On 23 April, St George's Day, it was opened by King George V, the King-Emperor, in the presence of around one hundred thousand people and, thanks to the very recent accessibility of the wireless, for the first time in history a monarch's voice was broadcast. An estimated ten million listeners heard the King introduce the delights of the Exhibition; despite his reputed personal dullness, it made him the post-war voice of patriotic hope.

Replying to his son the Prince of Wales who, as President of the Exhibition, had welcomed him, the King hoped the Exhibition:

'... may be said to reveal to us the whole Empire in little, containing within its 220 acres of ground a vivid model of the architecture, art and industry of all the races which come under the British flag... And we hope further that the success of the Exhibition will bring lasting benefits not to the Empire only but to mankind in general.'[2]

Ironically, despite the King's hopes and the concrete permanence of the stadium designed by Sir Robert McAlpine and Sons, the British Empire itself would only have another twenty-five years to go.

Victor Cavendish, having been Secretary of State for the Colonies since 1922, was deemed a highly suitable person to help organise the Exhibition, so the Cobbolds, as well as Charles and Pamela, would have had ease of entry and prime tickets for the performances. These included

---

[2] Quoted by A.N.Wilson in *After the Victorians*, London, Arrow Books, 2006.

the magnificent opening ceremony, attended by King George, Queen Mary – accompanied by her lady-in-waiting, Victor's wife, the Duchess of Devonshire – and the Prince of Wales, at which the guests were treated to a musical programme by the massed bands of the Brigade of Guards and Pipers, and a massive choir of ten thousand voices, formed and led by the popular composer Sir Edward Elgar.

Although the Exhibition's predecessor, the famous Great Exhibition of 1851 in the early days of Queen Victoria's reign, had been hugely successful, the number of visitors on this occasion was much greater. During its first week alone, the British Empire Exhibition attracted over three hundred thousand visitors, exceeding the Great Exhibition by seventy-five thousand. It must have been an extraordinary sight. A breathtaking array of pavilions and displays greeted the visitor, representing all the varied parts of the Empire. A replica of Old London Bridge, for example, led to the Burmese Pavilion with its pagodas, not far from the minarets and dome of the Malayan Pavilion. In the South Africa section, gold and diamond mining and ostrich farming were exhibited.

The Canadian Pavilion drew the crowds with a life-size statue of the Prince of Wales carved out of butter: an impressive feat, although the Prince said it made his legs look too fat! The great centre of the Exhibition, as of the Empire itself, was India, in the midst of which towered a replica of the Taj Mahal, with carpet-weavers busy at work in its courtyards. At night the whole Exhibition was electrically floodlit, and the amusement park came into life, with miniature trains on which Queen Mary loved to ride. She was delighted to visit the Doll's House, designed by Lutyens and named after her, with its original miniature royal portraits, its larder of real wines and jams and its tiny books in the library, handwritten by such current authors as Arthur Conan Doyle and Rudyard Kipling. It still survives today and is on display at Windsor Castle.

There were rodeos and exhibitions, sales of native crafts and motor shows, dance performances, concerts and parades. During the three months that it was open, the King and Queen visited several times, always finding something new to see, as did many of Europe's remaining monarchs and their children. In June, Boots the Chemist sent five thousand five hundred of its employees for a day's excursion to the

Exhibition by rail, in trains decorated with 'BOOTS' on the front of the engines, while the Prince of Wales gave each of his household staff a sum of money so that they could visit Wembley and enjoy it as much as he had. To celebrate his birthday on 23 June, he also arranged for the entertainment of one hundred war wounded soldiers at Wembley, who attended the Rodeo and toured the grounds and lake, finishing with an afternoon tea at which they received gifts of fruit, chocolate and cigarettes.

But as with many a happy parade, there lurked a slightly sinister element. A hall was built in the Stadium to show films, mostly purpose-made for the event, and to host meetings of a myriad of societies and good causes. On 18 June a meeting was held which was rather out of place amidst the goodwill and fellowship of the Exhibition: the Eugenics Education Society, shortly to become the Eugenic Society. In 1924 its second President since its founding in 1908 was Leonard Darwin, Charles Darwin's second youngest son. He thought the main task of the Society was to encourage the 'eugenically fit to have more children' and he deplored the consequence of a volunteer army in the Great War, because it depleted the number and reduced the proportion of superior, abler individuals. Darwin therefore supported the conversion to conscription.

Although the teachings of the Society were later to become discredited when they were adopted by the German Government, there were still many British intellectuals and notable figures of the 1920s who were members of the Society, as there had been earlier in the century. They now included the past Prime Minister Arthur Balfour, future Prime Minister Neville Chamberlain, and the lauded economist John Maynard Keynes. Even Marie Stopes, the saviour of women with her birth control advice and campaigning, was a supporter. However, unlike others associated with the Society, she saw contraception as the answer to society's fundamental problem – overpopulation – rather than it being a way of preventing the lower classes from reproducing.

As attractive as a healthy, intellectual population may have sounded, the implications were frightening. Whether its early British members saw it also as a way of ensuring some kind of supremacy of race, as well as intellectual supremacy, is not certain. By coincidence, the Society's Vice President from 1909-1911 had been Victor, 2nd Earl Lytton, Governor of

Bengal in the year of the Exhibition, and a grandson of Edward Bulwer Lytton, the author of *Vril: The Power of the Coming Race.*

Not long after the close of the Exhibition in early August, Pamela was delighted to be asked by Angy to be godmother to her first child. She and Charles attended the christening of the Hon Peter Algernon Strutt at Kingston Church in Lord and Lady Belper's Nottinghamshire village. Pamela was the only godmother amongst three godfathers, including Angy's favourite brother Rupert, and following the Saturday ceremony she and Charles were among a party of guests who were entertained for the weekend at Kingston Hall.

The christening was not the only cause for celebration that weekend. Pamela and Charles wanted to share with their friends the news that Charles had been made a director of Hambros Bank. It was what his father had intended for him and, apart from the prestige of the promotion, meant a significant increase in earnings. As Charles' professional commitments would increase, the couple looked for a weekday home in central London. They found Mansfield House in New Cavendish Street, in the highly desirable area just around the corner from Regents Park and Harley Street. A beautiful detached townhouse built around 1775, in a road of Georgian terraces, it still stands in the twenty-first century, renamed Asia House. Grade II listed, it retains many of the original features which Charles and Pamela would have enjoyed: the filigree plasterwork, elaborate marble chimney pieces and classical scenes painted onto the high ceilings and walls. That the road bore the surname of Blanche's family was no coincidence, since the Dukes of Devonshire had for many generations owned significant amounts of land in the area, in addition to their much-loved Devonshire House.

No doubt their friends Marcus and Doie Wallenberg would have been pleased for Charles on his appointment as a director of Hambros Bank. However, Marcus had not yet been given the equivalent honour by his family's Bank, the SEB, so there may have been a twinge of envy. But as the SEB under his uncle Knut's supervision was fast becoming a unique phenomenon in the Swedish financial world – a family-owned commercial bank and the centre of an active industrial group – his appointment three years later in 1927 would be worth waiting for. Doie and Pamela, firm friends, corresponded with each other but rarely had the chance to meet in those early days, for Doie and Marcus were still living a fairly nomadic lifestyle and so did not yet have a permanent home. Every summer Doie insisted on visiting her home at Glencruitten in Scotland with her young sons to see her family, leaving Marcus to his work and his yachting, but it rarely coincided with when Pamela was in Scotland.

In the meantime, Doie with her language skills was fast becoming fluent in Swedish so that she could integrate fully with her adopted country, whilst fiercely maintaining her own identity; she remained determined that she should not be seen by Swedish society as the hausfrau she so despised, even one who had married into one of the most significant families in the country. She enjoyed attention, but so did Marcus, and rather than sitting back and taking pride in his clever and witty wife, he seemed rather to resent it. As a result the couple openly competed for centre stage on many occasion.

If Charles Hambro had been centre stage for a little while following his promotion, his father Eric would shortly find himself thrust completely into the spotlight when, early the following year, the unexpected death of his father Sir Everard Hambro would set in motion a chain of events that would alter the dynamics of the family forever.

Chapter 20

The End of an Era

The following year, 1925, started well for Charles and Pamela. Charles was enjoying his new position as a director of Hambros Bank Ltd which, apart from giving him more responsibility, also involved him in more corporate entertaining – something with which Pamela was happy to help, although she still valued time to herself. With Charles' blessing, in early January she left him with their daughters Cynthia and Diana and went to Pontresina in Switzerland, an old resort and spa town 7 kilometres from St Moritz, perched 1800m above sea level. Among Swiss pine and larch forest, Pamela stayed in the magnificent Grand Hotel Kronenhof, one of the country's most luxurious hotels. She tried skiing for the first time and, with her talent for sport, took to it immediately, although not without a few tumbles.

Why she was in Switzerland is not certain: perhaps it was for the Ladies' World Figure Skating Championships, to be held there on 31 January, for Pamela had enjoyed skating since learning as a child on the lake at Holy Wells. However, that was some distance away in Davos. She certainly met up with friends in Switzerland, who reported back to Charles how well she skied and never stopped laughing, but part of the reason may have been to see her sister, Winifred. She and Algy had been living in Switzerland since about 1919, renting a house by Lake Geneva. It would have been a pleasant change of scenery for Winifred to travel cross-country to stay with her sister; better too for them to be on neutral territory to avoid any animosity between Pamela and Algy, of whom the family had still not managed to fully approve.

Neutral territory was what Switzerland itself had always been, remaining so during the Great War, although it had equipped its army in readiness for entry by any of the four countries that bordered it: these were two of the Entente Powers, Italy and France, and their enemies, the Central Powers of Germany and Austria-Hungary. Although Switzerland had been blockaded by the Allies during the Great War, it emerged generally unscathed, for an advantage of its neutral stance was that it kept its warring neighbours apart. It also made it an attractive place for international conventions, and Geneva was chosen as the home of the League of Nations, set up in 1919, which Switzerland joined in 1920. The aim of the League was to ensure war never happened again, and its main tenet was the new-found Rights of Man, which included those of non-whites and women. But while Switzerland may have hosted the League of Nations, the country did not practise all of its ideals: Swiss women, for example, were denied the right to vote at national level for another fifty years, until 1971, thus keeping them well behind the rest of Europe and, indeed, many other countries.

Winifred must have been deeply disappointed by Switzerland's attitude towards women, for in the years following the Great War it was otherwise an interesting place to live. It had become a haven for refugees and revolutionaries, a country which nurtured the competing political ideologies of communism and fascism, offering radically new concepts of society. Winifred was still an ardent Theosophist, and Switzerland had an academy of Theosophy attracting luminaries such as the psychoanalyst Carl Jung. In the early 1900s a Theosophist colony had been set up at Mount Verita – as the Theosophists renamed the mountain – near Lake Maggiore in the south of the country. The colony's members largely came from northern countries, particularly from the privileged sectors. Intent on searching for life's meaning, they embraced nature and practised vegetarianism, nudism, and free expression through dance. Winifred may have known some of its members although she and Algy, living at Lake Geneva, were too far away to be closely involved with the colony.

For some time Winifred had also been a fully-fledged socialist, and Switzerland gave her the opportunity to put her views into practice by helping those who had suffered from oppressive regimes. At some stage before moving to Switzerland Winifred had learned Serbian and travelled to the troubled Balkans, probably after the outbreak of the Second Balkan War in 1913 which had led to the Great War. Along the way she met and befriended the exotic Hungarian nobleman Count Mihály Károlyi, whose Roman Catholic aristocratic family had played an important part in the Empire of Austria-Hungary since the seventeenth century. Initially a supporter of the existing regime, Károlyi became increasingly left-wing and critical of the war, and in 1916, having married into another powerful Hungarian family two years earlier, he formed a new party called 'The United Party of Independence and of 1848', known generally as 'the Károlyi Party'.

The Party argued for peace with the Allies; they wanted looser ties between Austria and Hungary by abolishing the franchise and language requirements that allowed only a tiny fraction of the male population to vote and run for office before the war; and they wanted the right of women to vote and hold office, a principle of which Winifred strongly approved. With his aim of establishing an independent state of Hungary, Károlyi had made covert contacts during the war with British and French diplomats in Switzerland, supporting the goals which their countries represented as part of the Entente.

During the Great War the Austro-Hungarian Empire, of which Károlyi was still reluctantly a part, suffered greatly. Blockaded by the Allies, it suffered from fuel and transport problems and chronic food shortages, and from 1917 deaths from starvation were common. Upon its defeat, Károlyi established, on 25 October 1918, the National Council of Hungary, which demanded the end of the Empire. In the early morning of 31 October 1918, with help from the army, supporters of the National Council of Hungary, wearing the aster flower as their emblem, seized public buildings throughout Budapest in a revolution that became known as the 'Aster Revolution' or the 'Chrysanthemum Revolution'. The Prime Minister resigned and the former Prime Minister Istvan Tisza was murdered. By the end of the day the King of Austria-Hungary, Charles IV, had accepted the coup and appointed Károlyi as Hungary's new Prime Minister. On 16 November 1918 the Democratic Republic of Hungary was proclaimed, with Károlyi as President, marking the end of several centuries of rule by the Hapsburg Monarchy.

But also in November 1918 the Hungarian Communist Party had been formed by a group of Hungarian prisoners of war and communist sympathisers, and in March 1919 the Social Democrats, with whom Károlyi's National Council had been in alliance, albeit unhappily, handed power to the Hungarian Soviet Republic. In an effort to secure its rule the Communist Government resorted to arbitrary violence, ordering nearly six hundred executions, including those of the clergy. On 1 August 1919 the Hungarian Soviet Republic was ousted by the Romanians, followed by a counter-revolution by a militantly anti-communist authoritarian government. In trying to re-establish the traditional Hungarian political order, a 'white terror' ensued, leading to the imprisonment, torture and execution without trial of socialists, communists, Jews, and sympathisers with the Károlyi regime. Nearly one hundred thousand people were forced to leave the country; in anticipation of the troubles Károlyi and his wife, the Countess Katalin, went into exile in France in July 1919.

Winifred is known to have given moral and practical support to the couple, to whom she referred by their anglicised Christian names of Michael and Catherine, as well as other Hungarian refugees. Her family does not know how exactly she achieved this, but photographs of her and Algy at home in Switzerland in the early 1920s show them with the Károlyis, together with other intellectual friends such as the Swiss aristocrat Baron Reding, and Winifred LeSueur, an early member of the newly-formed Soroptimist Society, through which educated women in America and Britain sought to improve the position of women throughout the world. The Károlyis must have been particularly grateful for Winifred's support in 1923 when the Budapest Supreme Court confiscated Michael's lands, finding him guilty of high treason. At least Catherine owned a villa at Deauville in France, so they were not entirely bereft of somewhere to live.

Winifred and Algy must have found Michael to be a fascinating dinner guest. In 1925 he was aged fifty and had been a political reactionary since a young man. Many stories about his life had been published in the world's press as they occurred. In 1913, when Winifred and Algy were having their polite Society wedding in England, Michael was fighting a dramatic duel with his political adversary Count Istvan Tisza. As the *New York Times* reported on 3 January 1913, Count Tisza

263

was strongly anti-suffrage and for that reason an attempt on his life had been made the previous year. On 2 January 1913 in the National Club of Budapest, he offered his hand to Károlyi, the Opposition Leader, who refused to take it:

'... [Károlyi] ostentatiously thrust his hands in his pockets, declaring that after what had occurred it would be useless if he and Count Tisza pretended to be friends. Afterwards Count Tisza sent a challenge.'

The conditions Tisza set for the duel were that they were to fight until one of them was disabled, the only protection to be neck bandages. The two men fought for an hour with heavy swords, but 'Count Tisza, who is extraordinarily agile for his age, had the better of his opponent throughout, Count Károlyi being a big, heavy man'. Károlyi was badly wounded in the arm, at which point their doctors stopped the duel. The paper reported that the combatants were not reconciled and, rather ominously, that other duels were expected.

Károlyi hit the papers in March 1925 too, for his wife Catherine, once regarded as one of the most beautiful women in Europe, had fallen ill with typhoid fever while visiting America on her own and Michael was summoned to visit her. On applying for a visa he was told by the Secretary of State, who was conscious of his constitutional duty in the treatment of aliens and of the fact that Károlyi was suspected of being a dreaded communist, that it would be granted for the sole purpose of a temporary visit to see his wife; further, that he would be forbidden the right to speak in public while he was in the country. Michael was compelled to agree, even though this meant he was prevented even from responding to attacks made on him by the Hungarian press while he was there.

In Károlyi's defence, various English-speaking newspapers in America led vigorous attacks on the State Department for its gagging action: as a result, the Secretary of State relented, although with conditions attached. Károlyi was able eventually to return to Hungary in 1946 and served for three years as the Hungarian Ambassador to France, where he died in 1955. The Countess survived him by thirty years.

Pamela may not have met the Károlyis while staying in Pontresina but she would have been aware of the very different worlds she and her sister inhabited: Pamela married to a banker with very healthy prospects, Winifred living off financial handouts from their father and supporting socialist causes. The sisters looked very different too. Hemlines had gradually been rising: in England, ankle-length skirts had risen to mid-calf by the end of the war, and by 1925 hemlines were 14-16 inches above the ground. The fashionable silhouette of dresses disguised a woman's contours, flattening the chest and dropping the waist. Pamela followed the general trend but favoured the softer styles available, preferring to be feminine in her appearance, if not always in her demeanour. Winifred, on the other hand, had her dark hair cut very short in the latest fashion – the Eton crop: this was the iconic style which shocked many people, as it was so contrary to the notion that a woman's hair was her crowning glory. Winifred also wore very masculine-style clothes. She took to calling herself 'Freddy', in the fashionable way of changing female names to their nearest male versions, and had started smoking a pipe.

Her style had changed over the previous four years. An earlier studio photograph taken of her in 1921 in London by Bassano, photographer to the Royal Family and to the top strata of society, shows her with a softer hairstyle and pretty blouse, while her dark eyes gaze sadly at the camera, as though she is there against her will; perhaps she was, for the notion of having such a photograph taken does not seem in keeping with her unconventional self. Perhaps she was thinking of her son Toby, of whom she saw very little when he was small. As he grew older he sometimes visited his parents in Switzerland, as the many pictures of him as a teenager with Winifred show, although he seldom revealed much about his visits.

While Pamela was away, Charles was a very hands-on father for the times, although of course he was fortunate not to be a lone father trying to cope with the demands of work and children: he had plenty of domestic help, including Pamela's old faithful nanny, Jane Cottle. Nevertheless, he still spent as much time as he could with 'the Bubbas', as he called them, trying to get home from work in time to read them a bedtime story, which 'Cinders', the eldest at nearly four, loved, although three-year-old Diana, known as 'Di', would get restless. Writing to Pamela several times during January 1925 from his father's London home, Norwich House,

Charles gave her updates on the minutiae of their lives in her absence. Their spaniel Glen, and the cats Jock and Gracie, of which Pamela was very fond, had been treated by the vet for various ailments; Charles too was having treatment for some 'internal trouble', taking magnesia prescribed by his doctor, and as a result of a persistent sore throat had been told he should cut down on his smoking. From then on, he told Pamela, he would limit himself to '… one cig after each meal & one pipe after breakfast & lunch & dinner. No cigars.' The doctor was also going to give him something which would make him 'hate smoking and drink'.

Charles and 'the Bubbas' had enjoyed a trip to the zoo one Sunday to see the monkeys and lions and he told Pamela, clearly very pleased, that the girls had been very affectionate with him, smothering him in kisses. He had been to the cinema with his father to see a film – a silent, as 'the talkies' were still two years away – about 'a little woman whose hubby was a cad & she was so unhappy'; and he was 'fearfully busy' trying to organise the Bank's Dinner and Dance on 29 January, which was going to be a 'grand affair' with three hundred guests expected. Their ability to actually attend the event, however, would have depended on the weather that night. January 1925 would be remembered for the treacherous, unusually dense smog that enveloped London on the 10th and the 11th of that month, and which threatened to return. On 14 January there was another 'perfect pea soup fog, with everyone losing their way all over London', and there was no guarantee that it would not happen again on the night of the dance. Such was the poor quality of air in the city that 'pea soupers', a potentially lethal combination of natural fog and coal smoke, would remain a regular feature of London until the Clean Air Act of 1956.

In the sweeter country air of Kent, Charles was supervising various maintenance work at Pickhurst Mead at the weekends, and their car, the Sunbeam, was now ready for Pamela's return; its engine had been 'rejuvenated' by one of their staff and was 'looking very beautiful'. Charles was clearly missing their physical relationship and his thoughts turned to a subject they had obviously been discussing for some time: how to produce a boy. He passed on to Pamela some advice his doctor had given him:

'He says all the theories regarding periods, sides & times are proved to be incorrect. Because someone with one oviary [sic] can produce both sexes.

'He has a theory which he has tried with success many times. The husband to starve & become teetotal & the wife to take certain medicines he can give her. I am only to drink the minimum amount of wine & spirits for 3 months & go to bed every night hungry.

'You are to get fit & strong as possible taking stuff like champagne when you can. He said it doesn't matter if the woman comes or not!

'I've therefore arranged with him to write down all instructions & I start on the same tonight. I have no lunch & nothing to drink except a liqueur after dinner.

'You won't know me when you get back.'

That was pretty accurate, for just one week later he reported:

'I hardly know myself. Water, water, water & cough drops for smoke & a cup of coffee for breakfast & an apple. A piece of fish or some vegetables for lunch & 2 things for dinner. The only thing that troubles me is I'm so much fitter on it!! no throat, no tiredness in the mornings & I feel so hearty & energetic.'

Pamela would have been pleased to hear that, for they were hoping he would be able to join her in Pontresina on 31 January, from where they would leave for Paris on 5 February to enjoy a few days' shopping, arriving back in England in time to have 'a grand birthday party for Cinders' on the 13th . He asked if she could manage to get them 'a lovely big single bed' with a bath.

If Charles and Pamela were determined to have a boy, then according to the doctor Charles would have to stick to his regime for three months, until April, for the theory to work. But it seems they did not wait quite long enough before testing it: at the end of March Pamela fell pregnant, and would give birth to their third daughter on New Year's Eve that year, 1925.

Pamela was not the only mother to go abroad that January and leave her children behind, although at least she left them with their father. Her best friend Angy – Baroness Belper – had also left England at the start of January, taking her husband with her but leaving behind baby Peter, aged seven months. Angy and Algernon were going away for rather longer than Pamela, embarking on a voyage to New Zealand and Canada. Angy kept a detailed and vivid diary of their journey in her distinctive bold handwriting, which started with their saying goodbye to Peter at Kingston Hall, when his nurse Patti brought him down to the motor to wave goodbye:

'I cannot bear to leave him and squash him to me. He smiles & waves his little hand and will never know how unhappy I was.'

They were also leaving behind Algernon's children – 'the steps' as Angy called them – who came to see them off on their train for London, and cried 'bitterly'. The couple stayed overnight at the Hyde Park Hotel so they were ready for the 11am train the next day from Victoria station, dining at the Savoy with another group of well-wishers, including Angy's father, the Hon Douglas Tollemache. For much of the voyage they were joined by Pamela's father John, who of course had known Angy since her childhood and, unencumbered by Evelyn, was achieving his desire to travel again. John had his own little family group of well-wishers at Victoria, consisting of his sister Olive, who since her marriage had become Lady Cairns, his brother Ralph, son Ivan and son-in-law Charles.

While much of the world was still an unsettled and volatile place, the countries of the British Commonwealth were far enough away to be exciting but were comparatively safe. The travellers picked up their first ship, *RMS Ormonde*, in Toulon, where John and Algernon were pursued by a 'cocotte', as Angy referred to her: a woman who tried to sell them a basket containing a model of a female nude, which she insisted they would love. Their first port of call was Naples, where John joined Angy and Algernon onshore. John may have shared Angy's disappointment with the city, which she pronounced 'very dirty & smelly', although she was fascinated by Pompeii and appalled by the fact that the whole city had disappeared 'at the height of the season'. The voyage for John certainly started very promisingly, for on 18 January Angy refers in her diary to playing peg quoits and getting 'knocked out by Mrs Tolhurst, a 'pick-up' of JDC's', proving that even at the age of sixty-four he still had his attractions. Pamela would have been proud of him. John shared much of the journey with Angy and Algernon, all of them enjoying it very much, despite Angy suffering frequent bouts of seasickness.

Various practicalities meant Charles was not able to join Pamela in

Switzerland after all, and instead looked forward to her coming home at the end of January. The weekend before her return he took the girls to visit their great-grandfather Sir Everard, and told Pamela that he was 'really very well on Sunday & was in his motor pram when the Bubbas came down. They were awfully pleased to see him. I'm afraid his bladder trouble is not well yet & he loved your letter. Baby [Diana] gave him a big kiss from you.'

It was the last time the girls would see him, for Everard died of a heart attack a month later, on 26 February 1925, at home at Hayes Place. He was nearly eighty-three. Remaining involved in business until he was over eighty, he was physically active almost until the end, reliant on his electric wheelchair for only a short time before he died. Four days later Everard was buried in St Mary's churchyard, Hayes, next to the grave of his first wife Mary, and their little children Hermione and Maurice. His death was the subject of a major news item in *The Times*, where a lengthy obituary paid tribute to his achievements in the international banking world, his intellectual skills and his charitable work. The Bank of England too recorded their esteem of Everard as a member of its Court, praising him as one '... who, by his unvarying kindliness and courtesy and by his personal charm, has won the esteem and affection of every member of the Court'.

Two memorial services were held, one at Cornhill in the City, the other at Milton Abbey, where a great assembly of his Dorset friends and tenants gathered and where, in Sir Everard's pew, his head gardener of over twenty years, Mr Perkins, placed a magnificent wreath of amaryllis lilies, white azaleas and violets which had been grown in Milton Abbey's gardens. At Hayes too there was much mourning, for he had made the village his main home above Milton and had contributed hugely to the local community.

Everard's eldest son Eric, Charles' father, was now heir to Milton Abbey and Hayes Place, and the second Chairman of Hambros Bank. It was not a good year to take over, for 1925 saw a return to the gold standard, which had the effect of decreasing British exports and badly affecting commerce. The death of Sir Everard Hambro, Victorian philanthropist and Edwardian gentleman, now seemed to symbolise the end of one successful era for the family and the start of another

269

when things might never be as good again. But once the shock of his grandfather's death had lessened, Charles thought life was looking up, at least for him and Pamela, for the prospect of his inheriting Milton Abbey seemed just that little bit closer.

Chapter 21

Uncertainty

Sir Everard Hambro would have been greatly disappointed at what was about to happen to Hayes, his favourite estate, now that Eric had now inherited all his property. Comprising the two houses Hayes Place and Pickhurst Mead (and other smaller plots), Everard had regarded this estate as his home above Milton Abbey. Eric should have been able to maintain both magnificent estates as his father had done, but he had carried on spending and his love of roulette had continued. Unfortunately, so had his lack of success. It was soon clear that he would have a financial struggle but fortunately for him there was a potential rescuer in the unlikely form of Bromley Council.

Immediately after the war, between 1919 and 1922, over two hundred thousand homes had been built for the new war heroes to live in under Lloyd George's Coalition Government. But because of the post-war marriage boom many more were needed, and at a cheaper building price. In 1923, when he was Minister for Health in Stanley Baldwin's Government, Neville Chamberlain introduced a Housing Act, which provided attractive financial incentives to councils to build more houses to meet post-war needs and the demands of the new voting class. Shortly after inheriting the Hayes Place estate, Eric started discussions with Bromley Council for its development by Henry Boote, a Sheffield-based building company, into a massive new housing estate, the type that would soon be found all over the country. The end of the historical and beautiful estate was in sight.

Charles and Pamela were upset by Eric's plans, for it meant leaving

Pickhurst Mead. They must have hoped they could now have the house to themselves, as Everard's death made it possible for Eric and Sybil to leave Pickhurst Mead and move into Hayes Place mansion. Although by then Charles and Pamela had their London home, they had become used to having a country retreat, so much healthier for their children than London in those smog-ridden days and, for someone in Charles's position, expected by his clients. It should have been the case that the Hambros, unlike many landed gentry who by then had been forced to sell their estates, were able to hold on to theirs, for their financial security did not depend solely on inherited wealth but on their success in business. How frustrating then it was for Charles, aware of the effect his father's gambling was having on his finances, to see him parting with the estate after more than forty-five years of family involvement with the village which his grandfather had so loved. And Charles loved Pickhurst Mead. He had helped to nurture its beautiful gardens and spent much time preparing it for their first home as newly-weds. He and Pamela would now need to find somewhere else as their country residence, while Eric's plans for the estate as a whole meant he had no intention of taking up residence in Hayes Place mansion; he and Sybil would move into Milton Abbey instead.

Everard's death had left his much younger second wife, Ebba, a widow at the age of thirty-eight. Fortunately for the family, and no doubt taking a realistic view of the likelihood of her remarrying, Everard had not been so foolish as to favour her above his children. Instead, his Will left her: '... all the furniture pictures engravings drawings and articles whatsoever which shall be or have usually been in her boudoirs and bedrooms at Hayes Place and Milton Abbey...'; the lease of his flat at 1 Carlos Place, Mount Street, in Mayfair, which ran until 1934, to be paid for by his trustees from other monies; and the benefit of income from a trust fund of £50,000 whilst she remained his widow. On her remarriage the remainder of the fund and its income was to be divided between his four sons.

They would not have to wait too long. In February 1927, exactly two years after Everard's death, Ebba married Robert Stanhope Dormer, a grandson of the 11th Baron Dormer. Ebba's stepson Eric gave her away. She and her husband went to live at fashionable Greenham Common, in a large, newly-built house with a substantial amount of land which Ebba bought herself, presumably from the money she inherited from Everard. There she and Robert raised their children, who kept the house in the family until the 1980s.

From a wealthy Anglo-Irish family, the Whytes, Ebba had several sisters, two of whom had been killed when very young, together with their nanny, in a tragic accident in 1885 at the family's home, Hatley Manor in Ireland. One of Ebba's surviving younger sisters was called Estelle, and it would soon become public knowledge that she and Sir Eric Hambro were lovers.

It is probable that Eric met Estelle – whose full name was, grandly, Edith Estelle Ermyntrude le Poer Whyte – early on in his father's marriage. However, it is not known when she and Eric became lovers, and in fact, only three years after her sister's marriage to Everard, Estelle herself had married, on 20 April 1914. Her husband, Captain Leonard Gwyn Elger, was, like Everard and his sons, a keen golfer. He played for the same North Devon club as Angus Hambro, although was nowhere near his standard. Estelle and Eric may have met that way, and their paths are likely to have crossed at Biarritz at Everard's rented house and where the Hambro men also played golf.

Leonard Elger had already served in the army during the Boer War and in March 1915, aged forty-three, was appointed to No 5 Remount Squadron and sent to St German in France. In July 1917, while on duty, his horse bolted while he was riding and he struck his head on a tree. Knocked unconscious, he somehow stayed on the horse until it jumped a fence and he rolled off. He did not come to until the next day in hospital, when it was found he had fractured the base of his skull. Back in London, in the officers' hospital at Cadogan Square, it was at first thought that twelve weeks' leave and recuperation in the country would cure him of his headaches and dizziness, and the irritation which the noise of traffic caused him, and in November 1917 an Army Medical Board passed him fit for Home Service. But the following March a further examination found him worse than before: slow, finding it difficult to concentrate and easily fatigued by any mental effort, and still suffering headaches and dizziness.

Even so, he was considered able to carry out certain duties, although not fit to ride for the foreseeable future, and he was offered a desk job. As he wrote to a friend, the prospect of such a life, removed from action or adventure '... isn't good enough'. That same month he applied to resign his commission on the grounds of ill-health, which was granted, and he was awarded the honorary rank of Captain. He died on 17th April 1922 in Biarritz, in his fiftieth year.

For much of Estelle and Leonard's short marriage, they would either have been separated by war or living with the effects of his injury upon him. After she was widowed at the age of thirty-two, Estelle lived for a while at her brother-in-law Everard's flat at Carlos Place.

When Everard died, Eric was fifty-three and, as his father had done, was ageing well: still handsome, charismatic and, despite his extravagance, still rich. And as Chairman of one of the most successful merchant banks in Europe, he was high-profile and had influence, sitting on the Board of many illustrious institutions. Estelle clearly preferred older men for her husband, like Eric, was eighteen years her senior. The affair between Eric and Estelle had certainly started by late 1926. According to *The Scotsman*, a long-established and respected newspaper, it was following Sybil's trip to the Mediterranean in November that year that Eric made it clear to her, his wife of thirty-two years, that he no longer wanted to live with her.

Very fond of travelling, that trip Sybil took was one of many she made during their marriage, sometimes without Eric but usually with one of their children: Eric's work commitments, particularly since his father's death, did not allow him to join his wife very often. Their younger son, Charles' brother Richard, had been ranching in Argentina since 1921 when he came of age, and in 1923 Sybil sailed to Buenos Aires to visit him. Usually she and Eric managed to spend part of the winter together in Monte Carlo, but it seems the last time was in February 1925, when the Court Circular of *The Times* reported their being among the arrivals at the Principality's Nouvel Hotel de Paris.

During the rest of 1925 Eric and Sybil were seen together less and less frequently. That July Sybil went to the South of France with their daughters Zelia and Juliet, and again with them in August, in the middle of the British shooting season. Eric took a trip to Paris at the end of that year without his wife, returning to London in early January 1926.

There followed much separate to-ing and fro-ing. In late February 1926 Sybil left Milton Abbey, staying for a short time at Claridges Hotel in London, and eleven days later returned to Milton Abbey. She was not there for long, however. Within three weeks she was back in London again, leaving on 27 March 1926 with Zelia, by then aged seventeen, to go to Naples on a small Japanese ship which was bound for Japan.

Eric was also staying at Claridges in March, leaving there to return to Milton Abbey a couple of days after his wife and daughter's departure. Sybil and Zelia stayed in Italy for just under four months. After their return, in July Sybil went to a wedding without Eric, and then went away again. In her absence, in late October Eric stayed again in Claridges, this time for a few weeks, and then dropped the bombshell on Sybil, when she returned in November – that he wanted their marriage to end. After doing so, he spent the rest of the winter at Biarritz, returning in late January 1927, shortly before Ebba's wedding in the February.

It is highly probable that Estelle had been in Biarritz with Eric, and perhaps she stayed on there alone for a little while, for she does not seem to have attended her sister's wedding. Among the guests were her late husband's brother, a retired Major and his wife, presumably invited by Ebba. Perhaps her brother-in-law's presence was a deterrent to Estelle, who feared his disapproval if he suspected his late brother's widow was cavorting with a married man. Alternatively, perhaps her absence was because some of the Hambros had discovered the relationship and she did not want to confront them. However, as the only Hambro family members who attended were Eric, Zelia and a couple of cousins, she need not have worried. The other wedding guests included at least one person other than Eric who had enjoyed an extramarital dalliance: the Hon Mrs Dudley Ward. Although by 1927 her affair with the Prince of Wales had ended, she was still his close confidante.

It was coincidental that Sybil had been in Italy in 1926, for that year her daughter-in-law's sister, Winifred, was also there, having something of an uncomfortable time. She and her husband Algy had left England at the end of July for a motor tour of the Continent with two friends, Captain Arthur Mills and his wife Lady Dorothy, née Walpole, a well-known writer and traveller who had been the first white woman to visit Timbuktu. While Sybil would have been welcomed by the Italian Government thanks to the connections of her husband's family – Carl Joachim Hambro had played a vital role in the unification of Italy – Winifred would elicit a different response.

In April that year in Rome, an attempt had been made by an Irish aristocrat to assassinate Benito Mussolini, the Italian dictator. Violet Gibson, the would-be assassin – by coincidence a Theosophist like Winifred – only succeeded in grazing the bridge of his nose with her bullet, but that September another attempt was made when an anarchist threw a bomb at his car. The fascist leader was, understandably, a little sensitive, as were his many supporters. When just a week later Winifred, in a restaurant in Italy, allegedly made an insulting remark about Mussolini, it had results she never imagined: she was arrested and imprisoned.

There was scarcely a newspaper that did not report it, including papers in America, with headlines ranging from 'Political Arrest of an Englishwoman' to 'Peer's Niece in Italian Gaol', its reference being to her uncle, the 8th Earl of Dunmore, for the papers were all keen to state the fact that she was 'highly connected'. Her family was mentioned in various ways: John Dupuis Cobbold was usually 'the well-known Ipswich banker', and one paper spoke of her brother's marriage to a daughter of the Duke of Devonshire. Even Algy's connections were stated – the fact that he was a cousin of General Lord Cavan and of the author Douglas Sladen who, the papers pointed out, had written several books about Italy and, according to one report, was in fact an admirer of Il Duce.

According to Winifred's aunt Mrs Reginald Coke, with whom she and Algy had stayed before leaving England, the two couples had started from Belgium and then separated in Munich in August, when the Sladens were to go on to their flat at Villa al Mare. On 5 October 1926 Mrs Coke received a letter from Winifred written in French, headed, 'Prison, Volosca'. She told Mrs Coke that she was accused of speaking against Mussolini, had been put in prison and was not permitted to write in anything but French. Mrs Coke knew nothing more, telling the newspapers that Winifred was a woman 'of definite ideas and marked ability. She takes a great interest in problems that affect humanity.'

In early November 1926 the *Daily Sketch* was given the exclusive story of what had happened, referred to by countless other newspapers. Winifred had, it transpired, spent three days and three nights in prison before being released on bail on 5 October, pending her trial which was to take place on 18 November. The *Daily Sketch* published Winifred's letter to a friend in London, written when her ordeal had ended:

'I am writing to tell you it's all over. I heard today that the British Ambassador at Rome, who was away in England, returned and went straight to Mussolini about it, with the result that it was at once quashed.

'On Saturday October 3rd at Brioni, I was suddenly arrested and charged with having, on September 12 at Abbazia, spoken against Mussolini. I was taken by guard to Volosca and there imprisoned. The incident was that on September 12 we arrived in our car from Austria late in the afternoon and Algy and I went to Tornasie to have refreshments about 7.30pm. There a Hungarian acquaintance joined us, and there was no-one else there at all.

'This man immediately mentioned the attempt on Mussolini and began praising Fascism etc. I took the opposite viewpoint and we had a friendly discussion, and I completely forgot about it after.

'Apparently this Hungarian repeated this conversation at dinner that night to an Italian woman who dislikes us. She went straight to the authorities and denounced me. The Hungarian gave a written statement to the judge that I had spoken against Mussolini but he could not swear to what I had said or the words I had used. He could only say I had said one or two things. In my defence I denied this, and said I had only criticised Fascism academically and theoretically.

'After I had been three days and three nights in prison the British Consul at Fiume and Algy managed by tremendous efforts to get me out on bail pending trial.'

At least she thought that feeling in Abbazia was sympathetic towards her, and she said the prison was clean and the warders kind. Her adventure would not have done her reputation amongst her intellectual socialist friends any harm. One paper, with the headline 'WOMAN PIPE-SMOKER: Unusual Accomplishments of Mussolini's ex-Prisoner', spoke of Winifred's talents: not only could she speak Serbian, she was also an 'ardent Theosophist and Socialist, a very good swimmer and dancer, and she can smoke a pipe'. One paper even referred to her suntan, still something of a novelty amongst women of her social class, and which had only very recently become fashionable after the new French designer, Coco Chanel, accidentally acquired one on a yacht in the South of France.

To fellow Britons her story served as a cautionary tale for a while, illuminating the dangers of being in foreign climes. After all, if someone as well-connected and intellectual as Winifred, who was no shrinking violet and a seasoned traveller, could be imprisoned so easily, what hope for others? *The Scotsman* carried a 'Warning to British Travellers', saying that the British authorities were considering the issue of an official warning to visitors to the Continent to carry their passports with them in the streets and in all public places:

'… in order to minimise the risk of temporary imprisonment on any charge which may be preferred against them. Without going into the case of Mrs Algernon Sladen there is reason to believe that police authorities on the Continent do not always offer facilities to foreign nationals to communicate immediately with their Consul if they are arrested. In the absence of a passport two or three days may elapse before the identity of the detained person is established to the satisfaction of the police authorities, and this period is often spent in a prison cell.'

The piece also suggested that travellers to the Continent 'exercise discretion in their speech in public surroundings'. It cited the experience of an Englishman passing through France on his way to Italy who, irritated by French Customs officials, pronounced the formalities to which he was subjected as 'imbecile', whereupon he was promptly taken before a higher body and charged with contempt of the Customs. On proffering a £1 note for the fine in the absence of francs, the official refused to recognise it and the chap was marched under escort to a bank where he was able to convert it to the required currency. To add to his annoyance, he missed his train.

Young Toby would no doubt have been told of his mother's imprisonment once Mrs Coke had received Winifred's first letter. To divert him, his grandfather John Cobbold wrote to him at Stowe School, as he regularly did, in his usual chatty, kindly way, telling him of recent shooting achievements at Holy Wells: one hundred pheasants, fifty-three partridges, twenty hares and two woodcock. He told Toby that his Grandmama Evelyn was probably going to take him to the Pyrenees in December, and that she and his Aunt Pam would be going to see him soon, now that his cousin Cynthia had had her appendix out.

For that reason, although Pamela was sympathetic to her elder sister while not being surprised that her socialist views had got her into trouble, Winifred would have been very low down on her list of priorities, for having a five-year-old child with appendicitis in 1926 was a serious matter. Not until 1902, when King Edward VII's life was saved by what was then radical surgery – never previously used for appendicitis – had the general public been properly aware of the disease. But it was still closely associated with mortality. In the 1920s Cinders' age put her in one of the two categories at highest risk of death. Added to the fact that those in the Hambros' social class were – perhaps surprisingly – two-and-a-half times more likely to die from appendicitis than those in the lowest class, the risks for their eldest daughter were considerable. However, after a very trying time for Pamela and Charles, by the end of 1926 Cinders had made a full recovery.

Whilst amused by his sister-in-law's misadventure which he knew she would dine out on for months, Charles had his mind not only on his sick daughter but on his father's conduct. He knew that Estelle was no silly young flapper – she was a mature woman and held the office of Justice of the Peace – but even so, he knew that if her affair with Eric resulted in his parents' divorce, it could have wider adverse effects on the Hambro family. They had always put so much emphasis on the strength and importance of family ties, not only in emotional attachments but in running a dynastic business. Apart from his great-great grandfather Joseph, forced to have his mentally sick wife taken into care, the Hambro men had only ever been separated from their wives by death. Charles did not want to judge his father, who he knew had experienced much frustration working under Everard as Chairman of the family's bank, having to wait until the old man died before having the responsibility he always wanted; and he was well aware of his mother's determined independent streak and love of adventure, and the difficulties she had endured when she gave birth to Juliet.

But nevertheless, Charles must have feared for the family's future. Eric, in taking over Everard's role as Chairman, had stepped into big shoes, both professionally and personally, and his own financial situation had to be above reproach. A divorce from Sybil could be costly, and his gambling habit had not ceased. Charles was already concerned to find that his father had, in that November of 1926, sold through auction at Christies some very valuable paintings from Milton Abbey.

Fortunately, Eric's personal situation seemed to be having no adverse effect on his professional dealings. In 1927 and 1928, in a move of which his father and grandfather would have been proud, he arranged for Hambros Bank to raise massive loans for Greece. It was a country close to the Hambros' heart. From 1863 to the mid-1890s Greece had been one of the Bank's most important customers and, after a war with Turkey in 1923, it was in need of funds again. The loans Eric raised had extremely beneficial results for both that country and the Bank.

For Sybil, the last straw came at the beginning of May 1927 when Eric formally 'withdrew from cohabitation' and refused to live with her as a spouse. From an address in Berkeley Square, London, where she went to stay after leaving Milton Abbey, no nightingales sang but instead, on 1 July, Lady Hambro wrote a begging letter:

'My Dear Eric,

'It is now two months since you shut me out of my home – I wish you to know that I am ready absolutely to forgive and forget and let all bygones be bygones if you will receive me back and I will do all that I can to make you happy. I ask you to do this as we have not only our happiness to consider but that of our children.

'Yours affectly

'SYBIL'

He did not reply. On 13 July she wrote again, a short letter begging him to answer promptly. She received a letter dated 14th, from the address of Hambros Bank in the City:

'Dear Sybil

'I have your letter of 1st July and am compelled to tell you that resumption of former conditions is impossible either now or at a later time. My decision that an irrevocable break was essential in all our interests, was reached after long and anxious consideration and nothing that has since happened changes my views, which are final. Under no circumstances will I ever consent to return and I am sure it will be better for your own happiness if you recognise the inevitableness of the position, more especially as our adult children concur in this conclusion.

'Yours affly

'ERIC.'

The 'adult children' to whom Eric referred were Charles and Richard, who perhaps by then had come to realise there was little point their parents staying together. Her attempts at reconciliation having failed, Sybil took the next humiliating step and on 20 July 1927 presented a petition for the Restitution of Conjugal Rights to the High Court of Justice. Later abolished in 1970, at the time it was the step to be taken before presenting an actual petition for divorce, to enable the parties to think again before admitting defeat and facing the inevitable stigma that still accompanied it. The petition referred to the letters between her and Eric and his refusal to return and 'render her conjugal rights'. She asked for an order that those rights be restored – effectively that Eric return to her – and requested custody of their two daughters, Zelia, aged eighteen, and Juliet, by then aged eleven. There was an unbearable five-month wait before Sybil's petition was heard on 5 December 1927, when an order was made requiring Eric to return home to her 'and render to her conjugal rights'. Sybil also had to bear the embarrassment of the petition being announced in the national papers.

He did not return. Over the next twelve months Eric would continue to commit adultery with Estelle at Milton Abbey, his London house at 48 Upper Grosvenor Street, at Gleneagles in Scotland and at the luxurious Savoy Hotel, whose attractions, apart from the discretion of its staff, included up-to-the-minute art deco décor, an excellent resident jazz band and ensuite bathrooms in all the rooms. Coincidentally, three decades after Eric's dalliance at 48 Upper Grosvenor Street, the address would become infamous for the biggest sex scandal of the 1960s, when Margaret, Duchess of Argyll, was photographed there performing fellatio on a man who was not her husband: the notorious 'headless man' affair, so-called because his head was not captured in the frame, making him the subject of much fascinated speculation in Society, and the Duchess notorious.

There is little doubt that Pamela would have felt deeply for her parents-in-law, for she was very fond of both of them. To have the petition published in a national newspaper was a common enough occurrence, not reserved solely for the wealthy, although they tended to be the only ones who could afford to take such action. But it was nevertheless humiliating, and the fact that most of their social circle would see it, if they were not already aware of the situation, must have been excruciating for both of them. However, as the woman who had been deserted, it must have been far worse for Sybil.

At the same time, Pamela had also been thinking about her friend Doie and her marriage. Life should have been getting easier for her and Marcus for their hectic and nomadic lifestyle, dictated since they married by his training schedule in London, Paris, Berlin and New York, had finally become more stable. They had found somewhere permanent to live back in Sweden, near Stockholm, where staff were at hand to take care of everything, including their two boys – Doie had had a second son, Peter, in May 1926. But it seemed to Pamela, from Doie's letters to her, that the pair had started to drift apart. As Eric and Sybil had done, the Wallenbergs seemed to be spending an increasing amount of time away from each other, but unlike Eric and Sybil, the younger couple had been married for less than four years. To Pamela, the future generally looked suddenly less certain.

Chapter 22

Definite Ends

The Wallenbergs' marriage had started off well enough. After they met with Pamela and Charles in New York in late 1923, Marcus and Doie had stayed on in the city so he could continue his training there at Brown Brothers, the city's famous banking firm, and in early 1924 he was given industrial commissions to undertake in America by the Wallenberg's bank, the SEB, which involved the couple travelling all over the country. They both loved it.

The 'twenties were an exciting decade to be in the USA, for unlike Europe the country was experiencing an industrial boom. Vast modern buildings were appearing, creating golden opportunities in the building trade, and car manufacturers were springing up everywhere, making not only mass-produced motors that more families could afford but fabulous luxury models for film stars to enjoy: film stars who for the first time could be heard, not just seen. Just a few months before the Wallenbergs arrived in New York City, innovations in sound-on film techniques had led to the first commercial screening of short motion pictures, and by 1927 the first full-length feature 'talkie' would be made.

The increase in cars saw the creation of tourist attractions, and long-distance routes were made less tedious, and even fun, by the appearance of roadway cafés and neon signs, introduced just the year before. And when Doie and Marcus stayed somewhere en route during their travels, the chances were that the boom in electrical domestic appliances in the USA made their experience a comfortable one: certainly more so than Doie enjoyed in Sweden.

Like Pamela, fulfilling what was expected of her on the marital front, Doie had fallen pregnant very quickly after their wedding, and while heavily pregnant in May 1924 she went with Marcus to England, from where she could visit her family in Scotland. Marcus had to do some of his training in a London bank, so naturally did so in the international business department of Hambros Bank, of which his family were now a part and of which, that same month, his uncle Knut Wallenberg was re-elected a director. Whether or not Charles would have agreed with Marcus' view that Hambros was more old-fashioned than the American bank he had worked at, he knew Marcus could not deny the financial impact the Hambros had made internationally for more than a century.

Charles and Marcus saw much of each other in London in 1924. Pamela and Doie would have been pleased to meet up again too, although opportunity would have been limited that year: Doie must have returned to Sweden to give birth to Marc in the June, for undoubtedly Marcus would not have wanted his first child to be born outside his home country. Marcus made stipulations in his son's first year about his upbringing. In the event of his own death, his brother Jacob should be appointed Marc's guardian, and he expressed his desire that Marc 'should be given the opportunity to complete his studies in my native country'.

Whether Marcus returned to Sweden with Doie for the birth is not known, although it is likely that she and baby Marc accompanied Marcus when he went on holiday to France that August. The next month Marcus had to move to Paris for a while, so he could train at Credit Lyonnais, and there he rented an apartment, taking French lessons. As it was just a studio flat, up six flights of stairs with no lift, it is likely it was a lone trip for him.

A clever and competitive man, Marcus learned all about film techniques and quickly became an amateur movie buff, ahead of his time. Footage exists that he took of Doie and himself, with Pamela and Charles, in Berlin in late 1925, where that year he finally completed his training at a German bank. The film of the friends in a Berlin club shows Pamela and Doie wearing their very British cloche hats, no doubt among the decadently hatless throng – the emphasis in Berlin being firmly on decadence, for it was a fascinating city to be in at that time. Germany was still recovering, emotionally as well as financially, from its defeat after the Great War, and inflation had wiped out the savings of many middle-class Germans, leading to a strange mixture of despair and manic festivity that fuelled Berlin's artistic, musical and literary renaissance. The city welcomed with open arms the sensational black American jazz singer Josephine Baker in her flamboyant new show, *La Revue Nègre*, which opened in Berlin at around the time the two couples were there. She would shortly afterwards go on to cause a sensation in Paris in the revue *Chocolate Kiddies* with her overtly sexual 'banana dance', where she appeared naked except for a girdle of bananas.

At the end of 1925, as his training in Berlin was coming to an end, Marcus was made Assistant Manager of SEB, a position equivalent to Vice-President. The Hambros naturally were very pleased for him. Doie and Pamela always got on well. Their outgoing personalities meant they were both at ease in company, and each thought the other a jolly good laugh. Unlike Doie however, Pamela was less competitive with Charles than Doie with Marcus, and she did not have to endure Charles' absences for sporting purposes – in Marcus' case, tennis and sailing, the latter which Doie loathed. Having competed at Wimbledon in 1922 Marcus returned there in 1925, becoming the first Swede to play on Centre Court. During the winter of 1924-5 he had practised very hard, often competing with the top French players who led the world at that time, and twice a week practised against the great René Lacoste.

Then in 1926, following his and Doie's return to Sweden from Berlin, Marcus made his first appearance in Sweden in an exhibition match against a well-known Czech player. The match was hugely popular, attended by thousands, and was also an important social occasion; as the Swedish newspaper *Dagens Nyheter* reported, it was attended by the Swedish King and his children, the Crown Prince and his sister, as well as other members of the Royal Family, '... not to mention other celebrities, of which there were many'. Next to the Royal Box sat Doie and her father-in-law, Marcus Wallenberg Senior. Always pleased to be associated with the Royal Family, he would have been most happy to be seated near them for everyone to see, while his son would have loved the press reports, which enthused about his playing 'the entire match in an even and controlled manner but with enormous passion. His volley took the prize, however. No other Swede, and probably no other Nordic player, has such a stylish and effective stroke.'

Marcus was the golden boy again that May, when he helped Sweden beat Switzerland at Malmö in the second round of the Davis cup, although it was unlikely Doie was there to cheer him on: she was only eleven days away from giving birth to Peter. Marcus' luck ran out in July however, at Stockholm, when he and his fellow Swedes were beaten in the semi-final by France, whose team, comprising Lacoste, Borotra and Cochet, was regarded as one of the two best teams in the world. The other was Great Britain, whom France met in the final.

Doie got Marcus back after that – from tennis competitions, at least – for he developed a problem with his lungs that year. He continued to play non-competition games and remained committed to the sport, being credited with introducing a more modern and competitive attitude towards tennis in Sweden, where it had previously been regarded as an upper-class diversion. After a brief comeback in 1928 he became Chairman of the Swedish Tennis Association and an influential promoter of the sport, both inside and outside his country.

After Peter's birth, and once Marcus' part in the Davis Cup had finished in 1926, the couple had to think about settling down in Sweden, and entered into an agreement to rent Parkrudden, a villa rebuilt at the turn of the century for Baron Carl von Essen, who was married to Marcus' aunt Ruth. The refurbishment took some time, the house being partly equipped with furniture that Marcus and Doie had bought abroad, with French china, carpets and prams shipped by steamer from London. The family ended up spending the summer of 1926 in a private hotel while the work was being carried out, and then in the autumn, when the house was ready to move into, Marcus had to go abroad to have treatment for his lungs. Doie went with him, leaving the two boys with staff, so they had to move into their new home without their parents.

Doie's formidable mother-in-law, Amalia, was growing concerned about Marcus and Doie's continuing absence, during which time they were staying in Nice and Biskra, Algeria. Amalia hinted in letters to Marcus that it would be a good idea if Doie, at least, came home by Christmas; she felt the staff, although probably reliable, needed 'a housewife's guiding hand' – words that must have struck chill into Doie's heart. Nevertheless, Doie did come home, but not in time for Christmas.

She returned home in January 1927, with Marcus returning to Sweden in mid-February, after additional stopovers in Paris and London.

That year, 1927, was a good year for them – or at least, for Marcus. He was very pleased to be appointed a member of the Board of Directors of the SEB – now it was not just his friend Charles Hambro who was advancing – and he travelled extensively on business in Europe and the USA, constantly maintaining and building his network of contacts in the fast-developing industrial world, much of which he did without Doie. Marcus had quickly realised that his interest, and therefore his future, lay in industry rather than banking. He was quickly acquiring the experience and expertise that would make him the powerful and influential figure in Sweden that he would become, and establish the Wallenbergs as a formidable industrial dynasty.

It was not always his wish to be alone but his wife did like her independence, preferring her close-knit family to his. Every summer Doie spent six weeks with Peter and Marc and her own family in Glencruitten. Marcus went with Doie at first but the Mackay family's interests, being very literary, musical and artistic, were quite different from the Wallenbergs', and soon Marcus let her go on her own, spending those weeks sailing with his friends and family. In the winters, however, he would usually join Doie in Florida, where her father, Alexander, had developed his many business interests and owned an estate, where he hosted big family gatherings.

There were other sources of friction between them too. Back home in Sweden, Marcus would become annoyed when Doie – whose favourite saying was 'There's more to life than business' – invited writers and artists to Parkrudden. Given the chance, Doie loved to act, something she had enjoyed from her childhood and in which she had talent. In 1914, aged just fourteen, she had performed at the famous Theatre Royal in Glasgow in a programme of music hall entertainment. There she had the distinction of sharing the bill with a very popular singer of the time, Charles Coburn, singer of the song equivalent to a number one hit and which made him both famous and rich: 'The Man who Broke the Bank at Monte Carlo'. Of Doie's performance *The Scotsman* wrote, 'Dorothy Mackay, a singer of tender years, gave excellent impersonations of well-known comediennes...'

But to Marcus, any attempts by his wife to perform removed the spotlight from him, and served to separate them further, despite her successful efforts to integrate into his home country. Within the first few years of their marrying, Doie, with her skill in languages, could speak fluent Swedish and made many friends, which could only have reflected well on Marcus. Yet after moving into Parkrudden it became clear that they were drifting apart, and rumours were rife about their rows. Although their descendants have little detail about the deterioration of their relationship, one of them attributes some blame to Doie, 'for leaving a good-looking man on his own so often'.

However, it is hard to ignore the suggestion that he regarded himself and his family as superior to hers, and that she should therefore behave accordingly. This could sometimes be inferred from the attitude of the Wallenbergs generally towards others, as Charles Hambro discovered. The Hambros had maintained a very good relationship with the Wallenbergs, particularly with Marcus' uncle Knut, since the amalgamation of the BBNC with C J Hambro & Son in 1920; however, the Wallenbergs were less keen for their other bank, the SEB, to get involved. Marcus' father recommended to his elder son Jacob that SEB should decline, with thanks, the Hambros' invitation to become a permanent underwriter in its issuing of bonds, as he did not consider it a suitable proposition for them. Marcus' father wrote:

'We, of course, are able to judge industrial problems in an entirely different way than, for example, Hambros and, indeed, most other international banks. As regards other international transactions, we are also well equipped, since you, Jacob, as well as myself, are in a position to assess the nature of proposed business transactions, due to our constant travelling, language skills and excellent personal relations.'

Pamela and Doie saw each other when they could, and in the meantime it is known they wrote to each other. Unfortunately, the letters have since been misplaced. Pamela would have been anxious not to seem as though she were interfering or overtly offering advice to her friend. She may have thought that Doie's concerns about her marriage were just part of the ups and downs of any relationship. This was especially true in their circles, where physical separation between spouses was common where the husband had business obligations elsewhere to fulfil; and more

Lady Evelyn Cobbold (née Murray).

Angy (née Tollemache, later Baroness Belper).

Sir Eric Hambro (courtesy of
Hambro Family Archives).

Lady Sybil Hambro
(courtesy of Hambro Family Archives).

Remains of Holy Wells today – stable block from top garden.

The Brewery Tap Public House, Ipswich (formerly a Cobbold home), with the
Old Cliff Brewery behind.

Tomb of Carl Joachim Hambro in Milton Abbey.

Milton Abbey today (Photo: Ken Ayres).

so where the wife was not inclined to tow the line as a dutiful housewife, having interests of her own to follow. Unsurprisingly, such situations often led to one or both spouses having extramarital affairs.

For Pamela and Charles, married life was very different. They tried to be together as much as possible, and she often went with him on his business trips abroad, becoming well-loved by the fishermen in Iceland, one of their favourite destinations. Meanwhile in 1927 neither she nor Doie could know that in less than two years' time the Wallenbergs' marriage would be under a serious and permanent threat.

Chapter 23

Up and Down

With her best friend Angy travelling for over a year and Doie living in Sweden, Pamela did not see either of her friends very much during 1925. Neither woman was there to congratulate Pamela when she gave birth to a third daughter, another Pamela, or 'Pammie' as she would be called, on New Year's Eve 1925. The friend Pamela saw most often was probably her sister-in-law Blanche, and through her and Ivan she kept up with what was happening in the Cavendish family.

In 1925 the Duke had suffered a serious stroke, which had the effect of changing his character. From an easy-going, ironic and laconic man, he became bad-tempered and difficult to get on with. He took against two of his little grandsons, Blanche's nephews Andrew (later the 11th Duke), and his younger brother Billy, apparently because they looked more like their mother's family, the Cecils, than the Cavendishes. Evie, his Duchess, was particularly badly affected as Victor spoke to her little after his stroke, which made family mealtimes particularly difficult for others. This was not helped by the fact that, except at large parties, the couple used a room at Chatsworth called the Small Dining Room, considered by the rest of the family to be the gloomiest in the entire building.

Outside the immediate family, someone who felt the effects of his stroke particularly keenly was Victor's son-in-law Harold Macmillan; it was Harold's political discussions with Victor, with whom he had the best relationship out of all his wife's family, that had inspired him to consider a political career. Harold was grateful for the encouragement and support Victor had given him in his political aspirations, and had started campaigning in earnest for the Conservatives during the short life of Ramsay Macdonald's Labour government of 1924. His target constituency was Stockton-on-Tees, a northern town of which he knew absolutely nothing. However, he was helped in his campaign by his wife. Dorothy was accompanied in her campaigning by their three-year-old son and two-year-old daughter, much to Harold's distaste, but it all had the desired effect, for he succeeded at the next General Election of November 1924, becoming an MP under Conservative Prime Minister Stanley Baldwin. The same election saw Winston Churchill, a Liberal in the 1923 election, 'cross the floor' and become Conservative; he was elected MP for Epping and was immediately promoted by Baldwin to Chancellor of the Exchequer.

Dorothy's energy was boundless, her presence often formidable. Like her sister Blanche, upon marriage she would retain the title of Lady, while Harold, like Ivan, was referred to in humbler terms by his military rank. Dorothy's part in the election had included making 'women's gatherings' a feature of the party's campaign, her upbringing apparently influencing her organisational skills: she was said to have treated everybody, especially the women, as though they were servants or tenants at Chatsworth. In November 1926 Dorothy gave birth to their third child, Catherine, in a year that was a bad one for Britain generally, for the country experienced its first and only General Strike.

The roots of the General Strike partly stemmed from April 1925, when Winston Churchill was persuaded by the Governor of the Bank of England, Montagu Norman, to return Britain to the gold standard, at its 1914 rate of one pound to just under five dollars. The immediate result was an increase in export prices, and therefore a decrease in exports generally. As always, it was the miners who took the brunt. In 1925, 60% of mines were running at a loss which the mine owners could not continue to sustain. Nine out of ten miners in the export fields of Northumberland, Durham and South Wales were laid off. Instead of considering modernisation of the mines as a solution, the mine owners' union, the Mining Association of Great Britain, suggested a government subsidy as an alternative to reducing labour costs – in other words, cutting wages. Baldwin refused, saying that the Government would not attempt to control the country's industries: after all, his election meant that 'The people have repudiated socialism. They have repudiated nationalism.' The union proposed a pay cut to the miners, at which point Baldwin, in a change of policy, ordered an inquiry into the situation. In an attempt to avoid a strike, he met with both miners and owners, and came to accept that a reduction in labour costs was probably the only solution. In July 1925 Baldwin announced, 'All the workers of this country have got to take reductions in wages to help put industry on its feet.'

When it looked as though a strike was inevitable, his Cabinet decided, on the unusual basis of a vote, that a subsidy was preferable to a national strike, and agreed to protect the miners' wages for nine months.

In 1926 after the subsidy ran out, and after much further debate and negotiations, the miners were back where they had started the year before, faced once again with a choice of longer hours or less pay. Their slogan was born: 'Not a penny off the pay. Not a minute on the day.' When further talks between the two unions broke down, a miners' strike was called, beginning in early May 1926 and, as the miners were supported by the Trades' Union Congress, a General Strike began on 3 May, with the railwaymen, dockers and other public services striking in support.

It was estimated that nearly two million workers came out on strike. The whole country could have been crippled, but the Government had drawn up emergency plans in readiness, with Churchill in charge of the distribution of supplies. Rather as in the railway strike of 1919, but on a bigger scale, volunteers crucially did their bit: about three hundred thousand mainly middle-class men and women volunteered to do work previously done by strikers. Food was transported in convoys of trucks from the docks to central London by stevedores, while soldiers patrolled the streets with bayonets. Office workers and university students ran the buses.

The upper classes did their bit too. Those for whom hunting was a way of life acted as mounted police to patrol the great crowds in many cities; others drove trains, like Angy's brother had in the earlier railway strike. Lady Astor led a group of female volunteers to deliver the Royal Mail and Lady Curzon organised a car pool on Horse Guards Parade.

The General Strike lasted for nine days, during the first week of which four thousand people were prosecuted for violence. On 27 May Sir Eric Hambro chaired the AGM of Hambros Bank Ltd with Charles as the Company's Secretary, and after welcoming the Board to the very modern building at 41 Bishopsgate to which they had recently moved – a vital step, given the now inadequate size and state of the Bank's old premises – Eric referred to recent events:

'We are meeting today in troublesome times. When our last meeting was held most people in this country were of the view that 1925-26 would be a year of general improvement in the trade of this country; unhappily the shadow of the coal crisis, coupled with the general strike, has deferred that hope for the moment. The general strike is happily over, and it is inconceivable that a country which has been broadminded enough on all sides to settle such a question will not insist on an honourable and working agreement being arrived at between the parties at present concerned in the dispute.'

Unfortunately Eric was being rather optimistic, for a suitable agreement was not reached. Although the strike had ended in May, the miners continued striking until December, losing any public sympathy they may have had, and were forced back to work by starvation, subsequently accepting worse conditions than before. Meanwhile, Stanley Baldwin was determined to make general strikes illegal. Harold Macmillan and others including Robert Boothby, known as 'Bob', were in agreement in principal but also wanted to make sure that the conditions for a general strike did not recur. They wrote a short book called *Industry and the State*, arguing for collective bargaining between union and employer to be given statutory authority.

While the miners' strike continued during 1926, volunteers and the army helped to keep supplies of coal going, and the country tried to continue as normally as possible. For the privileged, that meant enjoying the season's shooting: it would take more than a strike to stop that. In August 1926, having recovered to a degree from his stroke the previous year, Victor Cavendish was able to honour the invitation that he and his wife had extended to King George V to join them for a few days' grouse shooting at one of their other estates, Bolton Abbey in Yorkshire. Ivan was pleased to be part of that select group, of which the men, after a hard morning's killing on Bolton Moors, were joined by the Duchess and

Blanche and another couple of ladies for luncheon, following which the men continued their sport until dusk.

Amongst those who were not directly affected by the strikes were Pamela's father – although the brewery probably suffered disruption due to transportation difficulties – and Angy and Algernon Strutt, for they were all still on their foreign tour. John wrote to his grandson, Toby, in May that year to tell him they had been to Honolulu, where Angy had bathed in the waters, and from where they were going on to Vancouver.

John was delighted when in June the following year, 1927, Blanche gave birth to a boy, John Cavendish Cobbold, the first of two sons for her and Ivan, and John's second grandson. As fond as he was of his two daughters, Ivan was thrilled to have a son, for now there was a future heir to the Cobbold empire. Pamela was pleased for her brother, even though she and Charles had still had no success in that respect, but they would not have exchanged their three girls for the world. Not that Pamela was an overly maternal woman: on more than one occasion she asked Doie, 'Why do we keep having to have babies?' Doie may well have wondered the same thing, but it was a bold woman in those times who chose not to reproduce upon marriage when there was no physical reason why she should not do so. Valuing time to themselves, both young women were happy to leave their children with nannies when occasion demanded, as was still expected in their circles, although Pamela's upper class background dictated this more than Doie's. All the more surprising, then, that given Dorothy Macmillan's aristocratic family, she was so taken by motherhood, apparently spending more time with her children than was considered proper for her class.

There was no doubt that Pamela loved her children. By the time her new Cobbold cousin was born, Pammie was eighteen months old. A beautiful, blonde good-natured child, Pammie was much teased by her sisters in the way that the older siblings are wont to do. The girls were all very different. Cinders, the eldest, had a stubborn streak and was strong-minded, yet was generally a good child. Di was much more flamboyant and inclined to be naughty. Pammie would remain the most beautiful of the three and retain her docile nature, as she grew older often trying to keep the peace between her sisters: perhaps because of their very different personalities, and the fact that there was only a year between them, Cinders and Di would never be very close throughout their lives.

At Easter 1927 Pamela took the girls to visit Angy and her sons, Peter, Pamela's godson, by then nearly three, and his brother Desmond, nearly one, at the family seat of Lord Belper. A charming photo of Angy's shows all the children on the lawn in front of the mansion, Kingston Hall, Angy's boys pretty and slight with golden hair and angelic features, Pamela's girls larger and sturdy. Cinders – still the image of Charles – fusses over baby Desmond on her knee, while statuesque Di sits slightly apart, looking regal in an elaborate daisy chain and headband; toddler Pammie and her older friend, Peter, ignore each other and pursue their own agenda on the grass. Perhaps as part of their birthday celebrations, the boys met up with the Hambro girls again that June at Felixstowe, the resort still loved by Pamela and Angy, with its long-standing Cobbold and Tollemache connections and its wide, clean beaches.

Being in Felixstowe that month also meant Pamela could easily visit Blanche and Ivan at Glemham Hall, and take the girls to see their new cousin. Ivan was busy developing the estate as a desirable one for shooting; after all, John had bought it so that his son could hold his own at that level of society into which he had married. As Ivan was invited by his father-in-law to shooting parties which included the King, there was always the possibility that His Majesty might in return accept an invitation to Glemham. In August that year Ivan was again invited by the Duke to join him and the King in a shoot at Bolton Abbey, this time with the Duke's brother and eldest son, and three friends of the King. And now that Ivan had a son, it was even more important that Glemham should be seen as an estate of quality so that its reputation could be passed on.

The years from late 1925 to 1928 were particularly good for Hambros Bank and therefore for Charles and Pamela. In November 1927 the Bank's reputation was recognised in *The Times*, in an article headed 'Great Financial Houses'. Hambros was one of eight banks, including Rothschild's, Baring's and J H Schröder and Co, of whose business the newspaper gave a summary and to which it attributed London's 'power and reputation'. Meanwhile, Eric as Chairman, with his fellow directors, voted to increase the Bank's capital by capitalising reserves and issuing shares. The Hambro family, who had acquired half the capital of the Bank when it merged with the BNCC in 1920, were now also able to increase their holding to a majority of shares and so take formal control.

In April 1928 Charles was honoured to be elected a director to the Court of the Bank of England. He was just thirty. His appointment was particularly notable because new recruits were no longer being drawn exclusively from the traditional merchant banking families as they had been before the war. Banking, as illustrated by families like the Hambros whose roots were founded in commerce, had not been an occupation of the aristocracy, yet like those occupations which traditionally had been the aristocracy's preserve – the Army, the Civil Service, the Church – banking too was affected by changes in recruitment and selection, and the Court of the Bank of England now included industrialists and other businessmen.

The Governor of the Bank of England, Montagu Norman, recognised Charles' unusual ability and realised he was one of the few bankers with first-hand experience of American finance. In Norman's view, Charles' knowledge was very valuable and the Hambro's long-standing friendship with the mighty Morgan family cannot have hurt either. By then, the role of New York and the dollar had become of major importance in the international monetary system. When Charles' grandfather, Sir Everard Hambro, served as a director of the Bank of England, London and its Stock Exchange had for centuries been the financial centre of the world. But during the Great War, New York had had the chance to move into the issuing of capital; until then, this was the main business of many of the British merchant banks, including C J Hambro & Son before it joined with the BBNC and moved towards trade financing. The increased importance of New York meant that by the 1920s the world's monetary system was effectively being run by two men: Montagu Norman, and Benjamin Strong, President of the New York Federal Reserve.

There were other reasons for Charles' appointment. Sir Everard had given exceptional service to the Court, so the renewal of the family representation was particularly welcome. Charles' age suited Norman's plans too, for young directors presented no immediate rivalry to his own succession. Norman – who naturally came from a banking family, and who had trained in the same American bank as Marcus Wallenberg, twenty-five years before Marcus – had been Governor since 1920. This was an unusually long time to be in office when his predecessors over the centuries had, with few exceptions, been Governor for only two years, and was the cause of some controversy. Prior to his appointment as Governor, Norman had been a director of the Bank of England during the Great War, when Britain's debt as a result of the hostilities reached £7 billion, and the role of the Bank, in maintaining stability and controlling inflation, was more crucial than ever.

If Charles had known that just eighteen months after his election the devastating Wall Street Crash would occur, he may have been less keen to accept his new position. Until then, in his calmer first year in office, he oversaw a radical change in the design of Britain's bank notes. New ten shilling and one pound banknotes were issued, for the first time printed in colour on both sides and incorporating complex machine engraving, swirling acanthus leaves and a centrally-placed watermark: something to take home to his daughters as a souvenir, an antique for the future.

Charles' appointment did not carry any great financial remuneration – there was a token payment to directors – but it was the honour and resulting professional kudos which was so valuable. The increasingly comfortable lifestyle that he and Pamela were starting to enjoy came from his share of the profits as a director of Hambros Bank, which continued to make wise decisions. In December that year, for example, the Hambros' continuing relationship with Greece was illustrated by the Bank's joint support of a loan of £4 million to the struggling Greek Government for three public work contracts, for improvements that were badly needed after the war. To do this, Hambros Bank invited applications from British investors for sterling bonds with an attractive return, thus minimising the risk to itself and maximising the benefit.

Pamela of course enjoyed all the benefits that went with being the wife of a successful banker in the 1920s. It was not that she put great store by materialistic things, for she valued above all the opportunity to be wild and free – she still was happier in Rannoch than anywhere else – and she relished the joy of spending time with their close friends. But she loved Charles and understood the importance of representing his success and that of Hambros Bank – and now she was under further scrutiny as the wife of a director to the Court of the Bank of England. Charles bought her exquisite jewellery, and their furniture in their London house was an elegant mix of the old and the modern. Chippendale chairs nestled with pieces by Le Corbusier, set against wallpaper by the celebrated duo Sybil Colefax and John Fowler. Art Deco was the style of the moment, while the most celebrated interior designer of the day was Syrie Maugham, wife of the writer W Somerset Maugham, just starting out on her career. Favouring light colours and mirrored screens, in 1927 she famously created an all-white salon in her house in London.

Syrie later redesigned the London pad that Eric Hambro had occupied, 48 Upper Grosvenor Street, and was soon designing for clients such as the Hon Stephen Tennant, Noel Coward and the future King Edward VIII. Syrie's decorative palette may have been neutral but her love life, for which she became almost as well known, was very colourful; she first married the pharmaceutical magnate Henry Wellcome, then enjoyed affairs with other business heavyweights such as Harry Selfridge, the retail chief. This was followed by marriage to W Somerset Maugham, a known homosexual, who himself had an affair with her good friend Beverly Nichols.

Three months after Charles' appointment, he and Pamela had the chance to celebrate further with friends they had not seen for a while when they were amongst several hundred guests at a huge Society affair in London: a coming-out dance given for Pamela's eighteen-year-old cousin, Rosemary Coke. Like Pamela, she was a great-granddaughter of the 2nd Earl of Leicester but through his second, much younger wife Georgina Cavendish, whom he had married as a widower. The venue was the grand London residence of Rosemary's grandmother, Viscountess Burnham, at 19 Grosvenor Square, where the 2nd Earl himself had lived for a while in the mid-nineteenth century.

With some of Pamela's Cobbold cousins, the Hambros were part of a guest list which provided a telling snapshot of British Society in the late 1920s. The majority of guests comprised the usual mix of British aristocracy, European royalty and exotically-named foreign ambassadors and their wives. However, on this occasion there was also a notably large proportion of non-aristocratic guests, something that was not the case ten years earlier. Unadorned by title, many still came from established and well-heeled families but now they were making their own living instead of relying upon family wealth, sometimes by choice but also out of necessity; their success lay in trade, industry, the media, politics, the arts and entertainment. Background was becoming less important than talent. Social mobility was on its way.

The two brightest stars of the Bright Young People were guests of the Viscountess; Mr Bryan Guinness and the Hon Diana Mitford, invited with her parents. That year eighteen-year-old Diana, the eldest of the six Mitford girls, had become secretly engaged to the charming twenty-three-year-old, one of the most eligible bachelors in London. The couple would marry six months after the dance, although their marriage would last only four years.

Those present at the party without a title included Henry 'Chips' Channon, an ambitious, social-climbing, bisexual American anglophile in his twenties who had immigrated to Britain from the country he had come to loathe. He would become an MP, a significant diarist and a close friend of Wallis Simpson, as well as a lover of the Duke of Kent and the dramatist Terence Rattigan. In 1933 he would cement his position in British Society by marrying into the Guinness family, Lady Honor Guinness. In 1927 she was simply a nineteen-year-old guest at Rosemary Coke's party, but she would eventually tire of his promiscuous homosexual dalliances during their marriage and leave him for a Czech airman.

Another untitled guest was a serious young man in the legal profession named Reginald Manningham-Buller who one day would be Lord Chancellor of Great Britain, and whose daughter would become head of MI5; while twenty-eight-year-old Henry Tiarks was, like his friend and Kentish neighbour Charles Hambro, a merchant banker working hard to maintain his family's reputation as part of one of the top merchant banks, J H Schröder and Co.

Amongst the many young ladies at the party who were contemporaries of Rosemary Coke, was one Joyce Phipps. A niece of Nancy Astor, the following year Joyce would marry Reginald Grenfell and become the well-known British entertainer Joyce Grenfell. Pamela and Charles would have been pleased to meet up with long-standing friends like the Cazalet trio. There was Victor Cazalet, by then Conservative MP for Chippenham; with him was his twenty-one year-old brother Peter, in the process of making the family's livery, Fairlawne, the world famous equestrian centre, and who before long would be married to Leonora Wodehouse, step-daughter of P G Wodehouse; and their sister Thelma, by then a Conservative councillor for the London County Council, the first stage of a significant political career. Perhaps Thelma chatted with Chips Channon that evening, for she would later be mentioned in his diaries as 'nice but tactless'.

Thelma's best friend Megan Lloyd George, daughter of the Liberal ex-Prime Minister, was invited too, with her mother Dame Margaret. The long-suffering wife of the notoriously promiscuous David Lloyd George, honoured because of her charity work, had that year become the first woman MP in Wales, while her daughter was appointed a Liberal candidate. Pamela would have been interested to meet them, despite their difference in politics.

Of particular note amongst the aristocratic guests was a future Lord Chancellor, twenty-one year old the Hon Quintin Hogg, later Lord Hailsham, while on a different plane altogether was the beautiful Hon Hugh Lygon. A friend and probably lover of the novelist Evelyn Waugh while they were at Oxford, Hugh was one of the young men, along with Stephen Tennant, thought to have been the model for Sebastian Flyte in *Brideshead Revisited*. The Lygon family clearly provided creative fodder. A long-running family feud over an inheritance which started with their forebears was the inspiration for the case of Jarndyce v Jarndyce in Dickens' *Bleak House*, while their family home Madresfield was the source of adoration and inspiration for artists. Hugh's father was William Lygon, 7th Earl Beauchamp, who was also at the dance with his wife, the Countess, and their daughter, Lady Lettice. Like his son, the Earl was also a model for Evelyn Waugh, who based his character Lord Marchmain upon him. The Earl's own homosexuality, which extended to rent boys and servants, was well-known in aristocratic circles, although the Countess was apparently unaware, as he was a devoted father. Pamela had met the unworldly Countess a couple of years previously, at the coming-out dance of her godfather's niece Joan Bromley Davenport, for which she had hosted a dinner beforehand.

300

The Countess did not know then what unhappiness would be thrust upon her and her family in the forthcoming years, for both her husband and her son would have an unhappy end to their lives. For all the ostensible acceptance amongst the upper classes of still-illegal homosexuality, in 1930 William would be outed by his brother-in-law the Duke of Westminster, for various reasons, largely political, and ordered by King George V to resign his official posts and leave England by midnight the same night. On being told of the Earl's homosexuality, the King reportedly said, 'I thought men like that shot themselves.' William spent five years in exile and died in 1938. Hugh would be killed in 1936 in a motor accident in Germany, aged thirty-two. Coincidentally, Pamela and Charles would one day come to have a permanent link with the Lygon family.

In August that same year, 1927, on the way to Loch Rannoch for their usual summer sojourn, Pamela and Charles visited Angy at Sandy Bay in Scotland, where she and Algernon, the boys and 'the steps' often stayed, and at the end of the Scottish season the Hambros looked forward to finding a new country residence. In October they took occupation, until the following spring, of a beautiful manor house in the Cotswolds. Netherswell Manor, at Stowe-on-the-Wold in Gloucestershire, was an Edwardian gem, built between 1903 and 1909 for Sir John Murray Scott and his family.

Pamela must have loved Netherswell's situation, set in beautiful countryside with excellent hunting, and the house itself was arresting. Designed by a popular architect of the day, Sir Guy Dawber, well known for his Arts & Crafts designs, the house with a riot of gabled roofs and oriel and bay windows stood alone at the end of a long drive. It was described variously as 'restless and Jacobean', and, by *Country Life Magazine*, as being in the 'scholarly Cotswold vernacular'. It was certainly grand. There were French interiors, fancy plasterwork, a Rococo study and a Louis XVI dining room. The house in Scott's day was stuffed with art works, tapestries, Sèvres porcelain and sculpture, and the garden ornamented with statuary from an historic French château.

Pamela and Charles were in fashionable company living in an Arts and Crafts country house in Gloucestershire. Not far away in Stroud, in a house of similar age, lived a younger cousin of Angy's. Born Winifred Tollemache, she had married one of the most lauded architects of the age, Detmar Jellings Blow, some years older than she. In 1914 he had designed and built Hilles, the house which was to remain the Blow family seat for generations. Winifred, familiar as she was with the Tollemaches' ancient Suffolk mansion Helmingham Hall, dearly loved the newer house and she and Detmar were living there happily in 1928 when the Hambros moved into Netherswell.

Although neither couple would ever know it, in the early twenty-first century Hilles would be the scene for, and cause of, tragic events within the Blow family. One of Detmar and Winifred's grandsons, Simon, would allege that Winifred was poisoned by Simon's uncle Jonathan, one of their two sons, because she intended to leave the house to both the boys rather than just to Jonathan. And in May 2007 it was at Hilles that Isabella Blow, the international style icon and wife of another grandson (also Detmar), committed suicide by drinking the weed killer paraquat.

But in 1928 all was quiet at Hilles, and at Netherswell the Hambros enjoyed their autumn, with Pamela riding and hunting and the girls happy. Not far away, at Swinbrook, lived the Mitford family. Cinders and Di Hambro started ballet classes, which they shared with one of the Mitford girls: it was very probably the youngest, Deborah, known as 'Debo' who, aged eight, was less than a year older than Cinders. Coincidentally, Debo would later come to have a further connection with the Hambro girls when she married their Aunt Blanche's nephew, Andrew Cavendish, thus becoming a niece of Blanche and Ivan. Andrew unexpectedly became the 11th Duke of Devonshire in 1950. As the Duchess of Devonshire, Debo would become known for reversing the dwindling fortunes of Chatsworth and turning it into one of the best-loved and accessible stately homes of England. Before then, in her less worldly youth, Debo stayed at Glemham as a teenager, and many years later still remembered the shock caused by Ivan:

'... it was the first time I had ever seen anybody drink gin before lunch. I did not dare tell my parents when I went home.'

Life at the end of that year was hectic but mostly enjoyable for Pamela and Charles. Unfortunately the same could not be said for their friends Marcus and Doie Wallenberg.

Chapter 24

Sex and Death

In September 1928, as Pamela and Charles were preparing to move into Netherswell, Doie Wallenberg found she was pregnant with their third child, due in June 1929. She and Marcus had continued to lead a hectic lifestyle involving much travel for business on his part. During the summers Doie still tended to leave Sweden to travel alone with their son Marc, by then aged four, and two-year-old Peter, to see her family in Scotland, and Marcus still sailed. Charles came into contact with the Wallenberg family regularly through work at Hambros Bank, although Marcus' direction had changed. Now aged twenty-nine, his banking training and experience had been channelled into another principal activity of the Wallenbergs – industrial ownership – in which they remain heavily involved in the twenty-first century. By the 1920s the Wallenberg family formed the largest concentration of ownership in Sweden. Their main involvement was the rehabilitation of weaker companies in order to recover loan losses, followed closely by the development of new companies which had the potential of becoming valuable customers of the family's bank, the SEB.

Marcus had discovered, especially during his trips with Doie to the USA in 1924, that his interest lay in industry rather than banking, and besides, his older and very experienced brother Jacob dominated that side of the family's business, which did not leave much room for Marcus. His industrial experience was increased in 1928 when he was appointed a director of the major Swedish company AB Diesel Atlas, founded by a Wallenberg in 1873, which was experiencing a severe depression.

Under the supervision of his father, Marcus acted as a troubleshooter and helped the company on its way to becoming a global concern, still trading today as Atlas Copco.

Doie had discovered early in their marriage her husband's single-mindedness and determination. A trip the couple made to Niagara Falls a few years earlier had sparked Marcus' interest in the production and distribution of electrical power, something which was relatively new and highly technical, and he had enthusiastically sent home to his father a report about the American power stations. Marcus then spearheaded a collaboration between Asea, Sweden's biggest electrical company, and its banker, the SEB, in which a power-holding company would be set up with the aim of acquiring concessions for the building of power stations and the distribution of electric power abroad. By 1928 the result was an enterprise attractive enough for the Wallenberg group to start buying shares in Asea. By the end of the following year, after Marcus also managed to see off moves by the American giant General Electric to buy part of the company, the Wallenberg Group was the largest individual shareholder in Asea.

Some thirty years later Marcus would be made Chairman of that company. In 1928, however, he was concentrating on gaining as wide a spectrum of industrial experience as possible. Not that he had abandoned his other interests. He still played tennis when he could, although no longer at international level, and this was the year that he had become a member of the Swedish Tennis Association. Marcus was also developing an interest in yacht racing, but the sport other than tennis which he had continued to love since a boy was hunting and shooting. As a child he had accompanied his father and other relatives on shooting trips – his uncle Knut owned an old hunting lodge near the border with Norway – and he enjoyed the rhythm that the regular shooting parties gave to each year. They were also very important for his social life: being invited to join the shooting parties of influential people, and ideally Sweden's Royal Family, was crucial to his attaining a position of status similar to that of his father and uncle.

So in late 1928 he was very pleased when he and Doie were invited by a member of the Swedish Royal Family to a wedding in New York, which was to take place on 1 December. However, Doie, in the first three months of pregnancy, did not feel up to a long sea trip, so Marcus went on his own, leaving Sweden on a ship with a group of fellow guests.

Described by the *New York Times* as 'one of the most brilliant society gatherings in recent years', the wedding was a significant event in that city because the bride, Estelle Manville, was the daughter of a well-known and wealthy American industrialist, and the groom was European royalty: Count Folke Bernadotte, a nephew of King Gustav V of Sweden. Amongst the guests at the plush wedding, at the centre of whose reception towered a seven-foot high wedding cake, were the groom's brother, Count Carl Bernadotte, and his wife Marianne, née de Geer af Leufsta, a Baroness by birth and a Countess by marriage.

Married for thirteen years, Marianne and Carl had three children aged twelve, eight and two, had lost another son at the age of two and, as a result of lack of success in various agricultural enterprises, were in a precarious financial situation. At the age of thirty-five, Marianne found herself in an unhappy marriage. She also found herself, in late November 1928, travelling to the wedding on the same ship as Marcus Wallenberg.

Handsome rather than beautiful, and tall, Marianne was six years older than Marcus. Ironically, echoing the meeting between him and Doie on a ship six years earlier almost to the day, the pair developed a friendship during that Atlantic crossing that became a love affair. In the aftermath of their ocean voyage, it is not known exactly how and where Marcus and Marianne's relationship was conducted. However, they moved in the same social circles and were seen at the same events, which means that Doie would often have been there too; she may well have chatted to Marianne in her acquired, yet fluent, Swedish, little realising that as she nurtured their daughter Anis, born in June 1929, Marcus was longing for the Countess instead of her.

As clever, confident women, able to converse with people on all levels, Marianne and Doie had much in common. But unlike Doie, Marianne shared the same interests as Marcus. She was interested in sport, sharing his enthusiasm for sailing, which Doie disliked, enjoyed hunting – a sport in which the academic Mackay family had no interest – and was a good shot. Marianne must have also accepted Marcus' lack of interest in reading anything other than what was necessary for professional purposes, or in following any other cultural pursuits;

he did not even indulge in political or ideological philosophising. Further, Marianne's background was aristocratic and she was well versed in Swedish society. For Marcus, the attraction of that must have been hard to ignore. Doie, despite her Cambridge University degree, strong intellect and varied cultural interests, was the product of a very different background and expectations.

But Marcus was not yet ready to consider a divorce. It was not that divorce was hard to obtain: in fact, in the 1920s it was easier in Sweden than in many other European countries including England. However, amongst members of the Swedish Establishment divorce was unusual and frowned upon, and Marcus was all too conscious of his and the Wallenberg family's position in the country to risk such approbation. For Marianne, with her own aristocratic background, married to a nephew of the King and with young children – although not as young as Marcus' – divorce was not something she could contemplate lightly.

So it was that their affair carried on for several years. Doie found out at some stage, quite how or when no-one is sure, and she confided in Pamela, including through their letters which unfortunately have been misplaced. Charles, no doubt, would have heard about the situation from his wife, as they discussed most things, and it may have made him regard Marcus in another light. After Marcus had done his training at Hambros Bank, the two men saw less of each other than they had done previously which may have made things easier. Whether anyone else in Marcus' family knew about the affair is not known. It seems unlikely as Marcus knew how they would disapprove, for it would have cast the Wallenbergs generally in an unflattering light. Despite their professional and social position in Sweden, on the personal front they liked to keep a low personal profile, and would not have liked being thrust into the limelight over an adulterous affair. But unless he and Marianne were scrupulously careful, their circle was bound to find out sooner or later.

Doie's woes must have made Pamela even more grateful for the fact that she had a loving, constant husband – then still a fairly rare characteristic amongst the upper classes – and one who had not echoed his father in straying. For Eric was still firmly with Estelle, failing to comply with the court order made in December 1927 under which he was to return home to Sybil within fourteen days. Until then she and

Zelia had been living temporarily at 18 Davies Street in Mayfair. A few days before Christmas 1927, when it became clear that Eric was not coming back, Sybil moved the two of them – it seems Juliet was still with her father at that stage – to the place that would become their permanent address, 54 Cadogan Square, one of the most desirable residential streets in London. The beautiful redbrick house, built in 1890 for Sybil's friend the 6th Earl of Cadogan whose family owned vast acres of London, must have cheered Sybil, who was very happy to be joined there as soon as they moved in by her younger son Richard and his wife, recently back from Argentina.

Determined not to inflict her unhappiness on her daughters, in early 1928 Sybil took Juliet and Zelia with her on two trips to Gibraltar. Meanwhile she applied to the court for an order that Eric pay maintenance to her, which was granted in July that year, obliging him to pay her periodical payments annually of £4,600, until further order of the court. The order was followed that November by another that gave her interim custody of Juliet, then aged thirteen; the question of Eric's rights of access to her, and of her education, was to be decided by the court four months later unless decided sooner by consent. Sybil was allowed to take Juliet abroad during that period if she wanted, and celebrated by taking her to Las Palmas three days later.

If 1928 was rocky for the senior Hambros and the younger Wallenbergs, 1929 would be an awful year for many. It did not even have an auspicious start. Pamela was sorry to learn in January that her mother-in-law, by then in Tenerife, had been forced to recognise that her long marriage was well and truly over, and had instructed her solicitors to prepare her petition for divorce. It was presented to the High Court on 11 February 1929 and named Estelle as Co-Respondent. After giving basic facts about the parties and the date of the marriage, the petition stated baldly, 'That since the date of the said marriage the said Sir Charles Eric Hambro has frequently committed adultery with Mrs Estelle Elger.' It went on to give stark but legally necessary detail of various dates when the adultery had been committed, and exactly where. The petition was served on both Estelle and Eric, who each had the chance to respond if they wished. Unusually in such cases, and perhaps unexpectedly, Eric did respond, denying he was guilty of adultery as alleged in the petition, and asking for it to be dismissed.

The three months between the presentation of the petition and the hearing, listed to take place in May 1929, were very difficult for Sybil and inhibited her usual sociable self, during which time her anxious daughter-in-law was keen to support her. By now Pamela was used to carrying out, with varying degrees of enjoyment depending on the company, the role of hostess, for which she was much admired; the combination of her wit and her wide reading always made a lasting impression, and the knowledge that she could laugh about the occasion afterwards with Charles helped her through the more tedious times. One event she would have enjoyed hosting to help out her mother-in-law took place in March that year, when she was one of several friends and relations who gave a dinner party in London before the coming-out dance of Charles' younger cousin, Pamela Martin Smith.

As a daughter of the marriage between Eric's younger sister, Violet Hambro, and Sybil's brother, Everard Martin Smith, the debutante was, unusually, a blood niece of both Eric and Sybil separately. Pamela assumed the role of hostess to relieve her mother-in-law of a duty that would have been unduly onerous at that particular time, and show support on the Hambro side.

Of the guests at the dance itself, those who almost certainly would have dined with Pamela included the Countess of Lytton and her younger daughter, twenty-year-old Lady Davina. Before she married Victor Bulwer-Lytton, 2nd Earl Lytton of Knebworth – with whom Sybil had worked in Room 40 during the Great War – the Countess had been Pamela Chichele-Plowden, a society beauty and the first great love of Winston Churchill's life. They had become engaged but she ended their relationship in favour of Victor.

Lady Davina's older sister, twenty-four-year-old Hermione, could not attend the dinner; she was still in India, where the Lyttons had lived from 1922 until 1927 while their father, Victor, was Governor of Bengal. Their grandfather had been Viceroy and Victor was born there. India was also where, like their parents, Hermione had met her fiancé Cameron 'Kim' Cobbold, Pamela's younger cousin. Kim and Hermione were engaged to be married the following year. Pamela would have enjoyed talking to the Countess and Davina, partly about the wedding plans but also about Victor's sister Lady Constance Lytton, a suffragette who had died too young in 1923 after an aggressively active political life in which she had been imprisoned several times, enduring force-feeding and other physical traumas which led to a heart attack and stroke.

Given Pamela's love of travel, she is bound to have asked Davina about their time in India. Leaving their elder brother Anthony in England, where he was training to be a pilot, Davina and Hermione had been fascinated by the country, and thrilled to live for a few months in the vast Government House, Calcutta, which they thought made even the grand Knebworth House feel like a cottage when they got home. They later moved for a while to Darjeeling, and travelled around the country by road and rail on the luxurious Governor's train, accompanied by an entourage of two hundred staff. Greeted like royalty, the family was entertained by the young Maharaja and Maharini. They could not know that the days of the Empire were numbered.

Leaving Victor to get on with his duties, the Countess and the girls had returned to England occasionally. Once, whilst back at Knebworth, they were shown a rare film made by the author of Peter Pan, J M Barrie, whom the family knew: he was godfather to Anthony's best friend. Tragically, Anthony would be killed in an air crash in 1933 at the age of twenty-nine, and Barrie would write the Foreword to Victor's book about his son, *Anthony: A Record of Youth*. Victor and his wife would also lose their youngest son John in World War II, so in the absence of male heirs on Victor's death in 1947, the Knebworth estate passed to Hermione.

Another pre-dance dinner party was given by an old friend of the Cobbolds and the Hambros, Bertram Gurdon, the 2nd Lord Cranworth, whose daughter Judith had been one of Pamela's young bridesmaids. Like the Lyttons, he and his wife had lived for some time abroad as colonists. One of the early British settlers in East Africa, he had made their home in Kenya. It had been taken over as a British protectorate in 1895, becoming a colony in 1904, and was an attractive proposition to impoverished and adventurous patricians like him. Kenya was an attractive country, with relatively friendly natives, beautiful rolling hills, fertile soil and abundant game. Bertram first went there in 1902, drawn by a love of big game shooting and a lack of cash: although he owned 11,000 acres of land in England, following the crash in agriculture at the end of the nineteenth century it was only worth £8,000. Kenya gave him the opportunity to increase his income by farming. After the administration was established and the railway completed, a settlement scheme was introduced in Kenya. By 1905 there were 600 emigrants and three years later the White Highlands were effectively reserved for Europeans. For the next thirty years Kenya was the scene of a unique, and some might say grotesque, attempt to transplant British country house life to the empire.

Having returned to England to fight in the Great War, Bertram fortunately was not in Kenya when the notorious 'Happy Valley' set came into being in the early 1920s. At the centre of this set was Josslyn Hay, the good-looking, promiscuous, bullying grandson of Lady Evelyn Cobbold's friend, the Earl of Erroll, whose wife was Pamela's godmother. Marrying an older woman, Josslyn moved to Kenya with her in 1924 when he was twenty-three. His louche behaviour, which continued after he became the 22nd Earl of Erroll in1928, would culminate in his murder, thought to have been committed by a jealous husband. Josslyn's story would become the subject of the book and film *White Mischief.*

Hosting the dinner party in their stylish London house, Pamela and Charles could afford to be particularly lavish at that time. At the end of that month, March 1929, the balance sheet of Hambros Bank reached its inter-war peak of nearly £34 million, whilst acceptances reached the unprecedented level of £12.5 million. Not that anyone could afford to be complacent. In his annual speech, Sir Eric explained that high interest rates in the USA had caused much uneasiness, and there was an additional threat that the Federal Reserve Bank over there would increase them further, to curb speculation. As a result, the demand for London acceptances had grown immensely in the previous few weeks, and as Sir Eric announced, '… one can say that practically the whole of the pre-war acceptance business is now back in London'. It was a heady time for the Hambros; the same could not be said, however, for their American friends, the Morgans.

But success in Eric's professional life did not alter the course of his personal life, for he still had the hearing of the divorce petition to deal with. It took place at the High Court on 17 May 1929, both he and Sybil having to attend. The Judge took into account her oral evidence and that of witnesses produced on her behalf, and referred to the fact that Eric did not defend the suit at the hearing after all. Sybil was granted her decree nisi, as well as full custody of Juliet. The decree absolute could be granted in a matter of weeks afterwards, once she had made her application.

The day after the hearing of the decree nisi, the pair found themselves for a second time in *The Times*' 'Probate, Divorce and Admiralty' section, an odd combination of items of bland public interest with intrusive personal announcements. It published details of the petition under the heading 'Decree Nisi Against A Knight' and included the fact that Estelle was the sister of Sir Eric's stepmother, and named two of the places where the adultery was said to have taken place.

The year did not get any better. While Pamela was seeing the consequences of her father-in-law's affair, as well as being privy to the one that was rocking the Wallenberg boat, her brother Ivan had become aware of an affair which, although remaining within the close confines of their own upper class circle for many years, would one day be exposed, for the victim was Britain's future Prime Minister, Harold Macmillan.

Ivan's sister-in-law Dorothy, after nine years of marriage to Harold, had become infatuated with Bob Boothby. It seems she had met him some time before July that year, for a friend of Macmillan's told him, not with the greatest sensitivity, that Dorothy said she planned to leave him. In May that year, a General Election took place. Macmillan was defeated in Stockton by the Labour candidate by a huge majority, in an election which saw Ramsay Macdonald back in power. Macmillan was devastated. He was also out of Parliament and back to relying on the salary he received as a junior partner in the family's publishing business – the senior partners were not keen on letting the junior ones become too involved. As consolation, in August Boothby invited him and Dorothy to his father's annual shooting party in Scotland. On the second day on the moors, as Boothby was waiting his turn to shoot, he was surprised to find his hand being squeezed affectionately. As he looked round, there stood Dorothy beaming at him. Her intentions were clear.

Although the Macmillans would have another child and remain married until Dorothy's death in 1966, in 1929 she began a long affair with the bisexual and promiscuous Boothby – also tipped to be Prime Minister – which lasted until she died, surviving Boothby's brief marriage

311

in 1935 to her cousin Diana Cavendish. Dorothy was not in the slightest bit discreet, talking to him passionately on the telephone and leaving love letters lying around. If Harold was Dorothy's stability, Boothby was her excitement, with his raffish air and his sexual magnetism. He was said to have had an affair with (amongst others) Ronald Kray, one of the notorious gangland brothers, and was a friend of Guy Burgess, the KGB spy.

Dorothy's affair with Boothby became widely known in Society circles but, thanks to the intervention of his friend Lord Rothermere, the newspaper baron, it never reached the press. King George V, when he heard about it, is said to have snapped, 'Keep it quiet.' In the book *Chatsworth: the House* by Blanche's niece by marriage, Deborah Cavendish (by then the 11th Duchess of Devonshire), there is a family photograph of Ivan at Christmas 1929, not long after the affair started, standing next to Harold Macmillan. Whether or not Ivan knew about it at that early stage –although if Dorothy told Blanche, then Ivan was bound to know – the photograph has a certain sad irony. Pamela is likely to have learnt about the affair either from Ivan and Blanche, with whom she was close, or from other members of their mutual circle.

Given Blanche's opinion of her sister's taste in Harold Macmillan, she was not surprised that Dorothy's attraction for her husband was short-lived. The result of the affair with Boothby was that the Cavendishes wrote off Harold as a failure – except, perhaps surprisingly, for the Duchess Evie. Although she had not cared for her daughter's choice of husband, when Dorothy strayed from what the Duchess regarded as the proper path, she became an unexpected ally of her son-in-law.

Whatever Pamela and Ivan thought of the affair, it was not at the forefront of their minds, for on 12 June their father had died, very suddenly, at home at Holy Wells. John Dupuis Cobbold was sixty-eight and had been ill for a very short time. A few months earlier, just after Christmas 1928, he had gone on a shooting trip to India and returned to Holy Wells in the middle of April 1929, apparently in good health. He had gone about his usual business and during the run-up to the General Election, just over two weeks before his death, he had chaired a public meeting in Ipswich on behalf of their MP Sir Francis Ganzoni at whose campaign meeting Pamela had made a speech ten years earlier. Yet something made him decide to make his Will, which he did on 21 May. Perhaps it was prompted by his hearing of Sybil and Eric's decree nisi a few days earlier: if he did not make a Will he would die intestate, which meant his estranged wife would automatically be entitled to a share of his estate.

On the day of the election, 30 May, John drove to Felixstowe in his open-top car and, as the *East Anglian Daily Times* surmised, had possibly contracted a chill, for the next morning he was unwell and unable to travel to Scotland for a fishing trip. Knowing his loyalty to the Conservative Party, his friends may have joked initially that it was the outcome of the election that had made him ill; although Ganzoni was re-elected at Ipswich, and nationally the Conservatives won the popular vote, it was not sufficient to secure them a majority in the Commons. That privilege belonged to Ramsay MacDonald's Labour Party, winning by a tiny majority. The result was a hung Parliament.

The next evening, 31 May, John took to his bed where he stayed almost continuously, yet it was not thought necessary to call a doctor for five days. Eventually, when there was no sign of improvement, two specialists were called but his condition worsened, until he fell into unconsciousness and died a few hours later.

No post mortem was held but John's death certificate said the cause was acute gastroenteritis. However, that in itself was not normally a cause of death, although the severe dehydration that can result from it could be. More likely that, as he had returned from India just a month earlier, he was suffering from something he had unknowingly contracted there – perhaps a virus, or maybe he had drunk contaminated water, the bacteria lying dormant in his system until he returned to England.

John's funeral three days after his death was held in the Suffolk village of Trimley St Martin, where his mother's family and some earlier Cobbolds were buried and in whose churchyard he owned a plot of land. There were so many people at the funeral that the tiny village church could not cope, and hundreds had to assemble in the churchyard in the brilliant sunshine of a warm summer's day. At least they did not need to worry about their attire: in his Will, John specifically said that no-one should go to the expense of buying mourning clothes.

The chief mourners were Lady Evelyn – still officially his wife, despite their separation – Pamela, Ivan and Winifred and their spouses, some of John's siblings, and Victor Cavendish, the Duke of Devonshire. Simultaneously a memorial service was held in Ipswich, at the Cobbolds' home church of St Clement, which hundreds more attended, and both churches were swamped by the floral tributes that were sent.

The Duchess of Devonshire must have been away at the time, for Victor told his wife about the occasion in a letter to her on 18 June after he returned to Chatsworth:

'I am glad I went to the funeral and I think Ivan was pleased. It was a nice simple service & there was a very big attendance. In fact, the church was not nearly big enough. A lot of people came down from London including my brother Dick.'

Apart from the vast throng of individual well-wishers, the many groups that were represented at the two services were a testimony to the extraordinary part that John had played in charitable organisations and the public arena, acknowledged in generous terms in the lengthy obituaries of both *The Times* and the *East Anglian Daily Times*; they also paid tribute to his many professional and sporting achievements.

Ipswich had already benefited greatly from the generosity of John and other Cobbolds, but he could not depart without leaving another gift to the city where he had spent most of his life. Ivan, as John's heir, was pleased to notify the Mayor of Ipswich that his father had left to the Corporation the beautiful oak panelling which adorned the walls of his writing room at Holy Wells; John's hope was that it might decorate a room in the Elizabethan Christchurch Mansion, once the home of his late uncle Felix which he had bequeathed to the city. The panelling, previously from an old inn that the Cobbolds owned, and before that in the house of a wealthy merchant, was valuable both in monetary and historical terms. A place was indeed found for it in the Mansion which, with its gardens, continues to be used by the people of Ipswich as Felix had intended.

John's children were shaken by the unexpectedness of his death. Pamela had always been much closer to her father than her mother, the more so since their separation. Winifred had benefited from his financial generosity even after she had married, and he had never judged her, despite her lifestyle and the differences in their political outlook. As for their brother, Victor Cavendish told his wife, 'I am afraid Ivan will miss

314

his father very much', while Lady Evelyn seemed to have been propelled into action by the funeral:

'It was very strange to see Lady Evelyn there very busy & fussing about. I went out for a walk with her in the morning round the garden and it was curious to hear her talking about her inheritances and speaking of John. She must be mad. She is really impossible.'

This suggests that Evelyn was anticipating John bequeathing her something, despite the very generous financial terms he had settled on her when they separated.

Victor paid his respects personally to other members of John's family in the next few days. The day after the funeral he visited Pamela and Charles, who were entertaining a friend of John's who had joined him on several big game expeditions, and also Pamela's sister Winifred. Victor's opinion of her was not complimentary; he found 'Mrs Sladen . . still very tiresome', but perhaps he was an unwilling recipient of her political ideals. After all, her socialist views would have been somewhat at odds with his, being one of the richest landowners in the country. At least he did not have the awkwardness of meeting Winifred's husband Algy; he must have taken himself off somewhere that day, avoiding the embarrassment of bumping into the ex-Governor of Canada who was familiar with his inauspicious past.

Victor took the opportunity while he was in Suffolk to visit Blanche and Ivan at Glemham, which he thought looked 'very nice', and to see his grandchildren whom he found to be very well; his latest grandson, John, he pronounced 'a capital little boy'. His impression from Ivan was that everything seemed to be in order in respect of his father's affairs. And on paper John's estate did indeed look very healthy, reflected two months later when Probate was granted to his three Executors, being Ivan, his brother Philip and a cousin. His net estate was valued at nearly £587,000, a value of around £3 million in 2011. John's Will was generous. Ivan was to reap the benefit of income from the sum of £50,000 which was to be invested for him, with Blanche to benefit if he died, and after that their son John Cavendish Cobbold could look forward to receiving both the income and capital on reaching twenty-one. Pamela was to have £5,000 which was to be paid to the trustees of her marriage settlement. Winifred was not mentioned at all, probably because of all the handouts she had received from her father, but £5,000 was to be invested for her son Toby for when he reached twenty-five.

Two of John's siblings, Ralph and Edith, were to receive a tax-free annuity; Ralph junior, his nephew, and various friends, would each enjoy a tidy sum; for those of John's Suffolk employees in his house, farm, stables or gardens who had served him for ten consecutive years, was a sum equivalent to one year's wages; and the family's beloved Jane Cottle, once Pamela's nanny and now nurse to Pamela's own children, would not only receive a year's wages but also an annual payment of £100 to be paid quarterly for the rest of her life, together with a cottage. And unsurprisingly, the beneficiary of the rest of his estate, after the debts and legacies had been paid, was Ivan.

Three months after the Grant of Probate, a Trust which John had formed in January 1918 making some of his land settled land, came to an end, and its Trustees – Philip, John's cousin Guy Cobbold, and another relation – obtained in August a further Grant of Probate of this land, valued at £18,000. Why it had been put in Trust, and for whose benefit, is not known, but it would have been a way of keeping a part of John's estate separate from that which passed under his Will, thus protecting it from challenge.

As John's heir, Ivan inherited his share of the Brewery, and although little changed on the practical front – he and his uncle Philip continued to run it as they had done with John – Ivan nevertheless knew that ultimately the responsibility was his. The combination of the burden of dealing with his father's estate and his grief made the rest of the year a difficult one for him, while Pamela continued to feel that in losing her father, she had lost a friend and ally. Her daughters too, missed their grandfather whom they would always remember as being funny and kind. Pamela feared for the future of Rannoch Lodge, and in that summer of 1929 was feeling so low that Charles decided that she needed a change of scenery.

Chapter 25

Another Storm Gathering

It was time, in the late summer of 1929, for Charles to find somewhere new to rent as their country house, somewhere which, as usual, would offer his wife excellent hunting. It had been a dreadful year for Pamela and she needed cheering up. But it had not been an easy time for Charles either, because in his position as a director to the Court of the Bank of England, he was only too aware of clouds gathering on the American financial horizon, those about which his father had warned Hambros Bank earlier in the year.

By contrast, in a lighter mood, throughout August that year Britain was the host of an unusual, but joyful, celebration. The Scouting Association, started by Robert Baden-Powell in 1908, was twenty-one, and a Coming of Age Jamboree was held at the massive Arrowe Park in Birkenhead. From all over the world boy scouts came, by road, rail and sea, fifty thousand of them from dozens of countries, to live together in one huge camp, celebrating the anniversary and reminding themselves of the importance of public service and the daily 'Good Turn'. Opened by Baden-Powell and the Duke of Connaught, a son of Queen Victoria, the Jamboree was a busy, crowded, muddy, unique event which acquired particular significance for Baden-Powell, when on the second day King George V, the Association's Patron, visited the camp and conferred upon its founder a peerage.

Boys and young men from countries as diverse as South Africa, India, America, Austria, Hungary, Czechoslovakia, Belgium, Poland and Germany, listened to Sir Robert's rousing speech, in which he talked of celebrating 'world fellowship and brotherhood'. Announcing, 'Here is the hatchet of war, of enmity, of bad feeling, which I now bury in Arrowe', he drove a hatchet into a barrel of arrows and sent the scouts out into the world, each of them to be his '… ambassador, bearing my message of love and fellowship on the wings of sacrifice and service, to the ends of the earth'.

In the same month that the scouts from Germany listened to the humane message delivered in an English park, many people in the boys' home country also attended a large meeting, at Nuremberg. One of several rallies held there, the host was the National Socialist German Workers' Party, otherwise known as the 'Nazi Party'. It too had an enthusiastic and driven leader, whose name was Adolf Hitler. Wishing to encourage all young people to learn about and support its ideals, the following year the Party would start its own youth movement.

Meanwhile, back in the Britain of autumn 1929, in the pretty Oxfordshire village of Swinbrook, life was about to change for Lord Redesdale (David Freeman-Mitford) and his family. Fortunately it was not quite time for his daughter Unity to catch her first glimpse of Hitler and become famously obsessed with him, for that would happen in 1933; for now her parents had more immediate problems to deal with. David Freeman-Mitford had invested in many ventures which were dependent on the American stock exchange, and had done very well so far. In 1926, mindful of the needs of his large family, and to indulge his love of having new projects to work on, he had sold the old family home, Asthall, and bought two properties. One of these was the lease of a huge, seven-storey London house at 26 Rutland Gate, Kensington, into which he installed a lift (of which his daughter Jessica later remembered he was immensely proud); the other was an old farmhouse above Swinbrook, which he extended and developed into what he considered to be a splendid modern family home, Swinbrook House. However, the family's fortunes were about to change.

In the USA that summer the economy had been uncertain, and on 19 October record share sales hit the stock market, culminating on 21 October, forever afterwards known as 'Black Thursday', in the Wall Street Crash. The crisis started early that day, when the sheer volume of selling – nearly 13 million shares changed hands in a few hours – caused prices to drop suddenly. The ticker tape started to lag behind, and as prices fell faster and faster, spot quotations began to show shocking collapses in value. Panic broke out. Orders to 'sell at any price' came in from frightened punters and boardrooms across the country, and the market turned into a clamour of dazed salesmen wading through a sea of paper looking for non-existent buyers.

At 11.30am the bottom truly fell out of the market. The Hambros' friends at J P Morgan & Co were living through a hellish nightmare of a time. At midday New York's leading bankers met at the Morgans' office, noticing with concern the huge crowds that had gathered outside desperate for news, their anger causing police riot squads to be called. After their hour-long discussion the bankers emerged and were surrounded by the mob eager to hear what Thomas Lamont, J P Morgan's senior partner, had to say. 'There has been a little distress selling on the Stock Exchange,' he announced, adding that the problem was 'technical rather than fundamental'. He reassured the crowds that the market was essentially sound, and it was simply undergoing a period of readjustment after four years of a strong bull market. Fortunately his assurance worked, for that afternoon the market started to recover. However, for many it was already too late. The country was forced to acknowledge that the boom of the previous few years, the spree of easy money and over-confidence, was over. Many small investors lost everything, while eleven speculators were said to have committed suicide.

In Britain, the initial fallout of the Crash was less traumatic than in the USA or Germany, and so long as the volume of world trade remained high, Hambros Bank and the other London merchant banks were not unduly hurt by the events. For a few British investors however, including Lord David Freeman-Mitford, it was potentially disastrous, and he had to take immediate action or face bankruptcy. Moving the family to live partly in a very much smaller house his wife owned in High Wycombe, called Old Mill Cottage, and partly in a tiny mews flat, previously a chauffeur's quarters, which he owned behind Rutland Gate, he knew it was vital to find tenants for both of his properties. He was very lucky, for he did not have to wait too long. Rutland Gate was let to a wealthy American woman, and Swinbrook House to Charles and Pamela.

With Charles Hambro's background, David Freeman-Mitford is

unlikely to have insisted on meeting his tenant beforehand, and must have been delighted knowing he would never have to send in the bailiffs to collect the rent. Charles too may have felt he already knew his landlord, whose sometimes eccentric views expounded in the House of Lords were frequently published. Any previous connection, apart from through their respective daughters' ballet class, was probably largely through Pamela's family. Her uncle Alexander, 8th Earl of Dunmore, was acquainted with Lord Redesdale through the House of Lords, and Alexander's daughter Marjorie, Pamela's cousin, was a friend of Nancy Mitford, a guest at Marjorie's wedding in 1926.

Accustomed as she was to older properties, Pamela would have found modern Swinbrook House refreshingly different, provided she could put up with some of its quirkier characteristics of which the older Mitford girls were not very tolerant: they had adored Asthall. Nancy, the eldest daughter, referred to the place as 'Swinebrook', which greatly upset her father, and they complained about the loss of freedom that the outbuildings at their old home had given them. The only daughter to love Swinbrook from the start was Debo.

The Hambro girls, Cinders, Di and Pammie, would have slept in the children's bedrooms on the top floor, where Nanny's room was, each bedroom painted white with a border of a different colour. The inside doors of the house were made of elm which Lord Redesdale insisted was 'damn good wood',[1] but Nancy said that even when it was locked, you could put your head around the visitors' bathroom door and see what was going on inside. In the dining room the table was made of two long pieces of oak, sixteenth-century style, which did not quite meet in the middle and bore the scars where the Mitford girls had sown seeds down the middle 'valley' and watered them.

The house had a large, warm, walk-in linen cupboard, just the right size for hiding in, where the Mitford children, including their brother Tom, held secret meetings. On the second floor, next to the governess' bedroom, was the schoolroom, big and airy, with bay windows, a small fireplace, chintz-covered furniture and a piano. It was separated from the visitors' and the grown-ups' rooms by a green baize door. In the

---

[1] Deborah Devonshire, *Wait for Me!* London, John Murray, 2010.

extensive grounds were tennis courts and stables, all essential to Charles and Pamela's lifestyle, and a chicken farm which Lady Redesdale had started as a profitable business and which was a particular favourite of Debo.

The Hambros, like the Mitfords, were regular churchgoers at the village church, but it is most unlikely that they would have been allowed to sit in the Mitford family pews which had been donated in 1914 by Lord Redesdale after winning a bet. They were, after all, only renting the house, whereas the Mitfords had an elevated status in the village. Lord Redesdale enjoyed the benefit of the 'living' at Swinbrook, which gave him the ancient right to choose a new vicar if the incumbent one died or left, and he also selected the hymns to be sung each week, insisting he did not want any 'damn complicated foreign tunes'.[2] The arrival of Pamela, Charles and the girls may have given the vicar a refreshing break.

Charles rented the house until about April 1931, when Lord Redesdale's finances had recovered sufficiently for him to move the family back to their home. Until then, for some of the time at least, Pamela enjoyed the excellent hunting in the area – Oxfordshire and neighbouring Gloucestershire – with the Heythrop hunt which had started in 1835. She already knew the hunt well for she had joined it when they were living at Netherswell. Even in the twenty-first century the hunt still boasts the stability of having only thirteen hunt masters in all those years, including Lord Redesdale's grandfather and father respectively on three occasions during the nineteenth century. Swinbrook was one of the estates which were of much importance to the hunt: Lord Redesdale and other local landowners, through whose estates the hunt ran, continued the awareness that had existed since it began of the importance of ensuring that the wildlife on their land benefited from a suitable environment. The hunt sometimes met at Swinbrook House, including on Boxing Day 1929, which would have delighted Pamela.

The Hambro girls too, were taught to ride. It is likely that Cinders and Di were enrolled in the Heythrop Pony Club, which had started in 1926, and Pammie, aged four in December 1929, may well have joined them. Charles shared Pamela's keenness for them to ride, with a view to

[2] Ibid.

their hunting when they were older; not only did he endorse the social aspects of hunting for both sexes, he did not believe women should be spared the necessarily bloody aspects of the kill.

Charles must have appreciated how lucky his family was in the light of the Wall Street Crash, although he was aware of what was happening economically in the rest of Europe, and it did not look hopeful. In October, just before the Crash, Germany's Foreign Minister Gustav Stresemann had died. Much lauded for rebuilding Germany's economy after the Great War, his death left that country without his skill and experience. Germany had been built on foreign capital, especially American loans, and it was very dependent on foreign trade. After the Crash the market for German exports would quickly dry up, leaving the country in dire economic straits and creating the right conditions for Hitler to increase his party's popularity.

Away from such gloom, the same month saw Pamela and Charles celebrating their tenth wedding anniversary and, whatever else they may have done to mark the occasion, she fell pregnant. They hoped very much that this time it would be a boy, for they were rather like the Mitfords: top-heavy in the female stakes, although Pamela would not have wanted to keep having children indefinitely until she had a boy. For one thing, pregnancy always curtailed her riding, so much to her frustration she was probably unable to do very much in the early days at Swinbrook.

Two months later another celebration in the Hambro family took place, although there were not many who joined in. On 11 December Sir Eric Hambro married Estelle, at Princes Row Register Office in London. For some reason – perhaps it was a quiet day for the Registrar – the ceremony took place half an hour earlier than the time actually fixed, which was midday. According to newspaper reports of the wedding of the 'well-known banker', there were only a few friends present, including Estelle's sister – a Mrs Keith, who must have been Maryanne Christina, their elder sister – and Eric's lawyer. After the ceremony a reception was held at the Savoy Hotel, after which the happy couple left for Milton Abbey. Why none of the family was at the ceremony is not known; perhaps Eric and Estelle did not want any fuss, and maybe Charles and his siblings went to the reception instead. Perhaps no-one went at all, for fear of appearing to approve and thus upset Sybil. The photograph in

The Scotsman of the occasion shows Eric looking content but strained, although he was by then fifty-seven; Estelle is tiny beside his still towering frame, her pleasant face framed by a huge fur collar as she holds a large bouquet and smiles gently.

If Eric looked a little strained it was hardly surprising, for apart from the emotional toil that the divorce had had on him – and he was not an insensitive man – his position as Chairman of Hambros Bank was becoming increasingly difficult. The Wall Street Crash made him consider the potential aftermath and its effect on Britain, and he was also acutely aware of his own financial position. He still enjoyed his gambling, although his luck had not improved, so he was increasingly aware that his personal finances were less healthy than they should be. Also, the day before the wedding he had learned that his plans for the development of Hayes Place estate may be disrupted, for the Parish Council had appealed to the National Trust to save the manor house.

Eric had signed an agreement with the Rural District of Bromley Council in December 1928, under which he would pay for the laying of the infrastructure for the new Hayes estate and the Council would carry out the work, but in May 1929 he had to complain to the Council through his solicitors that work had not yet started, and he was 'becoming very impatient at the delay in commencing these Roads'. Still occupying a large area of Hayes today, the new estate ended up taking longer to be built than Eric had anticipated. The problem was that Hayes in the 1920s was very rural, and the infrastructure necessary to support nearly a thousand new homes was extensive. Sewers and drains needed to be laid and roads widened, which took a good deal of time-consuming planning, and then came the hint of objection to the demolition of Hayes Place mansion.

It had been anticipated back in May 1928 that delays may occur, when a lengthy letter was published in *The Times* to coincide with the 150th anniversary of the death of William Pitt the Elder, in the house that he had built. The correspondents were the Lord Lieutenant of Kent, Lord Stanhope (a descendant of William Pitt the Younger), the Rector of Hayes and others, who paid homage to both of the former Prime Ministers and referred to the forthcoming development of the estate:

'The park which he [the Elder] planted with so much care will soon cease to exist; it is mapped out for building. The fate of the dignified house is uncertain.'

The writers appealed for the sum of £350 for a memorial to father and son to be placed in Hayes church to honour the 'talents, virtues and services of the elder and the younger Pitt', for none so far existed.

They were right to be concerned about the fate of the house itself. Given its history, its destruction would surely never happen today. But in the Britain of the mid-1920s historical houses like Hayes Place did not enjoy legal protection. The National Trust was relatively young, having been founded in 1895, and was still mainly concerned with protecting the countryside from development and obtaining greater access for ordinary people, rather than in the preservation of buildings.

Nevertheless, Hayes Parish Council (HPC) had a jolly good attempt, perhaps not least as a mark of respect to Sir Everard, who had been its first Chairman from 1895 until his death. Its clerk, a Mr William Plant, wrote to the National Trust on 10 December 1929, the day before Eric's wedding, saying that at a recent meeting of HPC the question was raised of whether steps should be taken for the preservation 'of the Mansion House in view of its historical associations'. He asked whether the National Trust 'had considered the acquisition of the house as an object of national interest and if in their opinion the Council could usefully assist in the matter'. A very brief reply was sent to him on 12 December, saying merely that the National Trust had not considered the acquisition of the mansion. No further discussion was invited. Eric must have been relieved when he heard that, for it seemed there was one less obstacle to the development.

If Charles regretted the potential destruction of his late grandfather's house, as well as potentially Pickhurst Mead where he and Pamela had started their married life, Pamela was deeply troubled by the fact that Ivan had discussed with her the necessity to sell not only the Rannoch estates but also Holy Wells, the Cobbold family home for one hundred and fifty years.

Pamela knew that talk of selling Rannoch was nothing new. In 1919, shortly before she married, her father had considered selling or renting out part of the estate, complaining to the Duchess of Devonshire about the stags and the grouse and wanting the roving life again. He did nothing about it at the time, probably due to the economically depressed market of the early post-war years. Then in March 1924 he went as far as putting it on the market: Rannoch Lodge and 26,000 acres of his land – just over half the total – including Camusericht shooting lodge, itself a handsome twelve-bedroomed property, its farmhouse, the fishing lodge at Dunan and the extensive fishing rights he owned. The rest of his estate, Talladh-a-Bheithe and Craiganour, were not included.

To Pamela's relief, given her love of the place and the fact that she wanted the children to have a chance to know it too, it did not sell. She had known that Ivan was bound to inherit the estates one day, and be free to do what he wanted with them, but in 1924 she had fondly imagined that her children would be almost grown up before that happened, that they still had years ahead of them all at Rannoch. When in 1929 John's death made the sale a real possibility, it was a shock to her.

It is unlikely that Ivan actually wanted to sell Rannoch. He loved Rannoch not only for its beauty but for its shooting, being well-known for his skill, and a Scottish shooting estate gave him somewhere other than Glemham to entertain the social set with whom he and Lady Blanche mixed, which occasionally included the King. But it was not only for social reasons. He had to keep up the family name in business, both the Brewery and the banking side and, as nothing breeds success like success itself, an outward show of it was necessary.

But the estate which had been the Edwardian gentleman's dream now needed to work for itself, to make money to justify its existence, and the years of the late 1920s were not good for that. John's estate had to meet massive death duties: the rate was 40% the year he died, increasing to 50% during 1930. And Ivan had to ensure that his mother's settlement could still be paid. Lady Evelyn would continue to be entitled for the rest of her life to the tax-free sum of £10,000 a year from John's estate under the terms of their agreement. It was a huge amount of money for that time.

However, Pamela could breathe again for once more Rannoch did not sell. But instead, Holy Wells was to be sold. She knew that really there was no point in Ivan keeping the Ipswich estate, for none of the family had use of it now that their father had died. Lady Evelyn, although legally John's widow, had no right to it as she had Glencarron and the mews house in Mayfair as part of her settlement; Ivan and Blanche had Glemham Hall, and Pamela and Winifred were married women. Although some shooting was to be had at Holy Wells, it was not known for it. It was too expensive to keep for purely sentimental reasons, even if those reasons included the fact that the estate had been in the Cobbold family since the late eighteenth century.

With Ivan living nearby at Glemham and his fellow director in the brewing business, his uncle, Philip Cobbold, at Tattingstone Park just outside Ipswich, a residence in the actual town seemed unnecessary. As a first step, Ivan and his co-Executors instructed the respected land agents Knight, Frank & Rutley to auction the contents of Holy Wells, which took place over two days in April 1930.

The sale was a mix of the historical, the cultural and the esoteric. There was beautiful wooden panelling from the dining room, transported from old merchant houses that the Cobbolds had bought generations earlier before they became inns, some panels carved with Jacobean designs of vine leaves and grapes and columns, some comprising paintings of a ship in full sail, an astronomer and a globe. From the library and a bedroom came old Chinese wallpaper in duck-egg green with flowers and foliage. Several of the ground floor rooms produced the 'trophies of sport' that the *Gentlewoman's Magazine* had described some thirty-eight years earlier: stag heads, antlers and skin rugs. Extravagant dining tables and delicate writing tables, elegant side cupboards and carved chairs, all of mahogany, could be bid for, along with Sheraton card tables and sideboards. The discerning collector of chairs could choose between those by Hepplewhite and those by Chippendale, some covered in leather, others in silk damask, which stood on deep Axminster or Wilton carpets, in rooms whose walls offered rich oil paintings and water colours – although the Gainsboroughs and other major artists were not included, too important to be left to the uncertainty of such a general auction. The gleam of brass bedsteads and candlesticks was reflected in wall mirrors and mahogany cheval glass, while the third decade of the twentieth century was represented by vacuum cleaners and refrigerators.

As for books, both fiction and non-fiction, there cannot have been a period or author that was not represented. There were sixty-four volumes of *Modern Novels*, and plays from the seventeenth century; histories of saints and of monarchs; classic works of literature such as Byron's *Childe Harold* and the works of Shakespeare and Dickens; dozens of copies of *Punch* and *Illustrated London News*; old volumes of Latin and Greek works; travelogues, atlases and books of poetry.

Neither was the ordinary or mundane excluded from the auction. Sandwich and flask cases, always kept conveniently close to the golf clubs and other sporting paraphernalia in the South Hall, formed part of one lot; items for sale in the footman's room included two mattresses and a towel rail, while from the chauffeur's room came nine blankets and three bedspreads. Even the linoleum laid in the servants' bedrooms could be bought.

The very fabric of the childhoods of Ivan, Winifred and Pamela – indeed, of the lives of the Cobbolds for the past one hundred and seventy years – was there for the world to see, up for grabs by the highest bidder. For the inhabitants of Ipswich itself, already saddened by John's death, the removal of the Cobbold family from Holy Wells where they had lived for so long was a cause of much regret, signifying the end of a long era and a reflection of the economic and political state of the times. But at least John's brother and son were still resident in the county, if not in Ipswich, and the Brewery, an essential part of the town's economy, continued to thrive. The future of Holy Wells mansion itself and its grounds would remain undecided until they were bought in 1935 by Lord Woodbridge, of a wealthy tobacco family; he gifted the grounds to the people of Ipswich, followed by their opening as a public park in 1936. The mansion, later falling into disrepair, would be demolished in the early 1960s. However, the orangery and stables still stand today and the park flourishes, with the old orchard where Pamela played and the lake where she skated both there for the modern visitor to enjoy.

The timing of John's death, four months before the Wall Street Crash, at least meant he missed the trauma that erupted from it, which would scar and change Britain. By the time the sale of the contents of his home took place, the Great Depression was on its way.

327

Chapter 26

The Country Erupts

The 1930s did not get off to a promising start. As the new decade began, the number of those out of work was just under three million. Unemployment – the defining characteristic of the Great Depression – had started to rise rapidly in Britain since January 1929.

The early years of the decade would come to be identified with greyness and drabness. But for the Hambro family it began on a very bright note, for Charles' younger sister Zelia was married on New Year's Day 1930, her twenty-first birthday, to a young Royal Naval officer, Lieutenant Patrick William Humphreys. The silver beads and diamanté embroidered all over the bodice of her ivory satin gown shone through the darkness of the winter's day and lifted everyone's spirits. Pammie Hambro, Pamela and Charles' youngest daughter, just short of her fifth birthday, was one of two young bridesmaids; their dresses were of chiffon velvet in different shades of blue, the colour of calm and stability, while the orange blossom which edged Zelia's train and veil, and the gold lilies in her bouquet, added richness and warmth to the scene.

The photograph of the couple in *The Times* shows the groom looking dashing in his naval uniform while Zelia, looking directly and almost challengingly at the camera, appears as tall as her husband, if not slightly more so. Height being a common feature in the Hambro family, at least amongst the men, she would still have been shorter than Eric, who was proud to give his daughter away at Holy Trinity Church in Sloane Street, London. The still-recent upheaval in the bride's family of the divorce of her parents and the remarriage of her father, which had

328

taken place just three weeks earlier, was dealt with tactfully. Although under different circumstances the reception might have been held at one of the Hambro family homes, this was no longer possible, and Sybil could hardly be expected to agree to its being held at Milton Abbey. After all, she had been replaced as its mistress by the new Lady Hambro: Sybil was now known as 'Sybil, Lady Hambro', denoting her past entitlement. Instead, Pamela and Charles hosted the reception at 18 New Cavendish Street in London, where even Winifred, although without Algy, was a guest.

The guest list was not huge but, as well as several of the groom's fellow officers, there were several senior Hambros including Eric's younger sister, Violet – for many years married to Sybil's brother, Everard Martin Smith – and several more of Sybil's family, including her step-mother Cecilia. The venue for the reception raises the question as to why Eric and Sybil did not simply hold it at a London hotel, which would have been suitably neutral territory. But then it would have been Eric's responsibility to pay for such a location, and his personal finances were becoming so increasingly precarious that Charles, his own son, sometimes had to bail him out from his gambling debts.

It was unusual to have a wedding on New Year's Day but not only was it the bride's birthday, her father and his new wife were leaving for South America at the end of the month for business, and were expected to be away for several months. At the beginning of May 1930 Estelle, perhaps anticipating how busy Eric would be on their return given Britain's financial situation, was to take herself off to Monte Carlo, where the summer social season was just starting, and settle herself into the luxurious Metropole Hotel, which then, as now, was classed as one of the world's best.

The Cobbolds too had their bright moment that year, when Pamela's second cousin Cameron 'Kim' Cobbold married Lady Hermione Bulwer-Lytton on 3 April at the church on her family's estate at Knebworth. It was a happier occasion than when the family had last met, which had been at John's funeral. Some of Pamela's favourite relations were there: Guy Cobbold, her uncles Philip and Ralph, her father's sister, Olive, and Ivan and Blanche. Her mother attended too; normally, given her attitude towards the Cobbolds, an invitation to the wedding of one of her late husband's family might have been greeted with a distinct lack of enthusiasm. However, as it came from the Earl and Countess Lytton of Knebworth, that was quite acceptable, and she knew there would be plenty more titled gentry to help her feel at home: old acquaintances like Lord and Lady Desborough, the Marquess and Marchioness of Salisbury, and the Countess of Balfour, could be relied upon to keep Lady Evelyn company. The presence of the now elderly Daisy, Countess of Warwick, would have helped break the ice amongst those guests who liked to gossip. Known mainly for her promiscuity and for being a mistress of Edward VII, she had by then become well-known as a socialist.

Other than aristocracy at the ceremony, there were plenty of other notables, such as Sir Edwin Lutyens, the architect, who was the Earl of Lytton's brother-in-law and had re-designed part of Knebworth's interior and its gardens; Lady Cynthia Asquith, daughter-in-law of the Prime Minister Herbert Asquith, and a highly respected author of ghost stories – rather fitting, given that Knebworth had belonged to Edward Bulwer-Lytton and whose architecture resembled something out of a gothic fantasy; and, as the Hambro children would have been interested to hear, the author of *Peter Pan*, Sir James Barrie. The stage manager and theatrical impresario Lilian Baylis, who that same month would create a storm in London with her production of *Hamlet* starring a young John Gielgud, also managed to find time in her busy schedule to attend the wedding.

Charles too was amongst friends. His cousin Jack Hambro, a fellow member of the family bank who himself was getting married in a few days' time, was best man while other members of the banking fraternity included Lords Baring and Revelstoke. Cameron Cobbold's grandfather Nathaniel Cobbold, who was Pamela's great-uncle, had been a banker with the family firm of Bacon, Cobbold and Co before it was absorbed into Lloyds Bank, and Cameron was in the early days of pursuing a banking career himself. As the twenty-six-year-old started married life, he could not know – although he may have hoped – that one day he would become Governor of the Bank of England.

To the bankers particularly, the wedding must have been a welcome distraction from the increasing challenges they were facing, and which were waiting to greet Eric Hambro in the middle of May on his return to Britain. Despite the pressures however, Eric continued to give his time to charitable causes, as Sir Everard had always done: he was, for instance, Chairman of the Royal National Pension Fund for Nurses, the charity which his father had set up when Eric was a boy, and in June that year he presided over its forty-third AGM. Eric had ensured that his eldest son was also involved in the cause, and at the meeting Charles was one of several who were re-elected as Council members, along with the Hambros' old friend, Jack Morgan.

Unfortunately Eric's worsening personal financial situation continued to manifest itself. In July, to the surprise of many in the world-wide agricultural community, Eric sold his entire herd of prize-winning Guernsey cattle. He had fondly raised this very old breed for years and the auction at Blandford, near Milton Abbey, was described in *The Times* as 'a landmark in the history of the Guernsey cattle breed'. Very high prices were paid for the beasts at the auction, particularly the bulls; one of them, described as 'the plum of the whole sale', was Fernhill Rose Lad, a famous prize-winning show bull which sold for 360 guineas. This handsome champion had been bought by Eric just three years earlier, for 350 guineas, and for two of those years he had gained reserve champion honours. What was Eric's loss was others' gain, including the keen American market which bought several of his cows and heifers.

Eric's personal finances may have been a cause for concern to his family but in his professional life he was as scrupulous as always. He set an example amongst bankers in encouraging action to help British industry through the troubled times. In May 1930 he was one of seventeen major bankers, including Lionel de Rothschild and the Chairmen of Lloyds and of Barclays, who agreed to serve on the Advisory Council of the Bankers' Industrial Development Company (BIDC). The BIDC was a new company formed with the aim of helping industry by considering schemes for rationalisation put forward by the basic industries; then, where the schemes were approved, it would provide the necessary money to carry them out.

A few days after the newspapers announced the formation of the Advisory Council, Eric presided over Hambros' AGM and pledged that, through participation in the BIDC, Hambros Bank would place its facilities for issuing loans more directly at the disposal of British industry.

Industry was the focus of many a politician's speech that year, including that of Stanley Baldwin, the ex-Prime Minister and Leader of the Conservative Party, when he went to address an open-air meeting in the grounds of Ivan and Blanche's home, Glemham Park, in June. Ivan, taking up the political mantle of their late father (to the satisfaction of Pamela, if not their elder sister), had continued to show support for the Conservative Party, hopeful that it may be returned to a majority in the Commons next time. Baldwin was determined to be the man who led the Party back to power, despite efforts by the two newspaper barons Rothermere and Beaverbrook, through their respective journals, to oust him as leader. In return, as *The Times* reported, he accused them of exercising 'power without responsibility'.

Baldwin recognised that it was important to restore prosperity to productive industry. He considered Britain's 'greatest industry' still to be agriculture, and said it was necessary to deal with the threats and help it grow. The audience of over ten thousand included hundreds of local farmers, who listened to him unfold his agricultural policy. It was necessary because, he said, agriculture was 'suffering from a fall in world prices and the over-production in certain countries of the world'. Suffolk was always an intensely rural county, and as Ivan pointed out as he introduced Baldwin to the crowd, their agricultural district was one which had 'been harder hit than any other district in the British Isles'. Ivan also took the opportunity, aware of the enmity between Baldwin and the press baron, to make a plea to Lord Beaverbrook, asking him 'to use his influence and undoubted ability to co-operate with the Conservative Party in attaining the object which they both desire'. He was met with rousing cheers.

Baldwin's solution to the agricultural problem lay largely in the need for town and country to understand each other so they could sympathise with each other's problems and support the other: agriculture and industry were closely linked, he said, and it was necessary for industrial districts to realise this, for a dwindling agriculture meant more surplus labour seeking work in the towns. He considered that people in England did not appreciate that, unlike industries like steel or coal, the majority of farmers in England were 'small men' whose businesses were scattered and generally were very small. Baldwin won their hearts when he said that townspeople did not appreciate 'the skill, inherited and acquired by the agricultural labourer'. He also spoke of the efforts of Neville Chamberlain who, as his Minister of Health, had devised a scheme for the repair and renewing of workers' cottages in the country, whereby such work could be done with minimal increase in the rents.

Town and country were certainly being linked just two counties further south, in Kent, although it was perhaps more accurately a case of country *becoming* town. Eric's plans for the development of the village of Hayes were proceeding, although still less quickly than anticipated. And there was more opposition to come from Hayes Parish Council (HPC). In March 1930 HPC had again approached the Rural District of Bromley Council, with which Eric had signed the deal. The task of spokesman fell once more to Mr Plant. He was already known to Bromley Council for having voiced HPC's other concern regarding 'the proposed layout of the Hambro estate', the plans of which HPC had only just been shown. On that occasion, three months earlier, Mr Plant had referred indignantly to the proposed destruction of seven cottages on the Hayes estate to accommodate the widening of the roads, and to the lack of reference to any plans to re-house the occupants 'or provide a similar class of property': hardly what had been envisaged by Neville Chamberlain. At Bromley Council a Mr Wall was instructed to deal with Mr Plant. Mr Wall learned that HPC viewed:

'... with considerable alarm the reduction of the already meagre number of cottages which are within the means of the working man to rent and would be glad to know what steps the RDC have taken in the matter and whether the Estate owners contemplate any cottage property in the lay-out'.

Mr Wall clearly passed on the concerns of HPC to Sir Eric who, conscious of his late father's reputation as a respected landowner in Hayes, would have been keen to deflect any criticism that he was not treating the tenants properly. Through his solicitors Eric swiftly replied to Mr Wall in a letter headed 'Hayes Place Estate – Housing of the Working Classes', saying that the road widening would only affect five cottages. That being two less than the seven about which HPC was concerned, it is presumed all the displaced were properly catered for.

The subject of the preservation of Hayes Place itself had not died down, either. With the National Trust's disinclination to take on the preservation of the building, HPC took up the mantle yet again. When Mr Plant wrote to Mr Wall in March 1930, it was to tell him that HPC and the Rector of Hayes were still considering whether the mansion was of sufficient value to make it desirable to save; meanwhile they were intending to preserve from the proposed development 'Dr Hussey's Well', an ancient well on land previously owned by a nineteenth-century Rector of Hayes of that name. Mr Plant wrote again on 22 April, enclosing a potted history of Hayes Place:

'... from which it would appear that for some 500 years a house has been situated on or near the site of the present Hayes Place, also that the present building appears to have been erected at some date between 1762 and 1766 and is therefore over 160 years old.

'The age of the building itself merits consideration as a national monument but of much more importance is the association therewith for over 30 years of one of the most famous families in English History, viz. the Pitt family Earl of Chatham & William Pitt.

'My Council feel that it would be an irreparable loss if Hayes Place was allowed to be pulled down and therefore most strongly recommend that the Rural District Council take such steps as are necessary to preserve for all times Hayes Place and sufficient land surrounding it as a place of historical interest, care being taken if possible to preserve the two trees mentioned in paragraph 10 of the precis.'

Alas, only those two trees, an oak and a chestnut, were considered for saving. On 13 June 1930 Mr Wall told Mr Plant that Bromley Council had 'taken all possible steps with a view to the preservation of the Mansion House but regret their efforts have not met with success', but that they would consider preserving the trees 'with which the names of Nelson & Wellington are associated'. Exactly what 'possible steps' were taken by Bromley Council was probably never made known to Mr Plant and HPC. Hayes Place was eventually unceremoniously demolished in 1933.

For many people in the small and ancient community of Hayes, the proposed plans for the new estate must have been deeply troubling. Apart from the worry about re-housing the tenants and losing its most historical building and lovely grounds, the village was about to change drastically forever. It had become used to the many day trippers coming from London on the train to enjoy its wide ponds and open spaces, but to have a thousand extra permanent families, and road after road of new houses and parades of shops where previously there had been gardens and parkland, must have been difficult to adjust to.

On the other hand, the injection of new blood and the improved infrastructure would have seen great advantages for the area. Living conditions would improve for most and, at a time when unemployment was very high, job opportunities increase: the new shops and school needed workers, and residents could commute into London where, in theory at least, there were further job opportunities. Each evening they could return to enjoy living in what was still quite a countrified environment, with Hayes village green and common, and the fields just outside. Hayes was in a better position to benefit from expansion than many parts of Suffolk, for although rural it was less intensely so than Suffolk, and since the late nineteenth century had enjoyed more efficient rail links.

While the work on the new estate gradually gathered momentum, Eric was kept informed at home at Milton Abbey. If he was not able to live the life of the country squire at Hayes, he tried to do so in rural Dorset with Estelle, including buying expensive gadgets for Milton Abbey like a Fowler 'Princess' steam engine built in 1910, which was such a fine specimen of its kind that it was eventually bought by a fairground operator and was still in use in steam rallies a century later.

While Eric and Estelle were still in the early days of their marriage, Doie and Marcus Wallenberg were coming to the end of theirs. Doie and Pamela's friendship had continued. When she heard of the death of John Dupuis Cobbold – just after she gave birth to their first and only daughter – and of the proposed sale of Holy Wells, Doie was naturally very sympathetic to Pamela. Although her daughter Anis gave her a lot of pleasure, life had not run smoothly for the couple for some time.

Marcus' affair with the Baroness had continued. Outwardly Doie carried on as if all was normal, performing functions as a member of a family whose importance was quickly spreading outside Sweden, and seeming, in public at least, to be a supportive – rather than subordinate – wife to Marcus. In May 1930 in her native Scotland, for instance, she dutifully performed the launching ceremony of a state-of-the art oil-carrying ship called *Laurel*, built to the order of a Swedish company. Not the most glamorous of duties but as the ship's main machinery was made and supplied by a Wallenberg company, Atlas Diesel, the presence of the attractive, outgoing Mrs Wallenberg, was appropriate, and must have added much-needed pizzazz to the occasion.

After carrying out her duties in Scotland, Doie probably spent some time with her family, and may also have had the chance to visit Pamela, who by then was seven months' pregnant. Two months later, Pamela gave birth to a much-awaited son. Charles Eric Axel Hambro, or 'Charlie' as he would always be known, was born on 24 July 1930. At last Pamela had provided Charles with his heir, the direct link with Carl Joachim Hambro. Even Pamela's mother was around to see her new grandson; Lady Evelyn had been in Norway for a while but returned to her London mews house, Mount Cottage, the week before the birth.

The name 'Axel' does not seem to have come from any of Charles' family but being Scandinavian it would have been a way of connecting with his Danish ancestors, although in later life Charlie would abandon it. Being the youngest of four, with three older sisters, he was at first doted on by the girls although as he grew up he would find himself being bossed about and teased mercilessly, especially by Di and Cinders.

Now it seemed that Milton Abbey would be assured of a continuing heir for after Charles inherited it from Eric, it would be able to stay on their side of the family. As though trying to seal the future of the estate, Charles and Pamela had Charlie christened in the Abbey church on 6 September 1930. Doie was there, delighted to be chosen as one of his two godmothers; the other was Mrs Carron Scrimgeour whose husband, like Charles, was ex-army and a city banker. Charlie's godfathers were an interesting pair. Lord Strathcona and Mount Royal, otherwise known as Donald Stirling Palmer Howard, was the Conservative MP for Cumberland North, whose Scottish-born grandfather had been a major Canadian financier, politician and supporter of women's education. Donald's father-in-law Gerald Loder, 1st Baron Wakefield, was a long-standing friend of the Hambro family in whose gardens Charles had pined for Pamela in the early days of their engagement.

Charlie's other godfather, Lancelot Hugh Smith, had a more racy pedigree. An old Etonian from earlier days than Charles, he was a bachelor and respected stockbroker but had some years earlier taken as his mistress a young lady called Gwen Williams; she was then working in musical comedy but would later become a celebrated novelist, under the pseudonym of Jean Rhys. When Gwen's landlady complained that she did not want 'tarts' in her house, Lancelot set her up in her own place in Chalk Farm. He later left her which devastated her, but he continued to provide for her financially, and to some degree emotionally, for some years. By the time Lancelot was appointed Charlie's godfather, Jean had had her first novel published, and her troubled personal life had moved on several times.

Later that September, Charles was elected a director of the Great Western Railway Board, joining his father in that position. The company, founded by I Kingdom Brunel, apart from owning the railway known affectionately as 'The Holiday Line', also owned ships and canals. The following month, Pamela went on her own – Charles being too busy mid-week to be able to join her – to the wedding of a friend of hers whose parents owned a house in North Berwick, Pamela's favourite golfing haunt. One of Society's 'It' girls, Rosemary Hope-Vere was witty and beautiful; this would turn out to be the first of three marriages for her. She was a close friend of the eldest of the Mitford girls, the novelist Nancy, who was also a guest with her sister Diana, by now the Hon Mrs Bryan Guinness. Apart from catching up with Society gossip, the wedding was a good opportunity for Pamela to see other old friends including Angy, whose son and Pamela's godson, the Hon Peter Strutt, was one of four pages with his brother Desmond.

In early 1931 Pamela and Charles went to Norway, as usual leaving the children behind. The new nanny they had taken on for baby Charlie was young and capable, and no doubt the children were taken to visit their respective grandparents, Evelyn, Sybil and Eric, at their three separate locations while their parents were away. The children adored Eric and Sybil, and were saddened that they were no longer together. Given the increasingly worrying state of the global economy, it is likely the couple's trip was for business rather than pleasure, although Pamela and Charles' connections with Norway were multiple, having conducted business with the country since the early nineteenth century. The Cobbolds still owned a house there and Charles had relations there: Isach Hambro, brother of Charles' great-great grandfather Joseph, had married a Norwegian girl and settled in her native country. Charles and Pamela returned to England on 23 March 1931 and went to their London house. The Court Circular column of *The Times* that reported their return also reported on the same day – although in a far more prominent place near the beginning, under the heading 'Buckingham Palace' – that Pamela's uncle Alexander, the Earl of Dunmore VC, had become a Lord-in-Waiting to the King. It was, of course, a huge honour, but it was not the most settled of times to take up such an appointment, for in 1931 George V was monarch of a country heading for trouble. In fact, the announcement immediately before that of Alexander's appointment was that in the evening the Prime Minister, Ramsay MacDonald, had an audience with the King.

After the Wall Street Crash, Britain's Government had not had an easy time. 'Hot' money had poured into London, which at first became a financial haven against the turbulent storms elsewhere. But once confidence in London began to falter, these foreign funds rushed out, leaving the City with a liquidity crisis of major proportions.

The Government was attempting to achieve several different, contradictory objectives: trying to maintain Britain's economic position by keeping the pound on the gold standard, balancing the budget, and providing assistance and relief to tackle unemployment. The King himself had voluntarily taken a cut to his Civil List to help the situation and lead by example. He was also supportive of the idea of a National Government – one made up of representatives from all parties – to tackle the crisis, hence the discussion with his Prime Minister. At that meeting in March 1931 MacDonald told the King that he had asked Sir George May, a financial expert, to form a Committee to look into Britain's economic problems.

At the same time the economist John Maynard Keynes published his own report on the causes of, and remedies for, the Depression. His solutions included an increase in public spending and the curtailing of British investment overseas. The Tory renegade, Oswald Mosley – then still married to his first wife Cimmie, for he had not yet met Diana Guinness – would have agreed with Keynes's proposal, for in 1930, as MacDonald's Chancellor of the Duchy of Lancaster, Mosley had proposed a public works programme as one of the best ways to cut unemployment. Further ways he suggested including the provision of old-age pensions at sixty and the raising of the school leaving age. These and other proposals which he put into the 'Mosley Memorandum' were rejected by many, including MacDonald himself and his Chancellor of the Exchequer, Philip Snowden. Disillusioned, Mosley resigned from office in May 1930 and, after a doomed attempt to win over the Labour party rank and file, set up his new party, the Fascist Party.

Ramsay MacDonald considered that unemployment was outside the Government's control, contrary to the public's view, which led to some defeats in local elections for Labour. The Cabinet dithered in a continuous state of indecision about how to deal with the economy, and the country limped on in an increasing state of crisis.

Money was being taken away from the City in ever-increasing quantities. Between mid-July and mid-September 1931, £200 million was withdrawn. In July 1931 Sir George May's report was published, which forecast a huge budget deficit and recommended that the Government should reduce expenditure by £97 million, including a £67 million cut in unemployment benefits. The Cabinet formed a Committee comprising MacDonald, Philip Snowden and others to consider May's report. John Maynard Keynes wrote to MacDonald describing the report as 'the most foolish document I have ever had the misfortune to read'. He suggested that the best way to deal with the economic crisis was to leave the gold standard and devalue sterling. Two days later, Charles Hambro's colleague at the Bank of England, the Deputy Governor, Sir Ernest Harvey, wrote to Philip Snowden to say that in the last four weeks the Bank had lost more than £60 million in gold and foreign exchange, in defending sterling. There was, he warned, almost no foreign exchange left.

Snowden's recommendations to the MacDonald Committee included the plan, based on May's report, to raise £90 million from increased taxation and cut expenditure by £99 million. £67 million of this was to come from unemployment insurance, the rest from education,

339

the armed services and elsewhere. The proposal to cut unemployment benefit was met with threats to resign.

The Cabinet met on 13 August but were unable to agree on Snowden's proposals. He warned that balancing the budget was the only way to restore confidence in sterling and that if his proposals were not accepted, sterling would collapse. When a further Cabinet meeting still failed to reach agreement about the best way forward, MacDonald returned to Buckingham Palace on 24 August and told the King he had the Cabinet's resignation in his pocket, and that he was considering resigning too. The King told MacDonald that he considered him to be the only person to carry the country through the crisis, and he hoped MacDonald would help in the formation of a National Government. He persuaded MacDonald that by remaining at his post, his position and reputation would be much more enhanced than if he surrendered the Government of the country at such a crisis. Although MacDonald realised that being part of a National Government would mean his 'death warrant', he felt he could not refuse the King's request.

Thus on 24 August 1931 the First National Ministry was formed. Some of MacDonald's old Labour Cabinet, like Philip Snowden, kept the same jobs. Other appointments included Stanley Baldwin as Lord President of the Council, and Neville Chamberlain as Minister for Health, both Conservatives. The Labour Party generally was appalled by what it regarded as MacDonald's act of treachery in this coalition, and expelled him from the party. He became leader of the National Labour Party and was Prime Minister of the new National Government.

The changes that the National Government immediately put into place would have long-term and drastic effects on the country. The cuts which the majority of the Labour Cabinet had judged to be necessary, but had been unwilling to put into place, were effected. The right to relief was exhausted after twenty-six weeks, and 'transitional payments' were to be paid after a rigorous 'family means test'. It was a policy which was vehemently hated, for the means which were tested included the income of the whole family. This meant that an unemployed father's dole money would be cut if the wages of his working daughter, who lived at home, were slightly increased. It led to family break-ups and bitter recriminations against the system and the officials who operated it. Families in receipt of the dole were put under a close and constant scrutiny of their circumstances. It became the subject of novels, like George Orwell's *The Road to Wigan Pier*.

Meanwhile money continued to be withdrawn in large quantities, and in early September the economic situation became extremely serious. Vital decisions had to be made by the Bank of England. On 9 September it established a Foreign Exchange Committee to deal with the currency crisis. As Charles Hambro was one of its original members, he was soon drawn to the very centre of the sterling arena, and his role at the Bank of England from then and for the next two years would be of great importance. The Board of Hambros Bank agreed that he should be relieved from his duties there for the time being to focus on his new role.

By Friday 18 September the decision to take Britain off the gold standard had become inescapable. It was no longer practical to have a currency which was freely convertible into gold, as gold reserves were now almost exhausted. Since the gold standard had been restored by Winston Churchill in 1925, the pound had been greatly overvalued, and the fixed rate of US $4.86 was to be abandoned so that sterling could find its own level without automatic readjustment by the Bank of England. Ramsay MacDonald, trying to escape the stress by spending a few days at Chequers, the country residence of Prime Ministers, was called back to London on that Friday evening to meet two of the Bank of England's representatives, and give his approval to the Bank's proposal. On Sunday the 20th Charles Hambro and the rest of the Court of Directors met to be informed of the decision and to raise the bank rate from 4.5% to 6%. Later that evening the Government issued a public statement. Within eight days the currency had depreciated by 26%, and soon much of the confidence in sterling had been restored.

Despite the image of sterling having changed, it still played an extremely important function in the world monetary system, so some form of regulatory control was still needed. The Foreign Exchange Committee had to consider a new plan. It was still meeting daily, so Charles was fully occupied. Jack Morgan, through his bank, told the Bank of England in early October that there was a large demand for sterling in New York at a price that was advantageous to them – a good opportunity to redress the balance of the past weeks. Unfortunately the new plan proved to be inadequate, and towards the end of the year sterling's value fell yet again.

It was a very trying time for the Bank of England, and its Governor, Montagu Norman, relied very closely on Charles, writing in his diary that Hambro was sitting next door, keeping him informed of all events. Charles was in fact acting almost as the Governor's personal assistant, and it has been recorded that the relationship between them was one of the most interesting in the City at that time. They were both very independent characters, yet they worked together very well.

Back at Westminster, despite opposition from several political corners, it was decided that following the formation of the First National Ministry, a General Election should be held to give the country the chance to elect its own members. It took place on 27 October 1931. On the Saturday before, Charles' father gave a speech in support of the National Government candidate, at Blandford, the town near Milton Abbey, which was reported in *The Times* as 'The Bankers' Warning: Sir Eric Hambro on the 'Ramp' Story'.

The 'Bankers' Ramp' referred to criticism raised against bankers during the economic crisis, following the Bank of England's unprecedented participation in Cabinet and inter-party deliberations. Eric referred to the 'nonsense' that had been written about this, saying that if a country's leading bankers did not give advice, however unpalatable, they would be accused of neglecting their duty. He reminded the audience that a bankrupt England meant bankrupt banks. He said that foreigners were 'rightly alarmed' at the state of Britain's Budget, the extravagance of the Government and the constant borrowing for the dole. Foreigners were wondering how long it would be before national bankruptcy was in sight, he told his audience, and it was not surprising that they were withdrawing their money from London. Unless the National Party was returned, he warned, the value of the pound would dwindle from 16/- to 10/- and even to 5/- . The result would be an enormous rise in the cost of food.

Eric was dismissive of the 'fanatical devotion' of Liberals like Lloyd George to the 'worn-out principles of free trade'. He was convinced that the only way the country could safely maintain a balanced Budget was to introduce carefully considered tariffs; a careful eye would then be kept

342

on all prices, and measures taken to ensure any increases were kept to a minimum. It was this protectionist stance that set the Conservatives apart from the other parties.

That same evening, Stanley Baldwin was giving a speech in support of bankers in Glasgow at the end of his tour of the industrial north. They were meeting, he said, on the eve of the most momentous election in living memory. The present crisis had been foreseen by many people except for the majority of the Labour Party, who had blocked their ears. The world had seen Britain live upon its credit – 'the greatest credit in the world' – for a century, always repaying its debts. 'We must ensure in our time that the words "Safe as the Bank of England" and "An Englishman's word" shall hold their truth and still ring around the world,' he entreated. People should remember that the depreciation in the value of money was 'a flight from the pound and a flight from currency': it was not, he said, a flight from the banks, which had 'held up their heads as models to the world'.

The majority of Great Britain appeared to agree with the Conservative Party's policies, for it gained 55% of the votes in the Second National Ministry, with 473 MPs elected. Ramsay MacDonald's National Labour Party came next, with 30.8% and 52 MPs, while the Liberals in third place managed just 6.5% with 33 MPs. MacDonald remained Prime Minister.

One of the most impressive results for the Conservatives was that achieved by Harold Macmillan who, having been devastated to lose his Stockton seat in the 1929 election, won it back with a resounding majority of over eleven thousand. It was a boost he badly needed, for he had been through a terrible time in the last two years. His wife Dorothy had continued her affair with Boothby, started in 1929, and was still being carelessly indiscreet about it; they saw each other every day, and often went away together. Soon the whole affair would be widely known, although it did not reach the press. However, knowing that so many people in his social circle and in Parliament knew of the affair was a terrible thing for Macmillan to bear. Dorothy also told him she wanted a divorce.

He had suffered further hurt and humiliation in late August 1930, when Dorothy gave birth to another daughter, their fourth child, and promptly told Macmillan that the father was Boothby. Inexplicably the birth was not registered until October and there was no name on the birth certificate. When Dorothy and Harold were invited by her parents to Chatsworth that Christmas, along with Blanche and Ivan and the other Cavendish siblings and spouses, Harold must have dreaded it for, apart from his mother-in-law's unexpected support for him in his marital crisis, the family's opinion of him remained unfavourable. He could not even find satisfaction in his publishing job, in which he continued to be deprived of any meaningful role. Hardly surprising, then, that during 1931 Macmillan had a breakdown, and in September was admitted to a clinic in Munich renowned for the treatment of severe nervous disorders. When he came out, he threw his efforts into the General Election. Boothby was fighting for a seat in Aberdeenshire and Dorothy left him to it, returning to help her husband with Stockton.

Charles meanwhile had taken on more responsibilities when in early November 1931 he was appointed a Sheriff for the County of London. At the same time his brother-in-law, Ivan, was made a Sheriff of Suffolk. The ceremony at the Law Courts at which they were sworn in, over which the Chancellor of the Exchequer Neville Chamberlain presided, provided a pleasant break amidst the gloom, and Pamela and Blanche were proud to support them.

For a little time, from Christmas that year for a couple of months, exchange rates stabilised and the bank rate was dropped from 6 to 5%, which provided some temporary relief to Charles and the rest of the Court of Directors. But it did not make any difference to the plight of the unemployed. During the first seven weeks of the means test operation, it had the effect of reducing or refusing benefit to 53% of claimants. By the end of 1931, seven hundred thousand households who had received benefit in early November had either been granted payments at a reduced level or been completely disqualified. That number of households meant that one million men, women and children were living in abject poverty. Many of the families in deepest poverty would remain destitute for years.

Christmas that year failed to happen for many British families. On a different level, by the end of 1931 Charles and Pamela were not having the best time either. While his father continued to be highly respected, always behaving with consummate professionalism, his own financial affairs had caused such concern in the Hambro family generally that Charles had decided earlier in the year that a direct eye had to be kept on him. In order to do so, he had moved his family to Dorset to live on the Milton Abbey estate.

Chapter 27

The Hunter and the Hunted

In the grounds of Milton Abbey, out of view of the mansion, stands a charming country house, Delcombe Manor, which was sufficiently important to be listed a couple of decades after Charles and Pamela came to live here during 1931. Built around 1750 re-using medieval material from the Abbey, its fairytale appearance would have enchanted the girls: in the Romantic Gothic style so popular in its time, it was all flint and gables and mullioned windows, with stone arches and slate roofs, and intriguing outbuildings to explore. The house looked out onto a very English cottage garden containing traditional kitchen beds, with a seven-acre paddock beyond, leading the eye across to the softly rolling hills of the Dorset countryside. A bluebell wood just along the lane provided the perfect trot for the girls on their ponies, which they kept in the large stables. There was even excellent hunting in the area for Pamela, with the Portman Hunt. It was an idyllic place to live.

Eric Hambro had put the manor house on the rental market that February, having had it restored and fully furnished, hoping he would be able to find some willing tenants for the summer season, from May to October. Charles saw that moving his family there would provide the perfect opportunity to keep an eye on his father whilst contributing to the coffers, without making it too obvious. With five large bedrooms and another three for servants, three reception rooms, two bathrooms and sundry utility rooms, as well as two adjacent cottages, it was a comfortable size for the Hambros, although not quite as large as they had been used to for the season: compared with Swinbrook it was small, but Pamela and Charles were there out of necessity rather than choice. Not that they did not like their new environment: on the contrary, for they were, after all, living on the very estate that Charles was intended to inherit from Eric, the place of which, as he had told Pamela upon their engagement, she would one day be mistress.

But they were aware of the potentially precarious position of the Milton Abbey estate, for once the Hayes Estate was sold, it would be the last significant inherited property that Eric Hambro retained. The new development at Hayes echoed what was going on in many other parts of the country. Only buildings which were likely to be useful survived. In May that year, Eric put up for sale by auction the remaining parts of the estate. Pickhurst Mead, Pamela and Charles' first home upon marriage, was advertised as 'A Modern Residence in excellent condition with vacant possession', and sounded highly desirable in the catalogue, yet it too was eventually demolished: as lovely as it was, presumably no-one wanted to pay a substantial price for a house that would be cheek-by-jowl with a new housing estate, however modern. After demolition, the only sign for posterity of the existence of Pickhurst Mead was the road named in the new estate as Pickhurst Lane.

Those 'useful' buildings on Eric's land that did manage to sell at the auction included The New Inn opposite Hayes Station, a free house 'with an old established trade and scope for great increase consequent upon the imminent development of the whole Estate'. After surviving several facelifts, The New Inn was still trading at the start of the twenty-first century.

Other useful plots were billed as 'Valuable building land suitable for the erection of Private Residences, Shops etc. possessing an extensive Frontage.' Eric was also selling, 'Attractive Cottages in the Village, comprising good small Residential Properties including first-class Sites suitable for rebuilding in conjunction with the general scheme for development.' A new lifestyle was about to be born: townies, who fancied living the country dream but still wanted easy access into London, could buy a little cottage with potential for expansion, or alternatively knock down the old dwelling and build their own dream home.

As a gesture to the late last resident owner of Hayes Place before the past was swept away, three roads on the new estate were named after him: Everard Avenue, Alexander Close, Hambro Avenue. In anticipation of the new development, Eric's younger brother Harold had, in September 1930, already sold his house, Hayes Grove, an eighteenth- century Jacobean-style house with 8 acres adjoining Hayes Common. It managed to escape demolition and in the 1950s would become a listed building. But the Hambros' occupation in Hayes had come to an end.

Thus the Milton Abbey estate became more precious than ever, sentimentally and practically. Charles was conscious of its being a testament to the family's hard work over the past eighty years: since Carl Joachim Hambro had bought it, much of the family's money and energies had been invested in it. Charles' grandfather Sir Everard had saved it after Harry's financial problems, and brought it under his line of descent. But to uphold Carl Joachim's wish that it stay in the family for perpetuity now seemed increasingly difficult.

Whether Eric's second wife was aware of the extent of his gambling and the uncertain position that her magnificent home was in, is not known. Estelle had her own interests to occupy her, including her responsibilities as a Justice of the Peace. She often stayed in London as social and professional commitments required, although she spent most of her time at Milton Abbey, returning in March that year as Pamela and Charles prepared to move into Delcombe Manor after their return from Norway.

Being in Dorset they managed that June to escape the worst of the aftershocks from the strongest earthquake ever recorded in Britain. With its epicentre in the Dogger Bank off the east coast of England, the earthquake measuring 6.1 on the Richter scale shook the country and its effects were felt as far away as France and Belgium. The Suffolk coast was particularly hard hit. Pamela's cherished Felixstowe took the brunt of it, whilst the pretty town of Sudbury suffered structural damage.

But there were enough rumblings of a different kind going on at Milton Abbey without having to worry about her home county. Pamela was all too aware of the need to keep a check on what was happening with her father-in-law, whilst trying to relieve some of the pressure on Charles who was dealing with the Bank of England's problems.

While she coped with that, her sister was having a very different time. In early April, while the rest of Britain confronted its financial difficulties,

Winifred and Algy had gone to Monte Carlo, a rather surprising venue for a pair of socialists. Maybe they were there to share the excitement of the third Grand Prix which was about to take place, but more likely it was for social reasons, for by 1931 Monaco had become a centre of cultural activity, thanks to its previous Sovereign Prince Albert I. A celebrated resident of the Principality was the Hungarian-born writer Baroness Orczy whose guests that month included Winifred and her husband. They must have known her through their other displaced Hungarian friends; like so many of them, the Baroness, born an aristocrat, had been forced to flee Hungary as a child with her family. Becoming an ardent anglophile, she settled in London and took a British husband. Long-known by 1931 for her novel, *The Scarlet Pimpernel*, she entertained the Sladens and others to dinner at her house, Villa Bijou, where they met Prince Albert's son, by then the Sovereign Prince Louis II.

The Baroness was clearly a sociable person, for in July she was back in London at a luncheon at the Ritz given by her neighbours in Kent where she had once lived. They were Lt General Sir Sydney and Lady Lawford, the parents of Peter Lawford, later a famous Hollywood film star. Aged eight, the precocious Peter was also at the lunch where the guests included Estelle Hambro, who must have found the mélange very entertaining.

While the Sladens were in Monaco, they were sheltered from seeing the difficulties experienced by so many people in the economic climate back home. While Britons were feeling the pinch and worried sick by the state of the economy, and others were facing life-threatening poverty, some of the very rich – although by no means all – continued to remain a breed apart; and some of the aristocracy, even those who were less wealthy than ten years earlier, gave the impression, publicly at least, that they were not affected by it. In July that year, for instance, there was a grand Society wedding when Lady Hermione Cobbold's sister Lady Davina Bulwer-Lytton married the Earl of Erne. Davina was upstaging her elder sister as far as the social standing of her husband was concerned and so her wedding took place in Westminster Abbey, to which the King and Queen sent presents and an even greater number of titled families turned out than to her sister's wedding. But as a cruel reminder that the gilded few are not exempt from suffering, Davina's marriage would last only nine years for her husband would be killed, aged thirty-two, in the war that was to come.

There were those who, mindful of the continued needs of charitable institutions in those straitened times, ensured they were not neglected. In June Charles and Pamela attended a charity ball at the Savoy Hotel in London, in aid of the Royal National Orthopaedic Hospital. Its title – the 'I'm Glad I Went' Ball – implies a reluctance on the part of the guests to attend, only to find themselves (presumably) pleased that they did. The Hambros, in affable company, are sure to have enjoyed it for they were part of a group of guests invited specifically by the Chairman of the Ball, the energetic Lady Melchett, awarded a DBE for her charitable works. They were joined by two of Winston Churchill's children, Diana and Randolph, and a beautiful nineteen-year-old woman, Miss Margaret Whigham. Named debutante of the year when she was presented to Court in 1930, she would later, after a marriage and various dalliances, become the Duchess of Argyll and achieve sexual notoriety.

Also that June, Eric opened up part of Milton Abbey to the public in aid of a nursing charity, along with Victor Cavendish at Chatsworth and the King at Sandringham. But Eric's sense of social responsibility may have contributed to his financial woes. In 1930 he had gone to Italy, with which the Hambros had long had an association, and in Rome had been impressed by an experiment supported by Italy's leader Benito Mussolini: the development of a system for the low-temperature carbonisation of coal. Eric saw this as being the ideal way to help Britain's coal industry. The greatest problem for Britain's mines was that fine coal, which formed a large percentage of their output, fetched a very low price compared with lump coal. Experts had long agreed that if a system of low-temperature carbonisation were available which could generally be applied, it would provide the remedy, because by such treatment fine coal could be turned into fuel of a value not merely equal to that of lump coal, but greater.

An Italian scientist, Commendatore Piero Salerni, was persuaded by Mussolini to concentrate on this possibility, and in November 1931 it was announced to the world, through the Carnegie Institute in the USA, that he had discovered the process. In December, Eric gave a widely-reported luncheon at the Savoy Hotel in London in honour of Salerni, who was the guest of honour amongst various captains of industry. Eric's visits to Italy in the 1920s, when he was a director of the Great Western Railway, had revealed his admiration for Italy's efficient railway system and his acknowledgment of Mussolini's talents – a view he shared with many in Europe, for no-one knew then how the dictator would later utilise his country's system. In his speech at the lunch as Chairman, Eric referred to Mussolini as the most far-seeing man of modern times, and acknowledged his, as well as Salerni's, contribution to the discovery. Eric saw the process as the 'salvation' of Britain's 'once-great coal industry': in fact, reported *The Times*, 'He was deeply convinced that this new industry would be the surest means of removing the chief cause of Britain's present crisis.'

But Eric recognised that it would require money, and that this was not the time to ask for finance from the Government or even from the public. According to the newspaper, he therefore decided 'to shoulder himself the responsibility for the provision of the initial funds'. He realised that in doing this he was departing from the traditions of British banking, whose sound rule it had been to finance only well-established industries. However, he said that in this situation he was acting not as a banker, but as a private individual who realised the country's urgent need for action. In funding it himself, Eric was not only going beyond the call of duty, he was taking action beyond that which the Advisory Council recommended. It seems inevitable that Eric's generosity contributed to his own worsening financial situation.

While Eric Hambro looked to Mussolini with some admiration – as many in Europe did at that time, either unaware of, or choosing to ignore, the full extent of the brutalities of his fascist regime – the Wallenberg family continued to reinforce their business relations with Germany. This was largely due to the active participation of Marcus Wallenberg Senior in European reconstruction work. In 1931 he was playing a particularly active and central role during the German banking crisis, acting as an adviser to the German Government in the reconstruction of German banks. He was also Chairman of a Court of Arbitration (the *Stillhalte*) set up to settle disputes arising from the war reparations arrangement between Germany and the Western Powers. His elder son Jacob managed with him the German business relations with their family's bank, the SEB, of which Marcus himself had been Deputy Managing Director since 1927.

In 1931, neither the Wallenbergs nor the Hambros could have imagined that eight years later the world would be embroiled in another war, started by Germany and supported by Italy. Marcus and Charles would come to play important parts in the resistance movement against Germany, but for now each was coping with his respective country's financial difficulties. While Charles dealt with the challenges facing the Bank of England, his friend was also about to face some hard decisions.

Shortly after Marcus took up his duties in SEB, his father had made him responsible for its loans to a businessman called Ivar Kreuger and his group of companies. Kreuger's family had made its fortune from matches, and Kreuger himself had the idea of turning the business into the leading provider of loans to the shattered economies of post-war nations during the 1920s. He raised cash through a number of share and bond issues in the US, and then loaned the money to national governments in exchange for match-making monopolies in those countries. Like the Wallenbergs, the Kreuger Group controlled a bank, international finance activities and an industrial complex.

As Ivar Kreuger acquired more and more companies, the Wallenberg Group viewed the growth of his empire with both alarm and scepticism, and it was right to do so. Kreuger promised fantastic rates of returns to investors, and he became the leading private lender to Europe; the American President Hoover sought his advice about problems affecting the global economy, and he consorted with Hollywood stars, including Greta Garbo, whom he had discovered whilst she was working in a department store. However, the loans he provided to countries such as Germany were returning much less to him than the amount he was promising to his investors.

Just days before the Wall Street Crash, Kreuger had made a massive $125 million loan to Germany, and it was at this point that his problems started. His financial methods were becoming increasingly devious. He had always sailed close to the edge of legitimacy, establishing a huge network of firms that bamboozled his auditors and bankers, and stashed cash away in secret subsidiaries in Liechtenstein and Switzerland, but now he began tactics that would be referred to in the twenty-first century as 'Enron-style' tactics: reporting profits when there were none and paying his generous dividends by attracting new investment or plundering existing ones.

The Kreuger Group had a normal overdraft facility with SEB during the 1920s, but at the beginning of the 1930s its borrowing increased significantly. Suddenly 7% of SEB's total lending was to Kreuger & Toll, the parent company, and SEB also guaranteed one fifth of the company's loans with other Swedish commercial banks. SEB had noted a tendency on the part of the Kreuger Group to delay its repayments, and so Marcus made sure SEB managed the loans more closely. At first the Group had provided collateral sufficient to cover the loans with a decent margin, but when share prices fell in 1931, the SEB forced the company to provide additional security as and when the loans came up for renewal.

It was soon clear to Marcus that the fate of the Kreuger empire was an issue that could affect the entire economy of Sweden. Towards the end of 1931 Marcus had serious discussions with Kreuger & Toll as a result of rumours circulating about the company's financial position. Marcus became acutely aware that he did not really know what Kreuger was up to, which was no doubt Kreuger's intention. It was a situation of grave concern to him, which must have worried Doie too.

Their domestic life was no smoother. In the late summer of 1931 Marcus had been hampered by several lasting symptoms of paralysis, which he first thought were the after-effects of hay fever. It later turned out to be diphtheria, a feared disease before the introduction of vaccinations and antibiotics. At the same time Doie, apart from knowing he was still having the affair with the Countess, was concerned about her parents, the Mackays, who were badly affected by the Depression. Until then, her father's various enterprises had been going very well. As recently as 1927-8 Alexander Mackay had commissioned a major Scottish architect, Sir Robert Lorimer, to carry out work on the family's Scottish estate Glencruitten, spending a good deal of money on substantially extending the house. But then came the Crash. Alexander managed to hang on to the estate in Florida, but it severely stretched his resources to maintain Glencruitten, which included woodland containing rare and protected species of tree specially selected by him: a keen conservationist, he had intended the woodland to be enjoyed long into the future. As it happened, the family did manage, albeit with difficulty, to keep the estate intact for some years to come, although eventually a substantial part of it was sold.

Doie was also concerned by the very high expectations that her husband had of their eldest son, Marc Jnr. In June 1931 he was seven, well able to read, so no doubt Marcus had, by then, shown him the worn brown piece of paper he carried in his wallet, written by his own father. It read:

'On 5th October 1900 Marcus Wallenberg, born on 5th October 1899, presented himself for the first time at the premises of SEB at Lilla Nygatan in Stockholm. On 12th February 1926 Marc Wallenberg, born on 28 June 1924, presented himself for the first time at the premises of SEB at Kungsträdgårdsgatan in Stockholm.'

Thus young Marc was placed in the family order of succession at an early stage. All too conscious himself of the importance of carrying on the financial dynasty, Marcus from the very beginning planned Marc's training in a way that would enable him to take over as head of the family. When Marc was born, Marcus had made provision that in the event of his dying, his brother should be appointed guardian – what Doie thought of this is not known, but doubtless she was unhappy, for the suggestion was that this should take effect even if she, his mother, was still alive – and he expressed his will that his son 'should be given the opportunity to complete his studies in my native country'. Despite his father's ambitions for him, 'Boy' or 'Boy-boy' as he was known, struggled throughout his school years, and would always be very anxious not to disappoint his father. By contrast, Peter, two years younger, was precocious and, as he grew up, found no problem with studying. He was also more assertive than his brother and had a will of his own. While Doie could see this causing problems of a different kind with his father, at least she did not have to worry about Peter in the same way.

Not that she saw much of either of the children on a daily basis, except during the summer holiday when Marcus would go sailing and she would take them to Scotland to visit her family, or when Marcus would let her take them to Båstad or Falsterbo in the south of Sweden: for in the time-honoured fashion of the upper class into which she had married, she and Marcus had eight indoor servants to take care of them all, so that time spent by the boys with their parents tended to be minimal. In 1931 their youngest, Anis, was still in the care of a nursemaid, and the boys, under the supervision of their nannies, were expected to occupy themselves outdoors from early in the morning until teatime, without the intervention of their parents.

Meanwhile rumours about the quarrels which the couple were having continued to circulate. The Wallenberg family itself has little information about the relationship between Marcus and his Countess and how much they saw of each other but Marcus, after temporarily recovering from the paralysis that had beset him, continued to travel a great deal for business, so opportunities could present themselves for meeting up, although given Marianne's own family commitments, it may have been easier for them to meet whenever Marcus returned to Sweden.

While Marcus and Doie battled with their problems, Charles battled with the financial concerns his father was giving him on the home front, and with those on the national front at the Bank of England. In October that year, 1931, Pamela was pleased to put aside briefly their worries to attend the wedding of Angy's favourite brother Rupert, at twenty-eight the youngest of the Tollemache family. Among the unusually large number of bride's attendants at the wedding in Oxfordshire were Angy's son Peter, Pamela's godson, the only page amongst twelve bridesmaids and slightly self-conscious in white satin, and Pamela and Charles' eldest daughter Cinders, pretty in geranium-red velvet with a headdress of leaves.

Pamela enjoyed the happy occasion with old friends of whom she was very fond. But as the end of the year approached, the Hambros and the Wallenbergs must have looked ahead with some dread at the coming year. For Pamela, her concerns lay in the financial uncertainty posed by her father-in-law and the toll it was taking on Charles. However, while being very worrying, this was different from the marital issues that her friend Doie faced. Pamela knew she still had the love of her husband and never doubted his faithfulness; they were still soulmates, and in the midst of their worries she must have thought back to their engagement, when they had stated that money did not matter, that they would be happy to live alone together in a cave above Loch Rannoch. They were still deeply in love.

Their closeness helped them steel themselves for dealing with the practical issues that they knew they would have to face as the new year approached, arising from Eric's lack of liquidity. But then something occurred which would eclipse that and set in motion an unforeseeable chain of events.

A few weeks before the end of 1931, Pamela had an accident while taking part in the Portman Hunt. It met that winter on 25 November, but not at its usual place. For many years, at least up to the Great War and probably afterwards, the Hunt's winter meeting place had been outside St Giles House, the seventeenth-century home of the Earls of Shaftsbury, in Wimborne St Giles, not far from Milton Abbey. The title was by then that of the 9th Earl, Anthony Ashley-Cooper, a friend of the Hambro family and grandson of the famous 7th Earl who had abolished child labour in the mines.

For years Anthony was happy to let the Hunt meet on his land, and had also allowed its followers to hold their annual Ball in the elegant state rooms of St Giles House. During the Great War, when he was elected Lord Lieutenant of Dorset, he allowed part of the house to be used as a hospital for the wounded, which may have affected its capacity to hold functions like balls, and earlier in 1931 his sister, Lady Harriet, had died: whilst in mourning, he may have felt it inappropriate to allow the Hunt to meet on the family's land that year.

So on this occasion it met instead in the grounds of the recently-founded Canford School in Dorset, a boys' boarding school housed in an early nineteenth-century mansion. The boys were given a special half-day holiday so they could follow the hounds, the whole school and many villagers watching enthusiastically as the hunt gathered.

At some point – it is hoped it was at the end, so that she did not miss out on the chase – Pamela was viciously kicked on the leg by the hunter she had chosen for that day. No-one knows what caused the horse to kick: Pamela was an accomplished horse-handler, as well as rider, and knew her horses well, so it is unlikely it was caused by anything she did, neither was it the season for insect bites. Perhaps it had been frightened by a noisy schoolboy.

A horse's kick has been calculated to have the same impact as a small car travelling at 20mph, so it would have broken her skin at the very least. It is likely she would have been attended to at the scene and then transported back to Delcombe Manor, to be seen by the Hambro's doctor. On satisfying himself that no bones were broken, the doctor would have dressed the wound and prescribed bed-rest, with a nurse to visit regularly to change the dressing.

The injury was slow to heal but then Pamela never healed quickly, a trait that was shared by her youngest daughter. This lack of natural healing ability, together with the state of medicine at that time, made her injury doubly unfortunate. The wound became infected and she developed septicaemia, a very serious condition generally known as blood poisoning. If not treated quickly the condition then, as now, was potentially fatal. Today it is treated by antibiotics; in 1931, despite penicillin having been discovered by Fleming three years earlier, it would not be available for general use until 1945. It meant that at the time of Pamela's injury, there was no commonly-accepted treatment for septicaemia: indeed, earlier that very year the subject had been discussed by physicians at the annual meeting of the British Medical Association (BMA) at Eastbourne. The condition had already hit the headlines in February, when the celebrated Australian opera singer, Dame Nellie Melba, died from septicaemia following facial surgery.

The BMA's discussion was reported in its Journal (BMJ) just the month before Pamela's accident. Fortunately it was not the sort of publication Pamela was likely to read, for it would have given her little comfort. There was, it said, a 'great lack of uniformity in practice' in treating the condition, which demonstrated 'the absence of convincing methods of therapy'. Many doctors had experience of treating isolated cases of septicaemia but not of treating a series of cases 'on truly scientific lines'. The article recommended that:

'A plan of campaign appropriate to the case in point should be decided upon and steadily continued, and the patient should not be disturbed by too many treatments. Panic on the part of friends is a frequent deterrent, but is pardonable; panic on the part of the medical adviser is sometimes fatal and is unforgivable.'

If the Hambros' doctor panicked, it is hoped he did not communicate it to Pamela. One option open to him was to operate, which could be

357

done where there was an infected accidental wound, but not always: the Professor of Surgery at Edinburgh University at the time, D P D Wilkie, recommended in the report that:

'... nicety of judgement is necessary in determining how much must be done, and when... In many cases it will be found that active surgery must be held in restraint until such time as the indications for intervention have become abundantly clear – in other words, the knife may be a lethal weapon if prematurely or incautiously applied...'

If Pamela was not operated on, a popular alternative was a 'bactericidal serum', which had to be used very early on and in adequate doses for it to be of any use, and even then its effect was doubted: such serums continued to be used because the theory of them was 'very attractive'. In all cases, it was suggested that 'Expectant measures' should be used, that is, those which aimed at getting control of the condition rather than curing it. Some physicians favoured using these measures above any specific remedy. The BMJ also advised that the measures should include rest and fresh air.

Pamela may also have received the benefit – if that is the right word – of other types of 'Expectant therapy', such as 'sunshine, both natural and artificial; eliminative measures for bowels and skin, such as hydrotherapy...' and intramuscular injections. 'Good nursing is imperative,' said the BMJ, and added, rather worryingly, 'and the personality of the doctor, who should be encouraging, resourceful and confident, is a great adjunct to success'.

So it was that the chance of success of Pamela's treatment was largely dependent on a calm, resourceful doctor, who was neither prone to panicking nor too fond of the surgeon's knife, in the midst of a largely sunless, British winter. At least the Christmas of 1931 was an unusually mild one, so she could be wheeled outside at Delcombe Manor to take the air. With such haphazard medical care and advice, it is incredible that whatever 'measures' were given to her appeared to have had some beneficial effect, for eventually she was up again. Nevertheless, Christmas that year would have been less active than usual for the Hambro family, as Pamela would have been entreated to take things very easy. However, at that stage her state of health cannot have caused too much alarm, for her mother took herself off just before Christmas to her Scottish estate

Glencarron where she stayed until mid January 1932.

Her father-in-law's usual winter adventures were also less exciting than usual that year, limited by financial considerations. January 1932 saw Eric and Estelle not in glamorous Monaco but in Brighton, spending the weekend with friends at the Royal Albion Hotel. It may not have been Nice or Cannes either, but the seaside town had not yet become the subject of Graham Greene's novel and was still regarded as smart, while the hotel (in which Greene would shortly stay), right on the seafront was, despite being over a century old, still elegant. In being frugal, Eric was no doubt thinking of the undertaking he had given to finance Salerni's carbonisation scheme – and just to keep his promise in the public eye, early in February Salerni himself referred to it in a speech at a public meeting in Sheffield, to where he had been invited so that the industrial city could persuade him it was the best place to build his plant. According to the report in *The Times*, the scientist '... promised to convey to Sir Eric Hambro, who is financing the scheme, the representations made to him'. There was no getting out of it now.

Eric still found the opportunity to continue as a member of the committee of the prestigious Prince's Golf Club in Sandwich, the President of which was the Prince of Wales (later king Edward VIII). Early 1932 was a particularly exciting time for golf-mad Eric, for the Club had the honour of hosting the Golf Open Championship. Charles meanwhile, believing that Pamela was on the mend, worked as hard as ever. On 20 January he was a guest at a dinner hosted by the Argentine Ambassador at the Argentine Chamber of Commerce, listening to the Prince of Wales as guest speaker, and to the Ambassador, talking about the special relationship between the two countries, which went back for well over a century. It was an important and timely topic, for in 1931 there was more British capital in Argentina than in any other country. Argentina was one of Britain's best customers not only for manufacturing but also for invisible exports like investments and insurance; Britain was Argentina's best customer for its grain and meat. However, since 1914 Britain's position in Argentina had been seriously threatened by competitors, and to try to change the position the British Empire Industries Exhibition had been held there in 1931, opened by the Prince of Wales. Times were too hard in Britain for its once-safe position in South America to be threatened.

While Charles pondered on the increasingly difficult financial situation both nationally and on the home front with his father, Marcus Wallenberg continued to have a hard time too. In early 1932 the Kreuger Group's situation became untenable, after increasing security had been pledged for the Group's loans with SEB. In February Ivar Kreuger announced from New York that he was in a severe liquidity crisis and quickly needed to borrow additional funds in Sweden, despite the fact that he no longer had any worthwhile security to offer. It transpired that he needed at least $2 million that very day to prevent the collapse of the whole financial structure of the Group. At first it was hoped that Sweden's national bank, the Riksbank, would step in, but it considered that the country's three leading commercial banks – including SEB – should face up to their responsibilities. At the very least, it wanted to be able to say that all the big banks were involved before it would consider using public funds.

Marcus was the one who had to deal with the situation, as his father was in Berlin at the Court of Arbitration and Joseph on holiday. He adopted a negative stance. Reports from the USA became increasingly desperate and the Government was called in, the Swedish Prime Minister pointing out that the prestige of the nation was at stake. A Swedish rejection of such a small credit could not be allowed to trigger the collapse of the Kreuger Group. A proposal was presented by which the Riksbank would lend half of a total loan of $3.2 million, while the three lending banks would lend one sixth each.

Marcus, with some relief, was able to get hold of his father that evening. He agreed with his son's approach and flatly dismissed the idea of granting any additional loans to Kreuger, confirming this to the Prime Minister, who stated that his confidence in SEB's management was greater than in that of the other banks, and that this was the reason he wanted SEB to take part in the transaction. Marcus Senior replied that for similar reasons, he wanted to stay away from the deal.

SEB's proposed part of the loan was finally taken over by the Riksbank, a move which was much criticised. The Riksbank now accounted for two-thirds of the loan and the two participating banks for one-sixth each. The loan was granted on the condition that Kreuger return to Europe immediately to present a detailed report on the position of his Group. But the meeting between the hunters and their quarry never took place. On 12 March 1932, at his bachelor pad in Paris, Kreuger shot himself.

At the time of his death, his bankers estimated he was the third richest man in the world. What was subsequently discovered about his financial dealings – including the discovery of forged bonds in his safe on which he had also forged signatures, which were then used as security against his loans – made it the financial scandal of the age. In the twenty-first century, comparisons with the disgraced tycoon Bernard Madoff would be made, although Kreuger was not a complete fraud.

Fortunately for the Wallenbergs, during Kreuger's last, increasingly desperate, six months, SEB had reduced its lending to his Group and increased the collateral to such an extent that the security still exceeded the total debt by more than ten per cent. The Wallenberg Group received new engagements to re-structure the Kreuger companies, with Marcus taking a personal interest in many of the companies involved. One of the acquisitions with which he and Jacob would remain closely involved was Kreuger's family company, Swedish Match AB, which still continues. Marcus had been able to turn a potential disaster for him and the Wallenberg Group to his advantage.

At least Marcus had been able to look to his father for guidance to help him with the problem; for Charles Hambro, his father *was* the problem.

Chapter 28

Om Mani Padme Hum

By the beginning of 1932 there was only one solution to safeguard the financial situation of Sir Eric Hambro and prevent the family facing the humiliation, and worse, the legal implications, of his going bankrupt. After much consideration by the Hambros generally, and after considering all alternatives, they concluded that the Milton Abbey estate, the jewel at the centre of the Hambro crown, would have to be sold. The place of which Charles had told Pamela she would one day be mistress, which he had looked ahead to passing to their son and onward for posterity as his great-grandfather had wanted, would be owned by strangers.

It was a ghastly time for them all. How far Eric accepted the fault was largely his is not known, but he surely could not have passed the blame for his roulette habit on to anyone else. By then the Bank too was doing less well than it had been, the effects of the Depression finally making their impact. The situation worried him sufficiently to make him decide, in March 1932, to resign as Chairman of Hambros Bank. One of Eric's last tasks in that role was on 22 March as a signatory, with several other major banks including the Wallenbergs' SEB, to a contract with the ever-needy Greek Government for an advance of £2.5 million on a League of Nations Loan, discussions about which Charles had also been involved. A week later, on 1 April, *The Times* announced under the section 'City news in Brief':

'Sir Eric Hambro, owing to indifferent health and a desire to have more leisure, is giving up his City activities and has resigned from the board of Hambros Bank. Mr R. Olaf Hambro has been appointed

362

chairman of the bank and retains his position as managing director.'

Coincidentally, that was not the only mention of the Hambros in that particular edition of the newspaper. Under the heading 'Ball', there was a piece about the South Dorset Hunt Point-to-Point Ball held the previous evening at the Dorchester Corn Exchange. It was a large affair, about four hundred guests, who danced to the band of the 11th Hussars. The piece mentioned those who took parties to the Ball, amongst them Pamela and Vanda Hambro, wife of Angus. Angus and Vanda lived at elegant Merly House, not far from Milton Abbey, and she and Pamela knew each other well. Neither woman seems to have attended the Ball with her spouse, and it is likely that the reason for the men's absence was Eric. While Angus, previously MP for South Dorset and on the way to being appointed Dorset's High Sheriff, was always busy with county activities, as well as his sporting obligations, he was probably at Milton Abbey that evening with Eric, no doubt supporting his retirement decision in the circumstances. Charles, as Secretary of the Board of Hambros Bank Ltd, was dealing urgently with the practicalities arising from his father's resignation from the chairmanship and setting in motion the handover of duties to his uncle Olaf, at the age of forty-five Eric's much younger brother. He was in no mood for partying.

Even the usually cheerful Pamela would not have been on top of the world that evening. It was not so much at the thought of Eric's resignation, for she knew that the Board considered Olaf to be tremendously capable, but more because of the burden that the extra work resulting from the changeover would put on Charles, at a time when he was upset by the decision – even though he knew it was the only one – to sell Milton Abbey. Pamela had been feeling stronger over the last few weeks, and while the various decisions were being made in her husband's family, she decided it would be a sensible time, as a precaution after her illness, to make her Will. This she did in the week before the Ball, on 24 March, signing it in her usual clear and strong hand before her two witnesses, a nurse and their parlour maid. She then she put it away, no doubt glad to have dealt with a slightly depressing task.

The timing of the Ball on Thursday 31 March was unfortunate, coinciding as it did with her father-in-law's announcement. However, as she was taking a party of guests, she was committed to going. The weather forecast for that day was not very promising. A moderate to fresh south-west wind was expected, with bright intervals between showers of rain or hail, and thunder at times. It was about 11 miles by road from Delcombe Manor to Dorchester, the county town of Dorset whose Corn Exchange was already famous as that which local writer Thomas Hardy had used as the model for Casterbridge.

Both women would have been driven to the Ball: Pamela by their chauffeur, perhaps picking up some of her party en route; Vanda possibly by one of their six children, for she and Angus had bought a Morris sports car the previous year so that their chauffeur could teach all the children how to drive.

In between entertaining their guests, the two women would have found the chance at some stage during the evening to catch up on the news. Vanda was fifteen years older than Pamela, but despite their age difference the pair got on well for Vanda was sweet and good-natured. They had plenty to talk about that evening. Vanda knew how important Milton Abbey was to her husband's family and how devastating the decision to sell it must have been. She knew, as all the close family did, about Eric's financial situation, and Pamela would have shared with Vanda her worries. For while the Hambro family generally was extremely wealthy, and Pamela had no reason to be concerned about Charles' prospects, she was aware of his continuing to pay off Eric's gambling debts and what the long-term effect could be on them. As for Milton Abbey, she knew it could have been another twenty years or more until Charles had inherited it from Eric, although they would still have been young enough to enjoy it – she fifty-two, he fifty-four – and she had so much hoped that one day it would belong to Charlie.

Their talking of inheritance may have made Vanda inclined to remind Pamela of the Hambro family history: that Vanda was Angus' second wife, for his first wife had died young, like so many other Hambro wives since the time of Carl Joachim Hambro. Vanda could have pointed out that, based on the past, the chance was that Pamela would never live to see Charles inherit anything, nor their children reach adulthood.

If Vanda had done so, then she would have been unkind, which was not in her nature, but it would have shown prescience. For at some time during that evening there was a thunderstorm, and somehow Pamela got caught in it. Although her family knows this happened, no record was handed down as to when exactly it happened or why she got caught. It is unlikely it happened as she arrived at the Ball: her chauffeur would have had a large umbrella ready to hold over her as she gathered up her gown and made quickly for the venue, trying not to get her feet, encased in slight evening sandals, too soaked. Perhaps it happened during the Ball, but there seems no reason for her to have gone outside. If she smoked, she could have done so inside, for smoking was fashionable and the place would have been full of fumes from elegant cocktail cigarettes and cigars. Neither did the Victorian building that was the Corn Exchange have a garden attached to it, for it was large enough to accommodate everyone in its ballroom, so Pamela would not have been sauntering outside while the band played. And at the end of the evening, the chauffeur would have made sure he was waiting for her right outside the building, again with an umbrella, to escort her to the car.

Of course, she may not have stayed at the Ball. Perhaps she left early and went on somewhere else with friends from her party, or joined up with Vanda and her friends; maybe she went home early and did as she always used to do when she needed cheering up, whether at Rannoch or at her childhood home at Holy Wells – jumped on a horse and galloped off, shouting into the wind as she rode.

Whatever she did, the timing was wrong. It was wrong because, although she may not have realised it, she had not yet properly recovered from the septicaemia and her resistance to infection was low. And it was wrong because it was only a few days into spring, when the nights were still chilly and rain was forecast, when even the healthiest person should make sure they are wrapped up warmly. Charles would have scolded her for getting so wet, and she would have laughed it off and told him affectionately not to fuss and gone to bed with a warm drink.

When a few days later she developed a temperature, she would have put it down to the chill she presumed she had caught, obeyed Charles for once, and stayed in bed. As she lay coughing, she would have told the nanny to let the girls talk to her from the safe distance of her bedroom doorway so they minimised their risk of catching anything; little Charlie would probably have been kept away altogether. When she started to become breathless, having longer periods of fever and experiencing a pain in her chest despite the cold remedies she was taking, they would have called for their doctor.

Bernard Septimus Hollick, aged fifty-three, was local to the Hambros, living about 7 miles away in the small market town of Sturminster Newton. He had qualified in 1901, long before the existence of the Royal College of General Practitioners, passing the Conjoint Exam, and becoming a kind of hybrid of a modern GP and a consultant. Since 1910 he had also been a member of the BMA, so was aware of their recommendations. He was most likely the doctor who had dealt with Pamela when she had developed septicaemia, so he would have been familiar with her history.

His diagnosis was what Charles had dreaded: pneumonia, and acute lobar pneumonia at that, rather than the less serious broncho-pneumonia. It meant that part of a lobe in her lung was infected. Like septicaemia, from which it often developed, it was still without a cure.

It is unlikely she was hospitalised, for it is hard to see what benefit she would have gained given the lack of treatment available. In the USA serums for pneumonia were being used; in Britain during the winter she fell ill, serums were still at the trial stage, trials being conducted by the Medical and Research Council in four centres around the country, in which every alternate case was to be given serum. But the nearest trial centre to the Hambros was in London, and it seems unlikely she would have been admitted there when her nearest hospital was Dorset County. Besides, it was a long way for such a sick person to travel, and there was no guarantee a serum would work.

With no medicinal cure, Dr Hollick would have treated the patient's symptoms instead. The main cause of death from pneumonia was circulation failure, so it was vital to keep Pamela's heart stimulated; she could have been given strychnine, camphor and oil for this purpose, or digitalis, which also controlled the heart's rate, but Dr Hollick most likely gave her oxygen, favoured by the BMA as the best cardiac stimulant. To administer this he would either have used a nasal catheter, blocking her other nostril with cotton wool, or if she would tolerate anything over her nose and mouth, a mask.

Most important in the treatment were fresh air and complete physical and mental rest. All unnecessary movement was to be avoided. Tepid sponging, carefully given, would have made Pamela more comfortable.

She would have been given plenty of fluid, and fluid only, during the first forty-eight hours. Dr Hollick would have looked for signs of her abdomen being distended, in which case she would be given an enema. If he were intending to give her any serum (notwithstanding that the jury was still out pending the outcome of the trials), he had to do so in the first three days to be of any benefit, when it could lessen the duration of the fever and bring everything to the necessary 'crisis'.

It was vital she have the necessary rest to keep her going and maintain her strength, so pain and insomnia had to be overcome. After five days, as long as her air passages were clear, she could be given morphine injections to help her sleep. Dr Hollick, whose (no doubt expensive) services Charles would not have thought twice about retaining for as long as they needed him, would have issued instructions to Charles and probably at least two nurses, who would take it in turns to watch her. The doctor would have visited each day to check on her progress. The main things to hope for were that her breathing would become easier and she would sleep.

As Charles watched over Pamela, the problems the Hambros had faded into insignificance beside his beloved wife's health: they were nothing compared with watching her suffering. All he could do was to make sure she was as comfortable as possible in her bedroom at Delcombe Manor, and pray.

To add to his problems, their four children had been in contact with someone who had whooping cough, for which a vaccine would not become available for another twenty years; although fatalities were low compared with other diseases, it was particularly unpleasant for children and could lead to complications. It was also highly contagious, so they were all put into quarantine. The only way the girls could see their mother without endangering her health further was by climbing a ladder to look at her through her bedroom window. For Di, then eleven, Cinders ten, and Pammie six, it was the last time they ever saw her, while Charlie, aged just twenty-one months, never had that chance, for on Saturday 16 April 1932 Pamela died, aged thirty-two.

As if to emphasise the terrible prematurity of Pamela's death, many of the mourners at her funeral were a generation older than she. The Cobbolds' dear friends the Hon Douglas and Mrs Tollemache, he seventy, she nearly so, who had known Pamela all her life; her uncles and aunts, like Philip and Cicely Cobbold and Ralph, grateful that at least their brother had not experienced the loss of his favourite daughter; Charles' relations, including his uncles Olaf and Angus and their wives, Winifred and Vanda; their Dorset neighbours, the Earl and Countess of Shaftesbury.

There were those for whose lives she had feared during the Great War, such as her brother Ivan, and her godfather Sir William Bromley-Davenport, who now knelt in the chapel of Milton Abbey and pondered on how they had survived against all odds, while she, young and vital and until lately, so healthy, was dead.

Some friends from her own generation were there, of course. Peter Cazalet, Pamela's talented riding friend, mused sorrowfully on the tragic irony of her death, originating cruelly from her much-loved horse. He would have been glad that Pamela, whose views he respected as she was slightly older than he, had managed to meet his fiancée Leonora Wodehouse, whom he would marry in December that year. There was Marjory Wyndham-Quin, whose nine-year-old daughter Pamela would never see become the 6th Marchioness of Salisbury; and organic farming pioneer Lady Balfour, niece of the Conservative Prime Minister.

There was one notable absence from her peers: her best friend Angy. She was in Morocco that month with three other women, including Iris Grenfell, their mutual friend since childhood. Receiving a telegram, Angy would have been devastated and distraught at not being able to get back on time for the funeral. Angy, who had once feared that Charles would take her best friend from her, had lost her after all to something far more permanent than marriage.

And, as a tragic illustration of the natural order turned upside down – the parent surviving the child – her mother, Lady Evelyn Cobbold. Now sixty-five, she was still full of energy, which was just as well, for her Hambro grandchildren now needed her attention. Their usually loving and attentive father was, just then, unable to give them anything, for he was inconsolable; and while Evelyn may not have been the most emotionally accessible of mothers to her children, she was, as she had demonstrated with young Toby Sladen, an attentive and kind grandmother.

Eric Hambro was there for his son, his own troubles temporarily forgotten, offering what emotional support he could, while at the same time feeling the terrible loss of a daughter-in-law of whom he had been very fond. He appreciated the presence of Montagu Norman, Governor of the Bank of England, who had taken time out of his hectic schedule to come to the funeral to show his support for Charles.

The funeral took place at 2.30pm on Tuesday 19 April in the Abbey church. It would be the last Hambro family ceremony that Milton Abbey would see. The *Dorset County Chronicle*, the newspaper which Thomas Hardy had so often scoured to provide authentic local detail for his novels, covered the occasion in respectful depth. The county was reminded that Pamela's husband, 'managing director of Hambros' Bank, a director of the Bank of England...' was 'the son and heir of Sir Eric Hambro, the great banker'. If the Editor had any inkling of Eric's troubles, or was aware of his recent retirement, this was not the time to mention it.

The coffin had been taken into the hall that morning, where it lay until the service in the Abbey itself. The *Chronicle* went on to report, 'The lid was almost hidden by many beautiful white flowers, out of which peeped the one word "Pam"'. The untimely death of one of the Hambro family which had been part of the county for so long, and the fact that four young children were left without a mother, greatly shocked the community. Villagers started arriving long before the service started, '... wending their way across the lovely park to the wonderful abbey, set with the mansion next door to it, the Dorset seat of the head of the Hambro family, in such incomparable surroundings encircled by a deep belt of woods'. If he had had the emotional energy to do so, Charles would have smiled bitterly at the irony of those words, knowing as he did that soon it would be the family seat no longer.

Mourners came not only from a wide geographical area but from diverse groups. Apart from the villagers there were 'many eminent people in society and in banking and commerce. Many distinguished Dorset families were represented too, in the large congregation.' Others travelled down from London by train, to be met at Wareham station by a fleet of cars, 'which bore them swiftly through the winding lanes in the heart of Dorset...'

As the mourners arrived, the organist played excerpts from the oratorios, including 'O for the Wings of a Dove' and 'I know that my

Redeemer liveth'. And then the service started, with a touch that was theatrical yet supremely touching:

'There came also to the great west doors of the abbey the two hunters of the deceased lady in charge of a groom, and with scarcely a movement they stood there while the coffin was borne from the hall to the abbey preceded by the surpliced choir from the parish church, with the cross at the head of the procession.'

The music was well known to the congregation: 'The King of Love my Shepherd is', the Psalm 'The Lord is my Shepherd', and lastly, 'Abide With Me'. They stood for the playing of the 'Dead March' from 'Saul' and then, to the singing of the Nunc Dimittis, followed Pamela's coffin out of the church. It was borne to a waiting car and then taken on the long journey to Scotland, where her burial, above Loch Rannoch, took place the next day.

On the same day as the burial, Wednesday 20 April, a memorial service was held at St Mark's Church in North Audley Street, London, attended by more relations and friends whose public engagements and other activities had prevented them from travelling to Dorset at short notice. With Pamela's uncle the Earl of Dunmore, her aunt Lady Muriel Gore-Browne, and even her maternal grandmother the Dowager Countess of Dunmore, whose advanced age brought home even more keenly the prematurity of Pamela's death, were two ministers from countries with which the Hambros had close connection, Greece and Denmark. Charles and Pamela's good friend the Hon Esmond Harmsworth, about to become Head of Associated Newspapers, stood with banker and supporter of the arts, Baron Frederic d'Erlanger, and several MPs. Pamela's sister-in-law and friend Blanche was there, of course, with two of her sisters, Lady Rachel and Lady Anne, and Pamela's dear mother-in-law, Sybil. Perhaps knowing that her husband's ex-wife would be attending, Estelle sent a representative, although why she was not at the funeral itself given that it was held at her home, is not known.

Brilliance and title there may have been, but none of that mattered as the mourners gathered that afternoon to pray for Pamela, and to think about Charles and the children she had left behind. The girls, if not little Charlie, had had their chance to see Mummy that last time through her bedroom window and, in the custom that still prevailed, were not allowed to take part in any valediction.

There was, however, an active part that Charles and their grandmother encouraged the children to play after Pamela's death. Her brother Ivan, having inherited their father's Scottish estates, gave to Charles a piece of land at Rannoch, on a hillside overlooking the Loch, so that his beloved wife could have a clear view of her favourite place on earth. After her burial Charles had a garden created around her grave, and would travel up regularly by train with the girls, especially Pammie, to keep the garden tidy. The children would choose and help Charles plant those flowers and shrubs which they thought Mummy would like, encouraged too by Evelyn, still a keen gardener.

At the entrance to Pamela's garden, just along the quiet lane from Rannoch Lodge, a tall set of iron gates was fitted, at the top bearing the letters 'OM', representing the Buddhist chant, Om Mani Padme Hum, and at the bottom, 'PH'. Today the surrounding land is densely planted by the Forestry Commission, while Pamela's garden is a wild tangle of trees and shrubs and undergrowth. Her view of Loch Rannoch now is obscured by foliage. Yet her grave itself is still accessible and, apart from a little lichen, is easily read. The plaque bears the inscription:

PAMELA
The ever beloved wife of
CHARLES HAMBRO
of Delcombe Manor in the County of Dorset
and the daughter of John D. Cobbold of Rannoch Lodge
Born at Ipswich on the Third Day of January 1900 AD
Departed this life on the 16th Day of April 1932 AD
'Eternally One with the Great Consciousness'

At each of the bottom corners of the plaque are again the initials OM: after a Christian funeral, Charles wanted to pay homage to her Buddhist inclinations. At the top and along the sides is engraved the juniper leaf, symbol of her mother's ancestral clan, the Murrays. Underneath the words is a large space, left blank for Charles' inscription to be added one day. However, the space remains empty, while the huge grave, clearly meant for two, holds only Pamela; for Charles was buried in the Hambros' family plot in Hayes churchyard, and with him lie the ashes of his second wife, Doie Wallenberg.

Epilogue

Aged just thirty-four when he was widowed, Charles Hambro was still a very attractive man. There were many women who, while sympathising with his loss, were delighted he was single. Although he was about to lose his entitlement to Milton Abbey, he was still rich, with the capacity for getting richer, and with contacts in the top echelons in the world. Women – some single, many not – made it very clear they would like to get to know him better. Even Angy, boasting in later life that she had had many lovers, hinted that Charles was one of them, although for many reasons it seems most unlikely.

But for the first two years after Pamela's death, his priority was their children, followed – out of duty and because it focused his mind – by work. The girls had been left hurt and bewildered by their mother's death, and at the beginning were too distraught even to sleep on their own. Charles let them sleep in his room, but in those days when separate sleeping arrangements for married couples were still common amongst the upper classes, such an unorthodox arrangement did not go unnoticed by Hambro relatives. However, his concern was that his daughters should recover their emotional equilibrium as soon as possible, rather than extending their misery for the sake of convention.

Charlie was bemused by his mother's absence but, being too young to understand its cause, was instead content with the attention of his father and his affectionate nanny. However, his nanny was young, and again some of the Hambro elders were concerned about the appropriateness of her living in the same household as Charles, the widower: tongues may start to wag, which would cause him aggravation and would not do his or the family's reputation much good. But once more, his concern was for his son: Charlie was devoted to his nanny, and at a sensitive time like this, Charles had no intention of changing her for an older woman just because of what people might think.

While Pamela and her mother may not have been particularly close, Lady Evelyn would nevertheless have been devastated by her daughter's death. Their relationship had been helped by the fact that Evelyn had always held her son-in-law in high regard, and now she made it clear to Charles that she was there for her grandchildren. She always found it easier to bond with children she admired, particularly good-looking ones, and she was especially fond of Di and beautiful Pammie. They would visit her in her London mews house, where she would take them out for ices at Fortnum's in Piccadilly, in those days a big treat, or to visit her own mother, their great-grandmother Gertrude, the Dowager Countess of Dunmore, still clothed in black out of respect for the late Queen, in whose service she had been. In later life, Pammie would recall:

'Every day Great-Grandmama would take out her horse and carriage and take any children or dogs for a ride around Hyde Park. She also loved to play cards, which she was very good at, and to do puzzles with us on rainy days, which Grandmama [Evelyn] also loved to do with us children as she got older.'

Knowing that the children could rely on affection from their mother's family, including their Uncle Ivan and Aunt Blanche who were very kind to them, must have helped Charles a good deal, enabling him to concentrate on work. Although he remained very occupied with his work for the Bank of England, as a director of Hambros he was still involved with major issues. But just when things seemed to be settling down following the transition in the chairmanship from his father to his uncle Olaf, another tragedy struck the Hambros. For at Pamela's funeral, a spectre had lurked in the shadows: death itself, not satisfied with what it had just taken but waiting to claim another who, while praying for Pamela's soul, had naively given thanks for her own life. Just four months after Pamela's death, Olaf's beautiful wife Winifred was drowned in Loch Ness. One of their three young sons, thirteen-year-old Jocelyn, a future Chairman of Hambros, was with her in the water, both swimming to the shore after abandoning their little boat whose engine had caught fire. Winifred was a strong swimmer, and Jocelyn, swimming in front, had turned to see her coping well, but when he looked again after reaching the shore, she had disappeared. Her body was never found.

It is hard to imagine how Charles and his uncle coped during the rest of that year. After Pamela's death, Olaf – a big, gruff-looking man, who would prove to be an excellent Chairman, although unlike Charles, introverted – had been a source of comfort and support to his nephew, but now he was suffering himself, and Charles felt unable to help him.

Disappointed by his father, grieving for his wife and worried for his children, Charles had to wrestle with new problems over sterling at the Bank of England, for the City was facing one of its worst crises. It was a terrible time for the country. Nearly three million people were registered as unemployed – 23% of the workforce. World trade was at a desperately low ebb as demand and prices slumped, and protectionist tariffs reared up around the domestic economies. Hambros Bank did not escape: its acceptances – the mainstay of its business, directly affected by world trade – and its balance sheet were both a third lower than at the end of the 1920s.

Three months after Pamela's death, Charles was given new responsibilities by Montagu Norman, who had appointed him the first full-time Executive Director of the Bank of England, to be in charge of administering the new Exchange Equalisation Account. This was set up by the Treasury with a special fund of £167 million, to be used to check undue fluctuations in the exchange rate. Charles began the job at a difficult time, when sterling was already under severe pressure, and at the end of November he was forced to abandon the idea of checking the decline in case the whole of the reserves were used up. Pamela would have been proud of him in his important role and stroked his worried brow, or made him laugh by making a joke out of his worries, but now he had to manage without that comfort. Nevertheless, he coped very well with a difficult job, and by September 1933 he had guided the Account through its difficult teething period and ensured a high degree of daily independence from the Treasury. Hard it may have been, but at least it absorbed him during the day and often into the night, so that he had less time and emotional energy left to think about Pamela.

Yet Charles must have felt certain events were rubbing salt into the wound. In May 1932, a month after Pamela's death, his father began negotiations for the sale of Milton Abbey. Although during the week he was living in his London property, Charles was still renting Delcombe Manor, so could not avoid being involved with the sale process. He was angry with his father for his financial recklessness, made worse when in June he watched Eric opening Milton Abbey's gardens to the public, as he had done annually for many years, as his own father Everard had done, knowing that it would be the last time he would ever do so. As the visitors paid their 1/6 entrance fee in aid of the Queen's Institute of District Nursing, they did not realise that it would be their last opportunity to wander around the beautiful gardens and park, and marvel at the architecture of the abbey church and old refectory.

The vast Milton Abbey estate was put up for sale by auction from 28 to 30 November that year. It was divided into 283 lots to make it more saleable, which resulted in the breakup of the estate and meant that not all of it was sold at first attempt. Charles and his uncle Angus, wishing to retain something of the family's link with Dorset, each bought some lots. One of the villages sold off as part of the estate was Winterborne Stickland. In 1934 Charles built a memorial hall there to replace its Reading Room, and gave it to the community on certain conditions, mainly that it bear his late wife's name forever. The Pamela Hambro Hall is still used in the twenty-first century, providing an important service to a busy community.

When she heard about her good friend's death, Doie Wallenberg would have been in touch with Charles very quickly, offering to visit him and her godson, Charlie. Visiting Charles may have given her a good excuse, after her annual visit to her family in Scotland, to delay her return to Sweden and the inevitable Wallenberg summer of sailing and hunting which she so loathed. In August that year, 1932, Marcus' uncle Knut transferred to him ownership of a large shooting estate, Skalstugan, in the north of Sweden, comprising 40,000 acres of alpine countryside and forests, forty fishing lakes and four large houses able to accommodate many. It was Doie's idea of purgatory. Here Marcus could fish and shoot ptarmigan and entertain his friends, who may well have included Marianne. For that relationship was set to continue, to the extent that by July 1934 Marcus and Doie decided formally to separate, and agreed the terms of a divorce.

Doie was to be given custody of the children, while Marcus would dictate the education and training of his sons if Doie were to leave Sweden. By contrast, he did not consider the education of their daughter

Anis to be very important, which must have galled Doie, especially given the apparent contradiction when the Wallenbergs endowed on her alma mater, Cambridge University, an annual prize open to both sexes.[1]

Marcus moved out of their house at Parkrudden in October 1934, renting a large apartment near the family bank. In October 1935 he and Doie were divorced. Marcus felt the stern disapproval of the Swedish Establishment, for divorce was still unusual in that country, even more so amongst members of the Establishment. But if Marcus was cold-shouldered, Marianne – whose divorce from Count Bernadotte had taken place in March that year – suffered far more socially as the guilty party in her marriage, for it was a positive scandal for a member of the Swedish Royal Family to be abandoned by his wife. For a while, Marcus and Marianne's relations with the Court were strained. Marcus used to play tennis with the King and make official appearances with him in his capacity as Chairman of the Swedish Tennis Association, and it took some time before Marcus and his wife-to-be were invited to the Palace for social occasions.

Not that Doie would have cared about their ostracism. She needed to get her future sorted out too. Her divorce settlement gave her Parkrudden and an annual allowance. She stayed there until around late 1935, by which time Marc was eleven, Peter nine and Anis six. However, she must have visited England often after her separation from Marcus, because by early December 1935 at the very latest, she and Charles Hambro were close enough not to mind being seen together at a charity ball at Grosvenor House, and their names reported in the society columns. On New Year's Day 1936, *The Times* announced their forthcoming marriage. Six weeks later, on Saturday 15 February 1936, beating the marriage in Sweden of her ex-husband to Marianne Bernadotte by three months to the day, and with Cinders and Di as bridesmaids, Mrs Marcus Wallenberg became the second Mrs Charles Hambro.

Pamela, overlooking Loch Rannoch, waited for her husband and her daughters to visit her, to tend the garden and tidy her grave.

Would it have pleased her that, according to Charles' step-daughter

---

[1] The Wallenberg Prize was for an essay on some subject connected with the language, history or civilisation of one or more of the Scandinavian peoples, and is still awarded in the twenty-first century, with a prize value of £500.

Anis, Cinders and Di had become so used to having their father to themselves after her death that in the early days of his second marriage, fuelled with jealousy against the new woman in his life (and, aged fifteen and fourteen, at that difficult adolescent phase), they made Doie's life intolerable? Would it have given Pamela satisfaction to know that Doie did not have Charles to herself even on their week's honeymoon, for he felt it necessary to take his two eldest daughters with them? Or would she have berated her girls for being so selfish and spoiling their father's chance of happiness?

If Pamela knew that young Pammie, who loved to make the journey to Scotland by train with her father, solemnly helping him in the garden and putting away the tools in the large shed he had built, had come to love her stepmother, would she have cried in jealous torment? Or would she have rejoiced that the child had found someone else to love and lessen the pain?

Would she have raged with indignation that Charlie should lose the nanny he loved to a new Swedish one, at Doie's insistence, and weep because the only mother he would ever know was his father's second wife?

And would Pamela have asked why this union had happened at all, her beloved husband with her close friend?

A man in Charles' position, still young, with serious professional responsibilities and four children, could not be expected to continue alone. Descendants of the Hambros and Wallenbergs would later muse that Charles and Doie's marriage had probably been engineered by Marcus himself, perhaps to atone for his guilt in straying. By uniting his ex-wife and his good friend who, after all, already knew each other, Marcus could feel he had done something positive. And his and Doie's children would be part of an extended family with Charles and Pamela's.

Fortunately it was an arrangement that both sides largely embraced. Pammie and Anis, step-sisters from a young age, would love each other dearly all their lives, and Anis would become close to and protective of her stepbrother, feeling for Charlie when, unlike his mother (but very like his stepmother), he proved to have no love of hunting or blood sports of any kind; this was much to the disappointment of Charles who expected his son to pursue such activities, for Cinders and Di loved hunting and were very good at it.

The Hambro children saw less of their stepbrothers Marc and Peter Wallenberg, for despite Doie having custody of them, Marcus insisted that they board during term time at Sigtuna School, a prestigious school near Stockholm, seeing their new families (including Marianne's) only during the holidays, while their sister Anis and their Hambro step-siblings would see the boys only when they came to England. When the children found themselves with a new Hambro half-sister, Sally, there were probably mixed reactions, and Pammie and Anis, despite the lack of a blood tie between them, would always be closer to each other than to their half-sister. Cinders and Di, like Marc and Peter, were sent to boarding school, so saw much less of Sally as she grew up, but at least the two girls were in England and therefore not far from the rest of the family.

Their father's marriage briefly introduced the Hambro children to some relations they had never met. Although, oddly, Pamela's sister Winifred did not attend her funeral and allegedly never enquired about the well-being of her nieces and nephew after their mother's death, she and Algy accepted the invitation to Charles' wedding. The cocktail party he and Doie hosted the evening before was the first time that Pammie, by then aged ten and allowed to watch the guests arrive, had ever met her aunt.

Pamela had not left her children and her closest friends without something tangible to remember her by. As Executor of her Will, Charles saw that their friend Peter Cazalet, with whom she shared a love of horsemanship and hunting, received her gift to him of her favourite hunter, Cocktail. Another friend, Olive Pike, was bequeathed Pamela's mink coat. To Angy she left her diamond clip brooch and all her gold bracelets: whether she might have changed her mind if she had known of Angy's boasting about an affair with Charles is not known, but she may have been amused to know the effect Angy had on Doie. Anis later recalled that her mother was a complete unknown, an outsider in England, when she married Charles; the fact that she had previously been married into one of Sweden's most significant families meant nothing in British social circles. As such, it seems Doie had to put up with the status quo, including the friendship of Charles with Angy, Baroness Belper: they had, after all, known each other for around twenty years. Angy frequently socialised with Charles and Doie in a threesome which Anis, despite liking Angy for being very amusing, said had been 'awful' for her mother. Perhaps Angy liked to feel she was a reminder to Doie of the existence of Pamela, of the fact that Charles had loved his first wife, her best friend, for a lot longer than he had been with Doie. Whatever Angy's reasons, Lord Belper must have thought the situation rather odd, but then his wife was always an irrepressible force, something of a law unto herself.

To each of their children Pamela left jewellery, to be passed to them when they reached eighteen or whatever age Charles thought fit. Cinders would have treasured her mother's emerald ring, Cartier diamond watch, and sapphire and diamond ring and bracelets; Di loved her rope of corals, her large fire-sapphire ring and two onyx and diamond bracelets. For Pammie there was a rope of small pearls, a smaller diamond bracelet and a cat's eye and diamond brooch. Charlie would come to treasure his mother's Coldstream diamond brooch, of particular significance as it was associated with his father's Regiment, and her three-string pearl necklace. The rest of her jewellery and personal ornaments were to be divided between the four of them as they should agree. Everything else was for Charles.

Although death took Pamela too soon, at least she was delivered from what was to come: for the world she left behind would – like her life – end prematurely, blown apart by yet another war. It was a war which would see her beloved brother killed in 1944, when a doodlebug fell on the Guards Chapel where he and Blanche had just celebrated their silver wedding; and her children sent by Charles to live with Catherine and Harry Morgan in America for fear their Jewish ancestry would be discovered. The Morgans, by then with their own children, offered friendship and security to the Hambro children, the close friendships between both families sustained through the next generation and into the twenty-first century.

But Pamela was deprived of the positive things, too. She missed the journey undertaken by her mother when, in 1933 and still in thrall to Islam, Lady Evelyn embarked upon her physical and spiritual journey to Mecca, subsequently publishing her book, *Pilgrimage to Mecca*. She did not see Charles become Executive Chief of the Special Operations

Executive (SOE), the resistance movement set up during World War II by Churchill, for which Charles was knighted, or his appointment as Deputy Governor of the Bank of England. She would have been so proud to see Charlie, who would marry a daughter of her friend, the younger Lady Lettice Lygon, become Chairman of Hambros Bank and Treasurer to the Conservative Party under John Major, for which he would be given a Life Peerage; and she missed her daughters growing up and sharing in their very different but interesting lives. All her children would give her and Charles many grandchildren.

Pamela would not have recognised the world that replaced hers any more than she would the life which her beloved Charles would lead, with another woman. No wonder a voice, born of the great energy which so fuelled her life, calls in that wild and lonely garden after her death.

Sources

Books

H Arnold Barton, *A Folk Divided: Homeland Swedes and Swedish Americans, 1840–1940*, USA, SIU Press, 1994.

Bo Bramsen & Kathleen Wain, *The Hambros 1779–1979*, London, Michael Joseph, 1979.

David Cannadine, *The Decline and Fall of the British Aristocracy*, London, Penguin Books, 2005.

Lady Evelyn Cobbold, *Pilgrimage to Mecca,* with Introduction by William Facey and Miranda Taylor, London, Arabian Publishing Ltd, 2008.

Denise Cush, *A Student's Approach to World Religions: Buddhism*, Hodder & Stoughton, 1993.

Andrew Devonshire, *Accidents of Fortune*, Norwich, Michael Russell, 2004.

Deborah, Duchess of Devonshire, *Chatsworth: The House*, London, Frances Lincoln Ltd, 2002.

Deborah Devonshire, *Wait for Me!* London, John Murray, 2010.

Roy Hattersley, *Borrowed Time: The Story of Britain Between the Wars*, London, Little, Brown, 2007.

Roy Hattersley, *The Edwardians*, London, Abacus, 2006.

David Landes, *Dynasties: Fortune and Misfortune in the World's Great Family Businesses*, United States, Viking Adult (Penguin Group), 2006.

Robert Malster, *250 Years of Brewing in Ipswich*, Ipswich, Malthouse Press in Association with Tollemache & Cobbold Brewery, 1996.

Jessica Mitford, *Hons and Rebels*, London, Phoenix, 1999.

Lucy Moore, *Anything Goes*, London, Atlantic Books, 2008.

Ulf Olsson, *Furthering a Fortune: Marcus Wallenberg, Swedish Banker and Industrialist 1899–1982*, Stockholm, Ekerlids Förlag, 2001.

Martin Pugh, 'We Danced All Night', A Social History of Britain Between the Wars, London, The Bodley Head, 2008.

Brian Scovell, Football Gentry, Stroud, Tempus, 2005.

Felix Walton, The Cliff Brewery, Ipswich 1723–1923, Ipswich, East Anglian Daily Times, 1923.

Charles Williams, Harold Macmillan, London, Wiedenfeld & Nicolson, 2009.

A N Wilson, After the Victorians, London, Arrow Books, 2006.

Brochures/booklets

Knebworth Estates, Knebworth House, Heritage House Group Ltd, 2005.

P A Thompson, HCC – History of Hayes (Kent) Cricket Club, 1828–1978.

Articles

Linda Bryder, The Medical Research Council and clinical trial methodologies before the 1940s: the failure to develop a 'scientific approach', J R Soc Med August 2011.

Sarah Cochrane, Assessing the Impact of World War I on the City of London, University of Oxford, 2009.

Lord Crathorne, The Crathorne Estate, accessed from Crathorne Arms, 21/12/2008, www.crathorne-arms.co.uk/crathorne/.

William F Howard, The Sweetheart of the AEF (published in New York Archives, Winter 2005), accessed from New York Archives, 2008, www.nysarchivestrust.org.

A-M Landtblom, P Fazio, S Frederikson, E Granieri, The first case history of multiple sclerosis: Augustus d'Esté (1794–1848), Published in Neurol Sci (2010) 31:29–33.

Alex Mitchell, Slains Castle and The Hays of Erroll, accessed from Docstoc, 2010, www.docstoc.com.

Perth and Kinross Fabian Society, 1971, The Acreocracy of Perthshire: Who Owns Our Land? accessed from Caledonia, 2008, www.caledonia.org.uk/land.

Tammy M Proctor, Family Ties in the Making of Modern Intelligence, the Journal of Social History, Volume 39, Number 2, George Mason University Press, Winter 2005.

Alan Sabey, *The British Empire Exhibition, Wembley, A Diary of Royal Visits and other Notable Events in 1924*, accessed from Studygroup, 2009, www.studygroup.org.uk.

Russell Sparkes, *The Enemy of Eugenics* (published in The Chesterton Review for Feb–May 1999), accessed from Secondspring, 2009, www.secondspring.co.uk.

Archives and Libraries

The British Library (local newspaper sources); Bromley Library (development of the Hayes estate); The Chatsworth Estate (Devonshire mss, Chatsworth, 9th Duke's Group and Diary of the 9th Duke of Devonshire); Eton College (The Chronicle; Charles Hambro and Ivan Cobbold); Hayes Library (history of Hayes and the Hambros); The London Metropolitan Archives (Hambros and banking); The National Archives (Sybil Hambro and Intelligence; Leonard Elger; Hambro divorce); The National Monument Records (Milton Abbey estate); The New York Times online (various); The Scotsman online archive (various); the Suffolk County Archives (history of the Cobbolds; letters of John Constable); The Times online archive (various).

Other Websites Accessed

(non-attributable information)
www.bbc.co.uk/bbcfour/documentaries
www.british-history.ac.uk
www.cheltenham4u.co.uk
www.cotswoldscottageretreats.co.uk
www.eugenics-watch.com
www.findmypast.co.uk
www.firstworldwar.com
www.galtoninstitute.org.uk
www.golfclubatlas.com
www.holkham.co.uk
www.iht.com/cgi-bin/search.cgi
www.isae.co.uk/history
www.knebworthhouse.com
www.measuringworth.com

www.mpthewarren.com
www.museum.guernsey.net
www.thePeerage.com
www.rmsmajestic.co.uk
www.sopse.org.uk
www.spr.ac.uk
www.statelyhomes.com
www.theosophical.org.uk/origins.htm
www.theosophical-society.org.uk
www.time.com/time/magazine
www.en.wikipedia.org/wiki/The Sketch
www.winstonchurchill.org/support/the-churchill-centre/publications/
finest-hour-online